W9-AAS-206

TAKING◆SIDES

Clashing Views on Controversial
Issues in Special Education

TAKING SIDES

Clashing Views on Controversial

Issues in Special Education

Selected, Edited, and with Introductions by

MaryAnn Byrnes
University of Massachusetts–Boston

McGraw-Hill/Dushkin
A Division of The McGraw-Hill Companies

Photo Acknowledgment
Cover image: © 2002 by PhotoDisc, Inc.

Cover Art Acknowledgment
Charles Vitelli

Copyright © 2002 by McGraw-Hill/Dushkin,
A Division of The McGraw-Hill Companies, Inc., Guilford, Connecticut 06437

Copyright law prohibits the reproduction, storage, or transmission in any form by any means of any
portion of this publication without the express written permission of McGraw-Hill/Dushkin and of
the copyright holder (if different) of the part of the publication to be reproduced. The Guidelines for
Classroom Copying endorsed by Congress explicitly state that unauthorized copying may not be
used to create, to replace, or to substitute for anthologies, compilations, or collective works.

Taking Sides ® is a registered trademark of McGraw-Hill/Dushkin

Manufactured in the United States of America

First Edition

123456789BAHBAH5432

Library of Congress Cataloging-in-Publication Data
Main entry under title:
Taking sides: clashing views on controversial issues in special education/selected, edited, and with
introductions by MaryAnn Byrnes.—1st ed.
Includes bibliographical references and index.
1. Special education. I. Byrnes, MaryAnn, ed. II. Series.
371.9
0-07-248056-4
ISSN: 1537-0739

Printed on Recycled Paper

Preface

Special education is full of questions, emotions, and opinions. Public responsibility for the education of children with disabilities is a relatively new endeavor that is still forging its identity and boundaries. Sometimes it seems that just as one set of issues is resolved, such as the creation of a range of services in public schools, a host of new challenges arises to take its place. Other issues, such as appropriate funding and inclusion, seem to defy resolution, despite long and thoughtful deliberation. Through *Taking Sides: Clashing Views on Controversial Issues in Special Education,* I invite you to consider some of the currently active issues in this volatile field.

A few basic principles guided the choice of selections for this book. Each reading needed to represent a widely held point of view on the question at hand. Other opinions surely exist, but the ones presented needed to be broadly held. Each had to employ solid reasoning; its position could not be easily refuted because of faulty logic. Finally, each selection, along with references for additional study, needed to be interesting to read. If an article did not captivate my attention, I did not want to include it.

Taking Sides: Clashing Views on Controversial Issues in Special Education has two major goals. First, to introduce key questions in special education so that readers can learn about the field from authors who have thought long and carefully about educational policy and practice. Second, to stimulate thinking and discussion so that readers can explore possibilities and debate the consequences of positions and actions. I hope you will find yourselves engaged and enlivened by the discussions these topics stimulate. Most of all, I trust that your thinking will contribute to constructive solutions to puzzles that demand careful thinking and care about all children.

This book includes 18 issues that address areas of active debate in the field of special education. I have grouped the issues into three parts. Part 1, Special Education and Society, introduces questions of social policy and practice. Part 2, Inclusion, highlights varied perspectives on this controversial philosophy. And Part 3, Issues About Disabilities, presents critical considerations about specific disabilities and therapies.

Each issue is framed as a question and begins with an *introduction,* which is designed to set the stage for discussion. Two readings presenting contrasting points of view come next. Each issue closes with a *postscript,* which summarizes the expressed points of view, suggests other points of view, and provides additional readings on the topic at hand. The introductions and postscripts also feature series of questions to stimulate your thinking as you weigh the topic at hand and its relationship to schools. Each question represents challenges to be resolved in the policy and practice of educating children with disabilities.

To expand your thinking, you may want to reference the *On the Internet* pages that precede each section. These contain a sampling of Internet site addresses (URLs) that present varied points of view as well as links to related sites and bibliographies for further study.

The YES and NO positions on every issue express strongly held opinions. You may agree or disagree with the authors, or you may find that your own view lies somewhere in between. You will likely identify additional perspectives as you study the issues more thoroughly. You will certainly find connections between issues. Perhaps class discussions will lead you to formulate a new and completely different response to issue questions. Doubtless, as you continue in your professional and personal life, your ideas will change and develop. What is critical as you read this book is to reflect on positions, options, and emotions so that you can decide what you think and use your opinion to guide your actions and decisions.

A word to the instructor An *Instructor's Manual with Test Questions* (multiple-choice and essay) is available through McGraw-Hill/Dushkin for the instructor using *Taking Sides* in the classroom. Also available is *Using Taking Sides in the Classroom,* a general guidebook that presents strategies for and examples of using the pro-con method in classroom settings. Faculty members using this text also have access to an online version of *Using Taking Sides in the Classroom* and a correspondence service, located at http://www.duskin.com/usingts/.

Taking Sides: Clashing View on Controversial Issues in Special Education is only one title in the Taking Sides series. The table of contents for any of the other titles can be found at the Taking Sides Web site at http://www.dushkin.com/takingsides/.

Acknowledgements So long as I have been in education, spirited debate about "the right thing to do" has been part of life. The reflection and critical thinking of these discussions have deepened my understanding of special education, introduced new perspectives, and resulted in more than a few changed opinions. I am very grateful for the assistance—individually and collectively—of many people. First, and most important, I thank the children, educators, and parents who taught me that almost anything is possible—not always easy, but possible; Prudence King, who introduced me to Taking Sides and who always works for consensus; Gary Siperstein, Suzanne Recane, Kym Meyer, Robert Hoffmeister, and Sarah Poissant, who introduced me to issues I had barely begun to consider; Karley Bailie, Cathy Cummins, Vanessa Hargrove, and Linee Scerra (graduate assistants extraordinaire), who explored, investigated, and debated with me; Ted Knight, David Brackley, Rose Gleich, and all the other McGraw-Hill/Dushkin magicians whose guidance and assistance were invaluable; and, of course, my husband, Joe, whose encouragement, optimism, and ability to weigh all sides of an issue make everything easier.

MaryAnn Byrnes
University of Massachusetts–Boston

Contents In Brief

Contents

Scot Danforth, a member of the School of Education of the University of Missouri–St. Louis, argues that America's trust in science has led to the creation of an array of artificial terms, such as *mental retardation,* that devalue individuals, have no basis in reality, and blunt the voices of those to whom they are applied. James M. Kauffman, a professor of education at the University of Virginia, cautions readers not to be overly distracted by criticism and asserts that special education is a relatively young profession that uses accepted research practices and self-reflection to generate reliable common knowledge of effective instructional strategies for students with disabilities who were previously excluded from schools.

James M. Patton, a professor at the College of William and Mary, argues that African American children are overrepresented in special education programs and that this overrepresentation needs to be addressed through the involvement of those who are culturally and interculturally competent. Donald L. MacMillan and Daniel J. Reschly, faculty members at the University of California at Riverside and Vanderbilt University, respectively, in examining the issue of overrepresentation, question the accuracy and usefulness of the mechanisms for assessing children and determining specific disabilities.

Teresa S. Jordan, an associate professor at the University of Las Vegas–Nevada; Carolyn A. Weiner, president of Syndactics, Inc.; and K. Forbis Jordan, a professor emeritus at Arizona State University, contend that the number of students identified as disabled is increasing at an excessive rate because of funding systems that encourage overidentification and discourage flexible, creative, inclusive school programming. Sheldon Berman, a school superintendent, and his colleagues maintain that districts have been careful and conservative in identifying children with disabilities but that enrollment and costs are increasing primarily because of the increased numbers of children with more significant disabilities.

Chester E. Finn, Jr., et al., educational policy experts and research fellows at the Hudson Institute, are involved in the third part of a multiyear study of charter schools. They affirm that every child is welcome in charter schools but hold that the requirements of IDEA, along with other regulations, often stifle creativity, limit resources, and reduce a school's flexibility. Nancy J. Zollers and Arun K. Ramanathan, a professor and a graduate student, respectively, at Boston College, maintain that the needs of many children with disabilities are swept aside as for-profit charter schools pursue their dual commitments to make money and raise test scores.

Hill M. Walker and Jeffrey R. Sprague, educational researchers at the University of Oregon's Institute on Violence and Destructive Behavior, describe the path that leads from exposure to risk factors to destructive outcomes. They argue that society must recommit itself to raising children safely, and they advocate strong collaborative arrangements between schools, families, and communities. James M. Kauffman, a professor of education at the University of Virginia, states that experts know what needs to be done to prevent emotional and behavioral disorders but that society as a whole has invented many reasons not to make prevention a reality.

Ashley Thomas King, bilingual coordinator in the Kwethluk (Alaska) Community Schools, concludes that court cases have hamstrung administrators so that they cannot equitably discipline students, regardless of whether a disability is linked to unacceptable behavior. Russell J. Skiba, an Indiana University faculty member and codirector of the Safe and Responsive Schools Project, writing after the passage of IDEA97, comments on disciplinary options that are available to administrators but questions the wisdom of the current system of school discipline, which he feels is heavily weighted toward exclusionary practices.

The National Council on Disability (NCD), an independent federal agency dedicated to promoting policies, programs, practices, and procedures that guarantee equal opportunity and empowerment for all individuals with disabilities, found that all 50 U.S. states are out of compliance with special education law, a condition that the council argues must be remedied by increased federal attention. Frederick M. Hess, an assistant professor of education and government, and Frederick J. Brigham, an assistant professor of education, both at the University of Virginia, maintain that increased federal monitoring will only deepen the separation between general and special education, drawing resources away from true educational excellence for all.

U.S. Supreme Court justice John Paul Stevens, writing for the majority of the Court, affirms the "bright line test," establishing that school districts are required by IDEA to provide one-on-one nursing services and any other health-related services that can be delivered by individuals other than a licensed physician. U.S. Supreme Court justice Clarence Thomas, representing the dissenting minority opinion, asserts that continuous one-on-one nursing services for disabled children are indeed medical and, as such, beyond the scope of congressional intent in IDEA. He concludes that such services are not the responsibility of special education programs within school districts.

Dorothy Kerzner Lipsky, director of the National Center on Educational Restructuring and Inclusion at the City University of New York, and professor of educational psychology Alan Gartner emphasize that IDEA97 supports inclusion as the best way to educate students with disabilities and discuss the ingredients that contribute to successful inclusionary practices. Daniel P. Hallahan, a professor of education at the University of Virginia in Charlottesville, fears that students with disabilities will lose access to necessary, specially designed instruction in the inclusionary rush to return them to the very classrooms in which they experienced failure.

Susan Shapiro-Barnard and her colleagues in the Institute on Disability at the University of New Hampshire affirm the positive outcomes of full inclusion at the high school level for students with significant cognitive disabilities. Public school administrators Gary M. Chesley and Paul D.

Calaluce, Jr., express their concern that full inclusion of students with significant cognitive disabilities does not provide appropriate preparation for successful life following school.

Harlan Lane, a faculty member at Northeastern University; Robert Hoffmeister, director of the Deaf Studies Program at Boston University; and Ben Bahan, a deaf scholar in American Sign Language linguistics, value residential schools as rich cultural resources that enable Deaf children to participate fully in the educational experience. Tom Bertling, who acquired a severe hearing loss at age 5 and attended a residential school for the deaf after third grade, favors the use of sign language in social situations but views residential schools as segregated enclaves designed to preserve the Deaf culture rather than to develop adults who can contribute fully to society.

Rex Knowles, a retired college professor, and Trudy Knowles, an assistant professor of elementary education, argue that federal mandates for all students to master the same curriculum fail to consider students' individual differences and needs. Jerry Jesness, a special education teacher, stresses that students who complete school without learning the basics will be ill-equipped to succeed as adults and that any program that avoids teaching these essentials fails to address the long-term needs of students.

Michael F. Giangreco, a research associate professor specializing in inclusive education, and his colleagues assert that untrained teacher assistants spend too much time closely attached to individual students, often hindering the involvement of certified teachers and nondisabled peers. Susan

Unok Marks, Carl Schrader, and Mark Levine, of the Behavioral Counseling and Research Center in San Rafael, California, find that professionally trained classroom teachers are often less prepared than some assistants to work with children in inclusive settings and that, unprepared to supervise assistants, they use this lack of knowledge to avoid teaching children with disabilities.

G. E. Zuriff, a professor of psychology at Wheaton College, challenges the differentiation between children who are diagnosed as learning disabled and those who are found to be slow learners, asserting that all children struggling in school deserve assistance. He questions the tests and assessment strategies that are used to determine the diagnosis of learning disabilities (LD), holding that LD is based on false comparisons to individuals with brain damage. Michael M. Gerber, a professor in the Graduate School of Education at the University of California, Santa Barbara, acknowledges that all the answers about LD have not yet been found, but he maintains that much has been learned in the process of exploring the unique learning characteristics of individuals who learn some subjects with ease and struggle mightily over others.

Edward M. Hallowell, director of a clinic that specializes in the diagnosis and treatment of attention deficit hyperactivity disorder (ADHD), discusses how he utilized his own diagnosis of ADHD to change the direction of his life and those of his clients, becoming more knowledgeable about brain functioning and implementing strategies that enhance daily life. Thomas Armstrong, an author and speaker specializing in learning and human development, is troubled by the fact that schools, doctors, and society have embraced ADHD as a real disorder. He raises questions about the reality of ADHD, the soundness of the diagnostic tools, and the motivation that leads society to create and believe in ADHD.

Lawrence H. Diller, a pediatrician and family therapist, asserts that the use of stimulants on children has risen to epidemic proportions, occasioned by competitive social pressures for ever more effective functioning in school and at work. Larry S. Goldman, a faculty member of the Pritzker School of Medicine at the University of Chicago, and his colleagues review 20 years of medical literature regarding the diagnosis of attention deficit hyperactivity disorder and the use of stimulants. They conclude that the condition is not being overdiagnosed or misdiagnosed and that medications are not being overprescribed or overused.

Issue 17.   Should Parents Choose Cochlear Implants for Their Deaf Children?   336

Thomas Balkany, Annelle V. Hodges, and Kenneth W. Goodman, of the University of Miami, argue that the Deaf community actively works to dissuade families from choosing cochlear implants for their children, preferring to have the decision made by Deaf individuals as a way to perpetuate the existence of a separate culture. The authors maintain that parents must decide whether or not their children receive cochlear implants, based on each child's best interest. The National Association of the Deaf (NAD), an education and advocacy organization committed to supporting the deaf and the hard of hearing, uses its updated position paper on cochlear implants to express concern that medical professionals will dissuade parents from considering the positive benefits of the Deaf community and choose, instead, a medical procedure that is not yet proven.

Issue 18.   Do Students With Disabilities Benefit From Participating in High-Stakes Testing?   358

Martha L. Thurlow, director of the National Center on Educational Outcomes, and David R. Johnson, director of the Institute on Community

Integration, both at the University of Minnesota, assert that high-stakes testing may hold many benefits for students with disabilities, especially if the tests are carefully designed and implemented. Pixie J. Holbrook, a special education teacher and consultant, maintains that high-stakes testing marks children with disabilities as worthless failures, ignores their accomplishments and positive attributes, and seriously limits their range of possibilities in adult life.

Introduction

MaryAnn Byrnes

I introduce... a bill... to insure equal opportunities for the handicapped by prohibiting needless discrimination in programs receiving federal financial assistance.... The time has come when we can no longer tolerate the invisibility of the handicapped in America.... These people have the right to live, to work to the best of their ability—to know the dignity to which every human being is entitled. But too often we keep children whom we regard as 'different' or a 'disturbing influence' out of our schools and community altogether.... Where is the cost-effectiveness in consigning them to... 'terminal' care in an institution?

— Senator Hubert H. Humphrey (D-Minnesota), January 20, 1972, on introducing to Congress a bill mandating education for children with disabilities (as quoted in "Back to School on Civil Rights," National Council on Disability, 2000)

Unfortunately, this bill promises more than the federal government can deliver, and its good intentions could be thwarted by the many unwise provisions it contains.... Even the strongest supporters of this measure know as well as I that they are falsely raising the expectations of the groups affected by claiming authorization levels which are excessive and unrealistic.... [This bill also contains a] vast array of detailed complex and costly administrative requirements which would unnecessarily assert federal control over traditional state and local government functions.

— President Gerald Ford, November 29, 1975, upon signing federal
legislation to mandate education for children with disabilities
(as quoted in *Congress and the Nation, IV*)

Special education was born of controversy. Controversy about who belongs in schools and how far schools need to stretch to meet student needs. The debate continues.

When was the first time you saw someone with a disability? Think hard about your school experience. What do you remember? Compare your recollections with those of someone one generation older—and one younger. The differences will be startling.

Chances are you remember The Room. Usually it was in the basement of the school. Hardly anyone went into The Room. Hardly anyone came out. The kids in The Room never seemed to be part of recess or plays or lunch or gym. The teachers were invisible, too. Sometimes the windows of The Room were covered with paper. Usually the shades were drawn. Kids in your class whispered about The Room, but no one really knew what happened "in there."

Likely, the students who went to school in The Room were older, bigger, and not as smart as most of the other kids in the school. They had few books to learn from and rarely studied any but the most basic academic tasks. No one really knew what happened to the kids in The Room once they left elementary school. There never seemed to be a Room at high school. Hard as it is to believe, those who made it to the inside of The Room may have been the lucky ones.

Less than 30 years ago, if you were the parent of a child with a disability, your local school had the option to tell you that your child was not welcome—that there was no place in the school for your child. The choices were few—you could teach your child at home (or just have him spend his days there); you could try to find a space in a kind school run by dedicated religious people; or you could have your child "put away" in a faceless institution for life. Try looking at Burton Blatt and Fred Kaplan's *Christmas in Purgatory: A Photographic Essay on Mental Retardation* (Human Policy Press, 1974) for a view of some of the worst options.

I remember The Room in the elementary schools I attended, but I never knew much about its students. I remember the Catholic school for girls with Down syndrome where I volunteered as a Girl Scout. The residents learned cooking and sewing while I was getting ready for high school and college. I never saw the girls outside the school and do not know what they did when they grew into adults.

I also remember the boys who sat in the back row of my classes and tried to avoid the teachers' attention. The teachers hoped that these boys would just be quiet and behave. The boys dropped out of school as soon as they could.

Many years later, in the early 1970s, I moved from being a fourth grade teacher to a special education teacher because I was intrigued with unlocking the puzzles that made learning so hard for some of my students. One of my early jobs was as a teacher in an updated version of The Room. It was my first experience in a small district. The day before school began, all the teachers and their students were listed in the local newspaper, along with the bus routes. I eagerly looked for my name, but instead of Mrs. Byrnes, I read "Emotionally Disturbed Classroom." For the entire time I worked at that school, I was the "emotionally disturbed teacher."

Times had changed a little since I attended school. My classroom was on the main floor, next door to the third grade; we had academic books to use; and we had lunch and recess with everyone else. But we were still different. Each day, my students and I needed to leave our room from 11:30 to 1:30 so that it could be used by the gym teacher while the gym was being turned into the cafeteria. Since there were only 10 of us, it seemed to be an easy solution to have us without a classroom space. No one seemed to care where we went or what we did during that time. Plenty of people were surprised to see us camp out in the library tackling "real" school work.

In contrast, I think about the schools of today. Children with learning problems that might be significant enough to be disabilities are the focus of concentrated attention. Trained professionals and researchers strive to understand disabilities and to address them with specific teaching methods and approaches. Parents and teachers actively consider ways to adapt instruction. Program options seem limitless. Many children with disabilities now grow into adults who hold jobs and contribute to society instead of spending their lives in isolation at home, in institutions, or on the streets.

Despite this progress, I still know schools in which students with disabilities are separated into sections of the school where no one else ever goes. There are still districts where no one thinks to include students with disabilities when counting up the number of new math books that need to be ordered. And once formal schooling ends, there are still many young adults who sit at home without jobs because there is no guaranteed support.

Has the promise of special education been met or exceeded? Has society done too much or not enough? Despite what feels like progress, arguments about special education continue. Many of them are included in this book.

As you consider the issues ahead, think about the people with disabilities you first remember. How would their lives have been changed by today's special education? What could be done to help them be more productive citizens? How have the dreams of Hubert Humphrey and the cautions of Gerald Ford been realized?

Recent History and Legal Foundations

The history of special education in American public schools is short and defined by legislation. Private or religious schools have long offered specialized options for students who are blind or deaf or who have mental retardation. Until the last quarter of the twentieth century, public options were largely limited to residential institutions and a few "Opportunity Classes" in public schools.

Following the civil rights struggles of the 1960s came the realization that another significant segment of children in the United States—those with disabilities—were not being afforded a quality education. Although a few states instituted their own policies and regulations regarding the education of children with disabilities, districts could still refuse to enroll children with disabilities.

Successful court cases in individual states establishing the right of children with disabilities to be educated led to the 1975 passage of federal Public Law 94-142, which requires every public school district to deliver a free and appropriate education to all children with disabilities. Renamed the Individuals with Disabilities Education Act (IDEA) in its 1990 and 1997 reauthorizations, the regulations connected to these laws form the foundation of special education for every state that receives funds from IDEA. In addition, individual states have constructed local legislation to clarify federal language or to extend commitments beyond the federal standard.

Even if districts chose not to seek federal funds and thereby sidestep IDEA regulations, the education of students with disabilities would be covered by other legislation. Section 504 of the Rehabilitation Act of 1973 is a civil rights statute prohibiting organizations that receive federal funds from discriminating against any individual based on a disability that substantially limits a major life activity. Reasonable accommodations must be implemented so that individuals with disabilities have equal access to the activities of such organizations. Curb cuts, lowered water fountains, and signs in Braille all came to be in response to Section 504. Since all school districts receive federal funds, Section 504 forbids the exclusion of students with disabilities, although it does not address education with the detail of IDEA.

The Americans with Disabilities Act (ADA), which was passed in 1990, expands the protections of Section 504 to the private sector. The ADA forbids businesses, governmental agencies, and public accommodations (other than churches or private clubs) from discriminating against any individual who has a disability that substantially limits a major life activity. The ADA carries the same responsibility for accommodations as Section 504 and impacts the practices of almost every employer. One of the most recently decided ADA cases established the right of golfer Casey Martin to use a cart as an accommodation during PGA Tour events so that his physical condition does not prevent him from competing.

Many people say that the elements of these laws are vague and undefined. Terms are interpreted differently across the states, and businesses struggle with the range of accommodations and the meaning of "reasonable." Clarity is often achieved through the resolution of legal challenges, some of which have reached the Supreme Court. Because of the continually changing natures of disabilities and society, a single court decision can radically alter the obligations of an employer.

The ground shifts for schools as well. For example, as you proceed through the readings in this book, you will encounter the debate between "least restrictive environment" and "free appropriate public education." Each term is critical to the development of a school's special education program, but each is also fluid in meaning. Federal law does not provide solid definitions that can be used with precision. Schools do their best to apply these terms to individual children with widely varying needs. As with businesses and the ADA, court cases about individual children continue to define what is "restrictive" and what is "appropriate."

Essential Terms and Concepts

Special education has its own unique vocabulary and terms, just as any other field. Being familiar with the concepts discussed below will increase your understanding of the issues ahead.

Disabilities.　All federal laws refer to the following list of disabilities: autism, deaf-blindness, deafness, developmental delay, emotional disturbance, hearing impairment, mental retardation, orthopedic impairment, other health impairment, specific learning disability, speech or language impairment, traumatic brain injury, and visual impairment. Autism and traumatic brain injury are recent additions to the list because their occurrence has increased. State laws frequently amplify the federal definitions of each disability with particular diagnostic criteria, satisfied through the administration of appropriate assessment tools in the child's dominant language. It is important to note that this list of disabilities does not include children who need instructional assistance solely because of language differences, cultural differences, or lack of instruction. In order for a child to be eligible for special education, the school's educational team must determine that a disability exists.

Federal definition of a child who is eligible for special education. According to IDEA, this is a child with a disability who is not making effective progress in school because of that disability and who requires specially designed instruction or related services in order to make progress in school. Federal legislation applies to individuals from birth to either the receipt of a high school diploma or age 22. In most states, public schools are charged with educational responsibility beginning on a child's third birthday.

Individual education program (IEP). IDEA requires each child's educational team, including parents, to meet at least annually to formulate this agreement, which describes the education of a child with a disability. The IEP outlines the impact of the student's disability, current educational status, necessary accommodations, the nature and amount of services to be provided to the child, and the goals and objectives that are the targets for each year. Services cannot be delivered—nor can they be ended—without a parent-approved IEP. Parents who disagree with evaluations or services have the right to seek redress through an administrative hearing or a legal suit. All educators are bound to abide by the terms of an approved IEP.

Related services. These supportive, noneducational services permit a child with a disability to participate in special education. Related services can include, but are not limited to, transportation, various therapies, mobility instruction, social work, and medical services for diagnostic or evaluation purposes.

Free appropriate public education (FAPE). This cornerstone of IDEA guarantees that special education and related services are provided at no cost to parents. The word *appropriate,* which has never been clearly defined, is the source of much controversy and litigation.

Least restrictive environment (LRE). Another key element of IDEA, this phrase refers to each school's responsibility to ensure that "to the maximum extent appropriate, children with disabilities...are educated with children who are nondisabled; and that...removal from the regular educational environment occurs only if the nature or severity of the disability is such that education in regular classes with the use of supplementary aids and services cannot be achieved satisfactorily" (IDEA, Section 300.550). Here, too, different interpretations of many undefined terms can lead to disagreement and litigation.

Continuum of services. Special education services take many forms and happen in many places. Inside the classroom, these can range from consulting with a teacher on the format of a test to team teaching a special educator and an English teacher. Outside the general education classroom, specialized instruction might be delivered to small groups of children with disabilities. A few children are taught in separate classes or schools (day, residential, or hospital) that enroll children with disabilities only. The entire spectrum of options, the continuum of services, must be considered when designing individualized special education programs.

Inclusion.   This term may be one of the first that comes to mind when special education is mentioned. Surprisingly, the word *inclusion* does not appear in any federal legislation. Its meaning differs across states, across districts, and even within schools, and it can change from year to year. Defining and applying this term has resulted in dedication as well as confusion, frustration as well as opportunity, creativity as well as litigation. The common element in all definitions involves increasing the participation of children with disabilities in general education classes.

Differing Orientations

Underlying the controversies in *Taking Sides: Clashing Views on Controversial Issues in Special Education* are three separate perspectives, each of which affects the way in which people envision a solid special education program. Although disagreements cannot always be reduced to one of these, it is likely that people who support differing sides of an issue question will also be on opposite sides of the following dynamics.

Medical or Educational Model?

The medical model of special education views disabilities as conditions that can be improved, remedied, remediated, or perhaps prevented. Medical model adherents seek a specific treatment or therapy to address the physical, psychological, or cognitive issues that result in school problems. Those who follow an educational model aim to address the impact of a disability on school performance directly. Proponents focus on improving educational success by teaching individual skills or employing particular strategies that sidestep the areas of difficulty. Is it wiser to deliver occupational therapy to increase the handwriting skills of a child with cerebral palsy or to teach the child how to use voice-activated software to enable his or her words to become print?

Special Need or Disability?

The federal list of disabilities does not mention children who need instructional assistance solely due to language differences, cultural differences, poverty, or lack of instruction. Neither does it include students who are gifted and talented. Yet children in each of these groups may not have their needs met in a standard classroom without extra attention. In addition, almost everyone can remember struggling with learning at one point in life. Despite these hurdles, special education does not help children who are covered by any of these descriptions unless those children also have disabilities. Special education is about the education of children who have disabilities rather than those who struggle. This delineation causes controversy. If we know children whose lives put them at risk for failure, should we wait until that failure occurs before we give them help, or should we expand special education to include them? If we expand special education by including these children, are we helping them or burdening them with a stigmatizing label?

Regular or Special Responsibilities?

Thirty years ago, millions of children with disabilities were excluded from school. Federal laws mandated their education, which initially occurred mostly in specialized locations by specialized teachers. Seeing these students grow, teachers and parents began to seek out special education services. In many districts, special education ceased being a stigma and became a desired and protected resource, particularly when budget stress increased class sizes. As the number of children receiving services increased, resistance rose to the expansion and costs of special education and to its separation from the overall school curriculum. This backlash resulted in tighter definitions that restricted services to those who are truly disabled and increased expectations that classroom teachers would assume responsibility for a wider range of children. Has the aura surrounding special education deluded people into thinking that there is a special magic to this part of education, or will legislators, teachers, and parents be frustrated by the limits to which one teacher's attention can stretch?

Understanding Controversy

Precisely because the issues surrounding special education are so powerful and the stakes for children are so high, it is vital that we engage actively in their resolution. To achieve this end, it is essential to recognize differences and collaborate to find common ground.

Disagreements About Applying the Law

Parents and teachers must come to agreement about the best way to meet the needs of a child with a disability. Honorable people may be equally committed to the goal of a free appropriate public education in the least restrictive environment but differ on the definition and application of these terms. Although few people would argue about the meaning of *free,* some parents and teachers prefer focused instruction in small groups of children with similar learning needs, while other parents and educators feel that the letter and spirit of the law can only be met when all children (regardless of individual need) are taught within the general education classroom all day. Two children may be very similar but have dramatically different special education programs because the preferences and reasoning of their educational teams differ dramatically. Since each child is unique and can only experience one option at a time, it is impossible to know which choice will lead to the best outcome. In fact, the "best" option may change as the child grows and develops.

Sometimes the differing interpretations of parents and teachers can result in heated arguments. The keys to coming to a consensus in this difference (as with all others) are listening, learning, and being open to new information and different perspectives. Equally important is evaluating each source of information and each course of action in a measured, careful way, even if it differs dramatically from what you feel is right. Often, putting yourself in the other person's place helps. Ask yourself, What would I do if this were my child? What would I do if I were the teacher?

As with most issues regarding children, the best solution is achieved when the adults involved put their attitudes, emotions, and pride aside to understand what the other person wants and why he or she wants it.

Disagreements About Interpreting Facts and Figures

While some of the issues in *Taking Sides* address decision making about individual children, others require the interpretation of objective facts. Analyzing these controversies requires a different approach.

For example, educators and legislators often argue about the significant increase in special education numbers and costs. While this is a debate that deserves examination, it is also one that highlights the importance of evaluating information carefully. The meaning of seemingly objective facts can change depending on the context that is used for interpretation.

Consider the following statement: "Student enrollment in special education programs increased from 3.6 million in 1976–77 to 6 million in 1996–97. During that same time, the total student population increased by only 4.4%" (Center for Special Education Finance [CSEF], *Resource*, Winter, 1999–2000).

A truly alarming increase. What a terrible situation! Truly, this is a system running amok. The number of children in special education has doubled while the number of children in schools has barely increased at all. There must be a way to slow this trend. At this rate there will not be any money to buy new books to meet new standards. Perhaps the law is poorly written. Perhaps districts are not evaluated closely enough. Perhaps parents are too unreasonable and administrators too ready to provide any service requested.

Or is it? Additional information might change the interpretation. The cited enrollment statistics begin with 1976, the first year after federal law mandated a free appropriate public education for all children with disabilities. In 1973 the Senate Labor and Public Welfare Committee documented "more than seven million deaf, blind, retarded, speech-impaired, emotionally disturbed or otherwise handicapped children in the United States... only 40 per cent were receiving an adequate education, and many were not in school at all" (*Congress and the Nation, IV,* 1973).

Millions of children with disabilities were not *in* school in 1976, so their addition to the rolls made a big bump. Many children were in institutions, which declined in size and scope as school doors opened. Many children became identified as having disabilities and entered the special education count— do the statistics subtract them from the "total student population"?

Searching out background information about statistics or seemingly objective facts can change your interpretation of their meaning and, with it, your position on the issue. Bringing to light the assumptions made by others may do the same.

Some believe that special education enrollments have risen due to the creation of "invisible disabilities" invented by those looking for a cause or an excuse for poor performance or any other way to get extra help for their children. Others contend that science is becoming more adept at understanding learning and behavior. In doing so, research identifies real reasons to explain why some students struggle and productive strategies to facilitate learning.

Some maintain that society has become looser and more permissive. Drugs and alcohol are more readily available. Also, children are not supervised the way they used to be and are influenced heavily by exposure to media representations of violent behavior. Others point to statistics on poverty, one-parent homes, three-job parents, and the disintegration of family and community supports to explain the increasing numbers of students who push the limits of courtesy, tolerance, and the law.

Some are proud that medicine is making remarkable strides, sustaining one-pound babies and victims of tragic accidents or chronic illnesses who live to come to school ready to learn. Others are concerned that these miracles of life require extensive support and extraordinary methods that are beyond the scope of schools.

Each point of view puts a different spin on the analysis of enrollment figures in special education. The interpretation you choose to accept depends on the argument you find most compelling. Careful deliberation of all information helps you formulate your own opinion.

Being Aware of Bias

We all bring to every discussion our own background and inclinations. We cannot help but apply these to the issues in this book. In fact, individual experiences may very well lead to creative options that change the course of a debate. As you begin to tackle your first issue, I offer the following reflections, gathered from students, parents, and colleagues.

Acknowledge and be mindful of your own experiences.   If you or a family member has encountered special education (or a lack of it), you will have formed strong opinions about its worth. If you have not had direct experience, your community's media coverage of special education may have shaped your thoughts. Recognize the impact of your experience, and consider its influence as you debate the issues.

Be cautious of solutions that claim to apply equally to every situation.   Two children with Down syndrome can be as different from each other as two "typical" seventh-grade children. Urban and suburban elementary schools pose very different sets of possibilities and limitations. Appropriate strategies in kindergarten transfer poorly to 10th grade. Ideas can usually be adapted but rarely be duplicated.

Think of possibilities rather than limitations. It is easy to say, "That can't be done," and be constrained by what you have already observed. Creative solutions emerge from asking, "How can it be done?"

Consider the impact of roles, motivations, and perspectives. Teachers come to their work because they want to help children grow and learn. Special education professionals believe in their ability to help children conquer the limitations of their disabilities and become productive learners and adults. Parents seek educators who are dedicated to helping children reach their potential. District administrators serve two masters. First, they believe in the power of education and want to clear financial and legal hurdles so that teachers can do their job as well as possible. Second, they understand that they are entrusted with the finite resources of a community and need to be answerable for their decisions in a way that will sustain the confidence of the citizens. Finally, legislators are committed to ensuring equal treatment and benefits for their constituents, whose lives span a wide range of circumstances.

Each of these roles demands responsibility and accountability. The tasks of each role shape opinions and decisions. The outlook of people inhabiting each role can lead to widely different perspectives, powerful arguments, and creative solutions. Consider the background of each of the authors as you evaluate their points of view. What in their backgrounds leads them to their opposite conclusions?

Final Words

As you read the selections in this book and discuss them with your colleagues, your challenge is to sort through competing arguments and information to form your own opinions about the education of children with disabilities. Perhaps you will have the opportunity to apply your point of view to an issue within your community or school. Perhaps you will discover practices in those schools that will change your opinion on an issue.

Controversies in special education are likely to endure. The topics will change, but there will always be argument about the right thing to do for children who seem to need so much. You might be tempted to search for global answers. You might find yourself frustrated by limited options. Or you might come to a unique solution that works perfectly for your district and your school.

As a special education administrator, especially in the spring, I often woke up in the middle of the night with a seemingly irresolvable problem running and running and running through my brain. Usually, it involved balancing competing views of how to help a child. None of the options seemed totally satisfactory. A wise friend suggested I let go of the feeling that I needed to solve the problem alone and, instead, ask others to discuss together the pros and cons of each avenue. This suggestion has always served me well as I struggled over issues of doing the right thing for children. I hope the issues in *Taking Sides* keep you thinking at night and that my friend's suggestion helps you come to your own resolutions whenever you think about educating children with disabilities.

National Institute of Mental Health

A branch of the National Institutes of Health, the National Institute of Mental Health (NIMH) is focused on generating and disseminating information regarding mental health conditions. This site contains information regarding the full range of behavioral disorders and conditions as well as up-to-date research information related to their existence, causes, and treatment.

http://www.nimh.nih.gov/home.cfm

Center for Special Education Finance

Established in 1992, the Center for Special Education Finance (CSEF) addresses fiscal and policy questions related to the delivery and support of special education services in the United States. This Web site provides access to CSEF publications, studies, and research activities.

http://csef.air.org

Center for Education Reform

This Web site is the home base for the Center for Education Reform (CER), a national, independent, nonprofit advocacy organization committed to education reform. The Web site contains information about school choice options and charter schools as well as a range of other efforts for changing schools.

http://www.edreform.com/index.html

The Behavior Home Page

Created and maintained jointly by the Kentucky Department of Education and the Department of Special Education and Rehabilitation Counseling at the University of Kentucky, this site has a wealth of information for individuals who seek information and strategies about the management of students with behavior difficulties.

http://www.state.ky.us/agencies/behave/homepage.html

Thomas B. Fordham Foundation

Affiliated with the Manhattan Institute for Policy Research, the Thomas B. Fordham Foundation supports research, publications, and action projects, with a special interest in education reform. This site contains a link to Rethinking Education for a New Century, a compilation of thought-provoking essays about the status of special education in today's schools.

http://www.channel1.com/users/hudson/

PART 1

Special Education and Society

It seemed simple enough in the beginning. All students have a right to an education. No excuses for not educating a child would be acceptable. Unfortunately, schools needed to be compelled by force of law to enroll all students. Once federal and state laws ensured enrollment, the boundaries of required services were interpreted as frequently by the words of litigation as by the decisions of educators. Opportunities for some are interpreted as limitations for others. As medicine becomes more sophisticated, disabilities become more complex. As budgets strain, the limitations of the commitment to educate all become increasingly contentious. As society changes, the definition of acceptable behavior evolves. The spirit and the letter of the law, which are not always clear, remain the source of heated discussion.

- Is Special Education an Illegitimate Profession?

- Are Minority Children Overrepresented in Special Education?

- Is Special Education So Expensive Because of the Way It Is Funded?

- Are the Doors of For-Profit Charter Schools Open for Students With Disabilities?

- Does Society Have the Capacity to Prevent Emotional and Behavioral Disabilities?

- Are Schools Limited in Their Ability to Discipline Students With Disabilities?

- Will More Federal Oversight Result in Better Special Education?

- Should One-on-One Nursing Care Be Part of Special Education?

ISSUE 1

Is Special Education an Illegitimate Profession?

YES: Scot Danforth, from "On What Basis Hope? Modern Progress and Postmodern Possibilities," *Mental Retardation* (April 1997)

NO: James M. Kauffman, from "Commentary: Today's Special Education and Its Messages for Tomorrow," *The Journal of Special Education* (vol. 32, no. 4, 1999)

ISSUE SUMMARY

YES: Scot Danforth, a member of the School of Education of the University of Missouri–St. Louis, argues that America's trust in science has led to the creation of an array of artificial terms, such as *mental retardation,* that devalue individuals, have no basis in reality, and blunt the voices of those to whom they are applied.

NO: James M. Kauffman, a professor of education at the University of Virginia, cautions readers not to be overly distracted by criticism and asserts that special education is a relatively young profession that uses accepted research practices and self-reflection to generate reliable common knowledge of effective instructional strategies for students with disabilities who were previously excluded from schools.

Thirteen categories of disabilities are contained in the Individuals with Disabilities Education Act Amendments of 1997 (IDEA97). To be eligible for special education, a child must be identified as having one of these disabilities. In fact, many teachers fret over the length of time it takes to identify a disability and to secure the special services needed to help a child progress in school. IDEA97 contains several sections dealing with the assessment of disabilities, as well as other sections addressing the avenues that parents can follow if they disagree with the decisions made by the school.

Special education law was developed to require schools to teach children who had been excluded as being "uneducable." In the last 30 years, definitions of disabilities have increased in sophistication. Teachers and researchers have struggled to identify and refine the practices that are most effective in increasing the academic achievement of children found to have disabilities.

During the same 30 years, the philosophies of postmodernism and cultural relativity gained prominence. First applied to fields such as psychology, sociology, and the arts, these theories decry the single version of history or reality often depicted by powerful, Eurocentric, white men who are out of touch with the breadth of human experience. Within the philosophy of postmodernism, previously mute voices—including those supporting feminism, alternative sexual orientations and life styles, and ethnic and racial identity—gain volume, power, and influence.

Instead of a single narrative defining "the way things are," postmodernists substitute myriad individual stories, supporting the idea that truth is based uniquely within the individual. Only when all the stories are heard—when no individuals are suppressed or oppressed because they are not part of a powerful elite—will society truly include everyone.

Applied to education, postmodernism connects with constructivist theories of learning and multicultural education, both of which place a high value on the experience of individuals as the foundation for learning. When postmodernism encounters special education, the very existence of disabilities is called into question.

In the following selection, Scot Danforth acknowledges that everyone involved in the field of special education cherishes the hope of improving the lives of children with disabilities. He offers, however, two very different versions of hope—one based on the "project of progressive social science devoted to the comprehension and correction" of disabilities, the other on the possibility that people limited by labels will speak out and, perhaps, overcome the tyranny of these disabling categories, which Danforth feels artificially sort children and silence their voices.

In the second selection, James M. Kauffman, in reflecting on the past and future of special education, expresses concern that critics of special education have forgotten the strides made during the last 30 years, focusing on shortcomings rather than accomplishments in this relatively new field. Providing examples of the empowerment that science has brought to those who were previously excluded from society and finding benefits in shared knowledge, Kauffman values the rigor of the scientific process, which builds on objective facts rather than unsubstantiated fads.

Danforth is concerned that overreliance on scientific verification of educational methodologies limits the range of possibilities for every child. Kauffman worries that without careful scrutiny, valuable learning time for a vulnerable child can be wasted.

As you read these selections, consider the opposing views. Has "acceptable learning" been defined so narrowly that labels are sought to separate those who vary even slightly? Or has scientific analysis been used to refine our understanding of intellectual development and the best practices that support it? Where is the boundary between a limiting stereotype and a descriptive term?

Scot Danforth

 **YES**

On What Basis Hope? Modern Progress and Postmodern Possibilities

Special education and hope seem to go hand in hand. Common sense tells us that individuals could not work to improve the lives of students with mental retardation without carrying and embodying hope in their professional practice. Despite the powerful and assumed role of hope in special education, it is an unexamined aspect of work in this professional field. My purpose in this paper is to provide a deep analysis of the philosophical and historical bases of hope in special education. I describe two separate and conflicting modes of hope: the modern version of hope as a project of progressive social science devoted to the comprehension and correction of mental retardation and other disability conditions, and a postmodern version of hope as an ongoing critique of the scientific ground and language by which individuals are habitually and casually devalued with disabling terms and identities such as "mental retardation." Although the modern version of hope promises a steady climb toward more enlightened findings and facts about mental retardation and services, for the postmodern mode claims that a critical dialogue is necessary, wherein professionals, parents, and, of course, labeled persons may confront, contest, and perhaps overturn the standard mental retardation construct.

Modern discourse in special education emerges from an American historical myth of scientific progress, what Gergen called "the grand narrative of modernism." This explanatory story extends from the Enlightenment rationalism of this nation's founding fathers to present day mainstream social science research to some faith-held, extrapolated future date when scientific knowledge and technological practice peak at a mastery of all necessary variables. This totalizing narrative links the revolutionary birth and subsequent political, economic, and moral rise of this democratic civilization with the deliberate advancement of science, industry, and technology. In the 20th century, this grand narrative of progress may be seen in the growth of interventionist social sciences (e.g., sociology, psychology, education, social work) and the many allied human service professions that ground their practices in these empirical research knowledges.

What does modernism mean for special education philosophy in the field of mental retardation? Modernist special educators hold that the profession

From Scot Danforth, "On What Basis Hope? Modern Progress and Postmodern Possibilities," *Mental Retardation*, vol. 35, no. 2 (April 1997). Copyright © 1997 by The American Association on Mental Retardation. Reprinted by permission of *Mental Retardation* and the author; permission conveyed through Copyright Clearance Center, Inc. Notes and references omitted.

should follow the lead of empirical social science to describe accurately the reality of mental retardation and identify the modes of intervention best suited to those conditions. From this perspective, hope lies in the gradual, scientific production of improved approximations of "truth" and the development of intervention technologies, practices, programs, and instruments "that work" according to the truth-clarifying research. Progress, the scientific development of increasingly accurate representations of human living and more powerful interventions to positively adjust that living, and the hope of helping special education students are taken to be conceptually and morally conjoined.

In stark and critical contrast, the post-modern professional concepts and practices of hope break from the modern tradition of progressive empiricism. Postmodern practices found hope not on the production of generalized, context-free facts about mental retardation and interventions but on the creation of human relationships and conversations in which "mental retardation" as a standard and overriding definition of self can be contested and more positive personal identities, roles, and activities constructed.

Proponents of postmodern positions critique modern empiricism and propose alternative possibilities for action. Postmodernists find the historical myth of scientific progress to be a socially constructed story of uncertain truth value, a narrative that relies on the naive assumption that human knowledge and ability are flowing in continuous motion through time toward perfection or eternal betterment. Lacking a transhistorical perspective from which to evaluate the truth value of modernism, post-modern scholars critique the sociopolitical effects of that narrative, finding it to be a dominating story with profound moral and political implications in the lives of the children served by special education programs. To postmodern special educators, the most notable result of modernism is not scientific progress but the reification of mental retardation as a "real" or "objective" phenomenon of human limitation and stigma in specific lives. Mental retardation, as fashioned in scientific discourse and daily practice, is perpetuated as a natural and unreproachable state, a ready and waiting deficient identity. From this critical analysis, new directions of hope allow us to ask: If the activities of modernist social scientists are not moving professional knowledge, practice, and hope for the improvement of children's lives forward, then how shall professionals, students, and families forge new forms of hope in special education? . . .

Modernism: Hope as Scientific Progress

Gergen noted that the:

> *grand narrative* of modernism . . . is a story told by Western culture to itself about its journey through time, a story that makes this journey both intelligible and gratifying. The grand narrative is one of continuous upward movement—improvement, conquest, achievement—toward some goal. Science furnishes the guiding metaphor. Had science not demonstrated the capacity to defy gravity, extend the lifespan, harness human energies, and

carry voice and image through the stratosphere? Because of individual's capacities for reason and observation, as expressed in our scientific attitude,
utopias were now within our grasp.

The dominant discourse among special educators in the field of mental
retardation claims the value of modernist research to discover the pieces to
the mental retardation puzzle and to find "what works" in practice with children and parents. The ultimate goal is to objectively unveil the approaches
and tactics that can be confirmed to produce positive effects in the education
and treatment of children with mental retardation. These "best practice" approaches, it is commonly stated, should then be generalized, encapsulated in
standard form, and dispensed for use by professionals throughout the nation.

Professionals, family members, and students who pioneer pathways that
are not supported by scientific knowledge, including those involved in inclusion programs and facilitated communication, are criticized by modernist
special educators as promulgating "long-odds approaches . . . [that] foster unrealistic hopes against formidable odds." From this vantage point, professional
and nonprofessional activities that are supported by social science research are
valued as contributions to a reality-based hope for concrete improvements in
the education of "exceptional" students. Such hope is viewed as "realistic" or
"truthful," unswayed by the power of overhyped fads and irrational emotional
currents. In contrast, those innovations and developments not sanctioned by
modernist social science are viewed as lacking a basis in reality. They are spirited "fanaticism," the long-shot pipedreams and tomfoolery of persons lacking
the reason of empirical science. . . .

How have modernist special educators arrived at such a faith in the
progress of social science? How has hope for the improvement of the lives of
persons called "disabled" come to be viewed as inherently dependent on the
progress of social science knowledge? . . .

American Myth of Scientific Progress

Perhaps in America, as in no other Western country, the idea of progress has
played the most powerful role in guiding and unifying a national sense of identify, history, and purpose. A New World burst forth from the political fervor of
the Enlightenment to launch a uniquely American brand of progressive mental-
ity. This American idea of progress, as it has developed through a wide range of
intellectual ideas and popular movements over the past 2 centuries, has enabled
citizens to create great unity in common interpretations of a victorious civilization rising up an ever-improving road. Stretching from the rationalism of the
founding fathers to the current incarnation of progress in the professional application of modernist social science knowledge as redemption for a variety of
social ills, this road brings us notably to our special education profession as
intervention for the "social problem" of students with mental retardation. Although the central cultural meaning of progress was recast in varying forms and
lights over those many decades, it remained ever closely tied to both modern
science and a nationalistic, optimistic American identity. . . .

Modernism and Interventionist Social Science

As the 20th century dawned, it became clear to many that the practical application of natural science knowledge had brought a particular kind of progress, a proliferation of an urbanized, industrial, and technological culture. America had its factories, bridges, tall buildings, and enormous cities. Yet, the apparent fall-out of this capitalistic/technological expansion was a variety of social ills, including school failure, delinquency, crime, and poverty. The cure for these social ills and the hope for social progress became entrusted to the imitator of natural science: the new, developing social sciences and the social science professions. An experimental science of humanity and society would be unleashed to intervene in spaces of imperfection and weakness, suffering and disorder.

No depiction of the development of modern social science would prove adequate to the task of explaining the common philosophical ground behind the geometric growth of the fields of psychology, social work, education, and special education in this century. My analysis, therefore, is limited to the career of one of the early creators of interventionist social science, Lester Frank Ward, a man who may rightfully be called the father of American sociology. Although it would be a foolish stretch to claim that special education science was born of sociology, a brief analysis of Ward's philosophy of an interventionist social science provides great insight into modernist special education assumptions about the necessary and powerful role of empirical knowledge in relation to hopeful professional practice. Ward's extension of natural science principles into the nascent field of sociology demonstrates both the attempt of social science to imitate the obvious successes of the natural sciences and the continuing narrative of progress newly imbedded in the hope to heal American society.

Lester Frank Ward developed a science of human, social living based within the principles and evident success of natural science, growing from a specific interpretation of the work of [Charles] Darwin. Although many claimed that society evolved in a manner analogous to biological evolution, relying on haphazard advancement via probability, Ward disagreed. He theorized two distinct forms of evolution: (a) the Darwinian mode of genetic or natural evolution that described the random and slow progression of nature to more perfect forms and (b) a conscious, intentional mode of social evolution in which people applied his scientific knowledge to push social improvement along at an increased pace. Because humans may understand the operations of evolutionary development in the social sphere, they should then intervene to artificially boost the natural process, making social progress more efficient and less time-consuming.

The power to know the truths of Nature... had gradually become the power to know the truths of Society. A rational social science would accurately describe human, social activity just as an earlier natural science had unlocked the laws of physical motion. Notably, as manifested in Ward's interventionist sociology, the modern social sciences combined the task of knowing truths with the related mission of affecting social change. A constantly improving comprehension of individual activity and social problems—a gradual but steady piecing together of the pieces of the puzzle—would place the new social science in the most hopeful position of all: the cultural and historical place of redemptive power. Human problems could be solved through the faithful application of an interventionist brand of modern social science.

Birth of Special Education as Interventionist Social Science

Where does the early development of special education fit in with this development of an interventionist, modern social science? More specifically, what was the connection between this social science and the work of early professionals and the development of early institutions in the field of mental retardation?

Space limitations in this paper demand that I address this issue in direct and brief fashion. The work of Henry Goddard in the first 2 decades of the 20th century provides us with a useful glimpse at the role of modern social science (namely, measurement psychology) in the growth of mental retardation as a construct and a legitimate professional field.

Conducting research at the Training School at Vineland with institutionalized, "mentally deficient" persons, Goddard was one of the first American psychologists to import and apply the intelligence testing instruments of Binet and Simon. The intelligence test allowed specialists to "objectively" classify persons along a graded scale, to separate the "normal" from the mentally deficient, and to classify the mentally deficient within ranges of intellectual deficit.

Goddard's application of intelligence testing to the identification and categorization of mentally deficient persons was important for two reasons. First, the importation of the mathematical schemes of measurement from natural sciences provided a dramatic boost of legitimacy to the fields of psychology and early special education. These disciplines and professions accessed a source of tremendous power and credibility within Western society through alliance with the assumed accuracy, progressive motion, and morality of modern science. It is not surprising that Goddard's utilization of intelligence testing at Vineland quickly led to his rise as a leading psychologist in the field of mental deficiency and Vineland as the preeminent research and early special education teacher training site.

The second reason that Goddard's use of cognitive measurement was important involves the theorized relation between mental deficiency, immorality, and a range of early 20th century social problems. Trent described Goddard, his professional colleagues at institutions for the "feebleminded," and the public at-large as subscribing to a general fear of "the menace of feebleminded." In both popular and the scientific publications, social vices such as criminality, alcohol abuse, unemployment, and sexual promiscuity were linked to mental deficiency.

... Specifically, mentally deficient persons, due to their pathology, were the purveyors of social vices. In accordance with prominent scientific thought at the time, feeblemindedness was assumed to be genetically inherited. As Goddard fully explained in his famous study of the Kallikak family, immorality was being passed on from one feebleminded generation to the next.

Perhaps the greatest insight into the early development of special education as a scientific practice based in intelligence testing can be gleaned from an analysis of the connection between modern social science and the hope to cure America of social vices in Goddard's work. Through the use of intelligence testing, Goddard claimed to have discovered a new class of feebleminded persons whom he called "morons." This group was undoubtedly the most dangerous of the feebleminded menace. Morons, according to Goddard, had the physical characteristics of "normal" persons and the intelligence of high-range mental deficients. In essence, Goddard claimed that there was an entire group of feebleminded persons who remained undetected, who had intermixed with the normal population, and passed by appearance for normal. Given the propensity of the feebleminded to commit acts of social misconduct, the existence of this class of morons in the general population was a frightening prospect. Evil was hidden among the population, but who could say where? (Or, more accurately, who?)

Goddard and his colleagues at Vineland proposed that intelligence tests be used to identify the "immoral element" for purposes of exclusion and population control. He and many professional leaders at that time advocated that the feebleminded be completely isolated from the mainstream in residential institutions. In addition, he joined the then-popular eugenics movement, supporting the surgical termination of the reproductive capacities of mentally deficient persons. Through exclusion and eugenics, Goddard believed that feeblemindedness could be wiped out through scientific intervention, thus solving the vast array of American social problems and ensuring the continued progress of this society.

At the recent crest of this wave of modern progress rises present-day special education, a field devoted to the practical improvement of the lives of a specific group of children commonly viewed as social or educational failures. Proponents of the centrality of modern social science to special education continue the story of a progressing science in relation to the hopeful mission of helping students with mental retardation and their families. From this modernist perspective, professional hope must rest on a faith in the grand narrative of scientific progress led by special education researchers.

But what if one, in agreement with philosophers Nietzsche and Foucault, holds no faith in the modernist story of progress? What if one does not believe that social science provides gradually improving pictures of social reality? What if the certain and upward motion of modern progress is viewed as neither certain nor upward-moving? Postmodern philosophers in many academic fields, including education and special education, are posing these and other critical questions about the truthfulness of the modernist account.

Postmodernism and Hope in Special Education

... A postmodern philosophy of special education asserts that the current governing story, the guiding scheme of modern social science, no longer provides a valuable basis for hope and unity in the struggle to educate children described as "mentally retarded." Postmodernists typically eschew any universal guiding story as deceptive and totalizing, providing not generalizable or useful facts but a harmful privileging of some knowledges and vocabularies over others of lesser sociocultural power. In brief, the modernist grand narrative cannot be determined to be objectively true. Its maintenance and re-creation in daily practice relies on the faith and actions of persons who believe in the American myth of historical progress. Post-modernists claim that adherence to this historical tale by professionals, students, and families perpetuates the belief that certain persons in society have a deficit condition called "mental retardation" that requires professional intervention and institutional control. As a result, postmodern educators encourage a professional shift from the primary explanatory story of modern social science to a pluralistic, conversational arena in which a multitude of smaller, nongeneralizable stories may be told by the diversity of participants in special education.

In the place of the dominating grand narrative, postmodernism supports a patchwork quilt of many stories, a provisional and ever-changing fabric honoring diverse cultural traditions and multiple versions of "the way it is." A place of many legitimate stories is an arena of dialogue and possibility, allowing individuals and groups to claim their voices, call out their own identities, and forge paths of action that need not comply with the scientific dictates of truth. The scientific goal of progressively finding and describing truth is thus replaced by the moral and political goals of supporting human freedom and community.

Postmodern special educators contend that the hope of educating and supporting children considered to have disabilities can no longer be fueled and conceptualized through the modern social science story, that "insuperable obstacles to this story's coming true" have indeed arisen. Scientific truth is in trouble.

Modern Truth in Crisis

... A number of movements described as postmodern or poststructural have struck at the very core of modern academic disciplines, contesting and undermining the underlying assumption that an objective world is knowable and may be established through the workings of a neutral, rational science. Gergen, in his analysis of the academic upheaval, stated:

> Most of the cherished beliefs that undergird the traditional goals of research and teaching are in eclipse. Some consider the demise of traditional assumptions to be an event little short of catastrophe, to part with the longstanding ideals of truth and understanding is to invite chaos, first in the academic world and then in society generally. Others feel an innervating sense that history is at a turning point, that a new and exciting era is in the making.

This "catastrophe" or "turning point," depending on one's perspective, is evident through much of academia as postmodern concepts have swept into writings in numerous disciplines, including anthropology, history, psychology, sociology, philosophy, and education. The intellectual stir in opposition to the domination of the modernist scientific project is rising in many bubbling caldrons.

Not surprisingly, the knowledge base of special education is the subject of similar doubt and critique from postmodern perspectives. Skrtic described special education as one of a group of professions based in modern social science that has suffered a crisis of legitimacy since the 1960s. This crisis gained initial impetus from Kuhn's analysis of the social and paradigmatic nature of science.

Kuhn's analysis removed scientific activity from the realm of cold rationality and redefined it in terms of social negotiations among perspective-bearing human actors. The truth-producing capabilities of science, according to Kuhn, do not depend on the strict performance of dry and neutral procedures but flex and change within the social and political interactions of scientists. What is held to produce the theoretical ground of authorized research in a given scientific field is a matter of social agreement among those scientists who have the status and reputation that allow them to declare certain theories and hypotheses to be better than alternatives.

... Often, modernist researchers have no or little awareness of how their paradigmatic assumptions form a field of assumed truths that greatly determines what aspects of living will be called "data," what data will be collected, how that data will be symbolized and manipulated, and what hypotheses will ultimately be supported by the inquiry. Parallel to [Sigmund] Freud's assertion that the hidden weavings of unconscious mental activity influence and determine behavior for reasons beyond conscious awareness, modernist researchers' unacknowledged paradigmatic framework surreptitiously provides the structural limitations, linguistic make-up, and conceptual substance of the knowledge they claim to "find" in the external world.

The alternative postmodernism should not be viewed as laying claim to a "better" paradigm; a new process holier than the modern, mechanistic way of constructing meaning; a more "truthful" outline for delineating "what is the case." Instead, we should understand postmodernism as a mode of critical vigilance maintaining that no means of describing reality holds universal privilege over alternatives. All descriptions are viewed as limited and partial, confined and influenced by the linguistic and sociohistorical contexts from which persons speak and write. They are understood to be contingent on the sociocultural context, the language community of the speaker, the knower's paradigmatic predisposition, and the historical situation in which the representation occurs.

Truth, Power, and Special Education

The greatest danger of modern social science, from a postmodern position, concerns the overwhelming authority generally accorded to both the modernist account and the bearers of that account. Knowledge and power are interrelated, integrated socially and institutionally. Each depends on and is supported by the other. The danger of modernism is tyranny in mundane forms, proceeding from what Foucault described as the "general politics of truth," the regime of power running through the social procedures and mechanisms creating truth and manifested within the applications of truth in social practice. What is made true applies power in the lives of those who are the objects of the truth.

For example, in special education, a series of "objective" and psychometric descriptions of a student can justify a mental retardation diagnosis and extrusion to a special education classroom. A child's social identity is quickly refashioned from "normal" status to debilitated learner through procedures of truth and power, processes whose credibility relies on modernist claims of "value-free," rational operation in depicting an "objective truth." The diagnosis makes up merely one moment of the powerful drama by which a person's social identity is constructed in stigmatized form. The on-going services provided by professionals and institutions continue this devaluation project by further reifying the mental retardation status in the life of the diagnosed and treated individual.

If, as the postmodernists contend, adherence to modernist grand narrative cannot be supported by claims to truthfulness or factuality, and if this history produces not so much hope as the social control of persons considered "abnormal," then special educators may choose to view special education science and disability as historical and bureaucratic artifacts of an international special education that may be questioned and contested on local levels. This practical contestation may bring about opportunities for the making of new stories, nongeneralizable tales of local identity generating valuable meaning for individuals and small educational communities. Students "disabled" by modernism may be re-defined or re-interpreted in terms and priorities that do not include disability concepts and descriptions.

As the hope generated by the myth of social science progress has faltered, space for the making of new versions of hope may arise in special education work with students considered to have mental retardation. Professionals may join with "persons who have disabilities" in their struggle to overturn disability constructs and roles in their own lives. Professionals can ally themselves with labeled persons, their families, and loved ones in efforts to transform social constructions of deficiency and incompetence into relationship-based and self-based understandings of personal power and efficacy. . . .

Postmodern philosophers propose that the sources of hope in the field of mental retardation services erupt from precisely those mouths and writing (or typing) hands that do not speak the language of science. Beyond, under, and beside the booming voice of science, that discourse attempting to conform the activities of many to the truth declarations of few, are voices of hope. These are the contributions of parents, students, family members, front-line practitioners, and program directors. Where the modern quest of a uniform knowledge that informs and limits practice has failed; where the science-prescribed methods to be used with students of a certain label or diagnosis are set aside as irrelevant intrusions on the local task of figuring out what to do and how to do it; where the many partners in the Individual Educational Plan (IEP) and educational planning process no longer depend on the promised progress of research to find a better way; in all these and other spaces where a more equal and open dialogue may be developed between practitioners, parents, and students, the hope of postscientific forms of knowledge abounds. The small stories and the soft voices so often devalued and silenced as subjective and biased, unscientific and unknowing, may become genuine and full participants in conversations about pressing matters in the day-to-day education of students labeled as having mental retardation.

Hope in Discourse Beyond Science

... The most important conversations occur in schools and homes, where labeled students, family members, friends, and professionals create practices and relationships far from the gaze of researchers and professional authors. These spaces offer the greatest opportunities for the cultivation of hope beyond modern science, for the arrangement of services in which the individuals involved can place their faith and trust. Small groups of 3, 5, 10, or 12 persons devoted to the well-being of an individual labeled as having mental retardation have the opportunity to set aside scientific talk and disability constructs in favor of language and relationships that value the labeled individual. Within such local circles, the stigmatizing identity of mental retardation may be tossed out and replaced with understandings that seek to protect labeled persons from stigma and devaluation. This reconstructive and relational task disavows universal concepts of progress for the sake of hope.

James M. Kauffman

 **NO**

Today's Special Education and Its Messages for Tomorrow

Characterizing today's special education is in many ways a dangerous undertaking. It is risky because no particular view is likely to be entirely accurate, and there is much diversity of opinion among special educators on nearly every issue. Furthermore, prognostication may make the forecaster look foolish. Had I been asked 20 years ago, or even 10, to guess what the future held, I would not have forecast the developments that have occurred in our field. I am thus acutely aware that my commentary about the meaning of today's special education for the future may be inaccurate and that in 10 or 20 years, or in even fewer, I will be embarrassed by my lack of understanding and foresight. However, in all candor, I am not very happy with most of what I see in our field today. I think we are in a period of considerable upset and danger, and our future could look rather bleak depending on how we respond to current pressures. Consequently, I offer a series of cautions about our present course.

The one sentence or metaphor that I believe best characterizes special education today is this: We are a middle-aged profession going through a profound identity crisis that includes self-destructive behavior. I refer here to the middle age of our profession's evolution, of course, not to the middle age of its members. Some might think that my characterization of special education merely reflects my own middle age or struggle with personal identity. Be that as it may, I offer more specific observations of our present-day characteristics and what they portend. Although there are exceptions, including individuals and pockets of our professional culture, I think the majority in our field could be said to have the following attributes: They are (a) ignorant of our history, (b) apologetic for existing, (c) preoccupied with image, (d) lost in space, (e) unrealistic in expectations, (f) unprepared to focus on teaching and learning, (g) unaware of sociopolitical drift, (h) mesmerized by postmodern/deconstructivist inanities, (i) an easy target for scam artists, and (j) immobilized by anticipation of systemic transformation.

Each of these 10 attributes has implications for our future, and I discuss [five of them] briefly. Because I am not single-mindedly negative and

From James M. Kauffman, "Commentary: Today's Special Education and Its Messages for Tomorrow," *The Journal of Special Education*, vol. 32, no. 4 (1999). Copyright © 1999 by PRO-ED, Inc. Reprinted by permission of PRO-ED, Inc., and the author. Notes and references omitted.

pessimistic about our field today, I conclude with a brief commentary on some positive characteristics that merit attention.

Apologetic for Existing

... [M]y impression is that some of our colleagues today see our very existence in public education as both unfortunate and avoidable. Their line of argument seems to be roughly as follows: If we had done our job as we should have, then we would quickly have worked ourselves out of business. Perhaps we should just quit special education now. The only reason we exist is that general education is flawed and we are evil co-conspirators, maintaining harmful domination over those we label as needing so-called special education. If we reform education in the right way, there will be no more need for labels or so-called special services because education will be a seamless and flexible web of indistinguishable supports for all students. We do not really belong in public education; we were grafted on as an ugly appendage when general education was weak and needed us to help maintain a stratified society by giving privilege to high performers and keeping the so-called disabled powerless.

... We are at a curious juncture in our profession's development a point at which the value of science in special education policy and practice is being attacked by those—including some special educators—who believe that special education has become an evil empire (see Walker et al., in press, for a discussion of such issues in behavioral disorders). Brantlinger, for example, uses concepts of postmodern, deconstructivist philosophy to condemn the presumed power of special education "traditionalists," which she sees as coercive of the powerless—those who, like herself, seek to transform education so that special education is unnecessary. If Brantlinger and others who condemn special education acquire the power of "voice" they feel they are now denied, it will be interesting to see not only whether they then loathe their own dominance but also whether students with disabilities benefit and what language, if any, is used to describe the students we now say have disabilities. Perhaps some prefer the role of victim and the pretense that difference and disability can be acknowledged without labels.

People who are apologetic about their very existence often self-destruct. They may accomplish their own demise in a variety of ways, including their imagined transformation to a new level of existence. If we are going to survive as a viable professional field, then I think we are going to need to change the way we view our legitimacy in public education and develop a sense of self-worth and pride in what we do. I would like to see us become unapologetic about our function, our identity, our distinctiveness, our visibility. I hope we can become unafraid to suggest that students *can* be better off for their contact with us, actually helped more than harmed by our services, including services delivered outside general education when that is appropriate. But many in our field today are preoccupied with an image as antisegregationist to the near exclusion of concern for our substance....

Unrealistic in Expectations

Today there is great unhappiness with special education and its outcomes, and unhappiness with general education, too. Rightfully so. Certainly, I agree that we need to improve outcomes. But what will happen if special education really works and general education does, too? That is, what would we expect to happen to the distribution of outcomes and our students' relative position in that curve if both special education and general education worked the way we think they should? What some reformers seem to be suggesting is that we should expect all children to be successful by a common standard—that is, that we should have the same high standards and expectations for all students and include all students in the same curriculum and assessment procedures, as if by some magic participation therein defines success. In the February 23, 1998, issue of *The New Yorker,* cartoonist Jack Ziegler depicted a California business executive exhorting a subordinate, "Damn it, Henderson, New York is *still* three hours ahead of us. Get on that!" Just as ludicrous would have been an educator saying, "Damn it, Kauffman, some students are *still* two standard deviations below average. Get on that!"

Special education can never be successful in terms of all or even most students with disabilities catching up with their nondisabled peers unless general education is really awful. In fact, if general education begins to provide truly effective instruction for all students, then we might expect that the population variance will increase and that the performance of students with disabilities will become more discrepant than ever from the mean. Perhaps our understanding of these problems at some level predisposes us to shy away from focusing on teaching and learning. After all, we tend to do things at which we are successful. If we ar unable to achieve the goal of helping students with disabilities learn academic skills within a standard deviation or so of the normal population mean, then why not turn our efforts to things more easily accomplished: placing children in neighborhood schools and general education classes and telling their teachers to collaborate?

Unaware of Sociopolitical Drift

I think many of us tend to forget that education, including special education, is a social welfare program of government. All such programs are under attack today, especially if they are conceptualized as entitlement programs. In fact, special education is being attacked in the popular media and by some special educators as a wasteful and ineffective government entitlement program that should be drastically downsized or eliminated. Government assistance of all kinds—except, perhaps, that offered to business and industry—is increasingly difficult to obtain. The prevailing opinion of our citizens, as reflected by the people elected to public office, is that government benefits for children at risk and their families should be smaller and harder to get. Today, more of our children are being reared in poverty and under conditions that we would expect to produce elevated risk of disability. Yet today sentiment is building against the increasing number of students served by special education and the increasing cost of such services. We are being told—and some of us are buying the big lie

—that government programs serving those with special needs, including special education, do not work and should be largely abandoned.

We are virtually certain, in my opinion, to be "downsized," possibly dramatically so in both the size of the population we now serve and the size of our budget. Perhaps a case can be made for turning back responsibility for some of the children we serve to general education. However, if we are to serve even the remaining students adequately, then surely we will need an increase, not a decrease, in the fiscal resources devoted to the task. Our expectations of our programs to normalize children have been unrealistically high, and our estimates of the cost of delivering high-quality services have been unrealistically low. Today, Americans want to ignore social welfare problems as much as possible, to abandon government commitments to all but the spectacularly needy, and to deal with what cannot be ignored by purchasing services from private vendors on the cheap. As a profession, we seem unaware that we are in grave danger of being torched by public sentiment and that some members of our profession are fueling the fire. Our vulnerability is being worsened by postmodern rejection of scientific evidence. Maybe we are attracted to any kind of claptrap if it seems to be capturing the popular imagination, as postmodern and deconstructionism are now doing.

Mesmerized by Postmodern/Deconstructivist Inanities

I recognize that mine may be an unpopular and risky position that in a few years will look silly or worse, but I now believe that some in our field today have taken a bad cognitive tumble into postmodernism and radical deconstructivist philosophy. I refer here specifically to essays on postmodern and deconstructivist descriptions of education, and more particularly of special education. In my view, their teachings undermine progress in serving the needs of students with disabilities. I am not able to identify any practical applications of these writers' work to special education or comprehend how applying their ideas might make a positive contribution to teaching students with disabilities or researching special education problems. This may reflect my own cognitive limitations, but if my assessment is widely shared among special education researchers, it may say something about the observation of an eminent scientist. "Consider this rule of thumb: to the extent that philosophical positions both confuse us and close doors to further inquiry, they are likely to be wrong." I do comprehend the value of context and understand the conditional nature of truth, but the recognition that scientific "truth" is tentative is not a uniquely postmodern insight, nor is the observation that science is affected by its social context a revelation of postmodernists.

The terms *posmodernism* and *deconstructivism,* though difficult to define precisely, are often linked (see Wilson, 1998). I refer to them together as "PD" to indicate the general notions that logical positivism (i.e., what we have come to know as science) is untrustworthy and that alternative ways of knowing or constructing truth have equal merit. The worldview presented by PD is singularly egocentric, as one's own experience (text or narrative) is the only one knowable. Much of the PD thinking put forward by educators is, in my view, based on nonsequiturs and serious misunderstandings of science. According to PD, disability is a social construction that we could eliminate (deconstruct, subvert, redefine), a view seriously at odds with the science of exceptionality. Elkind has suggested that postmodernism challenges the ideas of progress, universality, and regularity that are part of modern science. For example, Elkind noted:

> We acknowledge today that some phenomena, such as the weather, are inherently irregular. So too are phenomena such as the dispersion of cream in a coffee cup. Each time we place cream in a coffee cup, the dispersion pattern is different from what it was before. Some phenomena are, by nature, chaotic and have no underlying regularity.

First, it is important to understand that modern scientists do not claim to be able to predict all phenomena or all cases. In fact, it is precisely the irregularities in phenomena that give rise to shifts to new paradigms that can predict additional phenomena for which older ones could not account, bringing a new level of regularity and predictability to phenomena that previously were assumed to be chaotic. Second, the fact that some phenomena are or appear to be chaotic means neither that all are chaotic nor that the apparent unpredictability of a particular phenomenon will never be understood as a predictable sequence of events. Third, some chaotic phenomena are trivial for achieving a particular purpose in which they play a part. The fact that the dispersion of cream in coffee is chaotic in no way impairs our ability to predict with a high degree of accuracy, and with good effect, the color, taste, and caloric value of a given amount of coffee to which a given amount of cream is added. Likewise, the fact that an individual child's immediate response to a praise statement may be unpredictable in no way invalidates the use of social approval as a strategy for reinforcing desired behavior. Finally, the grand metanarrative of progress attributed to modern science by some proponents of PD is caricature, a clever and amusing set of exaggerations. But, if my understanding is correct, in the PD worldwide, caricature cannot be discriminated from reality.

The demise of the modern era and of logical positivism as the prevailing scientific paradigm are ballyhooed by those who speak—out of their academic element and inappropriately, I think—of a "paradigm shift." Many of those writers who urge a radical change in view invoke a book by Thomas Kuhn, who described the process by which science progresses from less defensible to more accurate and complete explanations of phenomena. But we are not experiencing a shift in scientific paradigm to postmodern or deconstructivist views in any sense compatible with the observations of Kuhn, who popularized the term *paradigm shift*. His treatise dealt only with how paradigms shift within science itself, in which replicable evidence in the positivist tradition is essential. "Any conception of nature compatible with the growth of science by proof is compatible with the evolutionary view of science developed here."

Those who say education paradigms are shifting have no reliable data—no proof—with which to create or legitimize a shift. In fact, PD rejects such proof as unnecessary. The changes of view proposed by PD are based on mere assertion. That is, the proponents of PD seem to suppose that a new paradigm can be created merely by saying or believing that science (that is, positivism) no longer provides valid explanations for our work. However, *scientific* paradigms are not shifted by chutzpah. A scientific paradigm shifts only if reliable, publicly verifiable data are obtainable in support of it; without the data, a new paradigm dies an ignominious death. Moreover, a new scientific paradigm does not necessarily discredit the old, as Kuhn has shown in the case of Newton's and Einstein's physics. Scientific paradigms offer solutions to problems; they are not merely interesting, novel ideas. Kuhn observed that "novelty for its own sake is not a desideratum in the sciences as it is in so many other creative fields." Nevertheless, in higher education, at least in the social sciences and humanities, data are often ignored for the glitter of novelty. . . .

So far, I see no evidence that PD approaches to education offer superior solutions to puzzles (in fact, as I suggested earlier, I am unable to discern what the solutions suggested by PD might be). The absence of better solutions to educational problems offered by PD suggests to me an alternative view of shifting paradigms in education. Researchers during the past several decades have provided clear problem-solving theory. Education may be considered preparadigmatic in that no consensus has existed that teaching and learning can be studied scientifically or that educational policy decisions should be based on reliable data. The rise of applied behavior analysis and the formulation of an explicit and testable theory of instruction may represent the shift to a scientific paradigm of education against which PD assertions are now being directed. An initial scientific paradigm may emerge over a period of decades, and there are always countercurrents that seek to discredit science or, once established, the scientific paradigm that ultimately becomes dominant. To me, a plausible explanation of shifting paradigms in education is that PD represents a struggle to discredit the paradigm that ultimately will be adopted because it solves problems better than the nonpositivist alternatives.

In the end—in science, anyway—the paradigm that wins the wars is the one that offers the most practical and reliable tools for problem solving. As the history of science shows, though, paradigms can be squelched, at least in the short term, by political philosophy or religious beliefs or superstitions. Positivism has won the day in the natural sciences for several hundred years only because political and religious authorities have allowed it to emerge from the dark ages. But persons who do not believe the scientific data or do not like them can still squelch scientific evidence in favor of political correctness, religious faith, or greed, as has been demonstrated by despots, religious zealots, some industrial giants, and occasionally by scientists themselves.

We should not underestimate the popularity of nonscientific and aggressively *anti*scientific beliefs today. Nor should we dismiss the danger of such sentiments and frames of mind for education. *The New Yorker* magazine of April 14, 1997 devoted its entire "Talk of the Town" feature to commentary on the mass suicide of Marshall Applewhite and his Heaven's Gate cult. Applewhite and his followers rejected evidence in favor of belief in the supernatural. *The New Yorker* commentary concluded: "Though science is stronger today than when Galileo knelt before the Inquisition, it remains a minority habit of mind, and its future is very much in doubt. Blind belief rules the millennial universe, dark and rangy as space itself." As if to provide supporting evidence, *Life* magazine subsequently featured an article on the recent resurgence of belief in astrology, hyped on its cover under the banner "ASTROLOGY RISING: Why So Many of Us Now Believe the Stars Reflect the Soul." Belief in astrology has burgeoned in the past 20 years, in the absence of any scientific evidence whatever to support its claims and in the face of reliable scientific evidence that its perceived "success" is a function of people's suggestibility and desire for personal validation.

Postmodern/deconstructivist philosophy would have us embrace the subversion of the concepts of disability and special education, particularly their positivist research bases. It suggests that the scientific way of looking at things is a cognitive house of cards created solely by White males, mostly ones now dead. In fact, it would have us believe that all apparent realities ar merely convenient constructions and power relations that need deconstructing. It is difficult, if not impossible, to construct a defensible philosophy of special education, or anything else, on the assumption that reality is always constructed to fit convenient power relations and fictions. Moreover, there is comic irony in the proposition that all realities are convenient fictions derived from power relations that enslave the powerless—except this one. It recalls the paradox embedded in any proposition made by someone who says, "I always lie." If we accept such notions we will be left with little or nothing but cognitive demolition debris. Guess who will be buried deepest in the rubble? Children with disabilities will be, of course.

The detonation of PD in our profession leaves us with profoundly weak defenses against the glossy assertions of charlatans that they have discovered something miraculous. We become easy marks for those peddling junk science and other frauds. Why wouldn't we believe a spaceship from comet Hale-Bopp might rescue us, if not our students, and transform our earthly vessels? Who is to say that it will not? I am reminded of the cartoon by Robert Mankoff in *The New Yorker* for April 14, 1997 (p. 6), with the caption, "What lemmings believe." Mankoff's drawing shows a stream of lemmings ascending into heaven rather than plunging off a cliff. As I have suggested elsewhere, our profession has a considerable history of enchantment by scam artists, and today's special education seems to me ripe for pied pipers.

An Easy Target for Scam Artists

In my view, PD philosophy helps make us sitting ducks for the quack—pun intended. The list of instructional and therapeutic procedures that have very little or no reliable data to support them is long. It would include such curious items as applied kinesiology and neurological organization technique (NOT) ocular training said to address learning disabilities, facilitated communication (FC), and a wide range of other new age nostrums. In some cases, these quack methods are popularized and sold shamelessly by special educators....

We have always had quacks, and we will have them in perpetuity. But PD notions of the invalidity of science and the arbitrary construction of truth have great potential for diverting us from progress and into perfidy. For example, in the 1990s, we have seen remarkable scientific progress in the positivist tradition in harnessing electronic technology to help individuals with highly specialized communicative needs to express themselves clearly, reliably, and independently. However, at the same time, we have seen the communication of some children with disabilities perverted by the inventive fantasies of "facilitators." What a cruel hoax—that some in our profession are now communicating *for* individuals with disabilities while pretending that these individuals are communicating for themselves. A predictable defense of such sham is that the phenomena of facilitated communication are beyond the reach of traditional scientific verification. This is the familiar dodge of accountability that is used by the magician, the charlatan, and cultist, or the astrologer.

My guess is that in 20 years or so many of those now believing in FC and other frauds will look back on today's quackery with considerable chagrin and wonder why they were so eager to play the fool. I think many of us will wonder why we thought we were about to be transformed, along with the rest of social science if not the world, by ideas that were disconnected from scientific method and not open to public verification. But even if we do not accept PD inanities and scams, we seem spellbound by the idea of systemic transformation, a notion that can distract us from the humbler task of ensuring the integrity and adequacy of *our* component of the array of services exceptional children need —special education.

... [T]he lure of postmodernism and radical deconstructivism is strong and growing. Anti-positivist sentiment is strong, and most citizens, including many teachers and teacher educators, have a very poor understanding of the methods and advantages of positivist science. We may well see even more virulent vilification and rejection of the scientific method by those who misunderstand the meanings and uses of evidence. Special education may lose much more of its focus on the scientific understanding of instruction and find itself lost in a cognitive dead end. We need to weigh very carefully the statements of those who would reform the foundational concepts of our field. We must think our way through the implications of propositions made with "little constraint from an external world of experiments and facts and numbers to limit the unleashed mind," especially propositions to subvert the idea of disability. We must remember that "disengagement from practice produces theoretical hallucinations." Minds unleashed from the constraints of external realities typically dodge responsibilities, leaving people with disabilities stuck in a social niche made more cruel by the avoidance of real-world issues.

A Note of Optimism

Our future looks bleak for many reasons, some of which I have addressed. We are a middle-aged profession that I believe is showing some signs of being "middle-age crazy," as the condition is called in the vernacular. As a professional group we seem to have lost our buoyancy, sense of purpose, and self-esteem. We appear to have forgotten much of our history, with two particular consequences. First, we tend to romanticize our profession's youth, when we were relatively free of regulation, definition, and responsibility, able to lead our professional lives ad hoc—without concern for the broader consequences of our actions. Second, we appear not to have learned much from our prior decades, as we seem ready to dismiss early mistakes as social aberrations and buy "new" ideas (or, if you prefer hype, "paradigms") with virtually no pragmatic analysis of their merits. This is not a pretty picture. If we are to get a grip on our situation and avoid decades of disastrous floundering, then we must do some serious stock-taking.

Our problem of conceptual foundations is not unique. Writers in many fields appear to be forcing a choice between common knowledge (universals) and idiosyncratic understandings of individuals or groups (constructivist knowledge). The differences in representation of truth are stark, and the consequences of rejecting common knowledge may be profound. But in the face of PD challenges, we can look with considerable confidence to the writing of numerous scholars in other fields who have studied the relationship of knowledge to culture and illuminated the value of common knowledge and truths that are independent of our idiosyncracies. The commentaries of several are particularly instructive and serve to give us hope that our profession will not abandon the science of human behavior for the alternatives:

> Some things in nature just are—even though we can parse and interpret such real items in wildly various ways. A lion is a lion is a lion—and lions are more closely tied by genealogy to tigers than to earthworms. (Of course, I recognize that some system of human thought might base its central principle upon a spiritual or metaphorical tie between lion and earthworm—but nature's genealogies would not be changed thereby, even though the evolutionary tree of life might be utterly ignored or actively denied.) (Gould, 1997, p. 17)

> No one can deny that science has often misunderstood the limits of its explanatory power, succumbing to a hubristic claim to the Truth. But hubris can be corrected without destroying the underlying confidence in the possibility of a common knowledge—or at least so one hopes. For without a common understanding, a common knowledge, prospects for coexistence among the world's many contending truths grow precariously faint. (Tolson, 1998, p. 12)

> How did they [liberal politicians since the 18th century] accomplish that [realize the goals of greater social justice]? Why, by identifying true (or nearly true) universals, such as the common origins, physiologies, aspirations, and feelings of all humankind, *and refuting the false ones,* such as the divine right of kings, natural slavery, and the general inferiority of women. Yes, by some scientists, and at various times, science has offered false universals, but those have been overthrown *only by better science.* And without reaching for true, or better-approaching-true commonalities, we would have only the idiosyncrasies of tribes, including those of whatever tribe you or I happen to belong to. (Gross, 1998, p. 48)

What these quotes have in common is the recognition that although individuals and groups may indeed see different truths from their idiosyncratic perspectives, there is also a body of information that is not only common or universal but able to free us from egocentrism and tribalism. Such universal knowledge—indeed, the admission of its existence and the recognition of its unique power to free people from separation into warring factions—is under serious attack as a modern failure. Nothing compels us to join the attack. The "modern" universal knowledge that has prevailed for several hundred years frees us as individuals and as a professional cadre to continue the pursuit of universally shared knowledge that brings the greatest liberation and habilitation to all people. The fact that contrary perspectives emerge should neither discourage us nor lead us to conclude that conceptual chaos is inevitable....

Looking only on the dark side is a serious mistake. Special education is a relatively young profession with a history that includes reliable empirical research on what works for students at the margins of the distribution of abilities and performance. We have considerable capacity for self-correction and finding order where others see disorder. We could turn our efforts unambiguously and forcefully to our historic mission of seeking reliable, common knowledge about how best to teach students with disabilities—researching and applying instruction that is intensive, urgent, relentless, goal directed according to individual need and delivered in the setting where it is most effective.

POSTSCRIPT

Is Special Education an Illegitimate Profession?

Danforth and Kauffman are both focused on the education and well-being of children in schools. Each is strongly convinced, however, that the viewpoint held by the other is not in the best interest of children.

Danforth asserts that normal learning differences have been magnified into labels that segregate and hobble children, causing adults to seek cures where none are needed. Like the perfectly thin model, the perfect learner may be an unattainable—in fact, an unnecessary—goal. According to Danforth, diversity in learning represents normal variation rather than a defect to be "remediated" by specially trained professionals.

In contrast, Kauffman worries that educators will be distracted by postmodern criticisms and lose direction. Significant learning differences exist, he says. Special education is still a new field. Educators are still seeking out the best way to meet the needs of children who have been on the outskirts of classrooms. However, noticing that individual attention helps some children learn, more teachers and parents seek that attention, whether or not their child has a disability. Kauffman concludes that perhaps the definitions of disability are not drawn tightly enough to ensure that the protection of the law is extended to those for whom it was intended.

The issues of postmodernism revolve around decisions of whose viewpoints are "in" and whose are "out." Those whose voices are "in" become important and shape policy and practice. Those who are "in" retain their influence by confining "others" to separate categories, which become less important. This view has been compared to the creation of maps (Smith, *Review of Educational Research*, 1999), in which boundaries are drawn to separate groups of people from each other. Smith maintains that the drawing of cultural or intellectual boundaries serves to create differences where none exist.

Rather than drawing boundaries to keep people out, modern science approaches to special education recognizes—and seeks to actualize—individual dignity and capability, according to Kleinert (*Mental Retardation*, 1997). Science, he says, uses descriptive terms and methods of systematic inquiry to demonstrate the potential within individuals who were previously "discarded as unteachable and of no value."

The polarity of this issue's points is expanded in discussions focusing directly on inclusion. Writing with William Rhodes (*Remedial and Special Education*, 1997), Danforth explores the idea that disability labels hinder inclusive education. If all children were viewed as individual learners rather than members of a category, they contend, teachers would easily accommodate individual needs instead of seeking assistance from specialists.

From another perspective, at least one proponent of modernist theories (Sasso, *The Journal of Special Education,* 2001) maintains that postmodernists have, in fact, found educating students with disabilities to be so difficult that their solution is to declare that differences have been artificially created. This declaration stifles systematic inquiry, abandoning the children to the very schools that once denied them access.

IDEA97 mandates that "services and placement needed by each child with a disability to receive [a free appropriate public education] must be based on the child's unique needs and not on the child's disability" (300.300(b)). Has the normal range of educational difference been forgotten in the race to seek scientific justification for special education? Or do the law's very words ensure that a child's needs are acknowledged and conveyed through the voices of his or her parents and teachers? Will the unique needs of all children be considered without the protection of law? Which will become invisible—the labels or the children?

ISSUE 2

Are Minority Children Overrepresented in Special Education?

YES: James M. Patton, from "The Disproportionate Representation of African Americans in Special Education: Looking Behind the Curtain for Understanding and Solutions," *The Journal of Special Education* (vol. 32, no. 1, 1998)

NO: Donald L. MacMillan and Daniel J. Reschly, from "Overrepresentation of Minority Students: The Case for Greater Specificity or Reconsideration of the Variables Examined," *The Journal of Special Education* (vol. 32, no. 1, 1998)

ISSUE SUMMARY

YES: James M. Patton, a professor at the College of William and Mary, argues that African American children are overrepresented in special education programs and that this overrepresentation needs to be addressed through the involvement of those who are culturally and interculturally competent.

NO: Donald L. MacMillan and Daniel J. Reschly, faculty members at the University of California at Riverside and Vanderbilt University, respectively, in examining the issue of overrepresentation, question the accuracy and usefulness of the mechanisms for assessing children and determining specific disabilities.

As far back as 1968, Dunn (*Exceptional Children,* 1968) examined the developing field of special education and voiced concern that African American children were being disproportionately placed in special education—that is, they were being resegregated into substantially separate classes for the mentally retarded.

Special education services, which are designed to provide educational support to children who are excluded from schooling because of a disability, also seemed to be the destination for children whose background differed from that of the majority culture. In an extensive history of the issue of overrepresentation, Artiles and Trent (*The Journal of Special Education,* 1994) cite confirming data collected by several studies, underlining concerns about students who differ by language proficiency and cultural learning style differences.

A mirror image of the same issue exists when the underrepresentation of minorities in programs for the gifted and talented is considered (Ford, *The Journal of Special Education,* 1998). McWhorter (*Losing the Race,* Free Press, 2000) posits that the belief that intellectual achievement is not compatible with black cultural identity affects the effort and achievement of African American children and youth.

Debate, discussion, and research of the issue of overrepresentation continues to be intense. *Research Connections in Special Education,* a biannual review of research sponsored by the U.S. Office of Special Education, devoted its Fall 2000 issue to a review of ongoing studies, promising strategies, regional perspectives, and contacts and resources. The front page of the issue highlights a quote from IDEA97: "More minority children continue to be served in special education than would be expected from the percentage of minority students in the general school population." *The Journal of Special Education* devoted the first issue of its 1998 volume to the issue of overrepresentation, presenting several dimensions of the dilemma. The following selections come from this thematic issue.

In the first selection, James M. Patton expresses his committment to educational equity in culturally competent schools. He contends that African American children have been consistently overrepresented in special education programs, and he maintains that this pattern is deeply rooted in a dominant culture that identifies students who do not do well in school as defective. Patton argues that the remedy to this unjust situation is an ethical discourse that fully includes the perspectives and knowledge of more African American teachers, researchers, and others who are able to critically look at educational practices.

Like Patton, Donald L. MacMillan and Daniel J. Reschly have also long considered the ways in which children become part of special education programs. In the second selection, MacMillan and Reschly take issue with the contention that overrepresentation exists. They find social class to be a stronger determiner of need for special education than race. They argue that faulty interpretation of statistics, the complexity of reporting the "category" of biracial children, and the unreliable operational definitions of certain disabilities contribute to the identification of a problem that does not really exist.

As you read these selections, consider the complex issues that are being presented. Does the problem reside in education's uneasiness with diverse learners or with researchers' interpretation of statistics? Is overrepresentation a stigmatizing attempt to continue segregation, deny individuality, and train students to "fit" into the majority culture, or is it a method by which to address educational need? What is the real problem, and what is the right way to address it?

James M. Patton  **YES**

The Disproportionate Representation of African Americans in Special Education

The overrepresentation of African Americans in certain special education programs (see Note 1) has been a persistent problem negatively affecting large numbers of African Americans and their families, the field of special education, and society at large. The sociopolitical and historical roots of the disproportionate representation problem addressed in this article predate the field of special education, with origins as early as 1619. They can be traced back to the arrival of Africans in America and their subsequent continuous, unequal treatment (Willie, Garibaldi, & Reed, 1991). The current reality of the overrepresentation of African Americans in special education classes perpetuates this sociohistorical legacy by allowing the general and special education enterprises to continue the creation of programmatic and classroom arrangements that jeopardize the life chances of large numbers of African American youth. The fact that disproportionately large numbers of African Americans are being persistently diagnosed as disabled and placed in special education programs constitutes a problem—for many of these students are inappropriately placed. The consequences, however, of such misidentification, classification, and placement are often deleterious. As an example, this problem is exacerbated by the fact that many African American youth today fail to receive a quality and life-enhancing education in precisely those special education programs in which they are often inappropriately placed (Heller, Holtzman, & Messick, 1982; Hilliard, 1992). In addition, the special education label borne by these students often serves as a stigma, producing negative effects on the bearer of the label and others interacting with the stigmatized individual (Goffman, 1963). Furthermore, while these students are in special education programs, they miss essential general education academic and social curricula. This limited exposure with the core academic curriculum continues the spiral of "lower levels of achievement, decreased likelihood of post secondary education, and more limited employment" (Markowitz, Garcia, & Eichelberger, 1997, p. 3).

Concerns about racial discrimination and violations of civil rights are raised when African American youth are consistently misidentified and disproportionately placed in special education programs. Recently, renewed at-

From James M. Patton, "The Disproportionate Representation of African Americans in Special Education: Looking Behind the Curtain for Understanding and Solutions," *The Journal of Special Education*, vol. 32, no. 1 (1998). Copyright © 1998 by PRO-ED, Inc. Reprinted by permission.

tention has been made regarding these issues. Reschly (1996) observed that this heightened awareness can be seen in recent reports to Congress and several initiatives funded by the U.S. Office of Education. The first initiative included a study conducted by the National Academy of Sciences of the National Research Council that critiqued the use of intelligence tests in special education and explored alternatives to these tests. This body noted the absence of "benefits" resulting from the use of these tests and their lack of pedagogical utility (Morrison, White, & Fever, 1996). A second initiative involved funding the National Association of State Directors of Special Education to examine policy issues around the disprotortionality problem and to recommend practical solutions. Although interest in this area has been recently piqued, renewed interest without a different analysis and different voices will not resolve this problem. . . .

The Overrepresentation Problem: Persistent Patterns

The overrepresentation of African American children and youth in special education programs for students with learning disabilities, severe emotional or behavioral disorders, and mental disabilities has remained a persistent reality even after more than 20 years of recognition. The literature is replete with causal factors that range from failure of the general education system (Artiles & Trent, 1994; Deno, 1970; MacMillan & Hendrick, 1993; McDermott, 1987; Townsend, Thomas, Witty, & Lee, 1996) to inequities associated with the special education referral, assessment, and placement processes (Harry & Anderson, 1994; Mercer, 1973). Yet, the problem of overrepresentation of African Americans persists even after causes have been unequivocally noted. We know and have known for years, for example, that, in spite of all the study and scripting of this issue, the proportion of African Americans identified as mentally disabled has not changed much from 38% in 1975 when those students constituted 15% of the school population. In 1991 they made up 16% of this nation's school population and 35% of the special education population (Harry & Anderson, 1994). Further, it is well documented that African American males are particularly overrepresented both in disciplinary practices (i.e., recipients of corporal punishment and suspension) and in certain special education categories and typically receive their special education in segregated classrooms or buildings (Harry & Anderson, 1994).

We also know that the labels associated with the sociocultural construction of the categories of mild mental disability, learning disability, and serious emotional or behavioral disability (SED) have definitional and validity problems with serious negative implications for African American learners. For example, Ysseldyke, Algozzine, and Thurlow (1992) observed that the arbitrary shifts in diagnostic criteria and frequency rates for the SED label coupled with the extreme variability in placement rates across the states call into question the validity of the SED category. These concerns and the attendant cultural variability of student behavior and teacher judgment place African American youth at great risk of being falsely labeled as SED. Similar arguments have been made for the educable mentally retarded (EMR) and specific learning disability (SLD) categories (Harry & Anderson, 1994)....

In spite of the presence of convincing data on the overrepresentation issue and the extant literature challenging special education processes that lead to identification and placement, this problem continues to persist. Its persistence will continue unless we reanalyze old premises and reconstruct new premises underlying the field of special education. An analysis of the deep structure foundations of special education will be discussed in the next section.

Special Education and Its Social Science Underpinnings

The dominant mode of inquiry in the field of special education has closely followed the "objectivist," or functionalist, tradition of theory development, paradigm construction, research approach, methodology use, and research applications (Bowles & Gintis, 1976; Skrtic, 1986). As a worldview, functionalism presupposes an objective, rational, orderly interpretation of social reality, whereby deviations to this view are placed under a pathology heading (Foucault, 1976). This functionalist framework leads persons to postulate that schools exist to transmit a body of "prescribed knowledge, skills, values, and norms that are essential for society" (Irvine, 1990, p. 2).... This functionalist narrative, enjoined by the medical and psychological grounding of the field of special education, explains deviations from the norm as deficits or pathologies (Skrtic, 1991). Students, then, who fail in general education are viewed as defective and consequently as needing some "special" system to organize itself, develop a different set of norms, values, roles, expectations and procedures to "fix" these "defective" students. Skrtic (1991) pointed out that the creation of the special education system to deal with these "defective" students removed the problem from the general education discourse and compartmentalized it into a separate special education narrative. This special education narrative, according to that author, includes a language that developed four assumptions that have reinforced its functionalist/psychological/medical origins. These mutually reinforcing assumptions are that "a) disabilities are pathological conditions that students have, b) differential diagnosis is objective and useful, c) special education is a rationally conceived and coordinated system of services that benefits diagnosed students, and d) progress results from rational technological improvements in diagnostic and instructional practices" (Skrtic, 1991, p. 152). Such, therefore, is the language used by many of the key special education knowledge producers who are writing the scripts for others to play.

Critical Theory and Special Education

This functionalist, or positivist, view fails to recognize the socioeconomic and political nature of schooling. Nor does it imagine the role played by schools and the special education system in maintaining the existing social and economic stratification order, thereby exerting ideological, social, and political control of African American learners.... [A] host of theorists, taking a more critical view, has created a body of literature that links school structures and processes, including those used in special education, with the values, attitudes, and needs that reflect the dominant social, economic, and political groups in this nation (e.g., Apple, 1981; Cherryholmes, 1988; Katz, 1971; Lipsky & Gartner, 1989; Skrtic, 1991). These critical, or conflict, theorists hold that education, and, thus special education, grounded in structured power relationships, is designed to serve the interests of the dominant social, political, and economic classes and to place African Americans in a disvalued position. As such, the structures, processes, assumptions, and beliefs of the dominant classes are deeply embedded in the special education knowledge base and its knowledge producers, thus undermining its theory, research, and practice. These theories, assumptions, and practices also are enormously resistant to change. This coupling of special education with the needs of the dominant social, political, and economic classes in society has resulted in the maintenance of a special education system that is unjust to African Americans. Many of those major knowledge producers, or "gods," in the field of special education have played an essential role in maintenance of this injustice.

Special Education Knowledge Production: A Missing Discourse

The overrepresentation discourse has not, to my knowledge, been discussed within an analysis of the social, political, and cultural contexts of the major knowledge producers in the field and the ontologies, axiologies, and epistemologies they employ. In the main, those who create, manufacture, and produce the knowledge base in special education historically have not included African Americans, especially those directly affected by overrepresentation. There exists in special education a mismatch of chasm proportion between the social, political, and cultural backgrounds and experiences of its knowledge producers and those African American learners studied, placed, and overrepresented in special education classes.

It is axiomatic that knowledge and the production of knowledge is not culture free. In fact, Gordon, Miller, and Rollock (1990) have postulated that social science knowledge production operates within communicentric frames of references, whereby one's own "community" becomes the center of the universe and the conceptual frame that structures thought. Knowledge producers in special education, as in other social science disciplines, shape the explanatory parameters of issues such as paradigm formation, definitional constructs, theory development, and choice of research methods—all important foundational concerns that shape the overrepresentation discourse. The nature of meaning and the stances taken by knowledge producers in the important knowledge production process are influenced by their cultural and ethnic identities, which shape their notions of what is "real," "true," and "good." Accordingly, the "pseudoobjective" nature of knowledge production and of those who produce knowledge is influenced strongly by the culture, assumptions, and beliefs that knowledge producers hold about the "other." If they lack knowledge, experience, or "insider" insight into the culture of the "other," their theories and constructs face serious construct and predictive validity challenges.

An examination of the special education knowledge base relative to African Americans will reveal that many knowledge producers have attempted to understand and explain the behavior and life experiences of African Americans through their own narrow cultural/ethnic perspectives and against an equally narrowly constructed cultural/ethnic standard (Gordon, 1985).... [T]he field's functionalist and positivistic core knowledge base further compounds the problem because of the culture-bound nature of this discourse and the limited explanatory usefulness embedded in this perspective. As such, many researchers and knowledge producers in special education generally explain and interpret the behavior of African Americans based upon their "outsider" beliefs and assumptions about the origins and meanings of behavior and the values placed on that behavior and the behaving person. Some have argued that this perspective represents a form of epistemological racism (Scheurich & Young, 1997; Stanfield, 1985).... A new set of enlightened cultural filters and discourses is needed to replace the current language and narratives used to maintain the legitimacy of current special education social and political arrangements. It is essential that these discourses include important ethical themes heretofore missing from most disproportionality narratives....

The Need for New Script Writers

The underrepresentation of African Americans and conscious others in the special education knowledge production process has had a strong impact on the character and nature of the knowledge that has been produced. Their relative absence from this story has limited some insightful knowledge production and, accordingly, our deep structure understanding of the disproportionality narrative.... New ways of knowing and valuing and new types of knowledge producers are called for. These knowledge producers are called upon to uncover the philosophical underpinnings of special education and replace them with a paradigm that expresses cultural "insider" knowledge, epistemologies, axiologies, and experiences that are social, political, cultural, and economic and that speak in multilectic terms (see Note 2). This grounding, then, by nature would require knowledge producers to understand and "be sensitive to the actual traits of populations under inquiry" (Stanfield, 1985, p. 411). In addition to rigor and methodological soundness in the inquiry process, this change calls for knowledge producers to develop a vast reservoir of cultural knowledge and experiences of African Americans, guided by "insiders" to this culture. This knowledge should serve to guide theory, research design, data collection, and interpretation (Stanfield, 1985). The need for this reformulated paradigm serves, then, as a special challenge to African American knowledge producers, as well as sensitive and caring non-African Americans knowledge producers.

Knowledge producers who would script the disproportionality problem with an ethic of critique, justice, and caring would offer the hope of replacing special education paradigms of domination and control with ones of liberation and emancipation. Resistance to such a paradigm shift is likely....

Concluding Statements

Artiles and Trent (1994) ended their treatise on the problem of disproportionate representation in special education by stating that some still find themselves asking the same basic question—whether or not overrepresentation is a problem. That is not a question that I have ever heard an African American special educator, sociologist, psychologist, anthropologist, barber, teacher, minister, social worker, custodian, business person, homemaker, or anyone else ask. Nor have I heard Latinos or Native Americans ask that question. We know the answer and it is *yes*. When this question is asked, the individual asking the question is usually from a European cultural background. The challenge and basis of analysis is to determine why this group, especially its knowledge producers, continues to beg the question. What is behind their question? It should be obvious to most people, professional and lay, that African Americans are overrepresented in large numbers in special education classrooms, particularly those for students with mild disabilities or emotional or behavioral disabilities. It is obvious, or should be, that many of these learners are misdiagnosed, mislabeled, and therefore misplaced.

It is obvious, or should be, that this reality has a historical legacy and has been (a) confirmed year after year by numerous scholarly studies, (b) recognized in U.S. law (the Individuals with Disabilities Education Act of 1990; P.L. 94-142), and (c) biannually confirmed by data from the U.S. Office for Civil Rights. It is obvious, or should be, that this reality is a symptom of a special education system run amok with many underlying problems in its deep structure philosophical and theoretical foundation, its ethics, processes, and practices. It is obvious, or should be, that its foundation, ethics, and practices have emanated from a set of knowledge producers outside of the affected population who have all too often created a system of false languages and knowledge production that continue to reinforce the dominant social, political, economic, and ethical order of things. Their beliefs, epistemologies, values, and presuppositions must be unveiled, analyzed, and made clear as an absolute precondition for resolving this problem—which has plagued this profession and nation for too many years. There is, however, a way out.

These same knowledge producers can begin to reevaluate their worldview, epistemologies, ethical themes, so-called objectivity, methodology, and practice in light of the many muted voices of African Americans. They could employ a language of ethical critique, justice, and caring in their work and inject social, political, economic, historical, and ethical discourse into all that they do. They could go to those who are "studied" to listen and hear. They could go to "insiders" for critical insights into the "other" and be guided by those insights. They could allow the "other," African American knowledge producers, to teach and lead them in their quest for knowledge production liberation. The challenge is not just with the dominant European knowledge producers. African Americans have an equally large leadership challenge.

A system is needed in special education that nurtures, develops, and allows for the voices of African American knowledge produces to be heard, confirmed, and affirmed. Their voices will more closely represent those who are studied, tested, identified, labeled, and placed in special education programs —often at levels well beyond accepted rates. It is through looking behind the special education ontological, epistemological, and axiological "curtain" and bringing to center stage the voices, narratives, and discourses of African Americans and sensitive and aware others that this problem can be resolved. The criteria needed for these new knowledge producers are the same ones needed for all of those participating in an agenda that turns the corner in resolving the African American special education overrepresentation problem. The training and continual development of liberating knowledge producers and practitioners should be conditioned by these criteria. Out of this reflection, growth, freedom, and progression could emerge a grand story. The denouement to yet another story that threatens this society could conclude in a way that liberates those most negatively affected, as well as those perpetuating these threats.

Author's Note

Preparation of this manuscript was supported in part by Grant No. H029J60006 from the U.S. Department of Education. Office of Special Education Programs, to the University of Virginia for the Center for Minority Research in Special Education.

Notes

1. The present analysis focused on the overrepresentation of African Americans in certain special education programs. I have addressed the underrepresentation of African Americans in gifted programs in other writings (Patton, 1992, 1995).

2. The term *multilectic* is used here to refer to a multitude of theses, their opposites, and their syntheses, as opposed to the Hegelian/Marxist dialectic.

References

Apple, M. W. (Ed.). (1981). *Cultural and economic reproduction in education.* Boston: Routledge & Kegan Paul.

Artiles, A. J., & Trent, S. C. (1994). Overrepresentation of minority students in special education: A continuing debate. *The Journal of Special Education, 22,* 410–436.

Bowles, S., & Gintis, H. (1976). *Schooling in capitalist America.* New York: Basic Books.

Cherryholmes, C. H. (1988). *Power and criticism: Poststructuralist investigations in education.* New York: Teachers College Press.

Deno, E. (1970). Special education as development capital. *Exceptional Children, 37,* 229–237.

Foucault, M. (1976). *Mental illness and psychology.* Berkeley: University of California Press.

Goffman, E. (1963). *Stigma: Notes on the management of spoiled identity.* Englewood Cliffs, NJ: Prentice Hall.

Gordon, E. W. (1985). Social science knowledge production and minority experience. *The Journal of Higher Education, 54,* 117–133.

Gordon, E. W., Miller, F., & Rollock, D. (1990). Coping with communicentric bias in knowledge production in the social sciences. *Educational Researcher, 19*(3), 14–19.

Harry, B., & Anderson, M. (1994). The disproportionate placement of African American males in special education programs: A critique of the process. *Journal of Negro Education, 63,* 602–619.

Heller, K. A., Holtzman, W. H., & Messick, S. (Eds.),. (1982). *Placing children in special education: A strategy for equity.* Washington, DC: National Academy Press.

Hilliard, A. G., III. (1992). The pitfalls and promises of special education practice. *Exceptional Children, 59,* 168–172.

Individuals with Disabilities Education Act of 1990, 20 U.S.C. § 1400 *et seq.*

Irvine, J. J. (1990). *Black students and school failure: Policies, practices, and prescriptions.* New York: Greenwood.

Katz, M. B. (1971). *Class, bureaucracy, and schools: The illusion of educational change in America.* New York: Praeger.

Lipsky, D. K., & Gartner, A. (1989). *Beyond separate education: Quality education for all.* Baltimore: Brookes.

MacMillan, D. L., & Hendrick, I. G. (1993). Evolution and legacies. In J. L. Goodlad & T. C. Lovitt (Eds.), *Integrating general and special education* (pp. 23–48). Columbus, OH: Merrill/Macmillan.

Markowitz, J., Garcia, S., & Eichelberger, J. H. (1997). *Addressing the disproportionate placement of students from racial and ethnic minority groups in special ed programs and classes.* Alexandria, VA: National Association of State Directors of Special Education.

McDermott, R. P. (1987). Achieving school failure: An anthropological approach to illiteracy and social stratification. In G. D. Spindler (Ed.), *Education and cultural process: Anthropological approaches* (2nd ed., pp. 173–209). Prospect Heights, IL: Waveland.

Mercer, G. R. (1973). *Labeling the mentally retarded.* Berkeley: University of California Press.

Morrison, P., White, S. H., & Fever, M. J. (Eds.). (1996). *The use of IQ tests in special education decision making and planning: Summary of two workshops.* Washington, DC: National Academy Press.

Patton, J. M. (1992). Assessment and identification of African American learners with gifts and talents. *Exceptional Children, 59,* 150–159.

Patton, J. M. (1995). Identifying and transforming the potential of young, gifted African Americans: A clarion call for action. In B. A. Ford, F. D. Obiakor, & J. M. Patton (Eds.), *Effective education of African American exceptional learners: New perspectives* (pp. 27–67). Austin, TX: PRO-ED.

Reschly, D. (1996). *Disproportionate minority representation in general and special education programs: Patterns, issues, and alternatives.* Des Moines, IA: Drake University, Resource Center/MPRRC.

Scheurich, J. J., & Young, M. (1997). Coloring epistemologies: Are our research epistemologies racially biased? *Educational Researcher, 26*(4), 4–16.

Skrtic, T. M. (1986). The crisis in social education knowledge: A perspective on perspective. *Focus on Exceptional Children, 18*(7), 1–16.

Skrtic, T. M. (1991). The special education paradox: Equity as the way to excellence. *Harvard Educational Review, 61,* 148–206.

Stanfield, J. (1985). The ethnocentric bias of social science knowledge production. In E. W. Gordon (Ed.), *Review of research in education* (Vol. 12, pp. 387–415). Washington, DC: American Educational Research Association.

Townsend, B., Thomas, D., Witty, J. P., & Lee, R. S. (1996). Diversity and school restructuring: Creating partnerships in a world of difference. *Teacher Education and Special Education, 19*(2), 102–118.

Willie, C. V., Garibaldi, A. M., & Reed, W. L. (Eds.). (1991). *The education of African-Americans.* Boston: William Monroe Trotter Institute.

Ysseldyke, J. E., Algozzine, B., & Thurlow, M. L. (1992). *Critical issues in special education* (2nd ed.). Boston: Houghton Mifflin.

NO

**Donald L. MacMillan and
Daniel J. Reschly**

Overrepresentation of Minority Students

The issue of overrepresentation was touched on in [L. M.] Dunn's (1968) classic article when he characterized the population of "educable mentally retarded [EMR]" as follows: "In my best judgment, about 60 to 80 percent of the pupils taught by these teachers are children from low-status backgrounds —including Afro-Americans, American Indians, Mexicans, and Puerto Rican Americans; those from nonstandard English speaking broken, disorganized and inadequate homes; and children from other nonmiddle class environments" (p. 5). The subsequent examination of this problem focused on the ethnic overrepresentation, largely ignoring the main effects of poverty and the interaction of poverty and ethnic group. Nevertheless, overrepresentation data have figured prominently in court cases... when introduced to support allegations of de facto segregation. Overrepresentation has been examined primarily in cases of children identified as mildly mentally retarded (MMR)..., but it has also been an issue concerning other disability categories (e.g., emotional and behavioral disorders [EBD], learning disabilities [LD]). In addition, concerns have been expressed over the "underrepresentation" of certain minority groups in programs for the gifted and talented.

Evidence of overrepresentation has focused on simple proportions of a given ethnic group (e.g., African American) qualified for special education in a given sanctioned disability category.... The underlying assumption is that the proportion of different ethnic groups in any category or program should be equal to the proportion of that ethnic group in the general school population if there is no discrimination. When the proportion of a given ethnic group enrolled in a given category exceeds the proportion of that ethnic group in the school population (i.e., in a district, state, or nationally), the interpretation suggested is that the disproportion is due to discrimination. It is important to note that ethnic proportions in clearly biologically determined disability categories (e.g., blind, deaf, orthopedic disability) and those cases of mental retardation considered severe and profound do not yield dramatic deviations from proportions one would expect. Efforts by the U.S. Office of Civil Rights (OCR) to monitor overrepresentation are restricted in the disability categories with which it is concerned; data from districts OCR monitors reflect enrollments in only

From Donald L. MacMillan and Daniel J. Reschly, "Overrepresentation of Minority Students: The Case for Greater Specificity or Reconsideration of the Variables Examined," *The Journal of Special Education*, vol. 32, no. 1 (1998). Copyright © 1998 by PRO-ED, Inc. Reprinted by permission. References omitted.

four categories (whereas 13 reporting categories are recognized under the Individuals with Disabilities Education Act of 1990 [IDEA]). OCR secures data on mental retardation, serious emotional disturbance (SED), specific learning disabilities (SLD), and speech and language impairments (SLI)... . This restriction of OCR reflects the absence of compelling, or even suggestive, evidence that a "problem" exists in the remaining IDEA disability categories with regard to overrepresentation. Two further points should be noted: (a) Among certain biologically caused entities there is "overrepresentation" of certain ethnic groups. For example, disproportionately high rates of PKU are found in White children, Tay-Sachs disease in Jewish children, and sickle cell anemia in Black children; (b) some studies do report a significantly higher incidence of biologically based disabilities among Black children and youth... .

Essentially, then, the "problem" of overrepresentation is evident only in the categories we characterize as "judgmental" disability categories—that is, those in which subjective judgments may influence decisions because the disabilities involved do not have a clear biological basis and in which contextual factors (what is tolerated in the specific environment, such as a third-grade classroom in a specific school building) are important and in which cases are filtered through the referral process of general education teachers... .

Calculation and Percentages: The Denominator Is the Key

As noted, simple proportions are employed to examine representatives. However, there are two different formulas used and they each provide a slightly different perspective on the "problem." Keep in mind that these calculations can be made for a school district, a state, or the nation. One estimate calculates the percent of children *in a disability category* who are members of a given ethnic group. That is, the first estimate asks the question, "What percent of the children classified as MMR are Black?" ... In this calculation, the number of Black children classified as MMR serves as the numerator and the total number of children classified as MMR serves as the denominator. Calculations using this formula are the most frequently employed and were cited in the litigations to demonstrate the magnitude of the overrepresentation of Black children in MMR... . [W]hen the *Larry P.* trial began in 1971, Black students constituted 10% of the California school enrollment, but 25% of the enrollment in MMR programs. The 25% figure was calculated based on the formula shown above.

A second formula that has been employed provides the "percent of group in category or program," and this estimate asks the question, "What percent of Black students are enrolled in MMR programs?" The same numerator serves (the number of Black children classified as MMR), but the denominator in this calculation uses the total number of Black children in the district, state, or national school population. This second formula provides a perspective on the percent of children in a certain ethnic group that are classified into one of the sanctioned disability categories. Typically, it is a much smaller percentage. For example, at the time of *Larry P.,* as noted, whereas 25% of the total MMR enrollments were Black, only 1.1% of Black students in California were enrolled in MMR programs.

The calculations are simple and straightforward, but the variables involved are not that simple and, in our opinion, warrant much closer examination.....

Why Is Overrepresentation a Problem?

In describing the work of the committee of the National Academy of Sciences, Heller, Holtzman, and Messick (1982) wrote: "Our initial question 'What are the causes of disproportionate representation of minorities and males in special education' became 'Why is disproportionate representation of minorities and males a problem?" (p. x). In fact, the overrepresentation of males in EMR at the time of *Larry P.* was greater than the disproportion of Black students, yet it did not elicit the same degree of attention or debate. The magnitude of the disproportion of Black students in Head Start, Follow Through, and Chapter 1 was at least as great as the overrepresentation of minority students in EMR, and yet these examples of overrepresentation have never been the subject of litigation or come in for criticism. Why is overrepresentation a problem when it appears in special education enrollments? The answer, we believe, resides in the perceptions held regarding the effectiveness of treatment afforded by the various programs and the perceived stigma associated with specific labels.....

Overrepresentation in EMR was viewed as "problematic" in part because the educational treatment provided students was perceived to be ineffective. In his opinion, Judge Robert Peckham described special classes as "deadend," "inferior," and "stigmatizing" no fewer than 27 times despite the fact that little, if any, evidence directly bearing on child outcomes was provided. Moreover, the cases ... heard prior to 1975 did, in fact, involve districts engaged in poor, and sometimes unethical, practices. These districts were targeted because they represented the worst in special educational practices, not because they were representative of typical programming, but the impression was given that such abuses were widespread. In both of these cases, the defendant districts and state departments of education agreed to several reforms imposed by the courts designed to remedy the poor practices—interested by some as an admission of complicity. It is less clear whether special education treatments for LD and SED are similarly perceived as ineffective or whether they simply suffer from a reputational bias by association and being subsumed under the umbrella of "special education services." ...

Need for Greater Specificity in Variables Under Study

Data bearing on overrepresentation involve linking information on the ethnicity of the child to the categorical membership of that child in one of the high-incidence disability categories—MMR, SLD, SED, and SLI. Moreover, data on ethnicity and categorical affiliation are typically aggregated across school sites to a district, across districts to the state, and across states to the national level. Although these data may provide a very crude approximation of what is happening nationally, a degree of caution is needed in interpreting the meaning and significance of the findings.....

Ethnicity

A box is checked on a school form determining the ethnic group to which a child belongs. One box, and only one, can be checked and there are no uniform guidelines applied from district to district within a state, let alone from state to state. Does a school employee decide the appropriate box based on the child's appearance? Does the parent select the appropriate box? Does a child's surname determine whether he or she is classified as Hispanic? If parents select the appropriate box, is there a box for "mixed"? Although variability exists in the method at the district level, by the time data are aggregated at the national level, it is easy to ignore this variability. The Office of Management and Budget's Statistical Directive 15 urges that racial and ethnic categories should not be interpreted as scientific or anthropological in nature; yet, that is exactly how they are treated in the OCR overrepresentation data set. For any ethnic category, " . . . we have to assume that everyone in the category belongs completely in that box" (Hodgkinson, 1995, p. 175).

In a recent article examining the utility of ethnicity in psychological research, [J. S.] Phinney (1996) concluded that "it is necessary to unpack the packaged variable of ethnicity" (p. 918). She went on to explain that "even within an ethnic group whose members share a relatively precise ethnic label there is tremendous heterogeneity" (p. 919). That is, they differ in terms of social class, income, education, generation of immigration, geographical region, and family structure. In discussing overrepresentation, it might be helpful to specify what aspect of ethnicity believed implicated in special education placements. Phinney distinguished between three aspects that may account for the psychological importance of ethnicity: "(a) the cultural values, attitudes, and behaviors that distinguish ethnic groups; (b) the subjective sense of ethnic group membership; and (c) the experiences associated with minority status, including powerlessness, discrimination, and prejudice" (p. 919). Illustrations of the heterogeneity among those who share an ethnic label were provided by [H. L.] Hodgkinson (1995) when he noted that in the United States there were a minimum of 3 million Black Hispanics (from the Caribbean, with dark skin, and who speak Spanish), and that Argentine immigrants are labeled Hispanic, yet are primarily of White European ancestry.

The case for "multiracial" children is even more confusing. The "one drop of blood" rule was applied to define a person as Black, but this rule was never applied to the defining of individuals as White, Asian, or Hispanic (Hodgkinson, 1995, p. 174). One school district in which the first author has conducted research reported that in cases of multiracial children the child is classified according to the mother's ethnicity *unless* the father has a Spanish surname, which overrides the mother's ethnicity. In another district, the child is classified as whatever the mother is "because that's the only parent we can be sure of." In yet another, the child is classified as whatever the parents want him or her classified. This was most evident in the case of *Crawford v. Honig* (1988), in which the schools refused the mother's request to administer to Desmond Howard a test of intelligence. Desmond's mother was Hispanic and his father Black, but on the school ethnicity code the box checked for Desmond was "Black." If his mother agreed to change his ethnicity (i.e., check the Hispanic box), he could be tested, but under the prohibition against testing Black children imposed by Judge Peckham in *Larry P.,* he could not be administered a test of intelligence if he was designated as Black. Under current ethnic categories provided in the U.S. Census, one cannot be a "little bit" of anything. Like pregnancy, ethnicity is an all-or-nothing entity. When we read that 25% of the children in EMR programs are Black, we assume that everyone in that ethnic category belongs completely in that box. However, "on direct measurement, the darkest quarter of the white population is darker than the lightest quarter of the black population" (Hodgkinson, 1995, p. 175). Hodgkinson concluded that "If a box labeled 'multiracial'—meaning any racial/ethnic mixing back four more generations— were added to the next Census, estimates are that 80% of blacks and a majority of Americans in general would check the box" (p. 176). Overrepresentation data require that a child be cast into one of the existing "ethnic boxes" and no further breakdown is provided. . . .

Ethnicity as Proxy for SES

As more Americans marry across racial and ethnic boundaries, the utility of ethnicity as a variable will become even weaker than it is today. . . .

In the United States, and particularly in the urban settings included among the 50 largest school districts in the country sampled by OCR, a disproportionate number of minority children live in poverty. Ethnicity and poverty are inextricably interwoven in our society and the OCR data (and other data sets used to inform us on overrepresentation) fail to break out cases of MMR, SLD, and SED by ethnicity *and* social class. We are willing to wager that in such a matrix, the intercorrelation between ethnicity and social class would be moderately high and that social class, and not ethnicity, would explain more variance in the rates of detection for these high-incidence disabilities, particularly MMR. When ethnicity is the only independent variable, interpretations tend to emphasize "the figment of the pigment."

Classification of Students Into Disability Categories

The second fundamental variable considered in the overrepresentation data is the classification into one of the sanctioned disability categories—MMR, SLD, SED, and SLI. . . . It is our position that this variable is fraught with a tremendous amount of error. In order to interpret overrepresentation data meaningfully, one must be certain that there is interrater reliability in the classification decisions, where the "raters" are the school site committees responsible for certifying that a child qualifies under one of the existing categories. . . . [D]ifferent states employ different criteria for children to qualify under a given disability category. Validity of the classification system refers to the extent to which membership in a given category determines the number of meaningful correlates of class membership. For example, in a review of state department of education IQ cutoff scores for defining mental retardation, . . . 81% of the states specified an IQ cutoff score, but the requisite cut scores ranged from 69 to 84. . . . [W]hat qualifies a child as mentally retarded or LD in one state differs from the criteria in other states. Overrepresentation data, however, do not make adjustments for such differences—if a child is called LD, the data treat all such cases *as though they represented the same psychological profile.* Clearly, this is not the case. . . .

Conclusions and Recommendations

Local and state departments of education have been sued in federal courts due to overrepresentation of minority students receiving programs and services that on the surface appear ideal—that is, programs in which (a) the pupil–teacher ratio is considerably lower than that in general education, (b) per-pupil expenditures are two to four times what is spent on general education students, (c) the child's program is individually tailored with written goals and objectives specified and evaluated, and (d) services are delivered by a teacher with specialized training. Despite these very desirable characteristics of special education programs, *something* weighs so heavily on the minds of critics that it more than offsets these apparently desirable features. This, in part, explains why the National Academy of Sciences panel posed the question, "Why is overrepresentation of minorities and males a problem?" We believe that the answer to that question is twofold. First, the treatments are perceived to be ineffective, with the positive features described above believed to be more than offset by the negative consequences derived from being removed from general education to receive services and the necessity of having a pejorative label appended in order to receive these services.

We also hypothesize that the attitudes held by many toward categories such as MMR and SED are both stronger and more negative when overrepresentation is evident because such evidence might reinforce negative portrayals and stereotypes of minority groups. . . . [T]he underrepresentation of minority group children in programs for the gifted and talented is also perceived as a problem. On the surface it might appear contradictory to object to *both* overrepresentation and underrepresentation unless one considers (a) the perceived benefits of the services and programs and (b) what these two sets of figures . . . suggest vis-à-vis the broader issue of racial differences in intelligence.

We have emphasized that overrepresentation data are descriptive and, as such, do not permit causal inferences, however tempting such inferences may be. We would also point out that interpretation of these figures as evidence of discrimination as identification and placement procedures must await additional evidence that the placements of majority students in these programs are "correct" and those involving minority students are "erroneous." Overrepresentation figures are not linked in any way to characteristics of the specific children of any ethnic group placed into one of the judgmental categories. Moreover, it is important to recognize that discrimination is a two-edged sword. Although we must remain vigilant in scrutinizing placement practices in order to prevent the qualification of *any* children for services for which they do not qualify and from which they will not benefit, we must be equally on guard to prevent the *denial* of access to services for which children do qualify and from which they are likely to benefit *because* of their ethnicity. Efforts to "correct" overrepresentation by denying services to children of a particular ethnic group that is "at quota" when one of those children needs the services and supports provided are equally repugnant and constitute educational malpractice.

We have pointed out the oversimplification of the ethnicity variable in the tabulations of overrepresentation in published reports. In addition, we presented evidence documenting the fact that many children categorized into any number of the judgmental categories do not evidence the criteria defining that category of children. When data are aggregated to a national level, the frailties of data at the school site level are lost and we come to believe that the figures reflect reality.... [D]ifferential diagnosis of EMR and LD in the early 1970s was important because the specific classification carried with it consequences for *placement and program*. If you were classified as EMR, you got a different functional program and it was delivered in a special day class. Conversely, the diagnosis of LD resulted in academic remediation delivered in a resource room. Since passage of P.L. 94-142, however, regardless of whether a specific child is classified as MR, LD, or SED, the specifics of the treatment or program are negotiated on an individual basis, ... and the placement is individually determined consistent with the least restrictive environment mandate....

We believe strongly that the extant evidence points to socioeconomic status rather than ethnicity as the risk factor for children encountering severe and persistent academic problems in our public schools. As poor as the data are on overrepresentation, the OCR figures continue to point to one primary disability category accounting for the overall excess of Black children in high-incidence disability categories—and that category is MMR. MMR and low socioeconomic status have been empirically linked for decades, and in urban settings the children currently being classified as LD closely resemble those identified as EMR in the past. How much unique variance in enrollment rates is explained by ethnicity after that explained by social class has been partitioned out? Relatively little, we suspect.... Special education services should be provided according to a child's need and not according to a child's ethnicity.

POSTSCRIPT

Are Minority Children Overrepresented in Special Education?

$\mathbf{P}$atton and MacMillan/Reschly agree on several points: Minority children, particularly African Americans, are reported to be overrepresented in special education. It is not likely that any one racial group is so different from another as to warrant the conditions as they are now represented, especially given the varying definitions of disability and race in today's society. All agree that an equitable society must educate all children based on individual needs, not on assumptions based on skin color, income, or language.

Patton speaks about the need to see education as other than a monolithic entity with one path to success. He challenges all educators to engage the perspectives of African Americans in an active dialogue to understand the historical and sociopolitical problems of overrepresentation. New and better models can be devised by a representative group of designers, he maintains.

Harry and Anderson (*The Journal of Negro Education,* no. 4, 1994) suggest that much of the overrepresentation stems from the fact that most teachers are white females faced with inflexible school expectations and a lack of knowledge about the learning styles and patterns of African American students, especially boys. The authors suggest that schools be reformed, with the assistance and collaboration of families, to recognize the strengths and talents of all students rather than seeking special education services for perceived disabilities.

Patton has collaborated with Brenda Townsend to compile a four-part series of articles (*Teacher Education and Special Education,* 1999, 2000) addressing issues of ethics, power, and privilege within the context of overrepresentation and teacher preparation. Beyond reviewing historical and political parameters, the series recommends ways in which educators can effectively increase cultural competence by using ethics of critique, justice, and caring (Starratt, *Educational Administration Quarterly,* vol. 27, 1991, and *Transforming Educational Administration: Meaning, Community, and Excellence,* McGraw-Hill, 1996).

In addition to carefully evaluating the way in which statistics are gathered and reported, MacMillan and Reschly suggest that the validity of some disability categories and the variability of special education across districts to establish a common language need to be reevaluated. They also state that special education is vastly improved and no longer represents stigma and limited options. They caution educators not to react to overrepresentation by removing valuable services from those who need them.

Artiles and Trent (*The Journal of Special Education,* 1994) combine the range of views. They analyze arguments of definition, service provision, poverty, and the tendency to confuse difference and disability, concluding that there are no simple answers to this debate. Acknowledging that some progress has been made, Artiles and Trent assert that global analysis needs to be replaced by careful study of differences by region, size of programs, and service options before conclusions are reached. They do not want to minimize the critical nature of overrepresentation but to refine the analysis in order to arrive at accurate solutions that truly benefit all students. In a later article, Artiles (*The Journal of Special Education,* 1998) advocates a sociocultural approach to overrepresentation, maintaining that only when researchers reflect on their own backgrounds and perspectives—as well as those of people of color—can this issue be effectively resolved.

How can educational patterns be fairly examined to identify the root of overrepresentation? How can the debate be effectively broadened to include the perspectives of African Americans? Can teachers be trained to effectively educate children with characteristics that differ widely from their own perspectives and backgrounds? Will this discussion change as society (and its institutions) becomes more multicultural? These are not easy questions to ponder, much less answer. But they must be raised and considered fully for the benefit of all children.

ISSUE 3

Is Special Education So Expensive Because of the Way It Is Funded?

YES: Teresa S. Jordan, Carolyn A. Weiner, and K. Forbis Jordan, from "The Interaction of Shifting Special Education Policies With State Funding Practices," *Journal of Education Finance* (Summer 1997)

NO: Sheldon Berman et al., from "The Rising Costs of Special Education in Massachusetts: Causes and Effects," in Chester E. Finn, Jr., Andrew J. Rotherham, and Charles R. Hokanson, Jr., eds., *Rethinking Special Education for a New Century* (Thomas B. Fordham Foundation & Progressive Policy Institute, 2001)

ISSUE SUMMARY

YES: Teresa S. Jordan, an associate professor at the University of Las Vegas–Nevada; Carolyn A. Weiner, president of Syndactics, Inc.; and K. Forbis Jordan, a professor emeritus at Arizona State University, contend that the number of students identified as disabled is increasing at an excessive rate because of funding systems that encourage overidentification and discourage flexible, creative, inclusive school programming.

NO: Sheldon Berman, a school superintendent, and his colleagues maintain that districts have been careful and conservative in identifying children with disabilities but that enrollment and costs are increasing primarily because of the increased numbers of children with more significant disabilities.

Legislators knew that establishing and maintaining programs for students with disabilities would cost money. No one knew how much or came close to an accurate prediction. Passage of the first special education law came with Congress's promise to pay up to 40 percent of the cost of educating children with disabilities. Annually determined through Capitol Hill negotiations, the actual funding appropriated has never come close to this promise; payments have ranged from 7 percent to 15 percent of this cost.

Despite continued underfunding, districts eagerly reach for any financial assistance available. To qualify for federal funds, schools maintain detailed records documenting compliance with special education laws and regulations. Students are counted annually, along with the extent of their time in special education. These figures are reported to the state and then to the U.S. Department of Education. Once budget wrangling ends, the total number of students with disabilities is divided into the funds available, and checks are sent to each state. After retaining some funds for the operation of overall special education activities, each state disperses the remaining federal funds among school districts. Sometimes the money that comes to a district amounts to less than $1,000 per student.

At the district level, schools begin budget formation in September for the following educational year. Estimating the cost of new textbooks and salary increases is relatively simple, especially when the number of students can be predicted based on current enrollment and when contracts are settled.

Predicting the number of students with disabilities and the extent of their needs is an entirely different matter. Who can tell when a child will have a tragic accident or anticipate a child who has not yet moved to town or reached the age of eligibility for publicly supported education? Nevertheless, the budget built early in one school year must anticipate the children who will require education a full 18 months later.

No matter how rich the school district, it seems that there is never enough money to go around.

In the following selection, Teresa S. Jordan, Carolyn A. Weiner, and K. Forbis Jordan explore the various ways in which states fund special education, and they conclude that most current systems encourage schools to identify more children as disabled to secure larger amounts of federal funds. The authors see this as counterproductive, limiting the flexibility of school districts and flying in the face of current efforts toward inclusion and site-based management. The authors describe several alternative funding mechanisms, all with an eye toward halting the practice of rewarding districts when they label children "disabled." They cite Massachusetts, for example, as a "trendsetter" state that is altering regulations and funding formulas to reduce reliance on special education.

In the second selection, Sheldon Berman, Perry Davis, Ann Koufman-Frederick, and David Urion analyze special education enrollment and funding patterns that followed the "trendsetting" policy changes in Massachusetts. Using data from districts throughout the state, and drawing parallels to national statistics, the authors find districts working assiduously to contain special education costs, struggling not to overidentify, and creatively building responsive programs. Despite these efforts, the authors say, special education expenditures continue to rise, driven by the increasing numbers of children with severe and complex needs and the shifting of costs to public schools.

As you read these selections, ask yourself whether federal funding helps to defray the cost of expensive education or creates rigid expectations that limit the creativity of schools.

Teresa S. Jordan, Carolyn A. Weiner, and K. Forbis Jordan

 **YES**

The Interaction of Shifting Special Education Policies With State Funding Practices

Introduction

In the current atmosphere of education reform, school finance litigation, regulatory changes, deregulation, and shifts in economic and political philosophies, increasing attention is being given to state funding systems for special education programs. The interactive effects of limited funds, mounting costs of some special education placements, and the federal interest in deregulation are resulting in greater scrutiny being given to special education programs. As schools strive to respond to shifts in policy and pressures for education reform, they are confronted with state funding systems for special education that are based on a different set of assumptions. Most current state funding systems for special education assume identifiable students, quantifiable program standards, isolated and measurable services, and auditable expenditures. As school districts change delivery systems so that children with disabilities are integrated into classrooms that also include students without disabilities, changes in local district budgeting and cost accounting systems will be required to provide special education expenditure data. Thus, state funding approaches will need to accommodate these new instructional arrangements.

Even before the dramatic changes in political control in 1994 and emphasis on inclusion of children with disabilities in classrooms that also contain children without disabilities, . . . the future of special education was uncertain. Funding levels for all education programs are being questioned because of the competition among various social services for scarce funds. . . .

For two decades, funding systems for special education in many states have allocated different levels of funding based on the child's disability classification. State funding allocations to provide programs and services for youth with disabilities typically have been based on instructional units, student weights, personnel reimbursement, reimbursement of the excess costs of educating these youth, or a flat grant.

From Teresa S. Jordan, Carolyn A. Weiner, and K. Forbis Jordan, "The Interaction of Shifting Special Education Policies With State Funding Practices," *Journal of Education Finance*, vol. 12, no. 1 (Summer 1997). Copyright © 1997 by The Association of School Business Officials International. Reprinted by permission. Notes omitted.

Recently, in an effort to provide a disincentive for local districts to identify and serve more children with disabilities, Massachusetts, Montana, North Dakota, Pennsylvania, and Vermont have enacted special education funding formulas that allocate funds on the basis of total school district enrollment and thus assume an equal proportion of students with disabilities in all school districts. Even though this approach may be attractive because of its simplicity and the elimination of the need to classify students to secure funds, a 1992 study reported that the statewide incidence of students in special education programs varied from just over 6 percent in Oregon to 17 percent in Massachusetts. State- and district-level incidence data indicate that children with disabilities are not uniformly distributed among states or among districts within a state....

The adversarial competition for funds between students without disabilities and students with disabilities may not be evident in all states, but events in Massachusetts illustrate that the conflict can occur. Since the special education reform legislation was enacted two decades ago, dramatic improvements have been achieved in Massachusetts. This legislation was praised as a national model; at the time, programs for children with disabilities were fragmented, under-funded, and highly segregated. After 20 years, over 96 percent of the special education students were being served in the public schools and no mentally retarded students under the age of 21 were in state institutions. However, the number of students receiving services was increasing and the costs of special education services and programs were rising faster than overall funding. In addition, residential costs were becoming a problem with $53 million being expended annually for 830 children, almost $64,000 per student each year. As might be expected, a backlash against special education occurred after overall spending constraints occurred in 1991.

Recently, in response to concerns about the effects of this earlier legislation, Massachusetts has taken two steps that may be trendsetters in the education reforms of the late 1990s that affect special education. First, the concept of the special needs child was redefined.... Second, the state's education reform legislation addresses the underlying challenge to provide a high quality education for all students. The presumption is that arguments over pull-outs, inclusion, and over-regulation will continue, but efforts to address the sufficiency of overall funding are expected to reduce the tension between general and special education. The state also changed its funding formula so that each district's funds for special education were based on total school population rather than the number of special education students being served....

The combination of programmatic reforms, fiscal constraints, and changing political philosophies suggest both the opportunity and the need to reexamine the ways that states fund special education programs and services....

Background

Even though most states had been funding special education for several years, the major impetus for full implementation of programs and services to serve youth with disabilities can be traced to the enactment of P. L. 94-142 in 1975.

Enacted in a climate of social reform, this federal law resulted in the promulgation of federal and state regulations that each child be provided with a free and appropriate education. The Congress took this action in response to federal court cases affirming the right of an education for children with disabilities, research demonstrating that all children can learn, and intense lobbying by special education personnel and parent groups. As a result of this legislation, children with disabilities were guaranteed:

- a free appropriate education
- a comprehensive evaluation
- an individualized educational program (IEP)
- related services
- due-process procedures
- placement in the least restrictive environment

Amendments were made to the original legislation in 1986 and also in 1990 when the title was changed to the Individuals with Disabilities Education Act (IDEA).

In 1994–95, about 5.4 million students were being served in programs for youth with disabilities; this represents about 11 percent of the total school enrollment. Spending levels have been estimated to be over two times the expenditures for general education, with less than 10 percent from federal funds, about 54 percent from state sources, and about 36 percent from local sources.

Program Delivery

Programs and services for children with disabilities are provided through both public and private schools with the private placement often being supported by public funds. Referrals are most often initiated by a teacher or parent who notices a difficulty. Following a diagnostic process, the eligible child's educational and service needs are identified and formalized in an individualized education program (IEP). Historically, the child then has been assigned to the appropriate special education for specific periods of time.

... [T]he majority of students receiving special education are served in their home districts. Many public school officials contend that private placements are very costly options that benefit affluent parents who can afford legal counsel; these parents have the economic power to challenge the contention that their child can be served in the public school setting.

For several years, special education procedures have been subjected to a variety of criticisms. Much of the programmatic criticism has been related to the practice of removing the child from the classroom either to receive special services or to be placed in a self-contained classroom on a full-time basis....

Additional concerns have been that special education has become a "dumping ground" for students who are more difficult to teach and that there is a tendency for students once placed in special education programs to remain there.

Another area of criticism has been the use of labels to categorize children with disabilities.... The labeling or classification process has been criticized because it often lacks validity and reliability, results in isolation of students, and may consume as much as 20 percent of the total cost of educating the student. However, continued enforcement of the classification procedures and regulations has resulted in the persistence of these problems....

These criticisms suggest that labeling students by disability and funding on the basis of these labels is not compatible with the current interest in providing more flexible programs and services for students with disabilities....

An additional issue is that some current special education program and service delivery systems are not compatible with either the movement toward decentralization in local school districts or the efforts to implement inclusion for children with disabilities. Decentralization calls for each individual school to make decisions about the educational programs and services to be provided for the school's children. Current education reform recommendations call for all students to be provided with needed programs and services in classrooms that also contain students who have not been identified as disabled....

Districts do not receive funds for children with disabilities when they try to meet the needs of students without specific identification. Most current state funding systems encourage districts to identify as many students as possible so that state funding will be higher. Initially, these systems were developed to ensure that funds would be provided for every identified student receiving services and that the more expensive forms of service received more financial support; however, the result has ben the segregation of students.

Effect of Funding Formulas

... When the values of weights are based on program types, the monetary value of a weight can encourage districts to classify students into a higher reimbursement category.... A uniform amount, or flat grant, for each child with an identified disability encourages districts to identify children with low-cost disabilities. Cost-reimbursement can encourage local school districts to become engaged in purposeful identification of students and fiscal accounting to maximize their state payment. A study of the effect of a change in Tennessee's funding formula for special education found that the number of children in a mid-level funding level category increased when the state used a weighted formula rather than a flat-rate system.

Commonly used state school finance formulas contain few incentives for serving children with disabilities in general classroom settings. State funding systems typically are based on traditional delivery systems that assume identifiable costs, services, and personnel assigned to special education. Cost accounting procedures require the assignment of staff time to a particular program, or in the case of special education to a sub-program. In an inclusion classroom, the time of the teacher would have to be assigned to the sub-program for each child with a disability as well as to general education. The record keeping and accounting burden would be significant. This is especially critical in those states that use a cost-reimbursement model in their state funding system. This funding approach tends to encourage schools to maintain status quo conditions. Higher funding levels for more intensive programs appear to result in the growth of these programs to serve children with disabilities in special classrooms.

Funding formulas influence the types of services and staff provided in a program. From a different perspective, when state funding systems are linked to location of service, the state funding system may not provide sufficient funds for local school districts that provide appropriate support services to students with disabilities. Thus, many state funding formulas may operate to the disadvantage of districts even if inclusion is judged to be the most preferable arrangement.

Current State Funding Practices

Traditionally, special education in many states has been funded as a separate categorical program.... Existing funding practices for programs and services for children with disabilities fall into four broad categories: pupil weights, instructional or classroom units, excess cost or percentage reimbursement, and flat grant. Pupil weighting and instructional unit systems typically are based on type of placement or disabling condition. Under the cost reimbursement method, state funds are based: (1) on allowable costs for programs and services or (2) on excess costs under which general program costs are deducted from the total expenditure levels for special education programs and services to determine the excess amount attributable to special education programs. Most states rely on a single funding method, but a few utilize some combination of funding methods.

Pupil weighting systems are used in 18 states; cost or percentage reimbursement methods are used in 11 states; flat grants are used in 10 states; and resource (i.e., instructional or classroom units) based funding is used in 11 states. In the 10 states that use the flat grant method, 5 states use the number of special education students to calculate the district's funds under the flat grant, and 5 states use population based funding (the district's total enrollment) to calculate the district's funds for special education....

Alternative Funding Responses

Various funding systems for special education are under discussion as efforts are being made to ensure that financing systems are compatible with the policy shift to inclusion of children with disabilities in the general classroom....

Delivery System Weights (DSW)

... The DSW option can accommodate a range of inclusion options. This formula does not include capital project funds that might be required for retrofitting classrooms or acquiring specialized equipment. *In contrast to funding programs for children without disabilities in which programs and services are reduced if funding is insufficient, school districts are required to provide programs and services (or a free and appropriate education) to children with disabilities consistent with the detail of the IEP. For that reason, the under-funding of special education programs does not reduce the services for these youth; however, if a financial shortfall occurs, the under-funding deficit is met by reducing programs for children without disabilities.* Thus, it is essential that sufficient base level funding be provided for children without disabilities.

The DSW funding methodology is different from traditional special education funding models.... It is still student-based, but is based on type of delivery system rather than type of disability.

The DSW funding model is currently used in several states and also was recommended in a recent study of schools serving American Indian students on Federal Indian reservation; these schools are funded by the Bureau of Indian Affairs (BIA).... These schools provided a unique opportunity for analyzing the effects of alternative funding models. Not only did they receive their funds in the form of a block grant, but also site-based management and decentralization were fully operational....

The DSW model was based on data from a cost study of BIA special education programs, an analysis of state practices, and information on preferred service delivery systems. The traditional service delivery approaches —consultation, resource, or self-contained—were reconfigured into a set of options that reflect current practices and recommendations: high service inclusion (HSI), moderate service inclusions (MSI), direct service (DS), and self-contained classroom (SC). The rationale for the new configuration was the need for a funding system designed to support recommended special education practices....

Based on the BIA cost study data, students in high service inclusion and self-contained classrooms were assigned a weight of 3.00, moderate service inclusion students a weight of 1.00, and students receiving related services a weight of 0.50.

This option is a form of per pupil allocation or child-based formula. Under this formula, the student's classification would be based on the provisions of the IEP. The amount of funds generated by this add-on weight would be based on the unweighted funding for students without disabilities.... Criteria for differentiating between *high service inclusion* and *moderate service inclusion* include the level (professional qualifications) and the quantity (time in person-hours) of service required. An example would be the proportion of an instructional aide's day required by a student and the number of students with whom a single aide could work at a given time.... This methodology is consistent with the theoretical assumptions about inclusion. Concerns would include the extent to which provision of related services within the general classroom would disrupt the general instructional program.

This latter approach for integrating the DSW funding methodology with the federal child count data is similar to the method used to fund special education under the Kentucky Education Reform Act. Special education directors in Kentucky supported the shift from the personnel unit methodology because it increased local flexibility and reduced the incentives for placing students into particular programs.

The DSW method recognizes differences in the educational needs of students among different school districts and requires that students be identified by the service being provided. Different amounts per student are based on the cost of the student's program. Local districts have flexibility in the use of funds, but, under this method, there is still no incentive to reduce services or change program or to determine that the child no longer needs the services or the special program. . . .

Population Based Funding (PBF)

. . . In 1996, the Congress considered using the population-based approach with an adjustment for the percent of poverty students in making state allocations of federal funds for students with disabilities. . . .

Massachusetts, Montana, North Dakota, Pennsylvania, and Vermont use the PBF method to allocate state funds for special education to local school districts. Vermont also uses the percentage reimbursement method. Motives for adoption varied from a concern about increasing costs to the desire to develop a funding system that would support inclusion.

The rationale for PBF is that a straight percentage of special needs funding should be allocated without recourse to testing or labeling. Districts then would not benefit from over-classification of students. A move to PBF at either the federal or state level would be a major shift in public policy. The economic incentives in many current state formulas to serve more children have been criticized, but this policy change would result in states and local school districts having a disincentive to either identify or serve children with disabilities. Since funding would no longer be based on programs being provided or the need for funds to serve children with disabilities, districts could use the released funds for other purposes. However, . . . currently available data document the contentions that children with disabilities are not equally distributed among either states or local school districts; therefore, the effect of a change to PBF would be that those states and districts with disproportionately larger numbers of children with disabilities would be penalized. This type of inequity was noted in the recent Ohio school finance litigation; the court noted the inequities that occur when the funding for students without disabilities is based on the residual that remains after funding has been provided for students with disabilities.

The primary rationales for PBF are that the number of students in special programs is increasing at an excessive rate because traditional state funding systems reward and encourage the over-identification of students with special educational needs. The assumption is that PBF would function as a block grant and that funding is based on a presumed percentage of children needing special education services; funds would not be attributable to a particular program or group of students. . . . The extent to which adequacy would be attained would be dependent upon the overall funding level. Local districts would have flexibility in the use of funds, and no penalty would be imposed for moving special needs students into general programs. The inherent assumption is that all districts have similar proportions of students with special educational needs.

PBF contains no incentive to identify students with special educational needs, and the district does not incur a gain or loss in state funds by identifying a student for a special program or moving a student from a special program to a general classroom. There is no incentive for over-classification; funding would not be dependent on labeling or classifying students. Funding would be predictable from one year to the next, but funding would not change if the districts had an increase in the number of students with special educational needs. . . .

Educational Overburden Index (EOI)

. . . This funding index is a proxy for the magnitude of educational need. The process involves development of an index for each district based on a selected set of variables that reflect the differing educational and socioeconomic conditions among districts. . . .

The first step in developing an EOI is to identify the educational and socioeconomic conditions that are to be considered in the index and then to select a set of common research-based variables or indicators for all school districts within a state. Data from the Decennial Census, state department of education, and local districts can be sources for the variables used in developing the index for use in the state funding formula. Potential variables include percent of students with IEPs, percent of unemployment, percent of children living below the poverty level, per capita income, percent of population with a high school education or higher, percent of youths 16 to 19 who were not in school and did not have a high school diploma (dropout), percent of persons with low English fluency, and percent of persons living elsewhere in a specific year (mobility). Data are converted into a common format to facilitate the statistical calculations that yield the EOI.

In the second step, districts within a state are clustered through the use of . . . two forms of artificial neural networks. . . .

Neural networks are information-processing systems that are able to deal with complex sets of multiple variables and group or cluster districts according to their relative needs without the traditional dependent variable. The first neural network assigns districts into groupings or clusters based on need. The second neural network refines the clusters by assigning each district an optimal weight reflective of its relative need in relationship to all districts in the state.

The results of this process yield a value that is converted into an index for each school district. . . . To determine the funding level for each district, the EOI [is] multiplied by the district's student membership to determine the number of funding units. This product [is] multiplied times the funding level per unit to calculate the district's state support level. In these calculations, the EOI is somewhat similar to population-based funding. However, unlike population-based funding in which the index is a uniform percentage for all districts, the EOI is a *variable percentage* applied to the district's membership based on each district's differentiated need.

The educational overburden index is different from the other methodologies in that it can be used to recognize cost burdens on school districts associated with the full range of special needs youth, i.e., children with disabilities, at-risk youth, limited English proficient students, and disadvantaged youth. The strengths of the index are that the concept: (1) is consistent with the current emphasis on inclusion, (2) can accommodate differences in cost conditions among school districts, (3) provides a research-based proxy for the special educational needs of all youth without requiring that students be labeled or be served in separate programs, and (4) empowers schools to create innovative educational environments in which the unique needs of each student can be addressed.

The two rationales for the... EOI are that the state's funding system should: (1) provide districts with sufficient flexibility to adopt creative reforms to improve instruction and learning and (2) recognize differences in the educational needs of students among different school districts without imposing additional paperwork. The... EOI would function as a block grant; therefore, funding would be based on the predicted overall educational need of the districts and funds would not be attributable to a particular program or group of students.

The level of funding is based on an assumed incidence of special needs students derived from district educational and socioeconomic characteristics, but the district does not incur a gain or loss in state funds by identifying a student for a special program or moving a student from a special program to a general classroom.... Funding would be predictable from one year to the next because allocations would be based on projected differences in the special educational needs of the district's student population....

Conclusion

... Funding systems have been used to promote implementation of regulations and encourage traditional delivery systems. The policy shift to inclusion of students with disabilities in the general classroom, the broad interest in school reform, and the desire to implement new instructional arrangements for all students are potent forces that are contributing to changes in state funding systems for special education.

Inclusion assumes that programs and services for students with disabilities will be provided in an integrated educational environment that may not be compatible with the premises in many current school finance programs. *The delivery system weights, population-based funding,* and *educational overburden index* funding models have several advantages. First, these models empower districts to use diverse systems in providing appropriate services for children with disabilities in the least restrictive environment. Second, from an administrative perspective, they are supportive of and compatible with the concept of inclusion. Third, even though the federal legislation and regulations may still require districts to label students by type of disability, these systems are much less prescriptive.... [A]ll three funding systems could be designed in a manner that would reduce the paperwork burden. However, the authors have a concern about the *PBF* because of its assumption of uniform distribution of need among school districts in a state. This perhaps would not be critical in a time of sufficient resources, but it has the potential of resulting in the under-funding of general education programs.

Given the perceived negative reactions to the level of funding for special education programs, the challenge is to reduce the adversarial relationships among special education advocates, school finance theorists, special educators, local district administrators, and state policymakers. These diverse groups should join forces in efforts to conceptualize and implement more responsive funding systems for programs to serve students with disabilities.

The Rising Costs of Special Education in Massachusetts

Introduction

Over the past decade states across the nation have seen rapid increases in the number of children requiring special education services. They have also experienced significant increases in the cost to school districts for these services. In states where additional funding has been provided to support education reform and school improvement, the rising costs of special education have consumed a disproportionate share of these funds, thereby compromising school-based and state-based efforts to support reform.

The causes of these increases, however, have been mis-diagnosed as the result of district policy and practice. In this case study of cost increases in Massachusetts, we determine that the increases schools have been experiencing have not been caused by school district policy and practice. In fact, just the opposite has been the case. School district policy and practice have been effective in containing and even reducing the percentage of children who require special education services in Massachusetts. Nonetheless, costs in Massachusetts have continued to increase....

[T]he root causes of these increases have been factors beyond the control of schools, such as advances in medical technology, the deinstitutionalization of children with special needs, privatization of services, and economic and social factors including increases in the number of children in poverty and the number of families experiencing social and economic stress. Although the focus of this paper will be on Massachusetts, national data on special education reveal that these factors are also influencing the increased number of special education children across the country....

A Case Study: Massachusetts

In the spring of 1996, the Massachusetts Association of School Superintendents (MASS) established a task force to study rapidly increasing special education costs across the state. These cost increases were significantly impacting school

From Sheldon Berman, Perry Davis, Ann Koufman-Frederick, and David Urion, "The Rising Costs of Special Education in Massachusetts: Causes and Effects," in Chester E. Finn, Jr., Andrew J. Rotherham, and Charles R. Hokanson, Jr., eds., *Rethinking Special Education for a New Century* (Thomas B. Fordham Foundation & Progressive Policy Institute, 2001). Copyright © 2001 by The Thomas B. Fordham Foundation. Reprinted by permission. Notes omitted.

districts' ability to implement the state's education reform program.... This study has been updated with new data in 1999 and 2000, and again for this paper.

... [T]he task force found that the financial challenges facing districts as a result of rising special education costs were exacerbated by Massachusetts' new education reform funding formula. This formula was built on the inaccurate assumption that school district policy and practice were responsible for the cost increases and that the state could force school districts to change their practices by under-representing the costs of special education in the formula. Not only did the formula set unrealistically low percentages for students in special education, but also it allocated less than half of what would be required to pay for services for these students.

Finally, the task force found that increases in the numbers of children and severity of disabilities in early intervention programs serving 0- to 3-year-olds and special-needs preschool programs serving 3- to 5-year-olds indicated that costs would continue to increase in the future....

The Reality of Special Education Costs in Massachusetts

The special education components of the state's education reform funding formula, known as the foundation formula, were built on the assumptions that school districts did not effectively contain costs and that they identified more children than necessary as having special needs. Specific elements of the formula were designed as disincentives to these practices. For example, in all areas other than special education actual enrollment within a district is used to build the foundation budget. Additional allocations are provided for the number of students who are from low-income families or who are in bilingual or vocational programs. In contrast, allocations for special education are based on a preset percentage of children in special education set at a rate lower than the state average. In addition, the cost allocations for providing services to in-district preschool, in-district K-12 students, and out-of-district placements are set at levels well below the actual costs that districts incur for these students. These disincentives were designed to cause districts to be more rigorous in their use of the eligibility standards and to encourage more cost-effective placement of students.

Analysis of Massachusetts enrollment data shows that these assumptions are not accurate. In fact, schools have done a good job containing costs. They have rigorously applied eligibility standards and provided regular education and inclusive programming for children as alternatives to special education services.

Special education enrollments as a percent of total enrollment reached a high in FY92 of 17.4 percent. After that, new eligibility standards were implemented statewide. Beginning in FY93 and continuing through FY97 districts applied these new standards, and enrollment declined to a low of 16.6 percent. With the exception of a "spike" in FY99, special education enrollment has remained relatively steady at approximately 16.7 percent.

Massachusetts special education enrollment increases are also well below national trends. Between FY89 and FY98, special education enrollment in Massachusetts grew at less than half the rate of growth nationally (31.7 percent growth enrollment nationally compared to 13.3 percent growth in Massachusetts).

In its 1997 study, the Massachusetts Special Education Task Force observed sharp increases in special education preschool enrollments and predicted that these would impact enrollments and costs in future years. In fact, current special education increases are indeed being driven by significant increases in special education preschool enrollment. Between FY89 and FY00, special education preschool enrollment in Massachusetts rose by 83.8 percent, while other special education enrollments increased by only 13.1 percent and total enrollment by 17.8 percent. School districts continue to contain costs and effectively apply the eligibility standards but are seriously pressed by a greater number of children entering school districts at age 3 with a disability diagnosis. This sharp increase in preschool enrollment is also present nationally; overall enrollments of children ages 3 to 5 are growing at twice the rate of children ages 6 to 21.

Costs continued to increase over the past decade as districts enrolled a greater number of children with more serious needs. The task force found that between FY90 and FY99 per-pupil expenditures in special education increased... from $6,675 to $10,249, while they increased by approximately one-third as much... in regular education—from $4,103 to $5,487. During this period, special education expenditures grew... at almost twice the rate of regular education expenditures.... The difference is even more significant when adjusted for inflation. In 1990 dollars, per-pupil regular education expenditures grew by only $186 or 4.5 percent, while per-pupil special education expenditures grew by $1,336 or 20 percent.

The Education Reform Act of 1993 resulted in the addition of $1.2 billion in state aid to local school districts. However, special education costs statewide increased by $476 million during those years, an equivalent of 38 percent of all the additional aid from 1993 to 1999....

The impact on education reform is clear when one compares the additional state aid provided to communities for education reform with the additional special education expenditures in those communities. The increases in special education exceeded the amount received in new state aid between FY93 and FY99 for 88 of the 300 school districts. For 36 more school districts, special education increases equaled between 75 percent and 99 percent of additional state aid. And for another 44 school districts, special education increases equaled between 50 percent and 74 percent of new state aid. This means that 56 percent of Massachusetts school districts spent the equivalent of 50 percent or more of new state aid on special education. There is no consistent pattern among these districts. They vary in size, wealth and region....

For most districts, the three primary causes of increased costs are students moving into the district with IEPs [individual education programs] requiring private placement, increases in the number of preschool children requiring special education services, and increases in the number of foster placements within the community requiring significant special-needs services. In fact, one factor in declining costs in some districts has been the movement of students with expensive private placements to another community. In all these districts, compromises have been made regarding implementation of education reform initiatives due to budget constraints presented by special education cost increases. Making headway on education reform is extremely difficult in the face of such increases.

Given the limited funds available to districts, even those districts with smaller increases in special education expenditures have had their education reform efforts compromised by a disproportionate share of new funds allocated to special education. In fact, the data the task force has provided may understate the problem. Most of the increases in regular education expenditures have simply covered the cost of inflation.

Significant increases in special education have the potential for starting a vicious cycle. Increases reduce the funds available for regular education classrooms, causing increases in class size and reduction in support services. These in turn make it more difficult for teachers to address the range of student needs in the regular classroom, producing more referrals to special education. This increases costs again, perpetuating the cycle. For many Massachusetts districts, education reform funds have prevented the perpetuation of this cycle by providing the infusion of new funds necessary to maintain regular education programs at a time of increasing special education costs. However, the price has been little improvement in regular education services for those districts—the original intent of the funding.

Associated Health Costs

Another cost trend impacting school districts is the increase in health and nursing expenditures. Over the past six years many school districts have experienced significant increases in the number of medically involved students who require nursing and other health-related care. These children are not necessarily classified as special education students, although they often receive extensive services.... [I]n analyzing the data on statewide health expenditures for school districts, we found that costs increased by 114 percent between FY90 and FY99....

At this point, we have not been able to secure data on how much has been expended for health education versus nursing services. However, we believe that the primary driver of costs in this area is the increasing number of students who need medical attention. This was not anticipated when the foundation formula was developed and remains an area of serious underfunding in the formula....

Ominous Trends

Based on increases in preschool and early intervention enrollments as well as trends in medicine and social services, we believe that special education costs will continue to increase well into the future. A significant factor in the increase in costs over the past decade has been the rapid rise in the number of children with moderate and serious disabilities who require special-needs preschool programs. Between FY89 and FY99, regular education enrollment rose by 17.8

percent. During this period, special education enrollment in all categories excluding preschool rose by 13.1 percent. However, special education preschool enrollment increased by 83.8 percent.

Preschool enrollment nationally has been growing at twice the rate of other special education enrollments. The increases in the Massachusetts preschool population parallel this trend.

Many districts reported to the MASS Special Education Task Force that not only were the number of children requiring special-needs preschool programs continuing to increase, but these children had more significant disabilities. These reports are confirmed by data provided by the Department of Public Health regarding children in early intervention programs. In FY92, 9,809 children were served by early intervention, with 59 percent of these children considered to have moderate or severe delays. By FY99, the number of children being served had increased by 105 percent.... However, the more ominous trend is that in FY99, the percent of children with moderate or severe delays had increased to 86 percent. Therefore the number of children with moderate to severe delays almost tripled during those years....

Major Causes of Rising Special Education Costs

Rather than school district policy and practice, the increases in special education costs are due largely to medical, economic, and social factors.

Changes in Medical Practice

Medical technology has advanced to such a degree that children who would not have otherwise survived due to prematurity or disability are now surviving. In addition, those whose disability would previously have placed them in hospital or institutional settings are now able to enter public school or private special education schools. The medical profession has also become increasingly aware of disabilities and is better able to diagnose them at an earlier age. Special education services are often recommended at infancy, and children are placed in early intervention programs. At age three, the responsibility for providing special education services is referred to the school district.

In particular, neonatology, the specialty of newborn medicine, has triumphed over the past decades. The last 20 years have seen increasingly premature infants survive at ever-lower mean birth weights.... Due to advances in medical technology, survival of children at a birth weight below 3.3 pounds has increased from 52 percent twenty years ago... to 90 percent today. Although this development is laudable, it has left us with consequences. Multiple studies have shown a close correlation between prematurity/low birth weight and subsequent developmental outcome. Many premature infants are left with lifelong developmental and neurological problems.

Of infants born at birth weights less than 3.3 pounds, approximately 10 percent will develop classic cerebral palsy with seizures, severe spastic motor deficits, and mental retardation. All of these children, approximately 4,950 annually over the last five years, will have multiple medical issues that will necessitate the expansion of medical and nursing capabilities within the school responsible for them.

Fifty percent of children born weighing less than 3.3 pounds will have significant cognitive difficulties without spastic motor problems. Half of these ... will have measured intelligence in the borderline to mentally retarded range.

The other half will have significant to severe learning disabilities.

The actual number of children with disabilities resulting from prematurity, therefore, has increased markedly over the past 20 years. In fact, those numbers have almost tripled as medical technology has improved.

Prematurity and its consequences are not evenly distributed across society. The children of poor and marginalized populations are more likely to be born prematurely and suffer greater difficulties from this than children of middle- and upper-income families.... Thus, the social and economic burden of educating children with significant developmental problems resulting from their premature births is not evenly or equitably distributed across communities. Urban and rural communities bear a disproportionate share of poverty and a greater share of the disabilities resulting from prematurity.

Medical advances have enabled other populations of students to attend school who would not have been able to do so 20 years ago. For example, two of every 1,000 full-term infants are born asphyxiated because of various medical events in the delivery process. This number has been very stable over the last two decades. Two decades ago, however, there was a 35 percent risk of death in the newborn period after asphyxia. Now nearly all these infants survive, and all come to school with significant to severe motor and cognitive deficits.

Another example is children born with epilepsy. Increasingly effective anti-seizure medications have allowed larger numbers of children with epilepsy to attend school on a regular basis. Although only 60 percent of school-age children with epilepsy were able to attend school without significant interruptions 20 years ago, now more than 95 percent are in school full-time. One percent of the school-age population has epilepsy; 85 percent of these children have significant special education needs. Given the treatment regimens that allow for full-time schooling, essentially all will require nursing supervision of their anti-seizure medications in school.

Children with autism represent another population that is increasingly able to attend school. Autism spectrum disorders (frank infantile autism and pervasive developmental disorders) appear to be present in roughly 2 percent of the population. It is not clear whether the apparent increase over the last 20 years represents an absolute increase in numbers or increased recognition. However, increasingly effective medical treatments for elements of behavioral dyscontrol in children with autism, coupled with more effective behavioral treatment modes, have allowed a larger percentage of children with autism to be educated in public school or consortium environments. These children generally require extensive and costly services within the school environment.

Twenty years ago, roughly two percent of the school-age population had a medical diagnosis that impacted upon their ability to function in school, both from an academic/cognitive as well as physical standpoint. Currently, conservative estimates suggest that 7.5 percent of the school-age population have a medical diagnosis that has such impact that these children cannot expect to prosper in school without significant multimodal academic and medical assistance in the school setting. The burden is placed disproportionately upon communities that have less access to contemporary treatment and intervention strategies.

The research necessary to implement effective treatments that prevent disabilities associated with prematurity, birth asphyxia, epilepsy, and autism is only now in its very earliest stages. As a result, the number of students with these disorders attending schools and requiring extensive services is likely to continue to climb for at least the first two decades of this century.

Deinstitutionalization and Privatization

A second factor impacting costs have been the deinstitutionalization of special-needs children and the privatization of special education services over the past decade. The best example is the Bureau of Institutional Schools (BIS). The Bureau of Institutional Schools was established within Massachusetts special education law to provide special education services for children residing in facilities under the control of the Departments of Mental Health, Retardation, Public Health, and Youth Services and the Country Houses of Corrections. However, in 1974, BIS primarily served two populations in state institutions. The first group was children with mental retardation; the second was children in hospital settings due to psychiatric or medical problems. BIS institutions and services for these populations were supported by state rather than local funds.

The number of children served by BIS, which has been reorganized as Educational Services in Institutional Settings (ESIS), has increased only slightly since 1974. However, the population is dramatically different from those served in 1974. Children with mental retardation are served directly through school district funds, either in programs within the district or in private or residential placements. This population, representing the majority of children served by BIS in 1974, is now the complete financial and educational responsibility of public schools. In addition, some children in hospital settings, who would have previously been served by BIS, especially those receiving psychiatric treatment, are also the responsibility of school districts. Currently, two-thirds of ESIS's caseload are incarcerated or detained youth served by the Department of Youth Services and the County Houses of Corrections, with the remainder coming from Departments of Public Health and Mental Health programs.

The shift away from state institutions toward a reliance on local school districts and collaborative or private placements is a positive one. It provides better services within a less restrictive environment. However, the financial resources to fund this shift have not come with the children.

Another example is a shift in policy at the Department of Social Services (DSS), especially in the new Commonworks Program. This program is designed to respond to the needs of hard-to-reach adolescents with multiple problems through out-of-home care. DSS typically has responsibility for out-of-home care but has sought to increase school districts' financial responsibility for children in the program. The Commonworks Program removes children from services they are receiving within a district and places them in private day or residential placements due to non-educational, family-related circumstances. School districts are then expected to share the cost of these placements. The request for proposals for lead agencies of the Commonworks Program contained specific references to the expansion of special education services, with DSS referring to school districts as a partner in paying for education services. DSS only set funding in place for educational services for 20 percent of the youth enrolled in Commonworks, however, creating an expectation that 80 percent of the youth enrolled in Commonworks would receive their educational services under cost-sharing agreements with school districts. The reality is that school districts lack the funding to support this new demand for services.

A third example is the increase in the number of children who are state wards placed in foster homes. These children receive services in public schools. However, the placement and movement of these children is controlled by DSS and the foster parent. The dilemma presented by the placement process is the large number of children placed in foster homes in some communities. In addition to the financial strain on these school districts, they are given late notification that a student with special needs will be placed in their community. A single foster home taking one special education foster child can require a school district to pay for an out-of-district tuition of over $30,000 plus daily transportation. The state does provide some additional funding for state wards, but no funding is available until the year after the costs are incurred. Plus, the funding is usually less than actual costs.

The children in both Commonworks and foster care deserve the services and education they receive. The problem is that both programs shift cost and responsibility from state level departments to local districts. Together with the deinstitutionalization of many children in ESIS, the financial and educational responsibilities now fall primarily on local communities without the funding to provide for these children.

Economic and Social Factors

A third cause of special education cost increases has been a higher percentage of children living in poverty. There is a correlation between poverty and special needs. . . . [B]etween 17 percent and 19 percent of Massachusetts children in primary grades lived in poverty for their early years.

The national data on children in poverty reveal that the percentage of children under six years of age living in poverty rose significantly during the 1980s and early 1990s to a high of 25.7 percent in 1993. The rate has steadily declined since 1993 and was approximately 18 percent in 1999. The high national level of children living in poverty since the 1980s may account for a portion of the increase in special education enrollments throughout the last two decades.

Adding to the impact of poverty is the increase in families experiencing social and economic stress. Many communities and school districts have seen increases in such indicators as child abuse and neglect, alcoholism and drug use, and dysfunctional family environments that lead to increases in children requiring special education services.

According to the Massachusetts Department of Social Services, reports of child maltreatment were more than two and half times higher in 1999 than in 1983, as was the number of cases of confirmed maltreatment through supported investigations. DSS's report *Child Maltreatment Statistics 1995* states that "families reported for child maltreatment displayed the following characteristics: substance abuse, poverty, economic stress (and the associated problems of poor housing and limited community resources), and a lack of specific parenting skills." ...

If the Commonwealth of Massachusetts and other states wish to address the financial dilemma presented by special education, they need to recognize that the major causes of cost increases are not school district policy and practice. Instead, they are advances in medical technology, deinstitutionalization and privatization of services, and increases in children in poverty and families experiencing social and economic stress. ...

The Foundation Formula

Rather than helping school districts adequately address special education cost increases, Massachusetts' education reform foundation formula exacerbates the problem by underestimating the percentage of children in special education programs as well as the cost of these programs. For example, in FY99 16.7 percent of the total student enrollment statewide was being served in special education programs. However, the foundation formula locked in a figure of 14 percent of student enrollment being served 25 percent of the time in special education programs. The formula adds an additional 1 percent for out-of-district placements ... [which] is particularly problematic. Given the small size of many Massachusetts districts, enrollment can vary widely, especially high-cost out-of-district placements. Out-of-district placements, in fact, can vary between 1 percent and 3 percent with smaller districts—those that can least afford it— experiencing the greatest variation. The formula makes no accommodations for these variations between districts.

More significant, the formula underestimates the cost of services for these students. ...

As special education costs continue to rise, the low estimates built into the formula remain inflexible and unresponsive to these changes. Consequently, they produce unrealistic estimates for districts' foundation budgets and provide no additional state aid to address the problem. Massachusetts' failure to adequately fund the costs of educating students with severe disabilities is compromising school districts' ability to implement the kinds of instructional improvements intended in the state's Education Reform Act. ...

Recommendations

... [P]olicymakers should be realistic about the rising costs of special education. The increases in serious disabilities within the population in general and the increase in the number of young children with moderate and severe disabilities will require greater expenditures in special education. Even though districts in Massachusetts are making their best efforts to provide regular education programs and services as an alternative to substantially separate special-needs programs, these regular education programs and services require additional resources. Learning disabilities do not disappear just because a child is not classified as a special education student. These are realities that policymakers need to face.

The long-term solution requires that the state and federal government support school districts in meeting the responsibility for special education. Communities, especially smaller communities, cannot meet the needs of children who cost the district over $20,000 each without compromising other programs, but, under current law, communities pay the bill. This places an unfair burden on local communities when the responsibility for these children is best addressed through the collective efforts of all citizens within the state and throughout the nation.

One proposal for addressing the increasing costs is to have the local community pay the educational costs and the state or federal government pay for medical, psychiatric, physical therapy, and/or occupational therapy services. Although schools should not be required to address medical problems, it is so difficult to define which service is educational and which is medical that we believe that the only effective approach is to increase both the state's and federal government's financial responsibility for special education.

On a federal level, the landmark Education for All Handicapped Children Act of 1975 established a federal commitment to pay for 40 percent of the excess cost of its special education mandate. This mandate has never been met, and the federal government currently contributes approximately a modest 12 percent of the costs of special education. Additional resources provided at a federal level would help relieve the burden on states and local school districts.

Conclusion

We face a challenging dilemma. Children are entering our school system with significantly greater special needs, and these needs are often identified at a very early age. The increased cost of special education services is seriously compromising regular education programs and education reform in states throughout the country. We need a solution that addresses the financial crisis emerging in many districts while at the same time meeting the real and substantial needs of these children. In addition, we need a solution that does not blame the children or those working with them and does not pit regular education against special education.

The Massachusetts Education Reform Act set ambitious new standards and dedicated significant funds for the improvement of education. However, for the majority of districts the increase in special education spending has meant that little of the new funds have been available for the improvement of regular education. For all too many districts the situation is critical. The long-term interest of children with disabilities will not be served by pulling resources from regular education classrooms. Action on the part of the state of Massachusetts and the federal government is imperative so that the needs of both regular education and special education children can be well-served and the goals of education reform realized. It would be tragic if education reform, increased funding, and public education in general were declared failures when, in fact, the experiment was never really tried.

The long-term solution lies in addressing the underlying causes of the special-needs increases—the medical, social, and economic issues that cause increasing numbers of children to require special education. We need to invest in medical research directed toward the prevention of disabilities in premature infants. We also need to invest in reweaving the social and economic support systems for families. These are difficult problems to solve, but we encourage our state and federal legislators to work toward these long-term solutions.

POSTSCRIPT

Is Special Education So Expensive Because of the Way It Is Funded?

The Center for Special Education Finance (CSEF)—the home page of which is at http://csef.air.org—estimates that the cost of educating a child with disabilities is 2.28 times that of educating a child without disabilities. Expenditures vary widely based on need.

CSEF researchers, who are currently studying the details of national spending, place the costs of special education in the context of decreasing funds for schools in general. In sharp contrast to the 1970s, fewer taxpayers have children in school today. The first priority of the majority is not education. As schools struggle to fund education reform, the unpredictable, individual, and unavoidable expenses of special education are cast into bold relief.

The solution, according to Jordan, Weiner, and Jordan, is a funding system that is not tied to specific groups. Currently, federal funds for at-risk students, bilingual children, children in poverty, and children with disabilities must be used to address the needs of their target population of students. Combining these into one block grant resource would reduce bureaucracy and eliminate the tendency to label students in order to receive funds.

Although they believe that schools are struggling to be reasonable about service delivery, Berman et al. see darker times ahead regardless of the funding system that is used. The beginnings of special education shifted educational responsibility from institutions and hospitals to schools. Managed care shifted financial responsibilities for medically related services from insurance companies to schools. The need for parents to work multiple jobs has shifted care responsibilities from families to schools. And tight fiscal conditions have shifted support responsibilities from social agencies to schools. However, Berman et al. say, money has not accompanied this shift of responsibilities.

Various methods of special education funding are being found wanting. For example, Alabama, Wyoming, Ohio, and Michigan have each supported special education through different systems. However, each state's mechanism was found to be illegal, resulting in the "encroachment" of special education into educational resources. The Ohio suit found the state's entire financing system for education to be inadequate and inappropriate (Verstegen, *CSEF Brief,* 1998).

There is agreement that special education is costly and that stressful financial times require difficult choices. Is this issue about the cost of special education or about scarce resources for all of education? Is this an argument about *how* to pay for the education of students with disabilities or *whether* to pay for the education of students with disabilities?

ISSUE 4

Are the Doors of For-Profit Charter Schools Open for Students With Disabilities?

YES: Chester E. Finn, Jr., et al., from "The Policy Perils of Charter Schools," *Charter Schools in Action Project: Final Report, Part III* (August 1997)

NO: Nancy J. Zollers and Arun K. Ramanathan, from "For-Profit Charter Schools and Students With Disabilities: The Sordid Side of the Business of Schooling," *Phi Delta Kappan* (December 1998)

ISSUE SUMMARY

YES: Chester E. Finn, Jr., et al., educational policy experts and research fellows at the Hudson Institute, are involved in the third part of a multiyear study of charter schools. They affirm that every child is welcome in charter schools but hold that the requirements of IDEA, along with other regulations, often stifle creativity, limit resources, and reduce a school's flexibility.

NO: Nancy J. Zollers and Arun K. Ramanathan, a professor and a graduate student, respectively, at Boston College, maintain that the needs of many children with disabilities are swept aside as for-profit charter schools pursue their dual commitments to make money and raise test scores.

School choice, a major component of education reform movements, offers parents alternatives to their neighborhood school. Intradistrict options range from open-enrollment programs to magnet schools, which focus on thematic education. Voucher programs grant families an amount of money that they can use across district lines to enroll their children in suitable programs. Finally, charter schools, which operate within the public school structure, are funded by direct transfers of funds from public schools. Depending on state law, charter schools can be created from the ground up or converted from existing public schools. The goal of these options is to offer unique programs to children, to stimulate creativity in public schools, and to increase academic achievement.

Charter schools are exempt from many of the rules that structure (some say bind) public schools. Freedom from union contracts and many state rules and regulations—combined with strict accountability for student performance—will, it is hoped, result in creative, innovative, nontraditional programs that offer more desirable alternatives for all children than bureaucracy-ridden neighborhood public schools. In turn, the possibilities created by charter schools will, it is hoped, stimulate public schools to move beyond their traditions and to become creative in turn.

Although charter schools are freed from many regulations, including union contracts, they are required to abide by federal laws, including those governing the education of students with disabilities. Lively discussions have emerged about whether or not students with disabilities are welcome in the world of charter schools—and whether or not they are well served there.

Chester E. Finn, Jr., Bruno V. Manno, Louann A. Bierlein, and Gregg Vanourek have spent years studying the operation of charter schools across the United States. In the following selection, they identify the range of autonomy and accountability that faces charter schools, but they also identify many roadblocks—some based in finance, others in policy—to serving all children as equitably as charter schools would like. They assert that charter schools should be responsible for upholding some regulations but report that others have been waived, hinting that the same should be done for students with disabilities. They maintain that charter schools are constrained by a morass of regulatory detail, the time it takes to fill out forms that are necessary to qualify for limited funds, and the rigidity of the laws that govern special education services.

Nancy J. Zollers and Arun K. Ramanathan evaluated the experiences of children with disabilities in a number of Massachusetts for-profit charter schools. In the second selection, citing numerous examples gleaned from teachers and parents, they contend that such students are welcome in charter schools so long as their disabilities are mild and easily addressed. They argue that the drive for profit and high test scores results in practices that discourage the enrollment of students with more complex disabilities and that "counsel out" students who do not fit into the standardized curriculum and behavioral expectations held by the managing company.

As you read these selections, consider the options that are open to all students. Are charter schools doing the best they can to open doors and create educational options for all children? Do the federal laws regarding special education strain the creativity of schools that are trying to break the mold? Or are the doors to charter schools not open enough to the full range of children and their needs?

Chester E. Finn, Jr., et al.  **YES**

The Policy Perils of Charter Schools

Introduction

... [T]he "Charter Schools in Action" research team has been to 14 states, visited 60 schools, and interviewed more than 1,300 individuals about the start-up difficulties that charter schools face. We also surveyed thousands of parents, teachers, and students regarding the accomplishments and failures of their charter schools.

In our first-year report, *Charter Schools in Action: What Have We Learned?*, published by Hudson Institute in July 1996, we began to examine the challenges that state and federal policies pose for charter schools and those who start them.... In this part of the project's final report, we probe those issues in greater depth....

The reason, of course, is that such policies powerfully shape the scope, adequacy, quality, innovativeness, and educational value of charter schools. To be sure, a good school needs a fine curriculum, good teachers, and all the other familiar elements. But whether it has a chance of succeeding as a charter school —even whether it's worth establishing in the first place—is deeply colored by the state policy environment.

Policy decisions made (or avoided) in Washington also impinge on charter schools, though to a lesser extent. There are a number of steps that federal officials could take to enhance the prospects for more—and more successful— charter schools, and some non-trivial ways in which present federal policies and programs dim those prospects.

In this paper, we offer some observations, criticisms, and suggestions for state and federal policy makers. Our assumption throughout is that a vigorous charter-school program is desirable. Those who dispute that assumption will not likely agree with much that follows.

Stronger and Weaker Charter Laws

Numerous attempts have been made by analysts to distinguish the "stronger" state charter laws from the "weaker" ones.... [T]he states where we have studied charter schools, though they house the majority of all U.S. charter schools,

From Chester E. Finn, Jr., Bruno V. Manno, Louann A. Bierlein, and Gregg Vanourek, "The Policy Perils of Charter Schools," *Charter Schools in Action Project: Final Report, Part III* (August 1997). Copyright © 1997 by The Thomas B. Fordham Foundation. Reprinted by permission.

amount to fewer than half the states with charter laws on their books. The reason, of course, is that our main unit of analysis was the school, not the state, and, being in pursuit of a representative sample of charter schools, we naturally turned to places with lots of them. Not surprisingly, those are states with relatively strong charter laws. It was pointless to spend time looking for charter schools in places where none exist, even if a state may have enacted something it calls a "charter" law. Nor, save for Wisconsin and the District of Columbia, did we linger over states whose charter laws have given rise to just a few schools. . . .

The result is that we find ourselves knowing a lot about the virtues and failings of state charter policies in jurisdictions that are commonly thought of as having "stronger" laws—and correspondingly less about places with weaker (or brand-new) charter laws. That is why we make no attempt here to rate or grade all U.S. charter laws. What we do instead . . . is outline significant differences between stronger and weaker laws [and] explain what we now believe to be the crucial elements of "genuine" charter programs.

We've identified seven of these elements, clustered under the headings of autonomy, adequacy, and accountability.

Autonomy

(1) Under a strong law, the state's charter schools are essentially self-governing, save for a few rules (e.g., open admission) that all must follow. They are accountable for their results but free to produce those results as they see fit. That freedom means, among other things, that the charter school is not legally part of a school district (unless it wants to be), nor are its daily affairs overseen by officials other than its own. Insofar as its fate rests in the hands of external decision-makers (e.g., the issuance or renewal of a charter by district or state authorities), ultimate decisions are made by disinterested parties rather than those whose own interests are affected by the decision. In practice, that usually means that a charter school's fate ought not rest in the hands of the district from which it "seceded"—or seeks to secede. That's why we favor multiple charter sponsors and appeals mechanisms, and why it's been our impression that state-sponsored charters often encounter fewer hassles and more support than district-sponsored schools.

(2) Charter schools come in many flavors and can emerge from many directions. Both new and conversion schools are possible (and desirable), and may be initiated by a wide variety of persons, groups, and organizations. The tests of their viability are whether they deliver the results they promise and whether anyone wants to attend them, not whether various interest groups and stakeholders give prior assent to their existence or whether they fit arbitrary categories of who should or shouldn't be allowed to run schools. To be sure, individuals and organizations seeking charters should be subject to criminal background checks,

credit checks, and other scrutiny of their general probity, honesty, and reliability. But it's wrong to bar charter operators because, say, they aren't certified
educators or are a profit-seeking firm.

*(3) Charter schools are automatically waived from numerous (state and local) laws,
regulations, and contractual provisions that go well beyond matters of curriculum and instruction.* They do not have to negotiate each exemption. It is
taken for granted—by virtue of getting a charter—that they can hire whom
they like, pay staff as they see fit, and retain or dismiss individuals as they
see fit.... They manage their own finances and other resources.... They are
not sideswiped by zoning laws, pension plans, or other non-education provisions. We've been struck by how often a seemingly strong charter law turns out
weaker than expected because of bureaucratic adhesions that have nothing to
do with curriculum or instruction.

Adequacy

*(4) Financial provisions for charter schools are fair, which generally means that they
are equal to those of conventional public schools.* They receive their full share
of operating revenues per pupil, auxiliary moneys (e.g., transportation, textbook aid, food programs), "categorical" funding, and capital. Though charter
schools may "buy back" various services from local, regional, and state agencies, they are under no obligation to do so if they can obtain better services (or
lower prices) elsewhere. Local and state agencies ... should be compensated by
the charter school for services they actually provide to it—and that the charter
school asks them for.

(5) A critical mass of charter schools is allowed to exist. Not until a significant
fraction—a reasonable conjecture is about 5 percent—of a state's pupil population has the option of attending charter schools will we have a genuine test of
their marketplace appeal or a satisfactory basis on which to appraise their educational value. And that, of course, is a level of participation that no state has
yet approached. The longer it takes to attain that level, the longer we delay the
arrival of definitive information about the appeal and efficacy of the charter
alternative....

Accountability

*(6) Only where a state has solid educational standards and good assessments in
place will we ever have truly satisfactory information about the performance of
charter schools vis-à-vis conventional schools.* This admonition goes far beyond
the charter law itself, of course, but is probably central to the long-term viability
of the charter idea....

*(7) Although charter schools should have most laws and regulations waived,
those regulations that remain (e.g., civil-rights laws, background checks of school*

personnel) must be scrupulously enforced. Honest enforcement mustn't be undermined by, say, legislated exemptions, unduly long waiting periods, or forgiveness provisions designed to allow misfunctioning charter schools to evade accountability. The charter movement is not well-served by tolerating schools that misuse public funds, discriminate on illegal grounds, or fail to ensure the well-being of their students. (Is this dictum compatible with the first one noted above? We believe so. So long as the regulations in place for charter schools are only those that are minimally essential, and so long as their enforcers are impartial and disinterested, the enforcement can be vigilant and swift.) . . .

To be sure, even charter laws that confer relatively little autonomy on a school as a matter of right . . . can make it possible for a strong and entrepreneurial leader to cut his school enough slack to do things very differently. . . . But it seems wrong to us to create charter programs where success depends on extraordinary individuals strong enough to circumvent the more onerous provisions of the law. That's too much like the "regular" system—where great schools often turn out to be run by mavericks who must disregard rules and bypass procedures in order for the school to succeed—and is surely not the right way to launch a reform movement! It helps explain our own impression that the stronger charter schools in states with weak laws are apt to be conversion schools, perhaps because they start with a certain kind of leader—one of those mavericks who already knows how to "work the system." Yet even the mavericks nearly always have tales of woe to tell about the agonies they suffered in transforming their school to charter status.

Other State Policy Issues: Financial

. . . [R]esource woes are the greatest single barrier to establishment of a large number of flourishing charter schools—and the one that state policymakers could do the most about. We do not believe that charter schools should be given preferential treatment in the allocation of public funds. But that's not the problem today. In almost every jurisdiction, charter schools receive less money than conventional schools and school systems. Yet they are expected to produce superior results. This strikes us as anything but a level playing field. We do not say that more money is needed or that charter schools (like many private and some conventional public schools) are incapable of providing excellent education on a shoestring. We welcome the cost-consciousness, efficiency, and productivity-mindedness that many of them display. We just don't think their present funding status in most jurisdictions is fair. And we think it has been caused in large measure by established education interests opposed to giving the charter experiment a proper test. Those interests have figured out that, if they cannot prevent this reform idea from being born in the first place, they can at least keep it malnourished. They take for granted, after all, that the money belongs to them, their institutions, and their accustomed overheads. To them, the notion that it's being expended by the public on behalf of children, and should follow those children to the schools they choose to enroll in, is a bizarre and alien thought.

Let us note [three] fiscal domains where charter schools in most jurisdictions don't get their fair share of resources today. The first of these warrants the most attention.

Capital, capital, capital   As we write, only one state has seriously begun to crack the facilities-and-capital nut for start-up charter schools.... It's not that an elaborate building is necessary for good education; some fine charter schools operate entirely in "portables," and some of them seem sanguine about doing so indefinitely. Some have also gone to considerable pains to beautify their portables. (A lot of "regular" schools have portables attached, too, these days.) Still, old, cramped, dim facilities, sans gyms, labs, libraries, and places to eat, can begin to pale after a year or two. Yet the cost of renting a usable facility, when it must be subtracted from already tight operating budgets, puts charter schools at a distinct disadvantage. The absence of capital funding also makes it hard to obtain computers and other major one-time purchases of durables that cannot be paid for entirely out of the current operating budget.

Most conventional public school systems have separate capital and operating budgets. The capital budget typically relies on borrowing—usually via bonds that are sold to investors and (much as the U.S. Treasury finances the federal deficit) paid off with interest over a number of years. The "full faith and credit of the state" usually undergirds these bonds, and sometimes state dollars help pay them off....

Charter schools, however, typically have just one budget. They have no access to bonds or other forms of public borrowing. And private vendors don't regard them as good credit risks, since they have little collateral and their very existence (hence their flow of operating dollars) is assured only for the term of their charter, rarely more than five years and sometimes just one or two years.

Charter schools are sometimes thought of as miniature school districts, and, in some states, their operating budgets are constructed that way. But one big difference remains between charter schools and regular districts: In many states, the districts can levy taxes and issue bonds—to be paid off from future tax revenues. (In other jurisdictions, the municipality is the taxing authority and the school system must work out its budget, including its capital budget, through the county council or city hall.) Charter schools have no such legal authority. And, from the standpoint of lenders, the fact that they rarely own their buildings and cannot count on even existing for more than a few years means that they aren't nearly so appealing or attractive as traditional private schools....

The basic formula   Charter schools' fragile operating budgets can be knocked askew by several oft-encountered features of state school-funding formulae and procedures....

Categorical funds   Besides general school allocations based on enrollments, many states have an array of "categorical" programs that support particular services and activities. These range from supplementary aid (akin to the federal program) for disadvantaged or disabled youngsters to pupil transportation funds, textbook funds, staff development programs, and curricular specialties (such as dollars earmarked for AIDS education or anti-smoking classes). It can be quite a long list. But the funding is not automatic. The school system or school must apply, filling out special forms for each program, sequestering and accounting for moneys received from that program, etc.

Obtaining and tracking these state dollars is much like federal categorical programs—and more of a hassle than private grants. There's usually much red tape involved—red tape that most charter schools are too thinly staffed to handle easily—as well as the likelihood of distorting the charter school's educational focus by accommodating the demands of the specialized program. Several Massachusetts schools, for example, have foregone funding from the Commonwealth's anti-tobacco education program because it insists on lessons that—whatever their merit—mess up the schools' carefully shaped curricula.

Turning a blind eye to these funding sources is, of course, easier when the sums involved are so small that the payoff to the school isn't worth the hassle involved in obtaining it. Yet every bit of funding foregone becomes another unleveling of the fiscal playing field—and another source of the fiscal disadvantage that charter schools commonly face today. Some sort of state "block grant" to charter schools would seem to us to make more sense....

Federal Policy Issues

More attention is now being paid to federal policies affecting charter schools....

First, as corporate entities—sometimes public, sometimes private nonprofit, sometimes profit-seeking—charter schools run into all the ways in which Washington is generally involved with the lives of other such organizations: from Social Security and tax withholding to occupational-safety and environmental standards, from minimum wage laws to rules for employee-retirement plans.

Second, as public schools, charter schools are subject to certain federal regulations that do not hinge on receipt of federal funds and therefore apply to all educational (but not necessarily other) institutions. The most important of these are a host of civil-rights laws that bear on student admission, staff hiring, accommodating disabled people, and so forth. Other examples involve the privacy of student records and pupil discipline issues, ranging from due process on the one hand to the mandated expulsion of weapons-bearing students on the other.

Third, charter schools are recipients (or potential recipients) of categorical education aid from dozens of programs, some very large (e.g., Title I, IDEA [Individuals with Disabilities Education Act], subsidized breakfasts and lunches), some middle-sized (e.g., bilingual education, vocational education) and others quite small. How well these programs (and the terms and conditions linked to them) serve charter schools and their pupils is an issue of great policy salience, and it is being examined through many . . . studies. . . .

Fourth, charter schools are beneficiaries of one smallish federal aid program targeted specifically at charter schools and state charter programs. . . .

Special aid for charter schools   As part of the "Improving America's Schools Act" passed in late 1994, Congress authorized a new aid program called the "Public Charter Schools Program." . . .

These funds are used mainly for schools' planning and start-up expenses, an area that, as noted earlier, most states have been loath to subsidize. So the federal aid is especially welcomed by new charter schools. . . .

This program today has few critics in the charter school community. It's the one thing that charter schools receive from Washington that "regular" schools don't get and thus a mild compensation for the unfair ways that the older and bigger programs typically treat charter schools. It isn't perfect, though. Three issues bear mentioning:

First, the fact that it concentrates on schools' start-up expenses naturally means it is not a source of ongoing budget subsidy to charter schools once they're launched. Thus, it does not offset ongoing shortfalls or unfairnesses in state funding formulae—or in the major federal aid programs.

Second, . . . the program's normal arrangement is that states must first apply for the money and then parcel it out among their charter schools. This can pose a problem in jurisdictions where the state education agency is hostile to charter schools.

Third, . . . it's important to note that—especially for schools serving large numbers of at-risk youngsters—this hand-out, nice as it is, doesn't compare to what they would get if they received their fair share from the "big" programs.

Inequitable help from the big programs   We have learned something about those big programs and their interaction with charter schools. Putting it simply, needy and otherwise eligible youngsters enrolled in charter schools are getting gypped. So are the charter schools themselves, schools that are under intense moral (and sometimes statutory) pressure to serve at-risk kids but that find themselves deprived of resources that would flow into conventional public schools serving such youngsters no matter whether the conventional schools did a good or bad job of meeting their needs.

So complex are programs such as Title I and the Individuals with Disabilities Education Act (IDEA) that, to the best of our knowledge, nobody yet has definitive aggregate data on the dollars from them that make their way into charter schools—or how those compare with funds reaching conventional schools enrolling similar kids. . . . We made a modest attempt to estimate the Title I and IDEA dollars received by charter schools in several jurisdictions in comparison with average funding levels for eligible youngsters attending conventional public schools in those same jurisdictions. In almost every instance where we were able to do this, we found lower aid levels for the charter schools. Even more significant, we found many charter schools that received no aid from these two big federal programs in 1996–1997 even though they enroll considerable numbers of disadvantaged and/or disabled pupils. In Massachusetts, for example, only 8 of the Commonwealth's 24 charter schools received any Title I funding and just 4 received IDEA money. In Arizona, about two-thirds of charter schools obtain Title I money and in California fewer than half.

Our overall impression corresponds to that of Central Michigan University's Mamie T. Thorns, who recently told a Congressional sub-committee, "Many [Michigan] charter schools do not receive some categorical funding because of administrative issues and the complexity of Title I eligibility," although she noted that 75 percent of the children attending charter schools in the state are eligible for Title I. . . .

What accounts for the short-fall? We see three main explanations.

First, and most basic, the federal programs themselves are not tailored to the contours of charter schools. Because the money does not "follow the child" to individual schools and the formulae are based on district demographics, many charter schools do not obtain the funds that they would if they were school systems rather than free-standing schools. . . .

So far as we can tell, Title I is especially unfair to charter schools with higher concentrations of disadvantaged kids than live in their surrounding districts. Moreover, program aid from Title I is typically allotted on the basis of the previous year's population of disadvantaged youngsters, leaving start-up charters completely stranded for their first year. (Massachusetts has negotiated an exception that allows it to base Title I funding for charter schools on anticipated enrollments in the current year. Why is this sensible arrangement not the norm?)

Second, charter schools must obtain their federal categorical funds through their state education agencies and, in many cases, also through their local school districts, neither of which can be counted upon to care about the well-being or even-handed treatment of charter schools. . . .

Third, the schools themselves are seldom equipped—in human terms—to maximize their aid. They don't have "federal program specialists" on staff to fill out all those forms, study the regulations, and interact with state and district bureaus. Except where a charter school is part of a larger organization with a business manager who is an experienced grant-getter, the school is apt to be thinly staffed in these areas. . . .

Regulatory concerns   When the new federal charter study was issued . . . , much was made of the fact that federal regulations were not found to be a major barrier to the launch of charter schools. Just 6 percent of charter directors reported that such regulations were a "difficult" or "very difficult" barrier to development and implementation of their schools. We find this disingenuous and misleading. School directors weren't even asked whether federal programs posed problems for their schools, or whether the burden of complying with program procedures outweighed the value of the funds received. Rather, "federal regulations" was the 15th item on a list of 17 possible "barriers"—and if they said yes to it, they were then asked to "list the federal regulations" that vexed them.

It's our impression that most charter directors don't think this way. Few keep a list of federal regulations at their fingertips. Indeed, because most federal education programs have their rules and procedures enforced by state education department officials, we suspect many charter heads do not even understand that those rules and procedures originate in Washington. Had the question been properly posed and explained, we believe that a strong majority of charter heads—especially in start-up schools—would have said that many of their daily headaches are directly or indirectly traceable to the red tape and idiosyncrasies of federal aid and federal regulations.

In principle, some of these can be waived—but not, importantly, the special education rules of IDEA. The same 1994 federal legislation that created the new charter-school aid program authorized the Secretary of Education—upon request—to waive rules and procedures of various programs run by that agency. Yet few such requests have been received—a fact that is also cited by federal officials as evidence that their regulations do not lay a heavy burden on charter schools.

That's not our interpretation. The fact that charter schools are so thinly administered is not just an impediment to grant-getting. It's also a handicap with respect to waiver-obtaining, a process that takes considerable time, effort, and sophistication. Moreover, requests for federal waivers must work their way up the governmental "food chain" through the district and the state before the Secretary of Education can even entertain them. Once they reach Washington, they must travel through a maze of boards, bureaus, and gatekeepers. It takes time, it takes a lot of paperwork, and it takes sophistication and tenacity to embark upon the process. The point is that here once again, as with aid distribution formulae, Washington's regulatory process starts from a completely different assumption than charter schools do. Uncle Sam takes for granted that schools must be tightly regulated until and unless they obtain waivers from specific rules. The charter concept, of course, is just the opposite: that schools should be free to decide these things for themselves so long as their results are satisfactory.

Special education deserves special mention here because it could pose special problems for charter schools. The reason disabled children come to charter schools usually seems to be because regular schools did not suit them and their parents. Often that's precisely because the regular school was following the procedures prescribed in IDEA and Section 504 (of the Rehabilitation Act); yet, for a variety of reasons, these were not satisfactory to the family. So they come to a charter school because it does things differently. Yet IDEA and Section 504 say, in effect, that no (public) school may do things differently with respect to educating disabled youngsters. The schools are very likely to find themselves caught between a rock and a hard place, the former being families seeking alternative strategies for working with disabled youngsters, the latter being a rigid and highly bureaucratized federal program. (It is no coincidence that IDEA is the only major program to which the Secretary of Education cannot issue waivers.)

As we have visited charter schools and spoken with parents and educators in them, we have found many families who do not want their kids "labeled" and do not want their educational needs met in cumbersome, standardized ways. The small, intimate, personalized settings of charter schools allow the needs of these kids to be met without the kids being viewed as peculiar. Yet these schools live in fear that one day a government "enforcer" will tell them that they must treat disabled youngsters exactly the same way the regular schools are compelled to do, thus vitiating the distinctiveness of the charter approach—

and very likely reducing the currently high levels of satisfaction that the parents of special-ed kids express about their youngsters' charter schools. (For example, two-thirds of the parents of disabled youngsters say that the charter school's curriculum and teaching are better than those of the school their youngster would otherwise be attending.) Charter schools also live in fear that one day a "$50,000 kid" will arrive on their doorstep—for example, a youngster who needs a full-time attendant of his own—and bankrupt them.

The 1997 IDEA amendments make explicit provision for charter schools to be eligible for federal funding, to be represented on state special-ed advisory committees, and so forth. But they also contain a provision that requires charter schools to "serve children with disabilities in the same manner as other public schools." Depending on how this is interpreted and enforced, it could be the beginning of the end of charter schools' ability to serve disabled youngsters in ways that their parents and the schools think best....

Conclusion

The policy problems outlined in this paper—state and federal alike—could be solved through fairly simple technical solutions: laws amended, regulations revised, procedures altered, formulas corrected, etc. Devising such solutions, however, is the easy part. The hard part will be finding the political will to override efforts by charter-school enemies (and false friends) to keep them starving and gasping, and the parallel efforts by special interests to preserve the programmatic status quo.

The next couple of years will be a time of testing. The charter movement itself is at a crucial intersection. One road leads to its growth into a bona fide educational option for millions of American families. The other leads to a continuation of its current "mom and pop" status, a smallish alternative for kids who have fared poorly in conventional schools—and to whom the conventional schools are just as glad to bid farewell.

Which road will be taken? Our sense is that the present political line-up in Washington and in many a statehouse is about as favorable toward charter school expansion as it is likely to be for a long time....

The window of opportunity is clearly open. How long will it stay that way?

We are struck by the possibility that strengthening the prospects of charter schools by solving the problems described in this report would also confer great benefit on regular public schools and their students. Such solutions would permit a degree of experimentation with alternatives that today are all but unthinkable in public education. We have little doubt that this would lead to good things for children. When it comes to making education policy, however, the interests of children only occasionally predominate.

Nancy J. Zollers and
Arun K. Ramanathan

 **NO**

For-Profit Charter Schools and Students With Disabilities

It's hard not to be drawn in by the rhetoric. Your public schools are failing. Your children aren't learning. The school system, choked by regulation and held hostage by unions, won't respond to your concerns. We will. We are America's "huge, vibrant, and creative" private sector. Our success is based not on compliance with government regulations or mandates but on creating the best product and attracting the most customers. We will revitalize the public school system with market-based competition. All we ask in return is something as American as free speech—the opportunity to make a profit. Think about it. What do you have to lose? Wouldn't you like to have a choice for your children?

That's the sales pitch. And it's a good one. Across the country, communities are considering turning over their public schools to private businesses. Businesses, always ready to seize an opportunity, especially in a market as potentially lucrative as public education, have been quick to respond. A number of management companies are investing in the business of schooling, and the concept that many of these companies have invested in is the for-profit charter school.

Companies find the charter school formula attractive: a steady flow of public money combined with exemptions from costly government regulations and school board requirements such as collective bargaining. In exchange for this funding and freedom, charter schools are expected to fulfill the terms of their charters, which usually have to do with improving student test scores over a fixed number of years.

... [W]e have been studying the way that for- profit charter schools in Massachusetts handle special education. Of the state's 33 charter schools, nine are for-profits, giving Massachusetts one of the highest percentages of for-profits in the nation. With more than 5,200 students, these schools have more than half of the entire charter school enrollment in the state. At the time of our study, five of these schools had been in operation for at least two years. [In 1998] four new for-profits opened. Our study focused on the five original for-profit charter schools, though we did review the applications of the new schools and interview a number of prospective parents.

From Nancy J. Zollers and Arun K. Ramanathan, "For-Profit Charter Schools and Students With Disabilities: The Sordid Side of the Business of Schooling," *Phi Delta Kappan* (December 1998). Copyright © 1998 by Phi Delta Kappa International. Reprinted by permission of *Phi Delta Kappan* and Nancy J. Zollers. Notes omitted.

Our interest in the for-profits' special education programs was provoked by reports that substantial numbers of students with disabilities were leaving the five original charter schools and returning to their local public schools. After we analyzed charter school applications, annual reports, and financial statements; interviewed dozens of parents, community members, and school and government officials; and reviewed government documents and memos as well as articles from the popular press and professional journals, a picture emerged of for-profit special education programs that sharply contrasts with the idyllic images of successful "inclusive models" that these companies have presented to the public. While they have done a decent job of including students with mild disabilities, for-profit charter schools in Massachusetts have engaged in a pattern of disregard and often blatant hostility toward students with more complicated behavioral and cognitive disabilities.

The source of this pattern is the very same factor that the companies that manage these schools use to explain their success—the profit motive. As they strive to make money and fulfill their promise to improve educational outcomes, for-profit charter schools often ignore special education law and treat students with more complicated disabilities as financial liabilities. This attitude has been reinforced by a state government that coddles charter schools while singling them out as examples of free-market accountability and innovation. All of this has occurred in the context of what many observers characterize as a "model charter school law."

Company Schools

Three management companies—Sabis International (a Lebanese company and the only foreign entry in the for-profit market), the Edison Project of New York, and Alternative Public Schools (now Beacon Management) of Nashville —were included in the first wave of Massachusetts charters. Beacon manages one charter school in Chelmsford and recently opened the Rising Tide Charter School in Plymouth. Sabis Educational Systems operates the Sabis International School in Springfield and the Somerville Charter School and recently opened the Sabis International School in Foxboro, a regional K-12 charter. The Edison Project currently operates two charter schools: Seven Hills in Worcester and Boston Renaissance. A fourth company, Advantage Schools of Boston, recently opened two regional charter schools, the Abby Kelley Foster Charter School in Worcester and the Mystic Valley Advantage Charter School in Malden/Melrose.

Considering the wide range of curriculum models adopted by nonprofit charter schools in Massachusetts, the curricular approaches adopted by the for-profit schools—especially those operated by Sabis, the Edison Project, and Advantage—are remarkably similar to one another. Each Sabis, Edison, and Advantage school uses a prepackaged curriculum developed by its management company. Each promises more instructional days, improved test scores, intensive instruction, extensive computer usage, and tight classroom discipline.

As for special education, all the for-profits pledge to educate students with disabilities using an "inclusive model" in which students with disabilities learn alongside their nondisabled peers. Their applications for charters contain strong nondiscrimination statements and language welcoming students with disabilities and touting the power of their curriculum models to accommodate students with varying levels of ability.

So far, the for-profits have generated mostly positive reviews. According to the charter schools' self-reports and local press coverage, parent and student satisfaction is higher than in local public schools. The for-profits' waiting lists are crowded with applicants. Their students have achieved remarkable gains on that all-important measure—standardized test scores. After some initial difficulties, the schools maintain that their inclusive models are working and reintegrating back into the mainstream many students who were mistakenly identified as disabled by the public school system. These results appear to confirm that the for-profits are a model for public education.

We do not challenge the for-profits' success at creating popular schools or improving test scores. We do, however, challenge the "success" of their special education programs and, based on that, the contention that they represent a model for public education.

Unwelcome Customers

Each of the original for-profits has a substantially lower percentage of students with disabilities than its local district. Charter school proponents tend to explain away this statistic by arguing that public schools over-identify students with disabilities, that all charter school students are "special," that labeling hurts students' self-esteem, and that charter school inclusion programs can facilitate the removal of the disability label.

This line of argument does not explain our findings. First, these for-profits serve far lower percentages of students with complicated disabilities than do local districts. Second, substantial numbers of students with disabilities, mostly those with more complicated disabilities and expensive needs, have left for-profits and returned to their local districts.

Massachusetts uses a noncategorical system that identifies students with disabilities by the "prototype" level (.1 to .8), based on the amount of time a student spends in the regular classroom. The state's charter school law exempts charter schools from serving students with .5 or higher prototypes, primarily students with severe disabilities who tend to be served in private schools. Even with this exemption, each of these for-profits serves a lower percentage of students in the moderate disability categories (.3 and .4) than do local districts.

As for returning students with disabilities to local districts, the worst offenders are the two Edison schools. According to figures provided to us by the Boston Public Schools (BPS), 21 students with disabilities have left Seven Hills and 40 have left Boston Renaissance over [a period of] three years. To put the Renaissance figure in perspective, BPS reports that during that same period only two students with disabilities left the five nonprofit charter schools in Boston. Since 26 of the 40 Renaissance students left in the 1997–98 school year, it is unlikely that this exodus resulted from start-up problems.

Both Sabis schools have also sent back students. "Sabis called and wanted to send back two .4 kids," reported a Springfield public school administrator. "I said no because they had a .4 program. The next day they called and said these students had new .5 IEPs [individualized education programs] and now we had to serve them." Similarly, the director of special education for Chelmsford, Carol Fredette, reported that 10 students have returned from the Chelmsford charter school. "They've been coming back all year—all grade levels —like a revolving door."

All the special education directors in districts with for-profits reported that charter school personnel were informing parents of students with disabilities that they would be better served in the public schools—a practice known as "counseling out." According to their reports and those of parents, for-profits begin counseling out during the enrollment phase.

Unlike public schools, charter schools have to recruit students (customers). Before Renaissance opened, representatives from the Edison Project canvassed Boston neighborhoods, promoting their model school and promising a safe environment, high standards, and a computer in every classroom and home. The other for-profits engaged in similar promotional campaigns. The responses to their recruitment efforts were dramatic—so dramatic that the schools were forced to conduct enrollment lotteries. Parents who won the lotteries were ecstatic. But once the for-profits began finding students with IEPs among their "winners," some asked parents to drop their children's IEPs and to accept nonbinding "learning contracts" without the procedural safeguards or rights attached to an IEP. Said a Chelmsford charter school administrator, "We don't use IEPs; we tell parents that you have the option of a learning plan. Every kid has one."

A typical example is the case of Blanca Diaz. A grandmother caring for her three grandsons with disabilities, Diaz won the lottery at Seven Hills. She reported that when school officials saw the boys' IEPs, they sent her a letter informing her that two of her grandsons could not be served by Seven Hills. Massachusetts and federal law expressly prohibit charter schools from discriminating on the basis of disability. Further, charter schools are required by law to take any student with a disability who wins the admissions lottery and to implement that student's IEP. According to Diaz, school officials never informed her of her right to enroll her grandsons. It was a week before the start of school, and she had already bought Seven Hills school uniforms for the boys. Assuming she had no choice, Diaz placed the two boys in the local public school.

Parents at the new Abby Kelley Foster Regional Charter School run by the Advantage company have also reported that they were counseled out. Mary Young has two sons, one nondisabled and one with a behavioral disability. Young stated that when her nondisabled son won the lottery and was accepted at the Advantage school, she asked if she could enroll her disabled son. According to Young, school personnel then informed her that "they couldn't discriminate, but they really couldn't deal with this kind of kid" and were "afraid that they'd just kick him out later." Dollie Luchie reported that she received similar treatment when she tried to enroll her significantly disabled daughter in the Advantage school. According to Luchie, school officials sent out a letter informing parents that siblings were automatically accepted. She stated that they quickly accepted her son but, despite her repeated requests for clarification, would not commit to accepting her daughter. The day school opened, she was surprised when a bus from the public school came for her daughter. When Luchie called the public school, they informed her that the charter school had asked for her son's records but not her daughter's.

Other students with disabilities were never even given the opportunity to choose a charter school. Sabis International moved into an existing middle school in Springfield. The building housed two self-contained classrooms of students with moderate disabilities (all of whom were eligible for the charter school), and it had just been remodeled to accommodate their physical needs. A Springfield public school administrator told us that all the students in the school except the students in the self-contained classrooms were informed that they would be welcome in the charter school. The students with disabilities were forced to leave their school.

For-profits have also counseled out students with disabilities after they began having behavioral problems. In the March 1998 *Kappan*, Peggy Farber reported on the case of Kylee Jones, a kindergarten student whom Boston Renaissance authorities attempted to counsel out after he displayed inappropriate behaviors such as tantrums. The parents filed a complaint in Kylee's name with the Office for Civil Rights, and Renaissance lost the complaint. What Farber did not report was that Renaissance had settled two previous complaints, one of which was nearly identical to Kylee's.

After Farber's article was written, another Renaissance parent, Renee Mitchell, filed a nearly identical discrimination complaint against the Edison school. Mitchell stated that, after her child began having behavior problems, he was repeatedly suspended, sent home early, and secluded in a separate classroom without an academic curriculum. Three weeks before the end of the 1997–98 school year, she reported that Renaissance authorities pressured her to place him back in the "failed" public school. Said Mitchell, "I wanted something better for my kid. They promised so much... family involvement, special-needs department, high emphasis on reading and math. I thought they would really listen to me. This has been a horrible nightmare."

Linda Alvarado won the lottery at Sabis International for her son Carlos. She reported that after Carlos began having behavioral problems, he was denied services, was repeatedly suspended, and was then placed in what Alvarado called "a holding cell." When Alvarado complained about this treatment, she was told that Sabis was a "semi- private school" and that her son would be better off in the public school. Assuming that she had to leave and after fruitlessly searching for a local Sabis administrator to whom to appeal the school's decision, she called the Sabis owner in Lebanon. "I actually had to call overseas to the owner. It was long, long distance."

In these and other stories parents told us, the pattern is the same. The for-profit charter school refuses to provide required services to a child with a behavioral disability, uses inappropriate disciplinary procedures, segregates the child in a separate "classroom," and eventually attempts to counsel him or her out of the school. The practice of repeatedly suspending a student without attempting to address his or her behavioral needs is, by itself, a crude tactic used to pressure parents to return their children to public schools. Parents who complain are considered troublemakers. . . . The Individuals with Disabilities Education Act (IDEA) requires that public schools provide a free and appropriate education to students with disabilities. Because they are public schools, charter schools cannot reject a student with a disability simply because their program isn't suitable for that student, a requirement called "zero reject."

IDEA also provides parents with extensive procedural rights when school officials want to change their child's placement or initiate disciplinary action. . . . When asked about the many reports that Massachusetts for-profits were counseling out students with disabilities, Edward Kirby of the Massachusetts Charter School Office confirmed that for-profit charter schools are "obligated to enroll without discrimination" and to provide necessary services. He also agreed that reports of counseling out could have a chilling effect on future attempts by parents to enroll their children with disabilities in for-profit charter schools.

But the truly disturbing aspect of these for-profits' actions is not their illegality. It is how they first raised and then dashed parents' hopes of providing their children with a better education. That many of these parents were recent immigrants who didn't know their legal rights renders these for-profits' actions even more suspect.

The Resources Myth

Charter school operators often complain that their small size and lack of funding make it difficult for them to serve students with disabilities. In 1995 we conducted a nationwide survey on charter schools and students with disabilities and found that many charter school founders were concerned that special education would bankrupt their schools. Chester Finn, the ideological godfather of the charter school movement, has questioned the cost/benefit ratio of special education and often cited its high cost as a threat to individual charter schools.

Certainly, special education is expensive. . . . Because state and federal reimbursements for special education fall far below its actual costs, school districts often strain to find the money to serve students with disabilities—especially students with severe disabilities. It would appear, then, that the fears that Massachusetts charter school operators have expressed about special education breaking their bank might be legitimate. And this, in turn, might lead charter school apologists to defend as a necessary survival tactic the way Massachusetts for-profits treat students with complicated disabilities.

An analysis of the way charter schools are funded in Massachusetts, however, reveals quite a different picture. Massachusetts charter school legislation stipulates that charter schools receive, for each student enrolled, "the average cost per student" in either the student's resident district or the district where the charter is located. This means that each for-profit receives roughly the same amount of money for each student as its local district spends on each student.... The total funding for the charter school is taken out of the local district's overall education funding.

We have already discussed how for-profits save money by serving substantially lower percentages of students with disabilities than do local district schools and by serving students with less complicated needs than those in local district schools. Compounding this saving is the fact that none of the for-profits have bilingual programs. These programs are expensive and heavily regulated. State law requires charter schools to implement bilingual programs if they have 20 or more students with limited English proficiency (LEP). All the for-profits except Chelmsford are located in districts with large numbers of recent immigrants and LEP children. However, none except for Seven Hills report an enrollment of 20 or more LEP students. Seven Hills reports an enrollment of 73 LEP students. And, according to attorney Jennifer Lopez, an expert in bilingual law, this makes the school's lack of a bilingual program a violation of state law.

Despite these statistics, each charter school receives funding based on its local district's substantially higher special education and bilingual expenses.... But even this tiny concession to the reality of higher district expenses is flawed because local districts run their own expensive and substantially separate programs, pay for expensive early childhood programs, contribute to collaboratives, or, in Boston's case, fund entire schools that are equivalent to the private school placements that for-profits are exempted from funding.

On top of this, for-profit charter schools' definitions of students in substantially separate classes don't compare to the reality of these classes in district schools. The noncategorical system doesn't provide any information about the specific disability needs of students. Sabis International characterizes 20 students who are a few years behind grade level and receiving remedial services as a substantially separate class. In a local public school, a substantially separate class often consists of a dozen students with moderate cognitive, behavioral, or physical disabilities who need expensive nursing services, therapies, adaptive equipment, and so on.

Adding this together, it's clear that the way the Massachusetts charter school law calculates average cost per student gives for-profit schools a major financial advantage over district schools. It creates a situation in which charter schools receive funding for students with disabilities or with limited English proficiency whom they are not serving, allowing them to spend more on regular education. Meanwhile, poor district schools pay for considerably larger numbers of students with disabilities or with limited English proficiency whom they are serving. Then, adding insult to injury, the for-profit charter school sends expensive students back to the same district, forcing them to use even more of their diminished resources on special education.

But it doesn't stop there. Massachusetts charter school law forces local districts to pay transportation costs for charter school students who need busing. The for-profits can also create a nonprofit foundation (a for-profit nonprofit), thereby attracting large private donations. By the end of the 1996–97 school year, Boston Renaissance, Inc., had pulled in almost a million dollars in private donations.

For-profits are also eligible for state and federal grants. All of them have received tens of thousands of dollars in federal charter school start-up grants. Renaissance, Sabis International, Chelmsford, and Seven Hills have applied for and received Title I grants for low-income students. Only Somerville did not apply for and receive IDEA grants for students with disabilities. As in the case of state funding, for-profits receive the same amount of IDEA money per student as their local district even though they serve students with less complicated needs.

Indeed, far from being starved for resources, Massachusetts charter schools are the richest schools in the state. They certainly receive more than enough money to serve students with "expensive" disabilities. Of course, each school does have to provide a sizable percentage of its state funding to its educational contractor in the form of a management fee (almost a million dollars by the end of the 1996–97 school year in Sabis International's case) or contract. It's hard to accept, especially for a parent of a student with disabilities, that a "public school" funded by Massachusetts taxpayer money could be too resource-starved to properly serve children with disabilities when that same school is paying tens of thousands, hundreds of thousands, even millions of dollars to a company in New York, Tennessee, or Lebanon.

The (Profit) Motive

The Massachusetts for-profit management companies don't exclude students simply because they don't like the trappings of special education. Their impetus for excluding students with disabilities derives from the profit motive. They understand that their survival and profitability depend on one factor— raising the test scores of regular education students. If they don't show substantial gains in test scores, they will lose their charters. Under these circumstances, students with disabilities, most of whom can't or won't perform well on standardized assessments, are liabilities. And, "from a school's perspective, finding a way to exclude the liabilities is a powerful means of improving performance."

This obsession with raising standardized test scores is reflected in the for-profits' curriculum and instruction. Sabis, Edison, and Advantage schools emphasize the basic math and English skills that are the focus of statewide assessments. Their schools have large class sizes, forcing their often first-year teachers to depend heavily on texts and technology. This packaged, standardized approach to curriculum and instruction is the linchpin of their long-term business strategy. All the for-profit companies are in the process of establishing nationwide networks of schools. To reap the advantages of economy of scale, Sabis, Edison, and Advantage use a single, easily replicated curriculum and system of instruction.

Predictably, this "McCurriculum" approach does not mesh with special education. If the for-profits are going to maintain their economy of scale, students must fit the school. Special education emphasizes individualized instruction, which often requires expensive supports and services. For-profits avoid this requirement by using what Renaissance calls a "responsible inclusion model." This means that they place students with mild disabilities in regular classrooms and provide them with extra instruction until they perform at grade level. Students with more serious cognitive deficits or learning disabilities are generally removed from the regular classroom for remedial attention or left in the regular classroom without appropriate academic instruction. This version of inclusion is inherently flawed. Most inclusion advocates believe that the true model, which emphasizes including all students with disabilities in regular education classrooms and integrating their therapeutic supports and services into the curriculum, is more expensive when properly implemented. . . .

Students with behavioral disabilities pose another problem for the for-profits. These schools see themselves as elite, "semi-private" institutions. The more exclusive they are, the better chance they have of attracting customers. Children with behavioral problems cause them to resemble the "out-of-control" public schools. Unless a child's behavior improves, he or she can't fit into an elite inclusion classroom. But changing behaviors takes time, expertise, training, and money—and, despite their abundant funding, it's evident from our interviews that for-profits don't want to waste resources on "problem kids." Instead, they use suspension and seclusion, and, when those methods don't work, they counsel the students out.

Again it's an Edison school, Boston Renaissance, that has been the worst offender on returning students. According to BPS, six of the 26 students who returned to Boston in 1997–98 were identified as having severe behavioral disabilities. None were identified by BPS as disabled when they entered Renaissance. Certainly public schools have not had a good track record with children with behavioral needs, but—unlike for-profits—they don't have the luxury of dumping their troublesome students on another school.

Where Does a Parent Go?

Do parents of children with disabilities who attend for-profit charter schools always have to call Lebanon to get answers? Is there anyone in Massachusetts they can ask for help—a board or an agency that would require a charter school to comply with the law?

According to the Massachusetts charter school regulations, the answer is yes. Parents of a student with disabilities who believe that a charter school is violating their child's rights can file a complaint with the school's board of trustees. If they are dissatisfied with the outcome of their complaint, they can file a complaint with the commissioner of education, who can refer the matter to the attorney general. In the event that the charter school is found to be in noncompliance with the law, the commissioner or the state board of education can revoke the school's charter. Parents can also file a complaint with the department of education.

It would appear that parents have plenty of avenues to address their grievances. It would also appear that for-profits can and will be held accountable by state agencies for their actions. Sadly, the realities of the charter school system and of Massachusetts' political climate make these accountability mechanisms practically worthless.

Let's begin with the possibility of filing a complaint with the for-profit charter school's board of trustees. Charter school supporters like to portray their schools as the outgrowth of a grassroots movement on the part of self-motivated parents, teachers, and community leaders. They paint a picture of concerned individuals coming together out of a mutual interest in improving local public education, organizing a board of trustees, and writing an application for a projected charter school.

Certainly, this was the case for many nonprofit charter schools. But in the case of for-profit charter schools, board members were often directly recruited by the school's management companies. Companies are forced into this tactic because the Massachusetts Charter School Law forbids a for-profit company from applying for a charter. However, the law does allow a charter school's board of directors to apply for a charter and then contract with a for-profit company for 100% of educational services. This provision is supposed to be a free-market mechanism that allows charter school boards to choose among competing contractors, picking the best service for the lowest price. But management companies use it as a way to apply for a charter indirectly....

By actively recruiting the very board members who are expected to "choose" them, management companies undermine the notion of board oversight. There is no indication in any of the press reports or charter school documents that any of these boards considered any educational contractors other than the ones they "chose." (So much for the free market.) Expecting such a board to "terminate a contract" for poor performance or to address a parent's complaint impartially is ludicrous.

... The last place a parent should go for assistance is the very state agency charged with monitoring charter schools—the State Charter School Office. In 1995 the forerunner of this office, the Executive Office of Education, headed by James Peyser, sent a technical advisory to charter schools providing a blueprint for "counseling out" students with disabilities. As our recent parent interviews revealed, for-profits have taken the state's advice to heart. There is no record in the charter school office that any subsequent technical advisory or legal memorandum was sent out to countermand the advice in this memo....

A Lost Opportunity

Charter schools in Massachusetts have been granted considerable advantages over local public schools. Many of the nonprofit charter schools are using these advantages to provide an excellent education for students with complicated disabilities, often for the first time in their school careers. Parents of these students are understandably enthusiastic about the charter school model. Many of these parents have had legitimate concerns about the public school system, and the opportunity to have a choice has been a transforming experience.

In the right circumstances, for-profit charter schools could also represent a powerful opportunity for students with complicated disabilities and for their families. As we have shown, these schools have the financial resources to provide an appropriate education for any student with a disability. Unfortunately, the basic interest of these schools in making a profit has often been incompatible with offering an appropriate education to students who require expensive supports and services. To parents of these students, for-profit charter schools do not represent a choice. If the politicians and the state officials who support the for-profit charter school concept are going to give parents this choice, they must protect parents' rights by enforcing federal and state laws.

Indeed, if we have learned anything from our study, it is the importance of enforcement, of requiring schools to be accountable for more than test scores. In the absence of accountability, for-profit charter schools will have the same incentive that public schools had before the passage of IDEA to exclude students with complicated disabilities and to ignore the rights that a generation of parents of children with disabilities fought so hard to acquire. After studying for-profits, it is clear to us that the much-maligned requirements of IDEA were adopted for the right reasons. As it stands, for-profit education in Massachusetts is re-creating the pre-1975 era, when public schools could choose whom they would educate and students with complicated disabilities were shunted away to institutions. In essence, the for-profits are becoming those pre-1975 public schools, and local district schools are becoming the institutions filled with their castoffs.

Parents of students with complicated disabilities shouldn't need another IDEA to give them a choice in public education. What they need is for Massachusetts politicians and state officials to set aside ideology and to make for-profit charter schools if not the most accountable schools in Massachusetts at least accountable to the parents whose tax dollars are the source of their profit.

POSTSCRIPT

Are the Doors of For-Profit Charter Schools Open for Students With Disabilities?

The difficulty of coming to a definite conclusion on the question of charter school accessibility for children with disabilities is evident in a November 1998 publication from the U.S. Department of Education Office of Educational Research and Improvement. *Charter Schools and Students With Disabilities: Review of Existing Data* presents an extensive compilation of studies and reports. Few of these studies compare practices across states. Also, many findings are contradictory. For example, while one study maintains that students with disabilities are underenrolled in charter schools, another contends that students with disabilities are simply undercounted or underreported. Although some papers mention special education costs as prohibitive, the Department of Education report's authors find no evidence that such expenses have ever threatened the financial existence of a school.

Finn et al. indicate that charter schools chafe under federal special education regulations and would relish the opportunity to design ways "to serve disabled youngsters in ways that their parents and the schools think best." Yet the very essence of IDEA97 is the individual education program (IEP), an educational plan that is developed by a team of parents and educators. From another perspective, if an innovative charter school enables a child to make effective academic progress without additional intervention, then the needs of the student are well served without an IEP. Is there really a conflict here?

Zollers and Ramanathan chafe under the possibility that students with disabilities are turned away from charter schools because they just do not fit. Yet there are many families who believe that the charter school is the best possible answer for their children. Some charter schools focus especially on children with disabilities. Is it possible that Zollers and Ramanathan interviewed a sample of dissatisfied parents without considering the responses of families who feel that charter schools are responsive and adaptive?

Charter Schools and Special Education: Balancing Disparate Visions (Ahearn, Rhim, and McLaughlin, 2000), an extensive survey/study of charter schools across 15 states, revealed that an average of 8 percent of the students enrolled in charter schools have disabilities, which is below the national average of 11 percent enrolled in public schools. This project postulates a "philosophical gap between the individualized, autonomous nature of charter schools and highly regulated (zero-reject) special education programs." The authors "propose that the greatest challenge facing charter school operators regarding special education is how to effectively commingle the two visions."

ISSUE 5

Does Society Have the Capacity to Prevent Emotional and Behavioral Disabilities?

YES: Hill M. Walker and Jeffrey R. Sprague, from "The Path to School Failure, Delinquency, and Violence: Causal Factors and Some Potential Solutions," *Intervention in School and Clinic* (November 1999)

NO: James M. Kauffman, from "How We Prevent the Prevention of Emotional and Behavioral Disorders," *Exceptional Children* (Summer 1999)

ISSUE SUMMARY

YES: Hill M. Walker and Jeffrey R. Sprague, educational researchers at the University of Oregon's Institute on Violence and Destructive Behavior, describe the path that leads from exposure to risk factors to destructive outcomes. They argue that society must recommit itself to raising children safely, and they advocate strong collaborative arrangements between schools, families, and communities.

NO: James M. Kauffman, a professor of education at the University of Virginia, states that experts know what needs to be done to prevent emotional and behavioral disorders but that society as a whole has invented many reasons not to make prevention a reality.

Emotional Disturbance: A condition exhibiting one or more of the following characteristics over a long period of time and to a marked degree which adversely affects a child's educational performance:

- An inability to learn that cannot be explained by intellectual, sensory, or health factors;
- An inability to build or maintain relationships with peers and teachers;
- Inappropriate types of behavior or feelings under normal circumstances;
- A general pervasive mood of unhappiness or depression;

- A tendency to develop physical symptoms or fears associated with personal or school problems;

The term includes schizophrenia. It does not apply to students who are socially maladjusted, unless it is determined that they have an emotional disturbance.

— IDEA97

The most well mannered child needs to learn acceptable behavior but may not always react appropriately, especially in times of stress, confusion, or fatigue. The happiest siblings will struggle over who gets the best seat in the car, for example. And everyone has a bad day from time to time. When a child experiences enough bad days in a short period of time, however, adults begin to wonder if a "real problem" exists and if those conditions are serious enough to fit the IDEA97 definition of emotional disturbance.

A large amount of time is spent talking about the increasingly troubled behavior of children. Of particular concern is aggressive behavior that creates difficulties on the playground and endangers the safety and comfort of peers.

Then there are the silent children, the ones who never act out but who experience internal pain and suffering. These are the children who do not call attention to themselves and are noticeable only by their severely bitten fingernails, their unkempt hair, their worried faces, and their failing grades. These children may not act out against others, but they may cause harm to themselves.

Children are being identified as troubled at younger and younger ages, and attention has turned to the schools. Isn't it the job of schools to fix such problems? Can't the schools do *something* to make the problems go away?

What should be done? Chalk the behavior up to an increasingly troubled society and try to adjust? Classify the children as emotionally disturbed and ask schools to enroll them in special education programs, surrounded by other children with similar problems? Consider them ill and ask doctors to prescribe medication? Blame poor parenting and urge families to provide stronger supports? Turn to the juvenile justice system?

Hill M. Walker has researched interventions for troubled and troubling behavior for over 40 years. In the following selection, Walker and his colleague Jeffrey R. Sprague trace the societal changes that continue to affect children and their schools. They forecast spiraling effects on society if students are not diverted from the path to societal violence and criminal behavior. They describe strategies that they maintain could be put in place to ensure that risks are reduced, cautioning that all difficult behavior can never be prevented.

In the second selection, James M. Kauffman, a pioneer in the field of special education, agrees that interventions can be designed. He is concerned, however, that society always manages to find a way to avoid taking action. Kauffman lists the range of ways in which society prevents prevention and urges citizens to conquer these obstacles for the benefit of children and society.

As you read these selections, consider the schools you know, the debates you have heard, and the your own responses. Should schools assume all this responsibility? Can anyone help children in today's society?

The Path to School Failure, Delinquency, and Violence

Some years ago, we were developing a program for intervening with very aggressive children who teased and bullied others during school recess. Ritchie, a second grader, was referred as a likely candidate for the intervention. During a playground recess period, he was being observed to see if he qualified for this program. Suddenly, for no apparent reason, Ritchie attacked a kindergarten boy about two thirds his size. He knocked the smaller boy to the ground and proceeded to choke him. The playground supervisor quickly broke things up and called the principal and school counselor, who escorted Ritchie into the school to call his parents. We wanted to know what was in Ritchie's mind that prompted the attack. "Can you tell us why you were choking that little boy like that?" he was asked. Ritchie looked up in utter amazement and said, "Well, it was recess!"

Sarah was a fourth-grade girl who was commonly regarded as a terror by her teachers and peers. Sarah was aggressive, smart, a natural leader, able to manipulate others, charming—and a pain in the neck. Billie Webb was a school psychologist who served Sarah's school part time and visited her school several times weekly. Sarah was a regular customer of Billie's each time she came to the school, and they were on a first-name basis. One day, the principal and counselor were waiting for Billie at the school's front door to tell her the latest things Sarah had done on the playground. Billie called Sarah into a conference to hear her side of things. The following exchange ensued.

"Sarah, I understand you've been having problems on the playground again." Sarah just stared at Billie, saying nothing. Trying to engage Sarah in a problem-solving process, Billie asked another question. "What do you think people will say about that?" Sarah thought a minute, looked at Billie, and said: "Well, Billie, some people might say you're not doing your job!"

These true case examples illustrate how aggressive, antisocial children and youth tend to think about themselves and the world in which they live. They are often self-centered and very inconsiderate of others. The standards they have learned for governing their behavior are different from those of others. Children like Ritchie and Sarah are reluctant to assume responsibility for their

From Hill M. Walker and Jeffrey R. Sprague, "The Path to School Failure, Delinquency, and Violence: Causal Factors and Some Potential Solutions," *Intervention in School and Clinic*, vol. 35, no. 2 (November 1999). Copyright © 1999 by PRO-ED, Inc. Reprinted by permission. References omitted.

actions. In very young children, these social characteristics are generally not destructive and can occasionally be amusing, even cute. However, in adolescents, they are highly destructive and anything but amusing.

Our society is producing thousands of children like Ritchie and Sarah who come from backgrounds in which they are exposed to a host of risk factors that can be very damaging over time. There are strong and clearly established links between these risk factors, the behavioral manifestations and reactions that result from exposure to them, the short-term negative effects on the developing child that flow from this exposure, and finally, the destructive, long-term outcomes that (a) too often complete this developmental progression and (b) ultimately prove very costly to the individual; to caregivers, friends, and associates; and to the larger society. . . .

As more and more young children experience a broad array of risk factors from the moment of birth, we are seeing increasing numbers who are following this unfortunate path, which too often ends in school failure and dropout, delinquency, adult crime, and sometimes violence.

Influence of Risk Factors

Risk factors operate at differing and sometimes overlapping levels. The contexts in which these risk factors exist include the family, school and neighborhood, community, and, finally, the larger society. Across these contexts, key risk factors can include poverty, dysfunctional and chaotic families, drug and alcohol abuse by primary caregivers, incompetent parenting, neglect, emotional and physical abuse, negative attitudes toward schooling, the modeling of physical intimidation and aggression, sexual exploitation, media violence, the growing incivility of our society, and so on. These risk factors provide a fertile breeding ground for the development of antisocial attitudes and coercive behavioral styles among the children exposed to them.

The longer one is so exposed and the greater the number of risks involved, the more likely it is that a young child will develop an aggressive, self-centered, and dysfunctional behavioral style. Taunting and provoking others, mean-spirited teasing, bullying, hitting, yelling, tantrumming, defying adults, and being cruel are examples of the early behavioral signs of long-term exposure to such risk factors. Too many children are coming to school with this behavior pattern already established; they are sometimes referred to as "early starters." That is, antisocial behavioral characteristics are manifested early in their lives primarily because of their early onset exposure to a host of such risk factors. These children tend to overwhelm teachers and peers with their destructive and highly aversive behavior. In adolescence, their behavioral characteristics often bring them into contact with the law from such activities as fire setting, cruelty to animals, burglary and robbery, assault, vandalism, drug and alcohol abuse, and so on.

Five specific risk factors have been identified through longitudinal research for both delinquency and youth violence. Adolescents who are involved in multiple risk conditions—(a) the mother and/or the father has been arrested,

(b) the child has been a client of child protection, (c) one or more family transitions has occurred (death, divorce, trauma, family upheaval), (d) the youth has received special education services, and/or (e) the youth has a history of early and/or severe antisocial behavior—are at severe risk for adoption of a delinquent lifestyle. The Oregon Social Learning Center and the Lane County, Oregon, Department of Youth Services (DYS) jointly developed this profile of risk factors on the basis of careful research and analysis of severely at-risk adolescents referred to the corrections department of Lane County. Any combination of three of these five risk factors puts the youth at an elevated risk for chronic delinquency and a host of associated problems. DYS has reported that a number of youth they see have all five of these risk factors.

The American Psychological Association, in its 1993 seminal report on youth violence, identified four factors that seem to propel at-risk youth toward violent acts:

- Early involvement with drugs and alcohol;
- Easy access to weapons, especially handguns;
- Association with antisocial, deviant peer groups; and
- Pervasive exposure to violence in the media.

These conditions combine destructively far too often among youth who come from at-risk backgrounds. Furthermore, we find that larger and larger numbers of at-risk youth are in states of rage and carry high levels of agitation because of the myriad abuses they've experienced. Such youth are more likely to react aggressively to real or imagined slights and act upon them—often with tragic consequences. They are also more likely to misjudge the motives and social intentions of others toward them because of the hostility and agitation they carry. As a result, they are frequently engaged in hostile confrontations, and they sometimes issue threats of bodily harm to peers, teachers, and others.

Short-Term Effects of Exposure to Risk Factors

Several negative short-term outcomes are produced by antisocial behavior patterns resulting from exposure to the above risks. In the short term, they include lack of school readiness, antisocial attitudes, high levels of aggression and agitation, rejection by peers and teachers, affiliation with deviant peers, inability to regulate emotional behavior, severe tantrums, refusal to abide by school rules and adult expectations, and so on. Very often the academic engagement levels and academic achievement of severely at-risk students also lag well behind those of their classmates as well as grade-level expectations. These factors set the at-risk child up for school failure and eventual dropout. If school dropout does occur, the risks for delinquent acts skyrocket. It is estimated, for example, that 80% of daytime burglaries across the United States are committed by out-of-school youth.

Thus, the risks to which larger and larger numbers of our children and youth are exposed tend to put them on a path leading to very negative, destructive outcomes. Unless they are diverted from this path relatively early in their lives and school careers, severely at-risk children are very likely to adopt antisocial behavior as a lifestyle choice during their later development.

Long-Term Outcomes of an Antisocial Lifestyle

The long-term outcomes of investment in an antisocial behavior pattern are very destructive and extremely costly to our society. These longer term outcomes quite often include the following: delinquency, school failure and dropout, dishonorable discharges from the military, severe depression, alcohol and drug abuse, violence toward others, lifelong dependence on social service systems, appearance on community mental health registers, incarceration, and higher hospitalization and mortality rates.

We find that severely at-risk youth have a high frequency of discipline problems in school, with many referrals to the front office initiated by their teachers. By the later elementary grades, they tend to have chronic disciplinary problems. These same students often begin having contacts with law enforcement in the middle and high school years (or earlier). There is a moderately strong relationship between a very high level of conduct problems in school and arrestable offenses committed outside school. To the extent that this relationship is consistent, it may allow for the earlier identification of at-risk students who are likely to become offenders outside the school setting.

For example, we've found in our longitudinal studies of antisocial youth that it is possible to make relatively accurate long-term predictions about the arrest status of at-risk fifth graders by using three simple school measures:

1. The number of discipline contacts the student has during the school year,
2. The amount of negative behavior a student typically displays with classmates on the playground and that is reciprocated by peers, and
3. The teacher's impression of the student's social skills as reflected in teacher ratings. . . .

We have the ability to find these at-risk children and youth early, but we generally prefer to wait—to not do anything—and hope that they grow out of their problems. In far too many cases, in the absence of intervention and appropriate supports for their emerging behavior problems, they grow into and adopt an antisocial behavior pattern during their school careers.

It should be noted that some students adopt an antisocial behavior pattern during adolescence but do not come from an at-risk background. These youth are referred to as "later starters." Although such students can become delinquent, they are much less at risk, as a general rule, than "early starters." Most will come out of this behavioral aberration within a few years. Occasionally, however, some of these youth will become severely delinquent and/or violent and retain their at-risk status into adulthood.

What Can Be Done?

What can be done to reduce and offset the effects of the risk factors to which more and more of our youth are being subjected? First and foremost, we need to reduce and eliminate as many of these risks as possible. As a society, we must recommit ourselves to raising our children safely and effectively. We seem to have lost our capacity to do so on a broad scale. Thousands of families are currently in crisis because of the stressors to which they are exposed (i.e., poverty, unemployment, domestic violence, drug and alcohol abuse, and so on). The resulting chaos negatively affects their children and provides a fertile breeding ground for the development of antisocial behavior.

Providing Parent Training and Supports

A very powerful knowledge base exists regarding parent–child relationships and the forms of parenting behavior that produce positive and negative outcomes in children. This knowledge base has provided the foundation for the development of a number of parent training modules, materials, and courses of instruction designed to teach positive and effective parenting practices. Providing supports, delivering respite care, and developing competent parenting skills are huge challenges that we as a society must confront in order to address this complex problem.

... [P]arenting practices that produce healthy, well-adjusted children... involve consistent, fair discipline that is never harsh or severely punitive; careful monitoring and supervision of children's activities, peer associates, and whereabouts; positive family management techniques; involvement in the child's daily life; daily debriefings about the child's experiences; and the teaching of problem-solving techniques. We have to find ways to provide opportunities for families to become aware of these parenting skills and to learn how to master them. Insuring that family resource centers are attached to "X" number of schools across a school district to provide parental access to this information is an increasingly viable option for addressing family needs in this regard. We should also teach these parenting techniques to all our youth prior to their becoming parents.

School-Based Prevention Applications

We need to make the school's role in the prevention of disruptive, antisocial behavior patterns an effective reality. We, as educators, tend to give lip service to prevention strategies but are generally unwilling to invest in them at the necessary levels because of suspicions about their effectiveness and worries about their long-term costs.... Primary prevention strategies use universal interventions, such as schoolwide discipline and behavior management systems, grade-level teaching of violence prevention skills, and effective instruction, which are designed to keep problems from emerging. Secondary prevention strategies are more costly, intensive, and designed for addressing the problems and skill deficits of children and youth who are already showing clear signs of their at-risk status. Primary prevention strategies are not of sufficient intensity and strength to effectively remediate the problems of children and youth who require secondary prevention strategies. Finally, tertiary prevention strategies are designed for the most severely at-risk children and youth whom schools must attempt to accommodate. Generally, their problems demand resources, supports, interventions, and services that cannot be provided by schools alone (i.e., wraparound services and interagency partnerships are necessary to accommodate the needs of these students and their families).

... We currently have a pipeline literally filled with at-risk students who are experiencing traumatic behavioral events and outcomes as they progress through it. If we respond only reactively and rely exclusively upon secondary and tertiary strategies, applied after these destructive events and outcomes are manifested, we will continue to invest larger and larger amounts of our resources in return for weaker and weaker therapeutic effects and outcomes. There will always be students who come to school with such severe behavioral involvements that secondary and even tertiary supports and interventions will be necessary from day one of their school careers. That said, however, we can make much greater and more effective use of primary prevention strategies in the school setting than we traditionally have.

As noted, universal interventions are used for achieving primary prevention goals. It is estimated that 80% to 90% of a school's student population will respond positively, at some level, to these universal intervention strategies. Those who do not respond to primary prevention approaches (anywhere from 5% to 15% of the school's population) select themselves out as candidates needing secondary and/or tertiary prevention strategies and approaches. However, for those students who require more intensive, individualized interventions (approximately 1% to 7% of all students), the existence of a well-designed and carefully implemented primary prevention base in the school setting provides a powerful context for their effective application....

The Importance of Supporting Schools

As a society, we have to give greater support to our public school systems, which are struggling to educate an increasingly diverse and at-risk student population. Our schools are expected to compensate for the damaging effects of the background risks to which so many of our students are now exposed; those unfortunate effects spill over into the school setting. At the same time, we seem to be withdrawing fiscal resources from basic school operations and making it increasingly possible for nontraditional schools to access those resources and to pull the better students away from public education. Weakening the ability of our public schools to accommodate a diverse student population is a dangerous movement in our society.

Near the end of his life, in a speech delivered in upstate New York, Mark Twain spoke eloquently and perceptively about the issue of investing in public schools. He related a true story about a Missouri township that was considering closing several of its schools because they were too expensive and regarded as not needed. A farmer who had heard of this planned move attended a town meeting where the issue was being debated at length. After listening to the discussion, the farmer observed that he didn't see how the township would save any money because for every school that was closed, they'd just have to build a new jail. A century later, this prophecy is coming true as our society systematically underfunds public schools and builds jails at a rate unprecedented in our history.

Collaborative Interagency Prevention Approaches

In our view, a far better solution is to create full-service schools that (a) have an expanded capacity to address the complex needs of today's school population and (b) can address true prevention goals through effective collaborations forged between schools, families, and communities.

... We need to build effective partnerships between families, schools, social service systems, public safety departments, churches, and other agencies to create the socializing experiences that will give all our youth a chance to develop along positive lines. ...

Conclusion

We have a violent history as a country, and many experts argue that we are, by nature, a violent culture. As a society, we should hold up a mirror and examine ourselves in this regard in order to take a good look at what we have become, how we got here, and how we might change for the better. ... The tragic spate of school shootings during the 1997–1998 school year offers grim testimony as to how the social toxins and violent images that increasingly pervade our daily lives are registering their negative effects upon our children and youth.

In spite of this grim picture, there are a few encouraging trends. According to recent annual reports of crime indices, adult crime seems to be on a downward spiral. It is imperative that we discover why this is the case and figure out how to make this trend continue. As we embark on a new century, we have the occasion to make a fresh start in this regard. We can ill afford not to.

NO

James M. Kauffman

How We Prevent the Prevention of Emotional and Behavioral Disorders

Prevention of emotional and behavioral disorders seems to be everyone's rhetorical darling, but I have come to the sad conclusion that most of our talk about prevention is of little substance. We often find ways to avoid taking primary or secondary preventive action, regardless of our acknowledgment that such prevention is a good idea. Other concerns take precedence, and as a result we are most successful in preventing prevention itself.

As a society, our actions often seem to thwart prevention of emotional or behavioral disorders at every level—especially primary and secondary prevention, but also prevention at the tertiary level. Primary prevention keeps disorders from occurring at all. It is focused on the universal application of safety and health maintenance interventions that reduce risk.... Once a disorder has emerged (become detectable), primary prevention is not possible; secondary prevention must be designed to keep the disorder from increasing in severity. The goal of secondary prevention is to arrest the growth of the disorder and, if possible, reverse or correct it....

Prevention of emotional and behavioral disorders sometimes occurs in our society and our schools, but it is not a predictable or pervasive phenomenon.... [T]hese programs reach only a very small fraction of those in need of them. Moreover, even if we had pervasive practice of what evidence to date suggests is best primary and secondary prevention, there is good reason to guess that emotional and behavioral disorders would still occur.... Nothing to date suggests that every such disorder can be prevented, although we have good reason to suspect that the pervasive use of our best primary and secondary prevention tools would reduce such disorders to a much lower level than we observe today. The problem I am discussing has much in common with other circumstances in which we fail to implement on a broad scale what we know are best practices, as in the case of teacher education.

If we show clear commitment as a society or as professional educators to prevention at any level, it is to tertiary prevention. We seldom hesitate to recommend intervention after a problem has become severe, protracted, and a clear threat to the community, even though our interventions are too late

From James M. Kauffman, "How We Prevent the Prevention of Emotional and Behavioral Disorders," *Exceptional Children* (Summer 1999). Copyright © 1999 by The Council for Exceptional Children. Reprinted by permission. References omitted.

and only have a small chance of success even if they are not too little. Attempts at tertiary prevention are responses to crisis and often devolve into angry and punitive behavior on the part of adults. By the time tertiary prevention becomes the issue, many people are so angry that physical containment of the child and punishment of the behavior are viewed by the general public and by many educators as clearly defensible interventions, if not the best. Preventive practices at the tertiary level are often ignored in favor of more primitive interventions that are counterproductive but satisfy the desire for revenge.... Supportive interventions that earlier might have been effective are, at this point, perceived by the public as effete, as well they may be. It is too late to get good effects from best practices at the primary and secondary levels; we have allowed those opportunities to pass.

The reasons we do not implement prevention systematically may be related to public attitudes toward children and their schooling, but we professionals have developed and use regularly an extensive repertoire of behaviors that are highly effective in precluding prevention. Our professional attitudes and actions contribute to the public's unwillingness to make prevention a concern that reliably results in preventive acts....

I caution here that preventive *educational* intervention is only one facet of a comprehensive preventive strategy, which involves families, multiple service agencies, local communities, and state and federal governments. Children and youths may show the earliest signs of emotional or behavioral disorders in non-school settings, and education alone cannot address the problem of prevention adequately.... However, the need for a systemic response to problems does not relieve us of the responsibility to make sure that each component of the system —in the present case, special education—functions properly. My particular concern in this article is the role of special education in prevention and how we avoid our responsibility....

Common Varieties of Prevention-Preventing Behavior

The gambits that stymie prevention are not mutually exclusive. In fact, they are often complementary. Like risk factors that are multiplicative rather than additive, they can become a witch's brew—individually not of great consequence, but combined a potent cocktail that easily wards off prevention.

Express Overriding Concern for Labels and Stigma

Perhaps the most frequent and fervid objection to preventive action is that the child will be labeled and stigmatized.... Either all students are treated the same or some are treated differently. Any student who is treated differently is inevitably labeled. We cannot speak of difference or needs without words (labels). Moreover, either our labels for emotional or behavioral difficulties signify concern (something unsettling, not positive) or they are worthless for describing what needs to be changed. The social reality of deviance cannot be hidden....

"Challenged," a euphemism of the 1990s, is already in our lexicon of deroga-tions. We need to use the least offensive labels that clearly describe the problem, but we need not believe the fantasy that the label *is* the problem or that a new label will fool people for long....

Decades of investigation suggest that stigma typically precedes a formal label for disability, that such labels do not add appreciably to stigma, and that formal labels may, in fact, assist in the explanation of disability and the for-mation of a more positive identity than is possible to achieve with informally labeled deviance. Nevertheless, antilabeling sentiment remains a powerful an-tiprevention force, particularly when it is wielded against the designation of children who are at highest risk of acquiring emotional or behavioral disor-ders. In fact, the sentiment against identifying any student as needing more or different treatment than another is so strong that I have heard colleagues ar-gue against use of the term "at risk" applied to individuals; we should, they suggest, speak only of high-risk *environments,* thereby ascribing only *collec-tive* characteristics. When we decline to use labels responsibly, the individuals whose problems they designate become rogues or unmentionables—those with unspeakable characteristics. Some may argue that "person first" language (i.e., "___ with ___" such as "child with behavioral disorder" or "person with mental retardation") is a partial solution, others that individuals do not actually *have* disabilities but are merely assigned them in some socially acceptable conspir-atorial fashion or have merely developed a *reputation* for behaving in certain ways, or that we should label only programs or services, not the people who re-ceive them. These are tortuous and self-serving philosophical games that delay and deny help to the suffering, whether they are the individuals who exhibit the problem behavior; those who must live, learn, play, or work with them; or those who simply care about them. When we are unwilling for whatever reason to say that a person has a problem, we are helpless to prevent it. In some instances, we call those who demonstrate such unwillingness to label a problem "enablers" because they support maladaptive behavior such as substance abuse or spouse abuse through their refusal to call it what it is. Labeling a problem clearly is the first step in dealing with it productively.

Most children with emotional or behavioral disorders are already labeled informally by their peers if not by adult authorities. They get the label du-jour among children for those who are misfits. Formal, adult labeling may, in fact, turn away some of the misunderstanding and rejection of their differences. Eventually, many of those with emotional or behavioral disorders are formally and informally labeled unequivocally, sometimes brutally. Their behavior often becomes so outrageous that its deviance cannot be denied. They become clients of a variety of.... social systems, including special education, mental health, and corrections. Their social spoilage is virtually assured by the fact that they did not have early and corrective treatment from these agencies....

Object to a Medical Model and to Failure-Driven Services

In the opinion of some, our labels should be abandoned because they reflect an inappropriate, medical conceptual model.... However, special education is much more aligned with the legal model than the medical model, and failure-drivenness is an inherent part of prevention. The mandatory and adversarial aspects of special education law ... bespeak special education's gravitation toward a legal rather than a medical model.

... To complain that special education is flawed or badly structured because it is failure-driven is to use non sequitur to prevent prevention. Prevention *is by necessity a* structure designed to avoid or attenuate failure.

Prefer False Negatives to False Positives

No one has yet devised no-fault prevention in education or any other field of human services. That is, every known prevention strategy produces false positives and false negatives—in the context of this discussion, children mistakenly identified as having emotional or behavioral disorders when they do not, and children mistakenly assumed not to have disorders when they actually do.... Primary prevention is weighted toward false positives, as the intervention is assumed to be a no-risk, or very close to no-risk, strategy. Medical and dental primary prevention strategies include vaccinations, water fluoridation, and personal hygiene routines that pose near-zero risk of negative outcomes for individuals who would not acquire a health problem were the prevention strategy not practiced, and the benefit to those who would otherwise acquire the problem is obvious. Secondary and tertiary prevention in the medical-dental fields is somewhat more controversial and involves weighing personal and economic costs against benefits of specific procedures.

In medicine, false negatives (overlooking cases of pathology) are the primary concern; false positives (seeing pathology where none exists) are not taken lightly, but the primary concern of physicians tends to be making certain that pathological conditions are not missed. In law, however, the opposite is true—false conviction is the horror to be most carefully avoided, not false acquittal. Special education is much more like law than medicine in its preference for the errors we know as false negatives.

In education, primary prevention of school failure, including the socialization failure known as emotional or behavioral disorder, has never been practiced with anything approaching the universality of vaccination, fluoridation, or personal hygiene in spite of evidence that primary prevention of school failure could be practiced with extremely low risk of harm to anyone. Major obstacles to implementing such primary prevention include disagreement about what is to be prevented as well as disagreement about the legitimate processes of achieving particular outcomes.

However, additional barriers to prevention at all levels are either (a) making the exception the rule or (b) justifying the familiar as acceptable. In making the exception the rule, the comparatively unusual case is used as the rationale for rejecting prevention. In the health area, an example is using the vigorous health of an aged person who has smoked cigarettes for many decades to disprove the link between smoking and ill health; in education, examples are using the reading success of a young child who was never taught phonics to disprove the necessity of explicit instruction to teach phonemic awareness ... or the successful adulthood of an individual who engaged in serious antisocial behavior in school to disprove the need for intervention programs for antisocial children. In justifying the familiar as acceptable, the pervasiveness of a phenomenon is used as a rationale for disinterest in prevention. In education, the pervasiveness of uncivil or antisocial behavior is often used as a rationale for inaction: "Boys will be boys," "Lots of kids, probably most of them, threaten to kill somebody," "Every school has its bullies," "In our culture and our school, it's normal for kids to be loud and disruptive." Antisocial behavior is seen as an ordinary discipline problem, not as an incipient or emerging pathology. We shrink from the early recognition of social deviance that, full-blown, we find intolerable.

Recent shootings in schools have brought the issue of prevention to public attention and highlighted our tendency to prefer false negatives to false positives. To date, the shooters have been students not identified for special education services, although in most instances news accounts of these children's lives clearly suggest that they had long histories of antisocial behavior prior to their opening fire in school. Some or all of these killers may be found through psychiatric examination to be legally "sane" (i.e., to be competent to stand trial and unlikely to be found "not guilty by reason of insanity"). Our preference as a society and as educators, it seems, is for absolute certainty that an individual has become deviant before intervening—for after-the-fact recognition of problems, not anticipation of them. To anticipate, we fear, is to prejudge, to pigeonhole, to spoil or corrupt or limit by our expectation. School authorities may now suspend or expel students who possess weapons or drugs on school property or at school functions. However, this is anticipation only of horrendous possibilities, and it is intervention only after contraband is found. Furthermore, such action frequently results in terrible miscarriages of justice because the policy of zero tolerance is reaction with a single, severe sanction to behavior without consideration of its motivations or context.

High-profile cases of school violence may raise issues of prevention in the minds of the public and many professionals, but these cases are probably not the most important. Less riveting by far, but much more important to prevention, are the less highly visible and more common antisocial acts of students. These often do not result in public outrage, and often there is no intimation that they are a result of psychopathology. Coercion, bullying, disruption, social isolation, and threatening behavior are examples of the kind of conduct that *should* induce preventive action by educators. Nevertheless, such behaviors often are *not* sufficient to trigger identification of the student as having an emotional or behavioral disorder, full-blown or incipient. They may simply result in the student's exclusion from general education classrooms....

Propose a "Paradigm Shift"

Perhaps it is understandable that we look for alternative conceptualizations, or what have come to be known as "new paradigms," that avoid the problems of misidentification altogether. Those who propose a paradigm shift may assert that it will obviate the need for classification of students. In the new paradigm, all students will be taught well without the need for distinguishably differ-ent instruction or behavior management strategies; because everyone will be treated as an individual, no one need be distinguished as a special case.... Consequently, prevention will be a pervasive and imperceptible part of school-ing. Prevention thus becomes at once a primary objective and impossible; we cannot prevent what we are unwilling to categorize as different from the typi-cal or normative, nor can we practice anything other than primary prevention if we are unwilling to categorize interventions as special (not normative)....

A related "paradigm shift" argument is that we must not see the problem as in the child but in the environment. It is a truism that behavior always oc-curs in and is affected by a social context (a social ecology), but recognition of this fact can become an excuse not to intervene because the "real" trou-ble is assumed not to be the child. Apparently, we would rather assess diffuse and nonspecific "blame" for the trouble than confront the fact that the child is in trouble and needs help. This observation does *not* mean that ecological problems can be ignored or that addressing all of the various environmental contributors to the child's difficulty is unimportant.... In the face of ecologi-cal complexities, it is easy to become overwhelmed and conclude that what *is* alterable will make no significant difference. The danger in shifting our con-cern to the environment in general is that we will do nothing in particular to change what we can. Prevention requires lighting one candle at a time, even if all darkness is not dispelled thereby....

Call Special Education Ineffective

Sometimes the ineffectiveness of special education is merely intimated; some-times the claim that special education has not "worked" or cannot work as currently structured is made directly and unequivocally....

Special education for students with emotional or behavioral disorders is in difficult straits for several reasons. First,... the meaning of "work" is un-clear: What would we expect to happen if special education actually "worked"? Would we (could we) actually "work ourselves out of business"? What is a realistic measure of our "success"? Should our success be judged simply by stu-dents' staying in school, not dropping out? Should we expect that there be no significant difference between the performance of those receiving special edu-cation and those not receiving it? Second, students are typically identified for special education services only after their problems have become chronic and severe, making "works" by the standards of their successful return to general education, loss of identity as disabled, or high school graduation and gainful employment improbable with any known intervention. Much of our effort is spent on tertiary prevention—waiting until the primary issue is containment and prevention of complications, when it is too late to have realistic hope of correcting or eliminating the disorder. Evidence strongly suggests that if chil-dren who exhibit the pattern of aggression called conduct disorder are not identified before they are about 8 years of age, their disorder is much like any other developmental disability—very unlikely to be reversed or eliminated. Third, special education is often attempted by teachers who are poorly trained and poorly supported by infrastructure, and under such circumstances it is difficult to imagine that the students' education would be either special or effective....

Misconstrue Least Intrusive, Least Restrictive Intervention

Americans have a strong preference for leaving people alone as long as they are not clearly and immediately endangering others.... Our enthusiasm for minimally restrictive environments blinds us to the fact that the consequence of minimum restriction now may be greater restriction later. In the placement of individuals with disabilities, including the treatment of mental illness, we emphasize placement in the least restrictive environment, often misconstruing this placement as the same environment in which those without disabilities can thrive....

However, the interventions that are least restrictive and least intrusive are those that can be implemented earliest in a pattern of behavior leading to more serious misconduct. After misbehavior has accelerated, the *formerly* least intrusive, least restrictive intervention is very unlikely to be effective. An emphasis on minimizing the intrusion and restriction of consequences without careful attention to the nature of the behavior pattern results in a chain of increasingly intrusive and restrictive but decreasingly effective interventions. Implementing preventive, least intrusive, least restrictive practices *in the long term* thus requires something counter-intuitive and typically thought to be unacceptable in our legal model: stepping in earlier, more proactively, and with more positive assertiveness to avert maladaptive behavior patterns by anticipating them rather than waiting for misbehavior to occur.

If we give priority to the least intrusive and least restrictive *response* to misbehavior rather than to the most effective *preventive* interventions, then we will forever chase our tail—always and inevitably be ineffectual in preventing the escalation of misbehavior.... We wait for misbehavior to escalate until the *presumed* least restrictive or least intrusive response is very likely to fail and the *actual* least intrusion or restriction (prevention) is very unlikely or impossible. The correction of this failing requires something that is anathema to many: identifying and serving a larger portion of the child population.

Protest Percentage of Students Served by Special Education

A commonly heard opinion today is that special education has grown too large, not only in the percentage of time, effort, and money that schools spend on it but in the number of students and the percentage of the population identified for services. In the case of emotional or behavioral disorders, this view is extraordinarily problematic, for it is abundantly clear that far less than half of the population of youngsters with such disorders have been identified for special education and that students with these disorders are typically identified for special education only after several years of very serious difficulties.

Prevention in an underserved population demands that more individuals be identified, not fewer or the same number. If cases are to be caught earlier, and if many cases are missed (i.e., they are false negatives for considerable periods of time), then we must be ready to embrace a considerable increase in the number of students identified—unless, as seems to be the case, we are willing to forego prevention.

Complain That Special Education Already Costs Too Much

Prevention costs more money *up front* than nonprevention. True, it may save money in the long term, but that is not the immediate issue for politicians, school boards, and taxpayers.... The inescapable fact is simply this: If we were to initiate preventive action on a large scale, then we would be stuck with a large, immediate financial cost.... The necessary tasks cannot be accomplished without an infusion of revenues to provide proper training and support to a huge increase in the number and quality of school personnel.

... Legislators are typically reluctant to embrace programs that will not produce immediate results and cost savings for which they can take credit. In short, the near-term financial cost of widespread preventive programs is a powerful but usually not articulated argument against their implementation.

Maintain Developmental Optimism or Use Ineffective Early Education Practices

Those who work with young children tend to be overly optimistic about children's development, leading to the assumption that early signs of behavioral difficulty do not predict a stable or increasing pattern of maladaptive behavior. Their assumption seems to be that the child will "grow out" of the problem. Preventive action—deliberate correction of patterns of social difficulty—is thus delayed until the problem has become severe. Moreover, many individuals who work with young children have an apparent bias toward developmental approaches that do not involve explicit teaching and correction of the first signs of maladaptive behavior, which foils prevention.

Denounce Disproportionality, Defend Diversity, Deny or Dodge Deviance

The preceding arguments may persuade us not to take prevention action, but there remain other arguments predicated on our society's ambivalence about cultural and behavioral diversity. Guilt for our past ignorance, insensitivity, and brutality about racial, ethnic, and cultural differences and fear of returning to or being accused of such horrors may keep preventive action at bay. I discuss the tactics to which our guilt and fear give rise under a common heading because these tactics are frequently used together as well as in combination with other prevention-stopping arguments.

Denounce disproportionality.   There is no denying that students of color, those reared in poverty or in the lowest social classes, and males are served in special education for children and youth with emotional or behavioral disorders in proportions considerably higher than their proportions in the general school population (a phenomenon that may be defined as overrepresentation). The facts are clear, and concern about the causes and consequences of these facts is not misplaced. Nevertheless, these observations can be used counterproductively to thwart early intervention and prevention.…

It is important to ask what causes the overrepresentation of any group in special education. Genetic differences are not acceptable as explanations of disproportional identification for special education services, but environmental circumstances are.… The environmental circumstances that lead to identification of disabilities fall into two major categories: (a) environmental circumstances known to heighten risk of disorders and (b) racial discrimination (i.e., racism in the social construction of disability or identification procedures).

Overrepresentation may be a result, at least in part, of racial discrimination in… a variety of… economic and social opportunities of parents that put children at risk for school failure. Racial discrimination creates conditions in which children and adults may strike out in anger and justifiable resistance to social control. These conditions must be addressed, but until they are corrected they may contribute significantly to the disproportional identification of students of color as having emotional or behavioral disorders.…

Overrepresentation may, of course, be at least partly a result of racial discrimination in the identification process.… Given overwhelming evidence of the underidentification of emotional and behavioral disorders of children and youth, a plausible hypothesis is that many students—both minority and nonminority—who should be identified are not.…

Overrepresentation of any group in special education or any other social service program is not a problem unless (a) the program is perceived as demeaning, there is an implication of hostile intent, or the program offers no benefit; or (b) the program is being provided to students who do not need it or is being denied to those who do. After all, it is the *under*representation of minorities in gifted education that is protested, precisely because gifted education is assumed to bring benefit to students and this benefit is being *denied* disproportionately to minority students.… Were identification of students for special education for those with emotional or behavioral disorders assumed to be beneficial, then the overrepresentation of minorities in such programs would likely not be the cause of protest (except, perhaps, by individuals unwilling to extend *benefits* disproportionately to minorities). But, as I discussed earlier, special education for students with disabilities is seen by some as thwarting opportunity, not as a helpful educational support. Perhaps, as I noted earlier, the problem is as much a self-defeating denial of the needs of students of all ethnic origins for special education as it is a racist or unintentional fabrication of deviance of children of color.

The rub for prevention is this: Disproportional identification of some groups for special education can be used as a rationale for nonidentification, nonintervention, waiting to take action out of fear that action will merely exacerbate the disproportion of the group to which the student belongs. The struggle against discrimination by race and class is not easy, and it includes resisting both the tendency to assume that disproportional identification can *only* be a consequence of unfair discrimination in identification for special services and the tendency to let an individual's color or social class inappropriately affect judgment of conduct.

Defend diversity.   In contemporary American educational jargon, differences are often lauded without thinking much about the differences among differences. Some differences are benign, but others are not.... In the desire to embrace diversity—difference—some may be tempted to extend acceptance to differences that are inimical to a just, multicultural, and benevolent society. In some instances, disrespectful or demeaning behavior towards others or rejection of academic learning may be defended as merely different from the ostensible white middle class standard or as an acceptable response to domination and oppression by the majority.

Prevention requires the recognition of diversity that is unacceptable. In today's social climate, however, there is reluctance to label difference unacceptable until it reaches the point of actual physical damage to another individual or to property. In the case of emotional and behavioral disorders, this means that there is pressure to allow behavior to escalate to extremely high levels before intervening, a response to difference that stops prevention in its tracks.

Deny deviance.   Differences of benign character should be accepted, if not celebrated. However, the harmful social conduct we call deviance must be discriminated from nonharmful difference. In contemporary American society there is a tendency to "define deviancy down" such that the consequences are deteriorating social justice and a lower level of benevolence. There is also a tendency to resist drawing lines that separate people into eligible and ineligible groups for any social service. Line-drawing has its costs of labeling and identity for the individual who is declared eligible, but refusing to draw a line has a more severe and an inevitable high cost—denial of service to that individual. We cannot have it both ways—special services and no eligibility lines....

There are a variety of ways to deny the deviance of children's behavior. Calling it mere cultural diversity is one such denial tactic. Another is saying that deviance and disability are social constructs and therefore somehow not "real." Deviance and disability are, indeed, social constructs, but so are childhood, adolescence, citizenship, success, social construct, democracy, justice, love, and nearly every other concept that we hold dear or that is necessary to a just and benevolent society. The point here is not that deviance is a social construct that can be changed arbitrarily but that it *is* changed—or people argue that it *should* be changed—in ways that prevent prevention. If we deny that an individual's current behavior is deviant, or that the behavior we wish to prevent is deviant, then it is highly unlikely that we will do anything to prevent it.

Sometimes we do not deny deviance but dodge responsibility for it. That is, we define behavior as deviant but claim that it is not a disability, concluding that it therefore does not fall within the purview of special education. The most common tactic is to conclude that a child is "socially maladjusted" or has a conduct disorder that is different from "emotional disturbance." Neither logical arguments nor reliable empirical studies support the distinction between social maladjustment and emotional disturbance. Furthermore, antisocial behavior, a form of social maladjustment that may be diagnosed as conduct disorder, is clearly among the most disabling emotional and behavioral disorders of children and youths. Unwillingness to include conduct disorder, antisocial behavior, or social maladjustment among the conditions for which special education interventions are appropriate is a dodge of responsibility for prevention that contributes to the unchecked acceleration of misconduct. If there is one emotional or behavioral condition for which every level of prevention (primary, secondary, and tertiary) is critical, it is conduct disorder. Dodging special education's responsibility for intervening early in conduct disorder virtually ensures that the child will become the responsibility of juvenile justice or another social agency specializing in tertiary prevention (containment)....

Suggestions for Attenuating the Problem

The arguments we can marshal against prevention must be taken seriously, as they raise important issues that we should not dismiss. Ignoring these legitimate concerns carries high costs, and I do not mean to demean them by pointing to the fact that they are often used to defeat prevention. My purpose is to bring into awareness the ways in which we may use them at the even higher cost of preventing prevention.

Myths—partial truths from which unwarranted generalizations or extrapolations are drawn—are pervasive in special education.... The arguments used to defeat prevention may be mythical if they occlude the larger truth that we would all be better off if we prevented serious misconduct. However, we must also recognize as myth any suggestion that we know in all cases precisely what behavior should be prevented and how to prevent it. Much of our knowledge of emotional and behavioral disorders is tentative. A great deal more research is required before we can, if ever, pinpoint for all children all the behaviors that should be prevented and prescribe the preventive action that is necessary and sufficient. Nevertheless, we now can identify many of the early signs of conduct that place children at very high risk for later negative life outcomes and describe preventive programs that can reduce these risks....

The attenuation of the problem will require assiduous attention to research and its application to instruction and behavior management. Prevention-supportive sentiments must be balanced by knowledge of the costs, both fiscal and personal. If we are to achieve a balance of preventive behavior and the cautions that should accompany it, we might seek answers to the following questions in the individual case:

- Is the behavior in question, either the behavior being exhibited or the anticipated behavior, one that elevates risk of negative outcomes?
- If so, is the behavior preventable or can risk be lowered by any legitimate means?
- What are the possible negative side effects or risks associated with preventive action?

- If we estimate that the risks of nonintervention outweigh those of preventive action, can we offer social support for those who implement the preventive action—develop a professional community that reinforces prevention through social approval?
- When we encounter prevention-preventing behavior, can we provide counter arguments that effectively remove the blockade?

Individually and collectively we might work toward the following goals:

- Establishing common standards for judging evidence of the effectiveness of preventive interventions at all levels (primary, secondary, and tertiary).
- Abandoning and publicly condemning interventions for which evidence clearly is not supportive or negative or that make tertiary prevention inevitable because primary and secondary prevention are highly unlikely if not impossible.
- Increasing our immediate positive attention to and, when possible, prompt financial and social support of primary and secondary preventive action, thereby creating a professional culture more supportive of prevention.
- Understanding negative reinforcement as the primary process sustaining preventive behavior and legitimizing its function in primary and secondary prevention (i.e., teaching others that the avoidance of problems can be legitimately rewarding).

POSTSCRIPT

Does Society Have the Capacity to Prevent Emotional and Behavioral Disabilities?

Walker and Sprague agree with Kauffman about the difficulties that children face and the consequences for society if children are not helped when the helping is easy. Examples of proactive, primary-level interventions abound. Among the many are Reach Out to Schools (Stone Center, Wellesley College), the Responsive Schools, Success4, and DARE (Drug Abuse Resistance Education). Each is dedicated to helping students develop strong social skills that lead to conflict resolution and problem-solving strategies for difficult times.

Webber and Scheuermann (*Behavioral Disorders,* 1997) foreshadow the list of risk factors experienced by children, augmenting them with recent public policy decisions that have further reduced community and family supports.

Noting that supportive counseling services have not been included in the current wave of education reform, Lindahl (*Education Week,* October 18, 2000) cites recommendations by the American School Counselor Association for a student-counselor ratio of 250:1 and an actual national ratio of 561:1. Lindahl contends that recommended levels of service could provide a safety net for students, teachers, and families, all of whom are struggling to meet the pressures of higher expectations.

The journal *Behavioral Disorders* dedicated a thematic issue (vol. 24, no. 4, 1999) to the topic of emotional and behavioral disabilities at the turn of the century. The wide-ranging articles in this issue contain expansions by Kauffman and by Walker and Sprague, as well as by others who are concerned with this field, especially as the number of students requiring intervention rather than prevention increases.

Walker et al. (*Behavioral Disorders,* 1999), noting that society often sees children as perpetrators rather than victims, expand on the conditions facing children today. According to the authors, the consequence of society's attitude is that, instead of improving their behavior, children learn to avoid those who serve to judge it and who could possibly help them.

Landrum and Tankersley (*Behavioral Disorders,* 1999) highlight the importance of early intervention as well as lifelong services. They emphasize that general education teachers must learn and apply successful behavior management strategies (secondary intervention) and that special education services should acknowledge the value of specialized settings (tertiary intervention) to improve the functioning of children who have developed problem behaviors. They warn that even perfect application of each level of intervention will not eliminate all incidences of problem behavior.

ISSUE 6

Are Schools Limited in Their Ability to Discipline Students With Disabilities?

YES: Ashley Thomas King, from "Exclusionary Discipline and the Forfeiture of Special Education Rights: A Survey," *NASSP Bulletin* (December 1996)

NO: Russell J. Skiba, from "Special Education and School Discipline: A Precarious Balance," *Behavioral Disorders* (in press)

ISSUE SUMMARY

YES: Ashley Thomas King, bilingual coordinator in the Kwethluk (Alaska) Community Schools, concludes that court cases have hamstrung administrators so that they cannot equitably discipline students, regardless of whether a disability is linked to unacceptable behavior.

NO: Russell J. Skiba, an Indiana University faculty member and codirector of the Safe and Responsive Schools Project, writing after the passage of IDEA97, comments on disciplinary options that are available to administrators but questions the wisdom of the current system of school discipline, which he feels is heavily weighted toward exclusionary practices.

R arely does a week go by without a media report about violence in schools. Politicians, school boards, teachers, and parents are all concerned. If there are no recent incidents to report, then the media covers efforts that have been put in place to anticipate and prevent violence—the installation of metal detectors in schools and new zero-tolerance policies, for example.

When the local press covers an incident of school violence that has incensed a community, it is not unusual for the report to note that the students involved did not receive the same punishment. Frequently, there is a comment that some of the youngsters involved were covered by special education and remained in school pending further evaluations while their peers were suspended, or that some suspensions were revoked pending special education proceedings. These situations incite feelings of frustration, unfairness, and confusion.

In the following selection, Ashley Thomas King reviews the sometimes conflicting, often confusing history of court decisions regarding the options for disciplining students with disabilities. Writing prior to the IDEA97 amendments, he relates conflicting guidelines faced by school administrators who strive to maintain an orderly school environment. While he acknowledges the importance of ensuring an appropriate education for all children, King maintains that true inclusion will be reached only when students with disabilities are held responsible for their own actions. King holds that being part of the larger society means being held accountable for the same behavior that is expected of everyone.

In the second selection, Russell J. Skiba, writing after passage of the 1997 IDEA amendments, finds that significant options are available for administrators. Although he acknowledges the delicacy of the balancing act between school inclusion and school safety, Skiba agrees that the entire shape of the current disciplinary system is unwise for both typical students and those with disabilities.

As you read these selections, think about situations that have occurred in your own school or town. What is the reaction when students who have committed the same behavior are treated differently? Are people glad that individual conditions and circumstances are considered or confused and angry when every student does not face the same consequence? Are suspension and expulsion effective in addressing undesirable behavior? What does each student learn from such a reaction to his or her behavior?

Ashley Thomas King

Exclusionary Discipline and the Forfeiture of Special Education Rights

A survey of exclusionary practices with handicapped students revealed a national pattern of *de facto* differential treatment: Handicapped children are less likely than their non-handicapped peers to receive in-school suspensions for disruptive behaviors and fighting, less likely to receive out-of-school suspensions for disrespecting rules or people and for abusing drugs, and less likely to be expelled for fighting, violating behavior codes, and bringing weapons to school (Rose, 1988). Special education students are accorded less severe consequences for all behavior categories except for certain extreme acts such as hitting an adult or committing a felony. Furthermore, as courts have heard cases concerning the discipline of special education students, they have tended to interpret IDEA [Individuals with Disabilities Education Act] in favor of the students, creating a legal basis for *de jure* differential treatment.

Educational Due Process Rights

State legislatures between 1852 and 1918 promulgated a right to an education through passage of compulsory legislation applicable, theoretically, to all school-age children within their jurisdictions (Bowen, 1981). Unfortunately, this did not always ensure equal participation by minority students, as the Supreme Court reminded the states in *Brown* v *Board of Education* (1954): "[the opportunity of an education] when the state has undertaken to provide it, is a right which may be made available to all on equal terms" (745 U.S. 691).

Traditionally, states have granted local schools wide discretionary authority in matters of discipline, and the courts, while placing some limits on this authority, have maintained that this general right is subject to forfeiture.

In *Wood* v *Strickland* (1975) the Supreme Court interpreted the Fourteenth Amendment as affording not a constitutional right but a "property" right to an education. Students could not therefore be deprived of an education without due process of law. The same year, the Supreme Court in *Goss* v *Lopez* set out the due process rights to which all students are entitled before their removal from school. These include notice of a hearing and the charges, and a hearing

From Ashley Thomas King, "Exclusionary Discipline and the Forfeiture of Special Education Rights: A Survey," *NASSP Bulletin*, vol. 80, no. 584 (December 1996). Copyright © 1996 by The National Association of Secondary School Principals. Reprinted by permission. References omitted. For more information concerning NASSP services and/or programs, call 703-860-0200.

where the student has an opportunity to question witnesses and evidence (419 U.S. 565, 42 L Ed 2d 725–729). *Goss* v *Lopez* also set a national definition for suspensions as no more than 10 days, and expulsions as periods in excess of 10 school days, and set the due process procedures for suspensions (42 L Ed 2d 729, 740).

The non-discriminatory 504 clause of the Rehabilitation Act (29 U.S.C. 794) clearly recognizes forfeitability: Handicapped children may be denied an education provided non-handicapped children would receive the same sanctions for the same infractions (Heumann, 1995). This is not surprising since the whole rationale for the 504 clause was to provide for the *equal* treatment of the handicapped. The Education for All Handicapped Children Act (EAHCA), on the other hand, proceeded from the premise that handicapped children, to enjoy "educational benefits" similar to the non-handicapped, would require special supports and services. Designating these entitlements as rights, EAHCA provided extensive due process protections to both the handicapped child and his or her legal guardians. As courts have heard cases regarding the discipline of handicapped students, the unequal legal status of special education students has become more apparent.

Exclusionary discipline is any practice that removes a student from school. The Supreme Court in *Goss* v *Lopez* set out what rights all students are entitled to before their removal. The following historical survey covers court cases involving suspensions and expulsions of handicapped students, both of which constitute exclusionary discipline. Their primary focus is upon the meaning of EAHCA.

Suspension and Expulsion: A Survey of Cases

In an early suspension case, *Mrs. A. J.* v *Special School District Number 1* (1979), a federal district court in Minnesota ruled that a school is not obligated to treat a student as handicapped because of a mere suspicion of a handicap. The court did find, however, that a 15-day suspension without an information hearing violated this regular students's due process rights as set down in *Goss* v *Lopez*.

In *Stanley* v *School Administrative Unit Number 40 for Milford* (1980) a district court in New Hampshire upheld the suspension of a learning disabled student because the tenth grade boy's disruptive behavior was judged to be the result of serious family problems (Golden, 1993). The court implied that a disability alone does not provide immunity from disciplinary sanction, and that there must be a linkage. The court's ruling avoided, however, what exactly would constitute a linkage.

The landmark case involving suspension was *Board of Education of the City of Peoria* v *Illinois State Board of Education* (1982). The federal district court ruled that a five-day suspension is not a change of placement under EAHCA and can therefore be applied to special students, in this case an eleventh grade learning disabled boy who verbally abused his teacher. The case is significant because the judge ruled on the issue of the linkage of misbehavior to a handicap: As long as no direct relationship can be established between the handicap and the misbehavior, the special education student may be suspended (531 F. Supp.

148). The court said the boy should have known better and that his handicap did not excuse the behavior. It is significant that the judgment assumed it was the link that required proof and the school could act in its absence.

In *Doe v Rockingham County School Board* (1987), a Virginia court took a position at odds with the earlier decision in *Mrs. A. J. v Special School*. As both decisions ushered from U.S. district courts in different circuits, however, these decisions have no controlling authority over each other. The federal judicial system is hierarchical, with the Supreme Court's rulings exercising authority over all federal Circuit Courts of Appeal, and Circuit Courts exercising authority over federal district courts within their circuit.

In *Doe v Rockingham* the possibility of a disability, even if raised after a disciplinary suspension, was ruled to invoke the "stay put" protections of EAHCA. Hence, the school was ordered to return the student to his regular placement pending evaluation. In *Hacienda La Puente School District of Los Angeles v Honig* (1992), the Ninth Circuit Court of Appeals also ruled that EAHCA procedural safeguards had to be applied whether or not a child had been previously diagnosed with a disability (976 F.2d 487).

In a recent suspension case in Pennsylvania, *Big Beaver Falls Area School District v Jackson* (1993), in-school suspensions were found to amount to actual suspensions since the special student regularly chose to leave the school rather than attend suspension (624 A.2d 806). Though the school did not intend to exclude the child from school, the effect of the student's leaving was found to violate the free, appropriate public education (FAPE) requirement of IDEA.

The first important case involving the expulsion of a handicapped student occurred in a U.S. district court in Connecticut and concerned a mildly mentally retarded student. In *Stuart v Nappi* (1978) the court pointed out that a failure to provide services—e.g., inappropriate placement—may substantially contribute to misbehavior. If this is the case, the court determined that the student must remain in her current placement until the matter is resolved (443 F. Supp. 1236). While a suspension of up to 10 days may be acceptable for special students, the court determined that expulsion was a change of educational placement under EAHCA and could therefore only be made by the Individualized Education Plan (IEP) team. The court also emphasized, however, that "[h]andicapped children are neither immune from a school's disciplinary process nor are they entitled to participate in programs when their behavior impairs the education of other children in the program" (443 F. Supp. 1237).

The *Stuart* court's reasoning was based on the interpretation that expulsion violates the Least Restrictive Environment (LRE) provisions of P.L. 94–142 by limiting the continuum of available placements (443 F. Supp. 1242–43). This implied that there can be no expulsion at all due to the LRE. Since the linkage of the girls' misbehavior and her handicap were not at issue in this case, and since the school was found to be at fault for misplacement, the matter of forfeitability did not come up in *Stuart v Nappi*. Nevertheless, the court's interpretation of EAHCA certainly favored the idea that special education rights could not be forfeited.

A short time later, a district court in Indiana came to a very different conclusion in *Doe v Koger* (1979). The major issue at stake in this case was the existence of a behavior-handicap linkage. The court concluded that schools are prohibited from expelling students whose handicap causes them to be disruptive. Inversely, if there is no linkage the student may be expelled and special educational services may cease provided a determination of whether the handicap was the cause is done beforehand (480 F. Supp. 225–26, 29). . . .

This was the first clear statement issued from a court stating that EAHCA rights are forfeitable. The court left unanswered, however, who determines linkage or how it can be determined. These questions were partly resolved two years later.

S-1 v *Turlington* (1981), heard in the U.S. Court of Appeals, Fifth Circuit, also dealt with linkage and forfeiture. In its ruling the court explained that before expulsion can occur, a trained and knowledgeable group must determine if the misbehavior is a manifestation of the student's handicap (635 F.2d 342). Furthermore, the court ruled that expulsion is a change of placement, invoking EAHCA protections (635 F.2d 343). The court maintained that suspension and expulsion are proper disciplinary tools for special students provided there is no behavior-handicap link; agreeing with the LRE argument of the *Stuart* court, however, the Fifth Circuit held there may not be a complete cessation of educational services (635 F.2d 347–348). Essentially, the court was allowing disciplinary exclusion of disabled students but not forfeiture of EAHCA rights.

Unfortunately, the Fifth Circuit provided a weak standard of linkage in this case. Denying that a student's misconduct can only be a manifestation of a handicap when the student is behavior disordered, the court found that stress may cause mildly mentally retarded or physically handicapped students to act aggressively (635 F.2d 347). In other words, determining whether a student knew right from wrong is not tantamount to determining if misconduct was or was not a manifestation of a handicap (635 F.2d 346). The simple possibility of this indirect linkage was enough to exculpate the students of sexual acts against other students, the use of profane language, defiance of authority, insubordination, and vandalism.

The Sixth Circuit Appellate Court similarly dealt with the problem of linkage in *Kaelin* v *Grubbs* (1982). In this case a 15-year-old educable mentally retarded boy was indefinitely suspended for hitting his teacher. As the school neglected to hold a hearing or address possible linkage, the court found the school had violated both the student's *Goss* rights and EAHCA. The court also held that indefinite suspension constitutes an expulsion, which is a change of placement; furthermore, if the misconduct is a manifestation of the student's handicap expulsion may not be used at all. In the absence of linkage, only when services do not cease did the Sixth Circuit feel that expulsion may be used (682 F.2d 602, citing *S-1* v *Turlington*). In other words, for the U.S. Sixth Circuit, EAHCA rights are not forfeitable.

Victoria L. v *District School Board* (1984), created an important precedent for the Eleventh Circuit regarding a school's unilateral authority to remove dangerous students. The court held that change to a more restrictive placement may be made immediately if a student's behavior endangers others (741 F.2d 369). In other words, there is an "dangerousness" exception to the FAPE and "stay put" requirements of EAHCA.

In *Jackson v Franklin County School Board* (1985), the Fifth Circuit reached the same conclusion. Here a 17-year-old learning disabled boy was committed by youth court to a state hospital after an act of sexual misconduct against another student. The court affirmed that the school did not have to readmit the student until it could devise an appropriate educational program (765 F.2d 536-537). In other words, the Eleventh and Fifth Circuit Courts agreed that in emergency situations, the student's right to FAPE may be forfeited temporarily in the interests of safety.

In a Fourth Circuit Appellate Court ruling the standards for linkage were extremely weak. In *School Board of Prince William County v Malone* (1985) a learning disabled youth's participation in drug trafficking at school was ruled to be a manifestation of his handicap since the boy had poor self-esteem, presumed to be from academic difficulties (762 F.2d 1210). Being a go-between in drug sales at the school increased the boy's peer approval within this subculture and therefore enhanced his self-esteem. The court concluded that even though the boy knew right from wrong, his disability prevented him from understanding the consequences of his actions (762 F.2d 1216) and expulsion was not permissible. The court declined to discuss whether forfeiture could occur had there been no linkage (762 F.2d 1218).

School Board v *Malone* allowed an extremely tenuous and indirect linkage between misconduct and a handicap. The U.S. Fourth Circuit Court upheld a district court ruling that had accepted a local hearing officer's and state reviewing officer's conclusion that the boy's participation in drug dealing *was related* to his handicap (762 F.2d 1211-1218). The school board had been arguing something else entirely, however, specifically, that his misconduct *was not caused by* his disability. In accepting such an indirect linkage the Circuit Court permitted the student's disability to exonerate his behavior since in its opinion the disability precluded the student from realizing the repercussions of his actions (762 F.2d 1216). It is hard to imagine how a student could distinguish right from wrong but not have any inkling as to the possible outcome of indulging in known misconduct. One may reasonably ask if there could be any misconduct *not* linked to a handicap given the conceptually fuzzy standards of the Fourth and Fifth Circuit Courts of Appeal.

In *Doe v Maher* (1986) the Ninth Circuit Court made important rulings on the issues of forfeiture and linkage. As with the decisions in *School Board* v *Malone, Kaelin v Grubbs,* and *S-1 v Turlington,* the Ninth Circuit held that there could be no denial of educational rights if the misconduct is a manifestation of the handicap (793 F.2d 1470). The Ninth Circuit, however, provided one of the clearest statements to date regarding what a linkage is and how to determine it.

The Ninth Circuit ruled that a direct causal relationship must exist between the misconduct and the student's handicap to invoke EAHCA protections. That is to say, the student's disability must significantly impair the student's ability to control his or her behavior. Indirect relationships, such as misbehavior resulting from a loss of self-esteem, or conscious misbehavior to gain attention or peer approval, were expressly rejected because the court felt that such conduct is not unique to handicapped children:

> As we use [the terms "handicap-related misconduct"], [t]hey refer to conduct that is caused by, or has a direct and substantial relationship to, the child's handicap. Put another way, a handicap child's conduct is covered by this definition only if the handicap significantly impairs the child's behavioral controls. Although this definition may, depending on the circumstances, include the conduct of handicapped children who possess the raw capacity to conform their behavior to prescribed standards, it does not embrace conduct that bears only an attenuated relationship to the child's handicap. An example of such attenuated conduct would be a case where a child's physical handicap results in his loss of self-esteem, and the child consciously misbehaves in order to gain attention, or win the approval, of his peers. Although such a scenario may be common among handicapped children, it is no less common among children suffering from low self-esteem.... (*Doe* v *Maher*, 793 F.2d 1480 n.8)

Regarding the method of changing a placement in response to a misconduct and of determining a misconduct-handicap linkage, the court pointed out the decision was to be made by a consensus of the student's IEP team. If consensus is not reached, the parents may call a due process hearing (793 F.2d, 1488–90).

The Ninth Circuit was equally unambiguous regarding forfeiture. It stated that expulsion is appropriate for special education students provided there is no linkage. In that instance, the school district may cease providing all educational services (793 F.2d 1471 n. 4, 1482), which is another way of saying that EAHCA rights may be forfeited. The certainty of these rulings for the Ninth Circuit region was put into doubt, however, when the state of California appealed *Doe* v *Maher* to the U.S. Supreme Court in *Honig* v *Doe* (1988).

The Supreme Court in *Honig* v *Doe* did not address the issue of a behavior-handicap linkage since it was not in contention in the case. Yet, the Supreme Court's interpretation of EAHCA in *Honig* v *Doe* has had important implications for the possibility of forfeiting EAHCA rights. Using the definitions set down in *Goss* v *Lopez*, the *Honig* court ruled that temporary suspensions of less than 10 days are permissible. A longer removal is also possible if the school secures parental consent for an interim placement. If agreement cannot be reached, the child must "stay put" in his or her current placement until review proceedings are completed. Only by showing that the return of the student is substantially likely to cause injury can a school overcome this limit through permission of a district court (484 U.S. 305, 98 L Ed 2d 709–710). California tried to argue that schools possessed discretionary authority to unilaterally expel students they deemed an immediate danger to themselves or others. The Court, in a literal interpretation of EAHCA, found otherwise. The justices ruled that *Congress did intend to strip schools of their traditional authority vis-à-vis special education students* (98 L Ed 2d 696). That is, there are no emergency exceptions to EAHCA's stay put provision. The Supreme Court agreed with the Ninth Circuit's opinion in *Doe* v *Maher* that schools may not expel students whose conduct is attributable to their disability but it left unanswered whether students whose conduct is not linked may be expelled.

In 1992 the Ninth Circuit made important rulings regarding who may determine manifestation in *Hacienda La Puente Unified School District* v *Honig.* Here a student who had been found not to meet special education eligibility criteria was shortly afterward expelled from school for frightening another student with a starter pistol. The Los Angeles Board of Education affirmed the decision but at the due process hearing to appeal the eligibility decision, the hearing officer determined that the boy was eligible and had been expelled for acts that were a manifestation of his disability (976, F.2d 489). The district and circuit court concurred, citing *Honig's* "no dangerous exception" judgment, and finding that all *alleged* disabled students are entitled to procedural safeguards under IDEA (976 F.2d 494).

The problems inherent in *Hacienda* and *Honig* could be seen in *M. P.* v *Governing Board of Grossmont Union High School District* (1994), where the district court lamented its powerlessness to counter abuse of IDEA. Here a student who was clearly not eligible for special education used IDEA's procedural safeguards to evade expulsion. As the court admitted,

> The "stay put" provision and the *Hacienda* decision, in conjunction, act to severely restrict school officials of their power to discipline and to maintain a safe school environment. Indeed, as this case suggests, if a child brings a gun to school, a parent or guardian's response could simply be to claim that the child is disabled and therefore bypass the laws' disciplinary procedures.... [T]he student responsible for bringing the gun escapes the consequences of the action. (858 F. Supp. 1048)

Discussion

In denying a schools' unilateral authority to remove dangerous or disruptive students, the Supreme Court's judgment in *Honig* took precedence over all earlier lower court decisions, including the Eleventh and Fifth Circuit Court rulings that recognized such authority. As can be gleaned from the survey, remaining unanswered questions are whether a student with a suspected disability is entitled to IDEA protections or not; whether educational rights are forfeitable when there is no linkage or if services may never cease regardless of linkage; and whether a direct or indirect linkage is required in a manifestation determination.

Without guidance on what constitutes a linkage, a school administrator takes a considerable risk in using exclusionary discipline with any special education student. If due process proceedings are called by the parent, and these reach court, it will not matter if the IEP team and the district hearing officer both conclude that there is no linkage—the determination could be overturned in court. Therefore, without a reliable standard, *the burden of proof shifts by default to the administrator....*

Can this be done? Several authors have suggested approaches, including searching the school records for behavior precedents or trying to evaluate behavior by disability category. But the sad reality is that if an administrator wishes to initiate exclusionary discipline with a special education student, the burden of producing evidence of no relationship between disability and behavior will rest solely with the school.... [W]hile one can assume that *Honig* may theoretically permit expulsion in the absence of linkage, in reality expulsion is not available as a disciplinary option with special education students. This is because without a clear definition of linkage, schools using it would be "in a legally precarious situation," and would be inviting administrative reviews and potentially expensive litigation. Facing this, it is advisable "to consider that a child's misbehavior is *always* related to his or her handicapping condition" (Yell, 1989, p. 67, emphasis added)....

This state of affairs has serious consequences. First, if manifestation is no longer debatable because attempting to disprove it is "legally precarious," then the matter of forfeiture is null by default. No matter what transpires, no matter how culpable the student may be, a special student must continue to enjoy an entitlement to a free, appropriate public education. Second, special education students, by virtue of their disability, in effect enjoy a special legal status and immunity from certain forms of exclusionary discipline. Third, and most important, by viewing all misbehavior as a disability manifestation we do handicapped children a profound injustice. We are saying, in effect, that they are not in control of their own behavior, that they are not capable of assuming the same moral responsibilities as their peers.

The U.S. Department of Education's Office of Special Education Programs (OSEP) position has long been that rights under EAHCA and IDEA are not forfeitable under any circumstances. OSEP's complete rejection of forfeiture has brought it into conflict with local school districts. In *Metropolitan School District v Davila* (1991), for example, a federal district court in Indiana barred OSEP from enforcing its policy forbidding cessation of services to properly expelled disabled students (Hartwig, Reusch, and Shaw, 1991). Given the deference of the *Honig* court to DOE rulings (98 L Ed 2d 693, 708), it will not be surprising if *Honig v Doe* is interpreted in a manner favorable to OSEP's official policy.

Justice Brennan, in speaking for the majority in *Honig,* stated that while schools were stripped of unilateral authority to remove dangerous and disruptive students, schools were not "hamstrung" by this: While a child's placement may not be changed during any complaint proceedings, this does not preclude a school from using its normal procedures for dealing with children who are endangering themselves or others (98 L Ed 2d 708). While the *Honig* Court did not exhaustively define what normal procedures were, it did include the use of study carrels, timeouts, and detentions. One area left unclear by *Honig* was, however, recently addressed in *Parents v Puyallup School District* (1994). The Ninth Circuit Court ruled that suspensions exceeding 10 days during the year may create a change of placement, but do not necessarily do so since *Honig* made no finding on the matter. That is, *Honig* did not create a 10-day cumulative limit (31 F.3d 1495).

But are "normal" disciplinary measures really secure? For example, there are only legal precedents for 5-day periods of in-school suspensions with disabled students (*Hayes v Unified School District Number 377* (1987) and *Doe* v *Maher*). Ellis and Geller (1993) recommend caution in using 6 to 10-day in-school suspensions for this reason. To address students bringing dangerous weapons to school, Congress passed the Gun-Free Schools Act, mandating expulsions of not less than one year for such actions. While IDEA was subsequently amended to give schools authority in weapons cases involving special students to immediately place them in an alternative-interim setting for up to 45 days, the one-year mandatory expulsion is not clearly applicable (20 U.S.C. § 415(a)(3)(B)(1995)). On the contrary, OSEP maintains that even when linkage is nonexistent in a weapon's case, educational services must continue for eligible students (Heumann, 1995, p. 16).

During the first half of this decade, legal challenges have been generally successful against schools attempting more restrictive placements for special education students (Yell, 1995). In such a litigious atmosphere, there is a palpable fear within school districts of taking vigorous action when the legal boundaries are unclear. . . .

An Outline of an Equal Treatment Model

Unequal treatment can be avoided but this will require the careful resuscitation of the twin concepts of forfeiture and linkage. An equal treatment model of exclusionary discipline, incorporating these principles, would:

1. Provide a strict and unambiguous standard for determining a direct relationship between a misbehavior and a handicap
2. Allow a manifestation determination to be made solely by the relevant special educator and the school psychologist
3. Place the burden of proof on the special educator and school psychologist to prove a linkage, not upon the administration to prove that a linkage does not exist
4. Disallow appeals of a manifestation determination entirely
5. Void or suspend an IEP in the absence of a linkage (forfeiture) for serious behavior code violations.

Unlike the courts, which have not been consistent on the issue of linkage, an amendment to IDEA should provide an operational standard for determining when a causal nexus exists between misconduct and disability. A strict standard describing a direct link is necessary, or the weakness of a *School Board* v *Malone* or *S-1* v *Turlington* standard would rationalize any behavior as a manifestation. A strict standard would require that the behavior could not occur in the absence of the handicap; it would also need to be shown that the handicap impairs the ability of the student to make proper judgments or exert sufficient self-control (a *Doe* v *Maher* standard).

A manifestation determination should be made by knowledgeable persons but this should not necessarily mean the IEP team because the question is a technical one. It is the special educator who is the primary educational advocate for the student. It is the special educator who has the responsibility of implementing the student's educational goals and representing the student vis-à-vis the school. He or she has the relevant specialized knowledge and experience to judge whether a student's behavior is a result of their handicap. The school psychologist also has the expertise to determine if a causal nexus exists. Their professional judgment should prevail.

Proof is the act of showing evidence for the truth of a proposition. *Placing the burden on administrators to prove that there is no linkage is both unfair and logically untenable*—it is a version of the fallacy of negative proof. It is simply not possible to prove the absence of a relationship. The best an administrator could do would be to show that no previous behavior pattern is extant in the records. It is a direct causal linkage that requires proof, not its absence.

Given a clear standard, a determination of manifestation must rest with the educational professionals intimate with the student and go no further. If their judgment can be appealed and taken to court then the educational system is weakened: Professional credibility will be undermined. Linkage is a technical, not a placement question: It should not be litigable. It is the purview of educational professionals, not attorneys.

If special education students are really going to be treated as the equals of their peers, and enjoy an equal right to an education, then they must be subject to the same disciplinary rules and penalties, including exclusionary discipline. If linkage cannot be shown, then for serious behavior code violations the right to a free, appropriate public education is forfeited, just as it would be for a non-handicapped student. An IEP would become inactive and would remain so for the duration of the sanction.

Conclusion: Toward Equal Responsibilities

One writer has suggested that educators accept and acknowledge the double standard that exists with regard to the discipline of special education students (Maloney, 1994), but this state of affairs need not be taken as permanent. It is Congress that has abdicated its responsibility during the last two decades in leaving it to the courts to legislate in its ommission. Suggestions have already been made in Congress to limit special education litigation by requiring mediation prior to due process and to allow schools to remove violent students, regardless of their disability (Hatfield, 1995). In Washington, the House Committee on Economic and Educational Opportunities has suggested amendments to address these issues in the next reauthorization of IDEA. Their draft bill contains provisions for normal expulsion or other appropriate disciplinary actions if there is a determination of non-linkage beforehand.

The forgoing discussion of forfeiture should not be interpreted as advocating the use of exclusionary discipline as a first option or as a preferred disciplinary tool—not in the least. But even an assertive discipline policy should not prevent schools from exercising exclusionary options when the circumstances merit.

It is time to stop trying to make amends for past mistakes. Because handicapped children were excluded prior to the Rehabilitation Act and P.L. 94–142 does not mean we should deny these children moral agency in the present. That is what the current system does if schools must assume that misconduct and a disability are always related.

If a student knows the difference, and still chooses the wrong, he or she is morally culpable, the Fourth and Fifth Circuits notwithstanding. When we allow handicapped students to assume equal responsibilities for their own behavior we will be taking a giant step toward genuine inclusion.

NO

Russell J. Skiba

Special Education and School Discipline: A Precarious Balance

Abstract

The 1997 Amendments to the Individuals with Disabilities Education Act brought together, for the first time, all of the disciplinary provisions pertaining to students with disabilities, attempting to guarantee a free and appropriate public education (FAPE) for students in special education while preserving a safe school environment for all students. Yet the discipline of special education students has continued to create controversy. Although the provisions are based on a long history of case law and administrative rulings that seek to protect students with disabilities from arbitrary exclusion, critics suggest that those provisions create a dual system of discipline limiting the options of school administrators with respect to school discipline. A review of the literature concerning school removal, however, provides little or no evidence that suspension and expulsion make any contribution to reducing disruption or violence, and some evidence that those procedures target certain populations disproportionally. In this light, it appears to make little sense to remove special education disciplinary protections, only to expose students with disabilities to procedures that may be both ineffective and discriminatory. Rather, seeking to move towards a unified system of discipline that implements effective and accountable disciplinary options will be more likely to preserve FAPE and guarantee safe and civil schools for all children.

Special Education and School Discipline: A Precarious Balance

Under current federal law, any student who brings a weapon to school is subject to a one-year expulsion. If that student is served in special education, however, bringing a weapon may still result in disciplinary removal, but a different, more complex set of regulations govern when and how that student may be removed. The amount of time that student can be removed is more limited, the nature

From Russell J. Skiba, "Special Education and School Discipline: A Precarious Balance," *Behavioral Disorders* (in press). Copyright © 2002 by *Behavioral Disorders*. Reprinted by permission of *Behavioral Disorders* and the author.

of the relationship between the act and the student's disability must be determined, and educational services must still be provided during the period of removal.

This difference in the treatment of students with disabilities who are violent or disruptive has created an intense controversy that continues to swirl around the disciplinary provisions of special education law. The often-heated controversy represents a fundamental clash between two basic values passed into law and supported by the courts: the right of students with special needs to due process and a free and appropriate public education versus the right of schools to implement procedures they see as necessary to protect the safety of students and teachers.

The guarantee of a free and appropriate education for students with disabilities is central to special education law in this country as it has evolved in the past thirty years. In response to a series of court rulings overruling the systematic exclusion of children with disabilities (McCarthy, Cambron-McCabe, & Thomas, 1998), Congress passed in 1975 what we now know as the Individuals with Disabilities Education Act (1997), relying upon a number of basic principles guiding the education of students with disabilities, including a free and appropriate public education and parental due process rights.

Though more recent in origin, the Gun-Free Schools Act (1994) represents an equally basic societal value, namely the right of students to learn, and teachers to teach, in schools that are free of weapons. Passed in response to national concerns about school violence, and at the height of a national movement toward zero tolerance, the act mandates a one-year expulsion for any student bringing a weapon to school. The law also requires the establishment of procedures at the local level allowing a case-by-case review of such expulsions, and that any legal violation occurring on school grounds be reported to law enforcement authorities.

In 1997 Congress passed the Individuals with Disabilities Education Act Amendments (IDEA 97), the most sweeping changes to the law since its inception in 1975. Those amendments were intended to codify case law and administrative decisions that occurred between 1975 and 1997. Among the most important and most controversial changes in the law were the IDEA 97 provisions governing the discipline of students with disabilities. Those provisions brought together in statute for the first time all of the rules that apply to students with disabilities faced with disciplinary action, seeking "a balanced approach to the issue of discipline of children with disabilities that reflects the need for orderly and safe schools and the need to protect the right of children with disabilities to a free appropriate public education (FAPE)" (Office of Special Education Programs, 1997).

Yet three years after passage of the law, educators and policymakers remain deeply divided on the appropriate balance between the individual rights of students with disabilities and the flexibility administrators need in order to ensure school safety. This paper will review the complex issues involved in the discipline of students with disabilities. Sections of the paper will review (a) the content, and some of the reasons for controversy, of the IDEA 97 disciplinary provisions, (b) the state of knowledge and practice concerning school suspension and expulsion, (c) alternatives to suspension and expulsion in promoting civil behavior and school safety, and (d) prospects for resolving the controversy concerning the discipline of students with disabilities.

IDEA 97 Disciplinary Provisions

Controversy about the law notwithstanding, special education law does not make it impossible for school administrators to discipline students with disabilities. Rather, balancing the tradition of free and appropriate public education with the need to ensure safe schools, it delineates a set of conditions under which students with disabilities may or may not be exposed to suspension and expulsion. Indeed, in some areas, such as the issue of "dangerousness," the IDEA 97 amendments provide administrators with disciplinary options not previously available.

But while it is not correct to state that special education law disallows suspension and expulsion for students with disabilities, it is accurate to state that the disciplinary requirements of the new amendments are highly complex, and perhaps not yet fully understood by either educators or policymakers. Part of this complexity stems from the multiple legal precedents that IDEA 97 attempted to weave together. For school administrators who may feel a need to act decisively on issues of school discipline, the sheer amount of procedure involved in removing a student with disabilities may seem to make disciplinary removal next to impossible.

However one may feel about the provisions of IDEA 97, those amendments did not simply spring up full-blown in 1997. With few exceptions, the disciplinary provisions are based on a history of case law and administrative decisions that go back to the initial passage of special education law in Congress. The following sections summarize the main provisions of IDEA 97 regarding discipline, review historical and legal precedents that informed each requirement, and where relevant summarize the arguments of advocates and critics of the provisions. [For further discussion of these provisions, readers are referred to excellent treatments in Yell (1998) and Hartwig & Ruesch (2000).]

Short-Term Disciplinary Removal

In the history of wrestling with the discipline of disabled students, two important principles have emerged. First, students who are disabled must to some extent be held accountable for their behavior—special education is not intended to make students immune from school suspension (McCarthy et al., 1998). Yet the desire to rule out arbitrary exclusion led to what might be regarded as the central tenet of IDEA: the guarantee of a *free and appropriate public education* (FAPE) for students with disabilities. Beyond a certain point, long-term suspension and expulsion may threaten the student's right to a free and appropriate public education. In *Honig v. Doe* (1988), the Supreme Court set a standard of ten days as the dividing line between typical short-term discipline and long-term change that triggers the FAPE guarantee for students with disabilities.

Beyond ten days, a disciplinary removal was considered a change of placement triggering the special education protections against arbitrary removal.

When does a disciplinary removal constitute a change of placement? The IDEA 97 regulations rely upon administrative rulings by both the Office for Civil Rights (OCR, 1988) and the Office of Special Education Programs (OSEP, 1995) to offer a set of guidelines that define *change of placement* for disciplinary removal as being (a) more than 10 consecutive school days, or (b) a series of removals that constitute a pattern by summing to more than 10 days in a school year. A "pattern" is judged by considering factors such as the length of each removal, total time removed, and the proximity of the removals to one another; responsibility for making that judgment rests with the IEP [individual education program] team. Whenever that change in placement criterion is met, students with disabilities must be provided with services that enable them to meet the goals in their IEP's.

It is an important point, sometimes misunderstood, that prior to the criterion of change in placement being met, there are no special requirements governing the discipline of special education students. For removals less than ten days that do not constitute a change in placement, special education students are treated no differently than other students; administrators are free to use any consequence that would be applied to all other students.

Long-Term Disciplinary Removal

The main provision of the Gun-Free Schools Act (GFSA) of 1994 is the mandatory one year expulsion of any student bringing a firearm into school. This provision of mandatory expulsion seems to create a legal quandary with respect to students with disabilities, apparently pitting the rights of special education students to a free and appropriate public education with the rights of schools to maintain a safe and gun-free environment.

Almost from the passage of the GFSA, amendments in Congress attempted to bring special education law into line with that act. The Jeffords Amendment to the Improving America's Schools Act (1994) introduced the concept of 45 day placement for students with disabilities in an Interim Alternative Educational Setting for possession of firearms. The disciplinary requirements enacted by Congress in IDEA 97 replace and extend the Jeffords Amendment, attempting to strike "a careful balance between the LEA's (local education agency) duty to ensure that school environments are safe and conducive to learning for all children, including children with disabilities, and the LEA's continuing obligation to ensure that children with disabilities receive a free appropriate public education" (Senate Report 105-17, 1997). A number of the IDEA 97 disciplinary provisions address the issue of long-term removal for students with disabilities.

Interim alternative educational setting.   Under IDEA 97, school personnel may unilaterally place a student with a disability in an interim alternative education setting (IAES) for up to 45 days for possession of drugs or weapons. The length of the disciplinary removal should not exceed the length of removal that other students would receive for the same offense.

A student with a disability may also be placed in an interim alternative educational setting if the district can demonstrate through "substantial evidence" that the student's current placement is "substantially likely to result in injury to the child or to others." Unlike a change in placement for weapons or drugs, however, removal for dangerousness cannot be made by school personnel without parental consent. Rather, the school or school district must petition a hearing officer in an expedited due process hearing for disciplinary removal.[1]

Like many of the disciplinary provisions of IDEA 97, the provision of the 45 day placement in an interim alternative educational setting has been the subject of controversy. Advocates hold that these provisions create a balance between FAPE and the need to guarantee safe schools by bringing IDEA 97 more into line with the Gun-Free Schools Act, and expand the authority of schools and school districts with respect to the disciplinary removal of special education students. Critics, however, argue that the law creates a dual standard of discipline, shortening the period of exclusion for students with disabilities, and that the high cost of interim alternative placements will draw resources away from the majority of children (Koch, 2000).

Parent appeal and the stay-put provision.   Due process rights are among the most fundamental rights and principles guaranteed under special education law. Parents of students with disabilities are specifically granted the right to appeal any change in placement, including any disciplinary removal that constitutes a change of placement. In order that these rights be respected during the process, a "stay-put" provision has evolved in special education law, such that a student cannot be moved from his or her current educational placement during appeal.

In the case of dangerous behavior, however, the stay-put provision may create substantial difficulty. This quandary was in fact the central issue in the landmark Supreme Court decision *Honig v. Doe* (1988). In seeking to expel two students with emotional disabilities, the California superintendent of public instruction argued in *Honig* that applying the stay-put provision to maintain students in their current placement regardless of the dangerousness of their behavior was untenable. The Supreme Court, however, responded that Congress had intended to remove the authority of schools to unilaterally exclude children with disabilities, and refused to issue an exception, even in the case of "dangerousness."

The disciplinary provisions of IDEA 97 represent a significant expansion of options for school personnel in the case of dangerousness. By allowing a hearing officer to place a student with a disability in a 45 day placement if a district can demonstrate that student poses a substantial risk of injury to self or others, the IDEA 97 provisions offer an additional option to administrators beyond what had been allowed by *Honig v. Doe*. In addition, IDEA 97 modified the stay-put provision somewhat for weapons, drugs, or dangerous behavior. Specifically, when a parent seeks a hearing or appeal of a placement to an interim alternative educational setting, the interim alternative educational setting becomes the "current" placement, in which the student remains while appeals are pending.[2] In short then, while the high court was unwilling to issue a "dangerousness" exception to the stay-put provisions of special education law, IDEA

97 has in effect created a dangerousness exception, under the authority of the hearing officer.

Other legal alternatives.   IDEA 97 also attempts to ensure consistency of special education law with other law regarding school safety by explicitly asserting that the law in no way prohibits an educational agency from reporting a crime to law enforcement authorities, or prevents law enforcement officials from exercising their responsibilities when crimes are committed in school. Finally, regardless of the limitations on disciplinary removal for students with disabilities under IDEA 97, the U.S. Supreme Court in *Honig v. Doe* ruled that schools may still seek a court injunction to remove a student that the district can show is dangerous, and for whom parents refuse to agree to a change in placement. If this option is successful, IDEA 97 disciplinary requirements cease to apply, as the child comes under judicial authority.

Manifestation Determination

The idea that a student cannot be removed from school because of his or her disability is central to the development of special education law in this country (see e.g., *Mills v. Board of Education of the District of Columbia* (1972) in which the court ruled that students with behavioral disorders could not be expelled for behaviors that could be expected to be related to their disability). Since the passage of P.L. 94-142, court precedents (e.g., *Doe v. Koger,* 1979; *S-1 v. Turlington,* 1981) have established that a student with a disability can be expelled only if there is no relationship between the misconduct leading to the expulsion and the student's disability. This criterion, which came to be known as *manifestation determination,* was reaffirmed by the U.S. Supreme Court in *Honig v. Doe.*

IDEA 97 pulls together prior precedent to offer guidance regarding the manifestation determination. Whenever a disciplinary action would result in a change of placement, a manifestation determination, conducted by the IEP team, must take place within ten school days of the decision to take disciplinary action, considering three questions. First, were the IEP and placement appropriate, and service and interventions provided consistent with the IEP and placement? If the IEP, placement, or services were inappropriate, the review cannot proceed, the behavior must be considered a manifestation of the disability, and the school district must take immediate steps to remedy the deficiencies. Second, did the child's disability impair his or her ability to *understand* the impact and consequences of the behavior? Third, did the child's disability impair his or her ability to *control* the behavior? If the answer to either of these questions is yes, then the behavior is viewed as a manifestation of the disability, and the child may not be subjected to standard disciplinary procedures.[3]

Although IDEA 97 provides more extensive guidance than was previously available, the process of manifestation determination may still be difficult and arbitrary in practice. The "ability to understand the impact or consequences" of one's behavior is a highly sophisticated internal process, as is the ability to control one's behavior. This difficulty is further magnified by the fact that there are currently no available measures validated for the purpose of making such distinctions (Katsiyannis & Maag, 1998). Forcing an IEP team to make these difficult distinctions in the absence of adequate assessment tools may reduce the manifestation determination review to a battle of wills, pitting school principals seeking to exercise the option of disciplinary removal against special education administrators seeking to preserve the rights of special education students.

Functional Behavioral Assessment/Behavioral Intervention Plan

Once a student with disabilities has been removed for more than ten school days, IDEA 97 requires that the school district conduct a functional assessment and implement a behavioral intervention plan. If a functional assessment and behavioral intervention plan are already in place, the IEP team must review that plan to ensure that it remains appropriate. Further, IDEA 97 requires that "as soon as practicable after developing the plan," the IEP team should be convened to take steps to develop and implement appropriate interventions.

Although fairly well-established in the field of special education, the term functional assessment is a new one for many principals and general education teachers. Functional assessment is generally understood as a behavioral technology originally developed in the 1980's for use with severely disabled, predominantly non-verbal students (Carr & Durand, 1985; Iwata, Dorsey, Slifer, Bauman, & Richman, 1982). In functional assessment, observations, checklists, and interviews are used to develop specific hypotheses about conditions that might be associated with a student's disruptive behavior.

Of all the disciplinary provisions set forth in IDEA 97, functional assessment seems to have the least grounding in specific legal precedent. In contrast to most of the other disciplinary provisions, there are no specific court cases or Office of Special Education rulings regarding functional assessment. Indeed, some writers within the field of special education have questioned whether the technology of functional assessment is sufficiently developed and has sufficient empirical support to be ready for generalization to all students with disabilities (Nelson, Mathur, & Rutherford, 1999).

In a broader sense, however, the new functional behavioral assessment/ individual behavioral plan requirements are consistent with at least the spirit of special education legislation. Since the passage of the original Education for All Handicapped Children Act, one of the guiding principles of special education has been the idea of individualized education. The requirement for individual behavior plans, and the functional assessment likely to make those plans more successful, is in some ways an extension of this concern with individual programming that meets the needs of students with disabilities. If the disruptive behavior of a student with a disability is related to his or her disability, then it only makes sense to ensure that an individual behavioral plan also be in place to remediate that behavior.

Still, it is not entirely clear that school districts are prepared to implement the IDEA 97 functional behavioral assessment requirements in a way that can meet the intent of the law. Without extensive research guidance with less severely disabled populations, many districts are using functional assessment methods developed for students with severe disabilities that have not been extensively tested in less restrictive environments. In addition, at the time of passage of IDEA 97, few districts had personnel trained in conducting functional assessment (Smith, 2000). It may well be that the mandates of IDEA 97 regarding functional behavioral assessment and individual behavior planning will stimulate research and practice toward more responsive behavioral planning for students with disabilities. On the other hand, in the absence of a well-developed technology and lacking trained personnel, it may be some time before school districts have the capability to conduct functional assessments that fulfill the law's intent.

Protections for Students Not Yet Eligible for Special Education

Another element of the IDEA 97 disciplinary provisions states that any child not yet determined eligible for special education services may assert their rights to IDEA disciplinary protections only if the school or district had prior knowledge that the child has a disability. The educational agency would be determined as having this prior knowledge if the parent had expressed concern in writing to district personnel about a potential disability, if the behavior or performance of the child demonstrates a need for services, if the parent had requested an evaluation, or if the child's teacher or other school personnel had expressed concern about the behavior or performance of the child.

It is important to note that this section of the regulations provides protections not only for students, but also for school districts. This provision protects students with disabilities in that a district or school cannot fail to identify a student it suspects may be disabled simply so that it may continue to apply standard suspension and expulsion practices to that student (Johns, 1998). On the other hand, the provision also provides some protection to districts that fulfill those obligations, since parents of a non-identified student facing disciplinary consequences may claim the protections of IDEA 97 only if certain well-defined conditions are met.

Summary

Students with disabilities are subject to the same set of disciplinary consequences as all other students for any disciplinary removal less than ten days, if the removal cannot be considered a change of placement. Whether a set of removals during the school year constitutes a change of placement is an IEP team decision, based upon the pattern of removals. Nothing in IDEA 97 prohibits multiple suspensions of more than ten days, so long as all services that the student is entitled to in the IEP are provided once the removals exceed ten days.

For long term removals, IDEA utilizes the interim alternative educational setting as an alternative to suspension and expulsion. School personnel may unilaterally place a student with disabilities in the alternative educational setting for drugs or weapons for up to 45 days. For a student deemed dangerous, school personnel may request a hearing officer to remand the student to an interim setting for up to 45 days. Parents have a right to appeal either decision, but the child will remain in the interim alternative setting while the appeal is being conducted. All of these provisions are dependent upon the behavior being a manifestation of the child's disability. If team review determines that the behavior is not related to the child's disability, normal suspension and expulsion procedures may be used, provided that services consistent with the IEP continue. For any disciplinary event cumulating to ten or more days, schools and school districts must conduct or review a functional assessment or behavior plan. Finally, students not yet determined eligible for special education may assert their right to IDEA disciplinary protections only if it can be shown that the district had prior knowledge that the student might be disabled.

The Controversy Over IDEA 97

The intent of the disciplinary requirements of IDEA 97 was to weave together previous precedents and decisions so as to bridge the gap between the treatment of special education and all other students in the area of school discipline. Yet whatever the intentions of the framers of IDEA 97, the new regulations have apparently not resolved the perceived conflict between FAPE and the Gun-Free Schools Act. If anything, the law passed by Congress and the implementing regulations promulgated in March, 1999 seem to have increased disciplinary controversy.

Critics say the law "ties the hands" of administrators in matters of discipline for special education students. "IDEA overrides state and federal zero-tolerance-for-firearms laws," says Julie Lewis, staff attorney for the National School Boards Association. "They contradict one another" (Koch, 2000, p. 200). The American Association of School Administrators (1998; Hunter, 1999) suggests that the law creates a "double standard" for violent and disruptive behavior. Parents of students expelled or referred to alternative schools for weapons or drugs may be confused about why a student in special education receives different treatment for the same offense (Koch, 2000).

Student advocacy groups, disability rights groups, and mental health professional organizations, however, hold that the provisions of IDEA in general, and the disciplinary provisions in particular, protect the fundamental rights of a class of children previously denied those rights. In response to previous abuses, all three branches of government have consistently asserted the right of students with disabilities to protections from arbitrary removal or change of placement. "Without due process, these students would be removed disproportionately by schools that decided providing services was too costly, time consuming or inconvenient," states Kevin Dwyer, President of the National Association of School Psychologists, and author of the USDOE/USDOJ *Early Warning, Timely Response* guide to school safety. "Withdrawing educational services from any student does not make our schools and streets safer" (Koch, 2000, p. 201).

These controversies have played out in sometimes emotional debate in Congress. Since the passage of the IDEA amendments in 1997, there have been numerous attempts to weaken or eliminate the disciplinary regulations of that act.[4] The latest were amendments in the Senate and House as part of the reauthorization of the Elementary and Secondary Education Act (Jones, 2001). The Norwood amendment (Amendment 13 to H.R. 1) would eliminate the mandated provision of special education services for children with disabilities who have been suspended or expelled for actions involving drugs, weapons, or aggravated assault and battery. The Sessions amendment (Amendment 604 to S. 1) would give State or Local Education Agencies broad authority to establish and implement uniform discipline policies regarding discipline and order for all children, unless the behavior in question represents a manifestation of the child's disability. The two bills are currently being considered in conference committee.

Although these amendments may significantly change the way in which schools handle discipline for special education students for the most serious of incidents, guns or weapons, they may or may not change procedures for the less serious incidents that constitute the largest proportion of school discipline. Much of the controversy centers on the extent to which IDEA disciplinary requirements deprive schools and school districts of tools, school suspension and expulsion, needed to ensure school discipline. Yet there has been little examination during the debate of those disciplinary tools themselves. How are school suspension and expulsion used in the public schools? What are the issues concerning the use of those procedures? How effective are they in reducing disruption or guaranteeing school safety?

What Do We Know About School Suspension and Expulsion?

Even before the implementation of zero-tolerance policy for weapons at the national level, suspension was among the most widely used of disciplinary options in America's public schools. Applications of zero tolerance appear to have further increased the use of school suspension and expulsion in school districts throughout the country (Advancement Project/Civil Rights Project, 2000). Many districts have enthusiastically supported the move toward tougher punishments, expanding the range of behaviors subjected to mandatory expulsion well beyond the federal mandate of weapons, to include drugs, alcohol, fighting, or offenses that take place off school property; some have extended penalties beyond a calendar year to two-year or even permanent expulsion ("Groups critical of no second chances school proposal," 1999).

Yet the increased use of suspension and expulsion as part of zero-tolerance discipline has also created controversy. Instances of students being suspended or expelled under zero-tolerance policies for seemingly minor events —possession of Midol, organic cough drops, nailfiles—has created a backlash against the unthinking application of school exclusion from groups of diverse political stripes. The Rev. Jesse Jackson has raised questions about issues of racial bias inherent in zero-tolerance and supports a "reevaluation all across the country of the absurdities of zero tolerance" (Wing & Keleher, 2000). At the other end of the political spectrum, the conservative Rutherford Institute has strongly criticized zero tolerance policies, arguing that they violate students' civil rights, and has provided legal defense to students involved in a number of zero tolerance incidents (Rutherford Institute, 2000).

At the heart of the matter, again, is the use of school suspension and expulsion as disciplinary tools. The following sections will review the current status of our knowledge concerning school suspension and expulsion. In general, those data raise troubling questions concerning the consistency, fairness, and effectiveness of school suspension and expulsion.

How Are Suspension and Expulsion Used?

School-based research has consistently found school suspension to be among the most widely-used disciplinary techniques (Bowditch, 1993; Mansfield & Farris, 1992; Rose, 1988). In one midwestern city, one third of all referrals to the office resulted in a one to five day suspension, and 21% of all enrolled students were suspended at least once during the school year (Skiba, Peterson, & Williams, 1997). Suspension appears to be used with greater frequency in urban areas than in suburban or rural areas (Massachusetts Advocacy Center, 1986; Wu, Pink, Crain, & Moles, 1982).

As might be expected with such high rates of usage, school suspension is not always reserved for serious or dangerous behaviors. Fights or physical aggression among students are consistently among the most common reasons for suspension (Costenbader & Markson, 1994; Dupper & Bosch, 1996; Imich, 1994; Menacker, Hurwitz, & Weldon, 1988; Skiba et al., 1997). Yet school suspension is also commonly used for a number of relatively minor offenses, such as disobedience and disrespect (Cooley, 1995; Skiba et al., 1997), attendance problems (Kaeser, 1979; Morgan-D'Atrio et al., 1996), and general classroom disruption (Imich, 1994; Massachusetts Advocacy Center, 1986; Morgan-D'Atrio et al., 1996). In fact, students are suspended for the most serious offenses (drugs, weapons, vandalism, assaults on teachers) relatively infrequently (Dupper & Bosch, 1996; Kaeser, 1979).

While more controversial, school expulsion appears to be used relatively infrequently as compared to other disciplinary options (Sinclair, 1999). In one of the few studies examining school expulsion, Morrison and D'Incau (1997) reported that expulsion appears to be reserved for incidents of moderate to high severity, although there is some doubt as to whether students who are expelled are always those who are the most troublesome or dangerous. Zero-tolerance policies, mandating expulsion for certain types of events, have apparently led to the expulsion of many children and youth who would be considered "good students."

Who Gets Suspended and Why?

There can be little doubt that certain students are at a much greater risk for office referral and school suspension. Students who have been suspended are more likely to endorse statements indicating an antisocial attitude (Wu et al., 1982). Students who engage in harassment, bullying, or violent behavior appear to be at greater risk of disciplinary action (Tobin, Sugai, & Colvin, 1996). Some students clearly account for a disproportionate share of disciplinary effort; in one study of middle school students in a large midwestern urban district, 6% of students were responsible for 44% of all office referrals (Skiba et al., 1997). Students who are suspended are also more likely to exhibit mental health problems (Eckenrode, Laird, & Doris, 1993; Morgan-D'Atrio et al., 1996).

Yet school disciplinary actions cannot be accounted for solely in terms of student behaviors. Teachers appear to differ greatly in their rate of disciplinary referral to the office; in one middle school in one study, two thirds of all disciplinary referrals came from 25% of the school's teachers (Skiba et al., 1997). School factors also strongly influence rates of suspension. Davis and Jordan (1994) reported high suspension rates in schools spending excessive amounts of time on discipline-related matters. Comparisons of schools with high and low use of school suspension indicate that low suspension schools have a lower student-teacher ratio and a higher level of academic quality (Hellman & Beaton, 1986), and pay significantly better attention to issues of school climate (Bickel & Qualls, 1980). Indeed, one national study found that school and district characteristics such as teacher attitudes and quality of school governance tend to be better predictors of suspension than student attitudes and behavior, prompting the researchers to conclude: "One could argue from this finding that if students are interested in reducing their chances of being suspended, they will be better off by transferring to a school with a lower suspension rate than by improving their attitudes or reducing their misbehavior" (Wu et al., 1982, p. 255–256).

Disproportionality in School Suspension

The expulsion of seven African-American students for two years in Decatur, Illinois represents the most publicized incident to date involving racial disproportionality in school discipline. Yet minority over-representation in school discipline is by no means a new issue. Both racial and economic biases in school suspension and expulsion have been studied extensively for over 25 years, with consistent results.

Socioeconomic and racial disproportionality in suspension.   The over-representation of minority and low-income students in the use of suspension has been consistently documented (Brantlinger, 1991; Skiba, Michael, Nardo, & Peterson, 2000; Wu et al., 1982). Virtually every study of school suspension including minorities for the last 25 years has found African American overrepresentation in school suspension, typically at a rate two to three times higher than that of Caucasian students (Costenbader & Markson, 1994; Glackman et al., 1978; Kaeser, 1979; Lietz & Gregory, 1978; Masssachusetts Advocacy Center, 1986; McCarthy & Hoge, 1987; McFadden, Marsh, Price, & Hwang, 1992; Skiba et al., 1997; Taylor & Foster, 1986; Thornton & Trent, 1988; Wu et al., 1982). Black students are also exposed more frequently to more punitive disciplinary strategies such as corporal punishment (Gregory, 1996; Shaw & Braden, 1990), and receive fewer mild disciplinary consequences when referred to the office (McFadden et al., 1992). Some have argued that African American overrepresentation in school suspension is not a matter of race, but is connected with social class (National

Association of Secondary School Principals, 2000). Yet suspension seems to be related to race above and beyond the effects of socioeconomic status. When economic status is controlled statistically, African American disproportionality in suspension remains (Skiba et al., 2000; Wu et al., 1982).

There is the possibility that African American students are suspended more because they misbehave more. In that case, disproportionality in suspension could be viewed as an appropriate response to higher levels of disruption. Yet school discipline researchers have found no evidence that African Americans misbehave at a significantly higher rate (McCarthy & Hoge, 1987; Wu et al., 1982). If anything, available research suggests that black students tend to receive harsher consequences for less severe or less objective offenses (McFadden et al., 1992; Shaw & Braden, 1990; Skiba et al., 2000).

Disproportionality of students with disabilities.   Research on rates of school suspension has also found disproportionate rates of school exclusion for students with disabilities. Studies of suspension in Kansas, Kentucky, Delaware, Minnesota, and national surveys have consistently found that students with disabilities represent around 20% of all students suspended, a disproportionately high percentage given that special education students represent around 11% of the population (Leone, Mayer, Malmgren, & Meisel, 2000). These data also indicate that the majority of behaviors for which students with disabilities are suspended are generally nonviolent in nature, and may not differ substantively from the behavior of nondisabled students.

It is difficult to know what to make of these data with respect to the argument that regulations prevent the discipline of students in special education. On the one hand, over-representation of special education students in school discipline creates some doubt concerning how much administrators are actually being limited in the suspension of those students. It might be argued, however, that the disciplinary disproportionality of at least some students (e.g., students with EBD [emotional and behavioral disabilities]) may be warranted by behavior that tends to be more extreme.

Suspension and Expulsion: How Effective?

The most important question in the use of disciplinary removal is the effectiveness of school exclusion. Unfortunately, there is little or no evidence showing that suspension or expulsion improves student behavior or contributes to overall school safety. The evidence suggests that suspension is ineffective for those students for whom it is used most often. Studies have found that up to 40% of school suspensions are due to repeat offenders (Bowditch, 1993; Costenbader & Markson, 1994; Massachusetts Advocacy Center, 1986), suggesting that this segment of the school population is decidedly not "getting the message" that disciplinary removal intends to teach. Tobin, Sugai, & Colvin (1996) reported that students suspended in sixth grade were more likely to be referred or suspended in middle school, prompting the researchers to conclude that, for some students, "suspension functions as a reinforcer... rather than as a punisher" (p. 91).

Nor are the long-term outcomes associated with suspension encouraging. The national High School and Beyond survey revealed that school dropouts were three times as likely to have been suspended as their peers who had stayed in school; suspension appears to be part of a constellation of factors, along with poor academics and low SES [socioeconomic status], predicting school dropout (Ekstrom, Goertz, Pollack, & Rock, 1986). Indeed, in some schools suspension appears to be used as a "pushout" tool; in these schools, repeated disciplinary removals are applied intentionally to certain students as a means of cleansing the school of persistent troublemakers who challenge school authority (Bowditch, 1993; Fine, 1986). Finally, over time, suspension and expulsion may be associated with an increased likelihood of delinquency. Criminal justice researchers have described gang involvement as a gradual process, starting with school alienation and requiring time to associate with those already in gangs (Patterson, 1992). Suspension and expulsion may thus accelerate the course of delinquency, by providing at-risk and alienated youth extra time to associate with deviant peers.

Summary

School suspension is among the most widely used disciplinary tactics in schools today, used for moderate offenses like fighting, as well as for minor offenses such as tardiness and disrespect. Yet there is currently no evidence that suspension or expulsion changes the behavior of difficult students. Rather, for troublesome or at-risk students, the most well-documented outcome of suspension appears to be further suspension, and eventually school dropout. Nor is there evidence that the use of suspension and expulsion makes a contribution to safer schools, and some evidence suggests that suspension is more widely used at schools with poor climate and less sound instruction. In an era almost defined by accountability, an instructional procedure that was used inconsistently, disproportionally targeted minorities, and was associated with increased school dropout might well be the target of a Senate investigation. It is indeed ironic that the most widely-used disciplinary tool in public schools, and the procedure at the heart of the special education disciplinary controversy, has just those characteristics.

A Comprehensive Model of School Violence Prevention

No less than five federally-initiated or federally-sponsored panels of national experts have been convened in the last five years to make recommendations concerning effective practice in violence prevention (Dwyer, Osher, & Warger, 1998; Elliott, Hatot, Sirovatka, & Potter, 2001; Gottfredson, 1997; Mihalic, Irwin, Elliott, Fagan, & Hansen, 2001; Thornton, Craft, Dahlberg, Lynch, & Baer, 2000); not one of those panels has included disciplinary removal as an effective or promising practice in addressing problems of youth violence. Rather, these reports, and the consensus in the field that they represent, indicate that it is possible to make a real difference in youth violence through preventive programs that teach students alternatives strategies for solving their problems. Consistently, effective programs have been found to be proactive rather than reactive; involve families, students and the community; and include multiple components that can address the complexity of school disruption and violence (Elliott, Hamburg, & Williams, 1998; Gottfredson, 1997; Hawkins et al., 2000). Indeed, preventive programs, while still emerging, appear to have more support for their effectiveness than do reactive and punitive approaches (Skiba & Peterson, 2000).

Recently, a comprehensive model of preventive discipline has begun to be supported by both research and mental health advocacy organizations as the approach most likely to successfully address the complexity of emotional problems and disruptive behavior in schools (American Psychological Association, 1993; Dwyer & Osher, 2000; Leone et al., 2000; Tolan, Guerra, & Kendall, 1995; Walker et al., 1996). The approach prescribes intervention at three levels:

- *Creating a Positive School Climate.* Targeting all students, effective schools implement schoolwide programs to encourage a positive connection between students and their school, and to teach alternatives to violence. Specific examples include unambiguous behavioral expectations, conflict resolution/peer mediation, bullying prevention, and proactive classroom management strategies.
- *Early Identification and Intervention.* A second level for violence prevention are selected strategies targeted for students who may be at-risk for violence. Just as important as identification, however, are programs that can provide support to alienated or at-risk youth, such as anger management or mentoring.
- *Effective Responses to Disruption and Crisis.* Effective responses and individualized programs are targeted toward a relatively small number of students demonstrating significant behavioral or emotional problems. Such options might include functional assessment, restorative justice, wraparound, school-based mental health services, and crisis management strategies.

Although the primary prevention model of school discipline and violence prevention is supported by some promising evaluations of comprehensive programs (Leone et al., 2000), more extensive study of both the model of comprehensive prevention and the individual components of that model is needed. Still, it might well be argued that the limited positive results for comprehensive alternatives to exclusionary discipline are far more promising than the largely negative results associated with the use of school suspension and expulsion.

The implementation of more effective alternatives for promoting school safety also requires improved training of school personnel in effective approaches to violence prevention. One must assume that school personnel do not rely on school suspension and expulsion because they enjoy excluding children from school. Rather, in many schools, there are simply few disciplinary tools available other than suspension and expulsion. Most distressingly, both regular and special education teachers commonly report feeling most under-prepared by their training programs in the area of classroom management (Calhoun, 1987; Leyser, 1986). Implementation of best practice in school discipline will require institutions of higher education to increase their training of teachers and administrators in dealing with student behavior, and especially in effective strategies that can contribute to comprehensive planning for school safety.

Resolving the Dilemma: Toward a Single Disciplinary System

In short, removing a student with disabilities based on disruptive or violent behavior is not ruled out by IDEA 97, but the conditions governing that removal are complex and difficult, yielding a perception by school administrators that the law has limited their options. It is difficult to see how policymakers can resolve the apparent conflict between the principles of due process and free and appropriate public education on one hand, and the desire to apply exclusionary discipline for purposes of school safety on the other. What are the options for resolution of the disciplinary dilemma?

Remedies within IDEA 97.   It is important to note that it is quite possible to resolve any special education/school discipline conflict at the local level, if school districts and parents can come to agreement. Virtually all of the due process procedures involving the stay-put provision and placement in an Interim Alternative Educational Setting are meant to resolve cases in which there is disagreement between parents and the school district. If parents and the school both agree to a 45 day placement for dangerousness, for example, the school district need not go to a hearing officer to request that placement. Certainly, the involvement of parents in both special education and in school discipline is an area requiring a great deal more attention in both practice and research.

Prior planning may also allow IEP teams to resolve disciplinary conflict well in advance of a disruptive incident. Apart from the specific disciplinary provisions of the law, IDEA 97 states that the IEP team should "consider, if appropriate, strategies, including positive behavioral interventions, strategies, and supports" to address the needs of students whose behaviors impede their own or others' learning (IDEA, 1997). For a student for whom behavior is an issue, the IEP team might, *a priori,* decide on an appropriate Interim Alternative Educational Setting should one become necessary, define the characteristics of a "pattern" of suspensions that would constitute a change of placement, and develop a functional assessment and individual behavior plan to prevent the occurrence of disruptive behavior. Prior planning and consensus should decrease the chances of conflict among team members if and when a student with disabilities transgresses against the school disciplinary code.

More extreme remedies: Repealing the disciplinary provisions?   Local remedies, pursued sincerely, may well resolve the vast majority of disciplinary disputes for individual students. Yet given the intensity of feelings generated by the controversy, one would expect policy disputes to continue. Critics of the IDEA 97 disciplinary provisions will probably continue to seek the repeal of disciplinary protections for students with disabilities, exposing those students to the same set of consequences faced by all other students. Yet if the purpose of that repeal is simply to regain the option of disciplinary removal for students served by special education, a review of the data concerning suspension and expulsion might well yield the response "Why?"

Suspension and expulsion continue to be among the most frequently used school disciplinary tools in general education, despite an almost complete lack of documentation that school removal is an effective procedure for improving student behavior or school safety. To meet the FAPE mandate, current special education regulations have constructed an alternative disciplinary approach whose purpose is to keep students in school, by using strategies (e.g. individual behavior planning) far more effective than exclusion in promoting positive social skills and behavior. There can be little doubt that the increased costs of that system, and the different treatment of students with disabilities, have indeed created tension between general and special education. But the question remains: Does it make sense to remove special education disciplinary protections regarding suspension and expulsion, simply to ensure that students with disabilities can be equally exposed to consequences that the preponderance of evidence suggests are unsound and perhaps discriminatory?

One must strongly empathize with those administrators who feel that IDEA 97 has limited their disciplinary options. Maintaining school discipline and ensuring school safety is a complex and difficult job, and anything that may make that job more difficult must be treated seriously. Yet if the only objection is that IDEA 97 limits the use of suspension and expulsion, then it might be said that the disciplinary options of schools were already distressingly limited, relying on strategies that may well be both unfair and ineffective in ensuring school safety.

One Effective and Accountable Disciplinary System

Given the gulf separating proponents and opponents of special disciplinary protections for students with disabilities, advocating for a single system of school discipline for both general and special education students might seem more than a little unrealistic. Yet proposals for a single disciplinary system have been made by both supporters and critics of IDEA 97 disciplinary regulations. Beverly Johns, past President of the Council for Exceptional Children and a staunch advocate for the rights of students with disabilities, argues that "Schools can eliminate a dual system of discipline if consequences other than suspension and expulsion are used" (Johns, 1998). The American Association of School Administrators, a vocal critic of the regulations, also advocates for a single disciplinary system, including mandatory alternative school placement for *all* children who are expelled, and full funding for special education programs (Hunter, 1999).

Any proposal for a unified system of discipline has to face the apparently conflicting demands of FAPE on the one hand, and school disciplinary measures meant to ensure school safety on the other. Yet it is critical to understand that these two principles come into conflict only under a certain definition of discipline. Defining school discipline solely or primarily as the ability to suspend and expel students for school disruption creates an ongoing conflict with special education law almost by definition, since the mandate of special education is to ensure continued education. The tension between the two systems is reduced or eliminated, however, if discipline is viewed, not as school removal, but as the comprehensive prevention of disruption through teaching appropriate alternatives to violence. The procedures and principles laid out in IDEA 97 are meant to protect students with disabilities from school exclusion, not from approaches that will improve their behavior. When discipline can be accomplished without school removal, the complex protections of special education law become largely irrelevant.

To reduce confusion and ensure equity for all students, a single system of discipline may well be the best course in the long term. Given the current state of best-practice knowledge in the field of school discipline, such a system would need to go well beyond disciplinary removal, to include the following characteristics:

- Suspension and expulsion are limited to only the most serious behavioral incidents.
- Preventive programs teach students alternatives to violence for solving their problems.
- Procedures are in place to identify troubled students who may be at risk for violence, as well as programs to help reconnect such students with their peers and classrooms.
- A broad array of responses to disruption reduce the need for suspension and expulsion, and individual behavior plans are developed for students with chronic behavior problems.
- Effective alternative school and in-school suspension programs are available to keep students who must be removed from class engaged in learning.
- The issue of minority overrepresentation in school discipline is being studied and addressed; that is, students of different groups are treated similarly for similar offenses, and overall disciplinary actions reflect the relative proportions in the population of various groups.[5]
- A disciplinary incident and critical incident data base is in place, and those data are used to evaluate the effectiveness of all school discipline and school safety measures.

It is important to note that such a proposal does not mean simply extending the protections of IDEA 97 to all students. Those elements of IDEA 97 that are both effective and logistically feasible for application to the broader population may make a contribution to a unified discipline system. But many strategies that have been shown to be effective in reducing student conflict and improving school climate, such as bullying prevention and violence prevention curricula, were developed and evaluated in general education settings. A unified system of school discipline would simply entail the application of those procedures that our best knowledge suggests are most likely to be effective in ensuring the safety of schools for all students.

Conclusion

The controversy created by the IDEA 97 may be less a function of the skill of the law's drafters than of the difficulty in reconciling two deeply held, but perhaps contradictory goals. Ultimately, it may be necessary to understand the futility of attempting to guarantee a free and appropriate public education to students with disabilities while at the same time retaining the option to exclude them from that education through suspension and exclusion.

Indeed, a review of both the special education disciplinary procedures and disciplinary removal in general makes explicit the fundamental irony of the special education discipline controversy. The disciplinary procedures that are at the heart of the controversy, suspension and expulsion, do not appear to make a positive contribution to school safety. Eliminating the IDEA disciplinary protections and exposing students with disabilities to more disciplinary removals might result in a system that appeared more fair, in the sense of treating all students equally. But given what we know about suspension and expulsion, it would also likely reduce the overall quality of American public education, by exposing more students to disciplinary procedures that are ineffective and perhaps discriminatory.

Focusing on a single, effective and non-exclusionary system of discipline for all students resolves the perceived contradiction between FAPE and school safety by addressing both of the primary values inherent in the special education discipline debate. Reducing the use of school exclusion as a consequence would obviate the conflict between school discipline and FAPE; there is no inherent conflict between FAPE and effective behavioral procedures that keep children engaged in education. Moreover, improving school discipline in general would likely increase the overall safety of schools, replacing procedures whose effect is largely negative with strategies that are at least promising in reducing school violence and disruption. The difficult, perhaps impossible, task faced by a dual system of discipline under current educational law is how to balance the basic values of FAPE and safe schools, given a set of disciplinary tools, suspension and expulsion, that appear incapable of guaranteeing either. In the long term, it will be more fruitful to have as our goal the development of a single system of discipline that relies upon procedures that are truly effective in promoting civil behavior and safe schools for all children.

Notes

1. For both placement in IAES due to drugs or weapons, or due to a ruling by a hearing officer that the student is dangerous, the removal may be extended at the end of the first 45-day period if school personnal are able to demonstrate that the child remains likely to create injury to self or others.

2. If, however, the school district petitions the hearing officer to extend that student's stay in the interim alternative educational setting past 45 days, then the student's placement prior to the interim alternative educational setting becomes the "current placement" in which the student must stay while appeals are pending.

3. If the manifestation determination review determines that, according to the above criteria, the disruptive behavior was not related to the student's disability, the student may be subjected to standard disciplinary procedures, including long-term suspension and expulsion. Yet even when there is no relationship between the behavior and disability, students with disabilities cannot be expelled or suspended for long periods without services. IDEA 97 reflects prior case law in requiring that services must be provided that enable the student to make progress toward meeting the goals in that student's IEP whenever a disciplinary removal constitutes a change in placement as defined above (*Metropolitan Sch. Dist. of Wayne Township v. Davila* (1992); *S-1 v. Turlington* (1981); see also the *New* letter (OSERS 1989) in which the Office of Special Education Programs declared that services consistent with the IEP had to be provided children with disabilities during a school expulsion).

4. Given that bills in Congress tend to be introduced and then dropped or combined with other legislation, it is difficult to arrive at an exact count of attempts to repeal the disciplinary provisions. A search of the Library of Congress THOMAS legislative information data base using the terms *IDEA* and *discipline*, however, yielded 17 pieces of legislation introduced addressing the disciplinary provisions of IDEA in the 106th session of Congress alone.

5. It might be objected that such a policy forces a "quota method" of discipline that would be inappropriate should minority students be responsible for a greater proportion of student misbehavior. Yet the absence of data showing that minority students are in fact responsible for a greater share of disruption suggests that, in cases of disproportionality of discipline, the onus may well be on the school district to show that statistical discrepancies in discipline are justified (see Advancement Project/Civil Rights Project, 2000).

References

Advancement Project/Civil Rights Project. (2000). *Opportunities suspended: The devastating consequences of zero tolerance and school discipline policies.* [online] http://www.law.harvard.edu/groups/civilrights/conferences/zero/zt_report2.html.

American Association of School Administrators (1998, September). Need for fairness creates state of emergency for IDEA. *AASA Online.* [online] http://www.aasa.org/Advocacy/legis9-16-98.htm.

American Psychological Association (1993). *Violence and youth: Psychology's response.* Washington, D.C.: Author.

Bickel, F., & Qualls, R. (1980). The impact of school climate on suspension rates in the Jefferson County Public Schools. *The Urban Review, 12,* 79–86.

Bowditch, C. (1993). Getting rid of troublemakers: High school disciplinary procedures and the production of dropouts. *Social Problems, 40,* 493–507.

Brantlinger, E. (1991). Social class distinctions in adolescents' reports of problems and punishment in school. *Behavioral Disorders, 17,* 36–46.

Calhoun, S. E. (1987). Are our future teachers prepared for the stress that lies ahead? *The Clearing House, 6,* 178–179.

Carr, E. G., & Durand, V. M. (1985). Reducing behavior problems through functional communication training. *Journal of Applied Behavior Analysis, 18,* 111–126.

Cooley, S. (1995). *Suspension/expulsion of regular and special education students in Kansas: A report to the Kansas State Board of Education.* Topeka, KS: Kansas State Board of Education.

Costenbader, V. K., & Markson, S. (1994). School suspension: A survey of current policies and practices. *NASSP Bulletin, 78,* 103–107.

Davis, J. E., & Jordan, W. J. (1994). The effects of school context, structure, and experiences on African American males in middle and high schools. *Journal of Negro Education, 63,* 570–587.

Doe v. Koger, 489 F. Supp. 225 (N.D. Ind. 1979).

Dupper, D. R., & Bosch, L. A. (1996). Reasons for school suspensions: An examination of data from one school district and recommendations for reducing suspensions. *Journal for a Just and Caring Education, 2,* 140–150.

Dwyer, K., & Osher, D. (2000). *Safeguarding our children: An action guide.* Washington, D.C.: U.S. Departments of Education and Justice, American Institutes for Research.

Dwyer, K., Osher, D., and Warger, C. (1998). *Early warning, timely response: A guide to safe schools.* Washington, D.C.: U.S. Department of Education.

Eckenrode, J., Laird, M., & Doris, J. (1993). School performance and disciplinary problems among abused and neglected children. *Developmental Psychology, 29,* 53–62.

Ekstrom, R. B., Goertz, M. E., Pollack, J. M., & Rock, D. A. (1986). Who drops out of high school and why?: Findings from a national study. *Teachers College Record, 87,* 357–373.

Elliott, D. S., Hamburg, B. A., & Williams, K. R. (1998). *Violence in American schools: A new perspective.* New York: Cambridge University Press.

Elliott, D., Hatot, N. J., Sirovatka, P., & Potter, B. B. (2001). *Youth violence: A report of the Surgeon General.* Washington, D.C.: U. S. Surgeon General.

Fine, M. (1986). Why urban adolescents drop into and out of public high school. *Teachers College Record, 87,* 393–409.

Glackman, T., Martin, R., Hyman, I., McDowell, E., Berv, V., & Spino, P. (1978). Corporal punishment, school suspension, and the civil rights of students: An analysis of Office for Civil Rights school surveys. *Inequality in Education, 23,* 61–65.

Gottfredson, D. (1997). School-based crime prevention. In L. Sherman, D. Gottfredson, D. MacKenzie, J. Eck, P. Ruter, & S. Bushway (Eds.), *Preventing crime: What works, what doesn't, what's promising: A report to the United States Congress* (pp. 1–74). Washington, D.C.: U.S. Department of Justice, Office of Justice Programs.

Gregory, J. F. (1996). The crime of punishment: Racial and gender disparities in the use of corporal punishment in the U.S. Public Schools. *Journal of Negro Education, 64,* 454–462.

"Groups critical of no second chances school proposal." (1999, January 27). *Baltimore Sun,* p. 4B.

Gun-Free Schools Act of 1994, Public Law 103–382, 108 Statute 3907, Title 14.

H.R. 1, The No Child Left Behind Act of 2001, Amendment 13.

Hartwig, E. P., & Ruesch, G. M. (2000). Disciplining students in special education. *Journal of Special Education, 33,* 240–247.

Hawkins, J. D., Herrenkohl, T. I., Ferrington, D. P., Brewer, D., Catalano, R. F., Harachi, T. W., & Cothern, L. (2000, April). Predictors of youth violence. *Juvenile Justice Bulletin.* Washington, D.C.: U.S. Department of Justice, Office of Juvenile Justice and Delinquency Prevention.

Hellman, D. A., & Beaton, S. (1986). The pattern of violence in urban public schools: The influence of school and community. *Journal of Research in Crime and Delinquency, 23,* 102–127.

Honig v. Doe. 484 U.S. 305 (1988).

Hunter, B. (1999, June). AASA supports single discipline standard in Juvenile Justice bill. *AASA Online.* [online] http://www.aasa.org/Advocacy/6-22-99norwood.htm.

Imich, A. J. (1994). Exclusions from school: Current trends and issues. *Educational Research, 36*(1), 3–11.

Improving America's Schools Act, P.L. 103–382, Sect. 314(a). (1994)

Individuals with Disabilities Education Act (IDEA), 20 U.S.C. §§ 1401 *et seq*; Individuals with Disabilities Education Act Amendments of 1997, Public Law 105–17, 105th Cont., 1st sess.; Individuals with Disabilities Education Act Regulations, 34 C.F.R. 300.1 *et seq.*

Iwata, B. A., Dorsey, M. F., Slifer, K. J., Bauman, K. E., & Richman, G. S. (1982). Toward a functional analysis of self-injury. *Analysis and Intervention in Developmental Disabilities, 2,* 3–20.

Johns, B. H. (1998). What the new Individuals with Disabilities Education Act (IDEA) means for students who exhibit aggressive or violent behavior. *Preventing School Failure, 42*(3), 102–105.

Jones, N. L. (2001, June 22). Amendments relating to the discipline of children with disabilities in H. R. 1 and S. 1, 107th Congress. *CRS Report for Congress.*

Kaeser, S. C. (1979). Suspensions in school discipline. *Education and Urban Society, 11,* 465–484.

Katsiyannis, A., & Maag, J. W. (1998). Disciplining students with disabilities: Issues and considerations for implementing IDEA 97. *Behavioral Disorders, 23,* 276–289.

Koch, K. (2000, March). Zero tolerance: Is mandatory punishment in schools unfair? *Congressional Quarterly Researcher, 10*(9), 185–208.

Leone, P. E., Mayer, M. J., Malmgren, K., & Meisel, S. M. (2000). School violence and disruption: Rhetoric, reality, and reasonable balance. *Focus on Exceptional Children, 33*(1), 1–20.

Leyser, Y. (1986). Competencies needed for teaching individuals with special needs: The perspective of student teachers. *The Clearing House, 59* (4), 179–181.

Lietz, J. J., & Gregory, M. K. (1978). Pupil race and sex determinants of office and exceptional education referrals. *Educational Research Quarterly, 3*(2), 61–66.

Mansfield, W., & Farris, E. (1992). *Office for Civil Rights survey redesign: A feasibility study.* Rockville, MD: Westat, Inc.

McCarthy, J. D., & Hoge, D. R. (1987). The social construction of school punishment: Racial disadvantage out of universalistic process. *Social Forces, 65,* 1101–1120.

McCarthy, M. M., Cambron-McCabe, N. H., & Thomas, S. B. (1998). *Public school law: Teacher and students' rights.* Boston: Allyn & Bacon.

McFadden, A. C., Marsh, G. E., Price, B. J., & Hwang, Y. (1992). A study of race and gender bias in the punishment of handicapped school children. *Urban Review, 24,* 239–251.

Menacker, J. C., Hurwitz, E., & Weldon, W. (1988). Legislating school discipline: The application of a systemwide discipline code to schools in a large urban district. *Urban Education, 23,* 12–23.

Mihalic, S., Irwin, K., Elliott, D., Fagan, A., & Hansen, D. (2001, July). *Blueprints for violence prevention (OJJDP Juvenile Justice Bulletin).* Washington, D. C.: U.S. Department of Justice, Office of Juvenile Justice and Delinquency Prevention. [online] http://ncjrs.org/html/ojjdp/jjbul2001_7_3/contents.html.

Mills v. Board of Education of the District of Columbia, 348 F. Supp. 866 (D.D.C. 1972).

Morgan-D'Atrio, C., Northrup, J., LaFleur, L., & Spera, S. (1996). Toward prescriptive alternatives to suspensions: A preliminary evaluation. *Behavioral Disorders, 21,* 190–200.

Morrison, G. M., & D'Incau, B. (1997). The web of zero-tolerance: Characteristics of students who are recommended for expulsion from school. *Education and Treatment of Children, 20,* 316–335.

National Association of Secondary School Principals (2000, February). *Statement on civil rights implications of zero tolerance programs.* Testimony presented to the United States Commission on Civil Rights, Washington, D.C.

Nelson, J.R., Mathur, S. R., & Rutherford, R.B. (1999). Has public policy exceeded our knowledge base? A review of the functional behavioral assessment literature. *Behavior Disorders, 24,* 169–179.

OCR Letter of Finding, EHLR 307.06 (Office for Civil Rights, 1988).

Osborne, A. G. (1998). The principal and discipline with special education students. *NASSP Bulletin, 82*(599), 1–8.

OSEP Memorandum 95-16, 22 IDELR 531 (OSEP 1995).

OSEP Memorandum, "Initial Disciplinary Guidance Related to Removal of Children with Disabilities from their Current Educational Placement for Ten School Days or Less." (OSEP 97-7).

Patterson, G.R. (1992). Developmental changes in antisocial behavior. In R. D. Peters, R. J. McMahon, & V. L. Quinsey (Eds.), *Aggression and violence throughout the life span* (pp. 52–82). Newbury Park, CA: Sage.

Rose, T. L. (1988). Current disciplinary practices with handicapped students: Suspensions and expulsions. *Exceptional Children, 55,* 230–239.

Rutherford Institute. (2000). Press release: Eighth-grade student suspended for saving friend's life: Rutherford attorneys file complaint in circuit court. [online] http://www.rutherford.org/courts/hot-cases.asp#18.

S-1 v. Turlington, 635 F.2d (5th Cir. 1981), *cert. denied,* 454 U.S. 1030 (1981).

S. 1, The Better Education for Students and Teachers Act of 2001, Amendment 604.

S. Rept. 105-17, 105th Congress, 1st Sess. 28 (1997).

Shaw, S. R., & Braden, J. P. (1990). Race and gender bias in the administration of corporal punishment. *School Psychology Review, 19,* 378–383.

Sinclair, B. (1999). *Report on state implementation of the Gun-Free Schools Act: School Year 1997-98.* Rockville, MD: Westat.

Skiba, R. J., & Peterson, R. L. (2000). School discipline: From zero tolerance to early response. *Exceptional Children, 66,* 335–347.

Skiba, R. J., Peterson, R. L., & Williams, T. (1997). Office referrals and suspension: Disciplinary intervention in middle schools. *Education and Treatment of Children, 20*(3), 295–315.

Skiba, R. J., Michael, R. S., Nardo, A. C., & Peterson, R. (2000). *The color of discipline: Sources of racial and gender disproportionality in school punishment.* Bloomington, IN: Indiana University, Indiana Education Policy Center.

Smith, C. R. (2000). Behavioral and discipline provisions of IDEA '97: Implicit competencies yet to be confirmed. *Exceptional Children, 66,* 403–412.

Taylor, M. C., & Foster, G. A. (1986). Bad boys and school suspensions: Public policy implications for black males. *Sociological Inquiry, 56,* 498–506.

Thornton, T. N., Craft, C. A., Dahlberg, L. L., Lynch, B. S., & Baer, K. (2000). *Best practices of youth violence prevention: A sourcebook for community action.* Atlanta: Centers for Disease Control and Prevention, National Center for Injury Prevention and Control.

Thornton, C. H., & Trent, W. (1988). School desegregation and suspension in East Baton Rouge Parish: A preliminary report. *Journal of Negro Education, 57,* 482–501.

Tobin, T., Sugai, G., & Colvin, G. (1996). Patterns in middle school discipline records. *Journal of Emotional and Behavioral Disorders, 4*(2), 82–94.

Tolan, P. H., Guerra, N. G., & Kendall, P. C. (1995). Introduction to special section: Prediction and prevention of antisocial behavior in children and adolescents. *Journal of Consulting and Clinical Psychology, 63*(4), 515–517.

Walker, H. M., Horner, R. H., Sugai, G., Bullis, M., Sprague, J. R., Bricker, D., & Kaufman, M. J. (1996). Integrated approaches to preventing antisocial behavior patterns among school-age children and youth. *Journal of Emotional and Behavioral Disorders, 4*(4), 194–209.

Wing, B., & Keleher, T. (2000, Spring). Zero tolerance: An interview with Jesse Jackson on race and school discipline. *Colorlines, 3*(1). [on-line] http://www.arc.org/C_Lines/CLArchive/story3_1_01.html.

Wu, S. C., Pink, W. T., Crain, R. L., & Moles, O. (1982). Student suspension: A critical reappraisal. *The Urban Review, 14*, 245–303; Massachusetts Advocacy Center (1986). *The way out: Student exclusion practices in Boston Middle Schools.* Boston, MA: Author.

Yell, M. L. (1998). *The law and special education.* Upper Saddle River, NJ: Merrill/ Prentice Hall.

POSTSCRIPT

Are Schools Limited in Their Ability to Discipline Students With Disabilities?

King laments the difficulties faced by administrators who are held to inconsistent and unclear court precedents that effectively prevent suspension or expulsion of students with disabilities, even if no direct link to a disability can be determined. He advocates for clarity of direction so that administrators can focus more on students and worry less about litigation. He holds that every student has the right to be held accountable for his or her own behavior and that special education laws often prevent students from being responsible.

According to Skiba, IDEA97 resolved some of the issues that King mentions, providing more latitude to schools and bringing more consistency to the mesh of special education and federal laws. Skiba does, however, question the broader issue of how an orderly school is achieved. He advocates for whole school change, arguing that every student—disabled or nondisabled—benefits more from a proactive approach that teaches and rewards desirable behavior than from the current punitive approach.

IDEA97 has made significant changes in the ability that administrators have to discipline students with disabilities. One of the most notable provisions requires teams to complete a functional behavioral assessment (FBA) whenever a student with a disability displays a behavior that could be punishable by suspension or expulsion. Through an FBA, teams determine what triggered the undesirable behavior and what need was filled by the behavior. Katsiyannis and Maag (*Behavioral Disorders,* 1998) argue that FBAs are a critical positive change and that they help teams to decide if a student's behavior is linked to his or her disability, how to teach more appropriate behavior, and whether or not the current program meets the student's needs. The authors do caution that although FBAs yield much valuable information, they require considerable time. Teachers will need to learn how to gather and analyze data to glean useful information.

When asked about the link between the individual education program (IEP) and behavioral difficulties, teachers reported that the IEP was so cumbersome, it was not often consulted for disciplinary issues (Butera, Klein, McMullen, and Wilson, *The Journal of Special Education,* 1998). If this is what teachers thought before an FBA became required, will this important new responsibility be effectively implemented?

Osborne (*NASSP Bulletin,* 1998) asserts that IDEA97 does provide options for schools but strongly advises educators not to wait until a behavioral crisis erupts in order to address a student's disabilities, especially those affecting expectations for school conduct.

ISSUE 7

Will More Federal Oversight Result in Better Special Education?

YES: National Council on Disability, from *Back to School on Civil Rights: Advancing the Federal Commitment to Leave No Child Behind* (January 25, 2000)

NO: Frederick M. Hess and Frederick J. Brigham, from "How Federal Special Education Policy Affects Schooling in Virginia," in Chester E. Finn, Jr., Andrew J. Rotherham, and Charles R. Hokanson, Jr., eds., *Rethinking Special Education for a New Century* (Thomas B. Fordham Foundation & Progressive Policy Institute, 2001)

ISSUE SUMMARY

YES: The National Council on Disability (NCD), an independent federal agency dedicated to promoting policies, programs, practices, and procedures that guarantee equal opportunity and empowerment for all individuals with disabilities, found that all 50 U.S. states are out of compliance with special education law, a condition that the council argues must be remedied by increased federal attention.

NO: Frederick M. Hess, an assistant professor of education and government, and Frederick J. Brigham, an assistant professor of education, both at the University of Virginia, maintain that increased federal monitoring will only deepen the separation between general and special education, drawing resources away from true educational excellence for all.

Federal and state laws regarding special education were written to compel school districts to design and deliver education to students with disabilities. The rules and regulations for IDEA97, the federal special education law, can be found in full at http://www.ideapractices.org/finalregs.htm. Hard copies of the regulations fill over 100 pages of the *Federal Register*, in tiny type. These regulations translate IDEA97 into operational elements, ranging from definitions of terms to the contents of an individual education program (IEP), to the substance, form, and timelines of communications with families, to reporting responsibilities to federal agencies. In short, the regulations guide the daily practices of schools.

Comparable regulations exist for Section 504 of the Rehabilitation Act of 1973. These regulations are designed to eliminate discrimination on the basis of disability in any program or activity that receives federal funds.

Beyond these, each state has its own specific statutes and accompanying regulations governing the education of nondisabled children and those with disabilities. Although there is much similarity between state and federal requirements, states are free to exceed federal requirements and to add unique local expectations.

Interpreting and implementing these layers of laws and regulations is not a one-time task. Changes in any of these laws mean changes in school practice. Parents who do not believe that the rights of their children are being preserved may seek resolution through administrative hearings or action before a state or federal court. As legal cases clarify the meaning of any of these laws, schools adjust to these interpretations.

As with most situations in which the weight of law is used to force action, the process of ensuring compliance is complicated and detailed. Each state is audited by the federal government periodically. In turn, states evaluate the performance of each school district. Some oversight takes place in regular reports of practices and finances. Periodically, more extensive study occurs during on-site visits to districts, which include record reviews and interviews with educators and parents. States and districts that refuse to correct identified faults run the risk of losing federal special education funds.

In an extensive study of federal monitoring and enforcement of elements of IDEA, the National Council on Disability (NCD) found that, despite more than 20 years of effort, there is not one U.S. state that fully and accurately complies with IDEA's requirements. In the following selection, the NCD delineates how the promises of IDEA—and the educational rights of children with disabilities—remain unmet by weak oversight procedures, poor follow-through, and lack of consequences for repeated failings. The NCD recommends implementing changes to ensure the civil rights of children with disabilities and a strong special education system.

In the second selection, Frederick M. Hess and Frederick J. Brigham, reflecting on the impact of federal regulations in Virginia, assert that the current emphasis on compliance forces districts to focus more on procedures than on children. Filling out forms according to regulation takes precedence over ensuring good programs for children. Also, money spent on compliance details reduces money spent on services for children. Hess and Brigham hold that strict adherence to rigid procedures creates an adversarial system that engenders distrust between families and educators and unnecessary divisions in school districts.

As you read these selections, ask yourself whether or not meeting the letter of the law prevents meeting the spirit of the law. Does holding states and districts to exacting standards help or hinder the implementation of an effective educational program?

Back to School on Civil Rights

Executive Summary

Twenty-five years ago, Congress enacted and President Gerald Ford signed the Education for All Handicapped Children Act, one of the most important civil rights laws ever written. The basic premise of this federal law, now known as the Individuals with Disabilities Education Act (IDEA), is that all children with disabilities have a federally protected civil right to have available to them a free appropriate public education that meets their education and related services needs in the least restrictive environment. The statutory right articulated in IDEA is grounded in the Constitution's guarantee of equal protection under law and the constitutional power of Congress to authorize and place conditions on participation in federal spending programs. It is complemented by the federal civil rights protections contained in section 504 of the Rehabilitation Act of 1973, as amended, and Title II of the Americans with Disabilities Act.

This report, the second in a series of independent analyses by the National Council on Disability (NCD) of federal enforcement of civil rights laws, looks at more than two decades of federal monitoring and enforcement of compliance with Part B of IDEA. Overall, NCD finds that federal efforts to enforce the law over several Administrations have been inconsistent, ineffective, and lacking any real teeth. The report includes recommendations to the President and the Congress that would build on the 1997 reauthorization of IDEA. The intent is to advance a more aggressive, credible, and meaningful federal approach to enforcing this critical civil rights law, so that the nation's 25-year-old commitment to effective education for all children will be more fully realized.

Background

In 1970, before enactment of the federal protections in IDEA, schools in America educated only one in five students with disabilities. More than 1 million students were excluded from public schools, and another 3.5 million did not receive appropriate services. Many states had laws excluding certain students,

From National Council on Disability, *Back to School on Civil Rights: Advancing the Federal Commitment to Leave No Child Behind* (January 25, 2000). Washington, D.C.: U.S. Government Printing Office, 2000. Notes omitted.

including those who were blind, deaf, or labeled "emotionally disturbed" or "mentally retarded." Almost 200,000 school-age children with mental retardation or emotional disabilities were institutionalized. The likelihood of exclusion was greater for children with disabilities living in low-income, ethnic and racial minority, or rural communities.

In the more than two decades since its enactment, IDEA implementation has produced important improvements in the quality and effectiveness of the public education received by millions of American children with disabilities. Today almost 6 million children and young people with disabilities ages 3 through 21 qualify for educational interventions under Part B of IDEA. Some of these students with disabilities are being educated in their neighborhood schools in regular classrooms. These children have a right to have support services and devices such as assistive listening systems, braille text books, paraprofessional supports, curricular modifications, talking computers, and speech synthesizers made available to them as needed to facilitate their learning side-by-side with their nondisabled peers. Post-secondary and employment opportunities are opening up for increasing numbers of young adults with disabilities as they leave high school. Post-school employment rates for youth served under Part B are twice that of older adults with disabilities who did not benefit from IDEA in school, and self-reports indicate that the percentage of college freshmen with a disability has almost tripled since 1978.

Findings

As significant as the gains over time are, they tell only part of the story. In the past 25 years states have not met their general supervisory obligations to ensure compliance with the core civil rights requirements of IDEA at the local level. Children with disabilities and their families are required far too often to file complaints to ensure that the law is followed. The Federal Government has frequently failed to take effective action to enforce the civil rights protections of IDEA when federal officials determine that states have failed to ensure compliance with the law. Although Department of Education [DoED] Secretary Richard W. Riley has been more aggressive in his efforts to monitor compliance and take formal enforcement action involving sanctions than all his predecessors combined, formal enforcement of IDEA has been very limited. Based on its review of the Department of Education's monitoring reports of states between 1994 and 1998, NCD found:

- Every state was out of compliance with IDEA requirements to some degree; in the sampling of states studied, noncompliance persisted over many years.
- Notwithstanding federal monitoring reports documenting widespread noncompliance, enforcement of the law is the burden of parents who too often must invoke formal complaint procedures and due process hearings, including expensive and time-consuming litigation, to obtain the appropriate services and supports to which their children are entitled under the law. Many parents with limited resources are unable to

challenge violations successfully when they occur. Even parents with significant resources are hard-pressed to prevail over state education agencies (SEAs) and local education agencies (LEAs) when they or their publicly financed attorneys choose to be recalcitrant.

- The Department of Education has made very limited use of its authority to impose enforcement sanctions such as withholding of funds or making referrals to the Department of Justice, despite persistent failures to ensure compliance in many states.
- DoED has not made known to the states and the public any objective criteria for using enforcement sanctions, so that the relationship between findings of noncompliance by federal monitors and a decision to apply sanctions is not clear.

DoED Monitoring Model

The oversight model adopted by the Department of Education is multitiered and multipurpose. The Office of Special Education Programs (OSEP) distributes federal IDEA funding to the states and monitors the SEAs. The SEAs in turn monitor the LEAs to make sure they are in compliance with IDEA. In this tiered oversight model, the same Department of Education office (OSEP) distributes federal funds, monitors compliance, and enforces the law where violations are identified. The politics and conflicts inherent in administering these three disparate functions have challenged the Department's ability to integrate and balance the objectives of all three.

Data Sources and Summary of Analyses

As mentioned above, NCD found that the most recent federal monitoring reports demonstrated that every state failed to ensure compliance with the requirements of IDEA to some extent during the period covered by this review. More than half of the states failed to ensure compliance in five of the seven main compliance areas. For example, in OSEP's most recent monitoring reports, 90 percent of the states (n = 45) had failed to ensure compliance in the category of general supervision (the state mechanism for ensuring that LEAs are carrying out their responsibilities to ensure compliance with the law); 88 percent of the states (n = 44) had failed to ensure compliance with the law's secondary transition services provisions, which require schools to promote the appropriate transition of students with disabilities to work or post-secondary education; 80 percent of the states (n = 40) failed to ensure compliance with the law's free appropriate public education requirements; 78 percent of the states (n = 39) failed to ensure compliance with the procedural safeguards provisions of the law; and 72 percent of the states (n = 36) failed to ensure compliance with the placement in the least restrictive environment requirements of IDEA. In the two remaining major compliance areas, IEPs [individual education programs] and protection in evaluation, 44 percent of the states (n = 22) failed to ensure compliance with the former and 38 percent of the states (n = 19) failed to ensure compliance with the latter.

Enforcement Authority

Currently, the U.S. Department of Education has neither the authority nor the resources to investigate and resolve individual complaints alleging noncompliance. The Department does consult with and share some of its enforcement authority with the U.S. Department of Justice (DOJ), which has no independent litigation authority. Yet between the date it was given explicit referral authority in 1997 and the date this report went to the printer, DoED had not sent a single case to DOJ for "substantial noncompliance," and had articulated no objective criteria for defining that important term. The Department of Justice, whose role has been largely limited to participation as an amicus in IDEA litigation, does not appear to have a process for determining what cases to litigate.

Overall Enforcement Action

Despite the high rate of failure to ensure compliance with Part B requirements indicated in the monitoring reports for all states, only one enforcement action involving a sanction (withholding) and five others involving imposition of "high risk" status and corrective action as a prerequisite to receiving further funds have been taken. The only withholding action occurred once for a temporary period and was overruled by a federal court. Overall, the DoED tends to emphasize collaboration with the states through technical assistance and developing corrective action plans or compliance agreements for addressing compliance problems. There appear to be no clear-cut, objective criteria for determining which enforcement options ought to be applied and when to enforce in situations of substantial and persistent noncompliance.

Recommendations for Strengthening Federal Enforcement

NCD makes the following recommendations to strengthen the capacity of both the Department of Education and the Department of Justice to more effectively enforce IDEA:

- Congress should amend IDEA to create a complaint-handling process at the federal level to address systemic violations occurring in a SEA or LEA. Congress should designate the Department of Justice to administer the process and allocate adequate funding to enable the Department to take on this new role. This new federal complaint process should be designed to complement, not supplant, complaint procedures and the due process hearing at the state level. The federal process should be simple to use and easy to understand by parents and students.

- Congress should amend IDEA to provide the Department of Justice with independent authority to investigate and litigate cases brought under IDEA. The Department of Justice should be authorized to develop and disseminate explicit criteria for the types of alleged systemic violation complaints it will prioritize given its limited resources.

- Congress should include in the amendment that the Department of Education and the Department of Justice shall consult with students with disabilities, their parents, and other stakeholders to develop objective criteria for defining "substantial noncompliance," the point at which a state that fails to ensure compliance with IDEA's requirements will be referred to the Department of Justice for legal action.

- Congress should ask the General Accounting Office (GAO) to conduct a study of the extent to which SEAs and LEAs are ensuring that the requirements of IDEA in the areas of general supervision, secondary transition services, free appropriate public education, procedural safeguards, and placement in the least restrictive environment are being met. In addition, the DoED Office of Inspector General (OIG) should conduct regular independent special education audits (fiscal and program). The purpose of the audits would be to examine whether federal funds granted under IDEA Parts B and D (State Program Improvement Grants) have been and are being spent in compliance with IDEA requirements. These audits should supplement OSEP's annual compliance-monitoring visits, and the audit results should be in DoED's annual report to Congress. To the extent that the DoED OIG lacks the subject-matter expertise to conduct program audits under IDEA, the OIG should contract with independent entities having such expertise when a program audit is necessary.

- The Department of Education should establish and use national compliance standards and objective measures for assessing state progress toward better performance outcomes for children with disabilities and for achieving full compliance with Part B.

- The Department of Education should consult with students with disabilities, their parents and other stakeholders in developing and implementing a range of enforcement sanctions that will be triggered by specific indicators and measures indicating a state's failure to ensure compliance with Part B.

- When Congress and the President approve an increase in the funding to be distributed to local schools under Part B, Congress and the President should appropriate at the same time an amount equal to 10 percent of the total increase in Part B funding to be used to build the Department of Justice's and the Department of Education's enforcement, complaint-handling, and technical assistance infrastructure to effectively enable the federal agencies to drive improvements in state compliance and ensure better outcomes for children.

Personnel Training Needs

Regular and special education teachers in many states are frustrated by the mixed messages regarding compliance from school administrators, local special education directors, state oversight agents, school district attorneys, and federal oversight agents. Teachers ultimately bear the responsibility to implement interventions and accommodations for students with disabilities, often without adequate training, planning time, or assistance. They must function within an educational system that often lacks adequate commitment, expertise, or funding to deliver appropriate services to every child who needs them. School administrators, special education directors, school principals, and agents of federal, state, and local governments must stop working at cross purposes and commit to working together to resolve, not conceal or ignore, these very real problems. If the Federal Government continues to refrain from taking enforcement action in the face of widespread failures to ensure Part B compliance, this atmosphere of questionable commitment to the civil rights of students with disabilities will continue.

Advocacy Service Needs

Pervasive and persistent noncompliance with IDEA is a complex problem with often dramatic implications on a daily basis for the lives of children with disabilities and their families. Too many parents continue to expend endless resources in confronting obstacles to their child's most basic right to an appropriate education, often at the expense of their personal lives, their financial livelihoods, and their careers. Students are frustrated—their skills undeveloped and their sense of belonging tenuous. When informal efforts have failed to end unnecessary segregation or inappropriate programming for individual children, many have used the rights and protections afforded by IDEA to successfully challenge these injustices. Advocacy and litigation have been essential to ending destructive patterns of recurring noncompliance. Litigation has resulted in important victories for the children involved and better outcomes for other students with disabilities by exposing and remedying systemic noncompliance with IDEA. Yet legal services are often far beyond the financial reach of many families of students with disabilities.

Children with disabilities and their families are often the least prepared to advocate for their rights in the juvenile justice, immigration and naturalization, and child welfare systems when egregious violations occur. Children with disabilities and their families who are non-English speaking, or who live in low-income, ethnic or racial minority, and rural communities, are frequently not represented as players in the process. These individuals must be included and given the information and resources they need to contribute and advocate for themselves.

Recommendations for Training and Advocacy

Accordingly, NCD makes the following recommendations:

- When Congress and the President approve an increase in the funding to be distributed to local schools under Part B of IDEA, Congress and the President should appropriate at the same time an amount equal to 10 percent of the total Part B increase to fund free or low-cost legal advocacy services to students with disabilities and their parents through public and private legal service providers, putting competent legal assistance within their financial reach and beginning to level the playing field between them and their local school districts.
- The Department of Education should give priority support to the formation of a comprehensive and coordinated advocacy and technical assistance system in each state. The Department should develop a separate OSEP-administered funding stream to aid public and private advocacy entities in each state in collaborating to expand and coordinate self-advocacy training programs, resources, and services for students with disabilities and their parents throughout the state. Elements of the coordinated advocacy and technical assistance systems should include:

  - The availability of a lawyer at every state Parent Training and Information (PTI) Center, a protection and advocacy agency, legal services, and independent living center to provide legal advice and representation to students with disabilities and their parents in advocating for their legal rights under IDEA.
  - Self-advocacy training programs for students with disabilities and their parents focused on civil rights awareness, education and secondary transition services planning, and independent living in the community.
  - The establishment of a national backup center with legal materials, training, and other supports available for attorneys working on IDEA cases and issues at the state level.
  - Expansion of involvement by the private bar and legal services organizations in providing legal advice to students with disabilities and their parents in advocating for their legal rights under IDEA.
  - Training in culturally sensitive dispute resolution to meet the needs of growing populations of citizens from racial and ethnic backgrounds having diverse traditions and customs. Multiple language needs and communication styles must be accommodated in all training.

Full compliance with IDEA will ultimately be the product of collaborative partnership and long-term alliances among all parties having an interest in how IDEA is implemented. For such partnerships to be effective, all interested parties must be well prepared to articulate their needs and advocate for their objectives. To that end, coordinated statewide strategies of self-advocacy training for students with disabilities and their parents are vital. To make this happen, NCD recommends the following:

- The Department of Education should fund additional technical assistance, training, and dissemination of materials to meet continuing needs in the following areas:

  - Culturally appropriate technical assistance, which should be available to ensure that American Indian children with disabilities, their families, tribal leaders, and advocates in every interested tribe can participate as full partners in implementing IDEA in their communities. Culturally appropriate training and technical assistance should be developed and delivered through the satellite offices of newly created disability technical assistance centers (DBTACs) managed and staffed primarily by Native Americans that serve American Indian communities around the country.
  - Training to enhance evaluation skills for parents to assess the effectiveness of their states' IDEA compliance-monitoring systems.
  - Training of the appropriate agents (officials, advocates, and other stakeholders) in the immigration and naturalization and child welfare systems in IDEA's civil rights requirements.
  - Training of the appropriate agents (officials, advocates, and other stakeholders) in the juvenile justice system in IDEA's civil rights requirements, how they apply within the juvenile justice system, and ways the law can be used to help minimize detention of children with disabilities in the juvenile justice system.

A Six-State In-Depth Sample

NCD looked in depth at a sampling of six states, using the last three monitoring reports to assess the compliance picture in those states over time. The first two of the monitoring reports for these six states (covering a period from 1983–1998) included failure to ensure compliance with a total of 66 Part B requirements. Only 27 percent (n = 18) of the 66 violations had been corrected by the time of the third report. Based on the reported data, in 73 percent (n = 48) of the 66 violations, either the six states still failed to ensure compliance or no compliance finding was reported at all in the last monitoring report.

To date federal compliance-monitoring and enforcement efforts have not fully dealt with the root causes of widespread noncompliance, and children with disabilities and their parents have suffered the consequences. This report details NCD's findings and recommendations for improving the effectiveness of federal efforts to ensure state compliance with IDEA and related legislation. NCD calls on Congress and the President to work together to address the inadequacies identified by this report so that children and families will have an effective and responsive partner in the Federal Government when they seek to ensure that IDEA's goals of enhanced school system accountability and improved performance outcomes for students with disabilities move from the language of the law to the reality of each American classroom.

IDEA mandates that school systems respond to the needs of individual children with disabilities, making education accessible to them, regardless of the severity of their disabilities. Teachers today know that education tailored to individual needs and learning styles can make all the difference in the quality of a child's learning, whether or not she has a disability. Very few public schools consistently and effectively deliver this individualized approach for all children. Accordingly, many children fall through the cracks, as performance on achievement tests across the nation demonstrates. Alternatives to traditional public education such as charter and private schools, as well as political calls for vouchers, indicate growing public dissatisfaction with schools that do not educate all children effectively. IDEA calls for a responsive public education system that meets the individual learning needs of students with disabilities. It also contains a blueprint for the future of public education—where no child is left behind, and all children have an equal opportunity to gain the knowledge and skills they need to fulfill their dreams.

Ultimately, the enforcement of the civil rights protections of IDEA will make a difference to every child, not only children with disabilities. At the national summit on disability policy hosted by NCD in 1996, more than 350 disability advocates called for a unified system of education that incorporates all students into the vision of IDEA. NCD's 1996 report, *Achieving Independence,* presents the outline of a system in which every child, with or without a disability, has an individualized educational program and access to the educational services she or he needs to learn effectively. IDEA leads the way in reshaping today's educational system from one that struggles to accommodate the educational needs of children with disabilities to one that readily responds to the individual educational needs of all children.

NO

**Frederick M. Hess and
Frederick J. Brigham**

How Federal Special Education Policy Affects Schooling in Virginia

Federal special education legislation has an honorable heritage and a laudable purpose. Unfortunately, the manner in which Congress and the executive branch have pursued that purpose now impedes the ability of state school systems to serve children in both general and special education.

The current system of oversight and resource allocation focuses less on educational attainment and more on procedural civil rights. Problems result from the federal government's use of this legalistic approach. In most areas of education, Washington offers supplementary funding as a carrot to encourage desired state behaviors. The challenge of compelling states to abide by federal dictates in special education, however, has produced a reliance on procedural oversight with deleterious effects for the federal-state partnership in education.

Under the present system, educators are restricted in their ability to make decisions regarding how best to assist children with disabilities. Instead, in response to federal dictates, states press school districts toward a defensive posture in which educators may spend more time attending to procedural requirements than to students' instructional and behavioral needs. Most discussions of reforming special education at the federal level ask what policy changes would alleviate this problem of excessive proceduralism. We suggest that such an approach is too narrow, that over-reliance upon procedural regulation actually arises from Washington's attempt to compel behaviors with insufficient incentives or guidance.

While seeking to get states to do its bidding with respect to children and youths with disabilities, Congress has provided neither inducements for them to cooperate nor flexibility in how they comply with federal direction. Lacking the capacity to implement special education policy on its own—considering that it does not operate public schools or employ their teachers—Washington has instead relied upon micro-managing state procedures and using the threat of legal action as a primary enforcement tool.

Lacking explicit federal direction or support, state officials cope by crafting their own muddled guidelines. This permits the state, like the federal government, to forestall messy conflict over details regarding program eligibility

From Frederick M. Hess and Frederick J. Brigham, "How Federal Special Education Policy Affects Schooling in Virginia," in Chester E. Finn, Jr., Andrew J. Rotherham, and Charles R. Hokanson, Jr., eds., *Rethinking Special Education for a New Century* (Thomas B. Fordham Foundation & Progressive Policy Institute, May 2001). Copyright © 2001 by The Thomas B. Fordham Foundation. Reprinted by permission. Notes omitted.

and services by pushing such questions down to districts and schools. Principals and teachers complain that the nested levels of governance deepen the confusion as the rules grow more convoluted and cumbersome at each stage.…

The Federal Role in Special Education…

The IDEA [Individuals With Disabilities Education Act]

In making special education law, Congress and the executive branch have relied heavily upon judicial precedents rooted in the Equal Protection and Due Process Clauses of the 14th Amendment. Whereas most federal legislation is framed as a compromise between competing interests and claims, this more absolutist orientation means that special education policies turn on endowing claimants with an inviolable set of rights. That mindset is illustrated by the "inclusion" proponent who prominently argued, "It really doesn't matter whether or not [full inclusion] works… even if it didn't work it would still be the thing to do."

Under the IDEA, a satisfactory program is defined as one that adheres to due process, regardless of its results. Critics suggested that this orientation fed lower expectations for students with disabilities. In response, the 1997 IDEA reauthorization sought to emphasize academic performance by insisting upon "meaningful access to the general education curriculum to the maximum extent possible" for students with special needs.…

Section 504

In theory, states are free to disregard the IDEA. The only federal sanction is the ability of the Office of Special Education Programs (OSEP) to withdraw IDEA grants. These grants amount to less than ten percent of state special education spending. This apparent freedom is illusory, however, because any state that fails to comply with the IDEA's requirements would still be liable under Section 504 of the Rehabilitation Act of 1973. Section 504 is designed… "to eliminate discrimination on the basis of handicap in any program or activity receiving Federal financial assistance." Although it supplies no funding, Section 504 applies to any entity receiving any federal funding, meaning that all states must abide by its directives.…

Although the IDEA offers guidelines regarding various disability conditions, the provisions of Section 504 are so nebulous that it becomes extremely difficult to distinguish students entitled to special education services from those not entitled. As one administrator said, "In my opinion, IDEA is much more precise, much more specific.… 504 is the same as saying, 'you have a problem here.' [Anybody can identify some problem] 'substantially limits' [a life activity].… What's the line there? So you're wide open."

Special Education in Virginia

Special education comprises a substantial share of Virginia's K–12 educational expenditures. Between 1995 and 1998, special education students made up 13 percent to 14 percent of the state's student population, while the special education budget consumed 23 percent to 25 percent of the state's education budget....

In Virginia, federal special education directives are interpreted and implemented by a designated group of professionals in the state Department of Education (DOE). Within the larger DOE, headed by the state Superintendent of Education, is a directorate for special education headed by a Director of Special Education and Student Services (SESS). Historically, the directorate for Special Education did nothing else. In 2000, DOE merged "Special Education" with "Student Services," the unit responsible for activities such as school health and safety. Despite this reorganization, Special Education remains relatively isolated from the other areas of the DOE. In January 2001, SESS included 23 positions devoted to oversight of special education. These individuals include specialists in learning disabilities, emotional disturbance, mental retardation, early childhood, and severe disabilities. Not one member is explicitly charged with coordinating policy with the other parts of the DOE.

Virginia's DOE essentially runs parallel school systems, one staffed by special educators for students with disabilities, the second staffed by general educators for everyone else. Each side exhibits distrust and frustration with the other. A local special education administrator observed, "People in general education don't listen to us or even ask us about the kids in our caseloads." A state-level administrator said, "We have consistent problems with some of our districts," explaining that the state deals with such challenges by using legal and administrative sanctions to coerce general educators into "playing ball." General educators voice reciprocal concerns. One administrator spoke for many, saying, "I have all I can handle right now without attending to students with wildly varying educational and behavioral needs." ...

The current structure ensures that special education policy decisions are mostly made by people removed from actual school practice and from the general decisionmaking process for K–12 curriculum and instruction. This makes it less likely that services for students with special needs will be integrated or coordinated with the larger educational program.... The structure of the DOE helps to divide general and special education personnel, while encouraging professionals to think differently about different categories of children, despite Congress' insistence that its goal is to eliminate distinctions among students.

Special Education Litigation

Despite the visibility of special education cases that reach the courts, such actions are relatively rare in Virginia. The most common legal or quasi-legal actions are complaints and due process hearings. The Commonwealth devotes considerable time and energy to these. Due process hearings are a quasi-judicial, adversarial procedure overseen by part-time hearing officers trained by the DOE.

Between 1992–93 and 1999–2000, 799 due process requests were filed with the DOE.... All such requests require formal notification to the Department that the plaintiff is exercising his right to a due process hearing. Ninety-three percent of these requests were filed by parents. The remaining 7 percent were filed by school districts, usually when the district was concerned that parents were refusing to allow it to provide the services it deemed appropriate. These figures indicate that formal legal proceedings may be less of an issue than critics sometimes fear.

Of these 799 cases filed, 586 were resolved in the same year. Of the 586, 176 (30 percent) led to decisions by a hearing officer while the rest ended through withdrawal of the complaint or settlement prior to a hearing. Of the 176 decisions rendered, three-quarters were resolved wholly in favor of the school district. The other 25 percent either favored the parent or split the difference between parent and district.

There are at least two ways to interpret these outcomes. One is that a substantial percentage of the requests filed lack merit. A second is that some schools respond to parental concerns only when faced with the threat of legal sanctions. A significant number of hearing requests are withdrawn after districts make concessions....

The larger problem is not the number of formal complaints or their resolution, but the incentives that this legalistic mechanism creates for local educators. Presently, the desire to avoid legal sanctions and officer-ordered costs and services is the clearest incentive for schools to make extraordinary efforts to serve students with disabilities. Such efforts may cause the district to divert resources from other worthy purposes. Educators have cause to focus on what services and accommodations will forestall complaints, rather than on which are cost-effective and educationally appropriate. The result is that districts are caught between a desire to "cut corners" on special education expenditures and the impulse to provide services in order to avoid the threat of legal action. By encouraging schools and parents to adopt adversarial roles, the legalistic emphasis makes cooperative solutions more difficult and shifts the focus of decisionmaking from educational performance to the avoidance of potential liability.

The Institutional Shape of Special Education

Here we examine three key program dimensions used by the federal government to define special education and to ensure that it is delivered in an acceptable manner....

FAPE and LRE

The key IDEA mandates affecting instruction and student placement are FAPE (free appropriate public education) and LRE (least restrictive environment). FAPE addresses the elements of a student's education program, although LRE addresses the integration of disabled students into the general education system. Often, the two mandates embody contradictory impulses. Legal scholar Anne Dupre has observed, "The friction between 'appropriate' education and 'appropriate' integration has baffled the court and led to a confusing array of opinions on inclusion." While educators must attend to both considerations, in

Virginia it appears that the balance is tipped in favor of inclusion, even at the cast of effective education. An attorney who often represents parents of children with disabilities said, "[t]he intensity of the programs offered for students with mild disabilities fell after the push for more inclusion. Now we more often have to pursue formal action to get these students the services they need."

The most difficult aspect of FAPE involves the meaning of "appropriate," which is clearer for some disabilities than others. Few question the need for Braille tests for students who are blind or ramps for those with limited mobility. For students with less obvious disabilities, however, program appropriateness ought to take into account curricular demands on the student as well as the larger educational context of the school....

Although the challenge of validating the appropriateness of a given student's educational program is daunting, it is overshadowed by the problems surrounding the LRE requirement. Few areas of special education are as controversial. Much effort is invested in determining the LRE for individual students, closely watched by a group of educators and advocates who call for "full inclusion" of disabled youngsters in regular education classes....

In Virginia, as a result of the push for "inclusion," many of the services formerly available to students with mild disabilities... have been cut back or eliminated. Such programs frequently have been replaced by "collaborative" or "consultative" models, in which students with special needs are enrolled full-time in general education classrooms. One result has been that a continuum of placement options has ben replaced with a starker choice between intensive (for example, self-contained) classes and limited services (for example, enrollment in general education programs). This shift has left both general and special education teachers with fewer ways to respond to the needs of students, which reduces their ability to make effective professional judgments about what works for children in their schools....

The current approach to FAPE and LRE fails to resolve the tension between maximizing achievement and maximizing integration, leaving these competing desiderata to be worked out by administrators, teachers, and parents without clear guidelines. Yet educators are blocked from using their professional judgment in weighing these two imperatives and are subjected to administrative or judicial review and sanction if deemed to have proceeded in an inappropriate manner. In other words, district officials are granted an ambiguous autonomy and expected to make appropriate decisions but are prevented from relying upon their professional determinations of efficiency and efficacy in reaching those decisions. The system is faintly redolent of a star chamber in which one is not sure the criteria to which one is being held.

Funding

One of most significant impacts of FAPE is on state education funding. Because Congress has imbued disabled children with particular rights, the state is legally required to give budgetary priority to their needs. States are legally vulnerable to charges that they have failed to provide adequately for students with special needs, while parents of general education students cannot make similar claims.

The consequence is that states have a difficult time making the case against the provision of even very expensive special education services and tend to fund these by dipping into the pool that would otherwise fund general education. . . .

Monitoring Special Education

In theory, federally inspired monitoring ensures that special education programs provide an appropriate education to all eligible students. In reality, the monitoring focuses more on procedural compliance than on either the appropriateness or effectiveness of the education being delivered. Given the lack of evidence that procedural compliance equates to more effective services, it is not clear that federal monitoring is effectively promoting quality special education. Moreover, such an emphasis undermines teacher professionalism by forcing educators to invest significant time in managing procedures and documenting processes, rather than on instruction.

OSEP's policy, adopted after the 1997 IDEA amendments, monitors states predominantly by requiring them to conduct self-studies. A key problem in this process is that the reporting requirements are both complex and vague. For example, the phrase "free appropriate public education" sounds straightforward and easily implemented, but a closer look proves otherwise.

Assuming that "free" means no cost to the parents, interpreting this part is straightforward. But, what does "appropriate" mean? In order to define this term, one must first determine the goals of the education program and ask the question, "Appropriate for what?" The IDEA is silent on that point, meaning that this question must be revisited in the case of each student. OSEP plainly is unable to monitor the "appropriateness" of a given decision in the case of a particular child. Therefore, it winds up monitoring processes and procedures —for example, the way that the decision was made. In practice, the guidelines are daunting, elaborate, and time-consuming even for many special education professionals—let alone the parents and students they are intended to protect. As one state official commented, "Monitoring used to be a part of my job, now it's all I do. Running the monitoring program has become my whole job."

Virginia's SSEAC [State Special Education Advisory Committee], which is supposed to identify critical issues and advise DOE on carrying out special education programs, scrapped its entire agenda for 2000–2001 in order to concentrate on the issue of program monitoring. The state DOE has had to add additional staff to handle these responsibilities.

In early January 2001, the SSEAC met to discuss the self-study that comprises the initial stage of Virginia's federal monitoring. At the beginning of the meeting, a facilitator asked each committee member why he or she had given up the time to attend this particular meeting. The most common response was to attain closure on the process. The facilitator pointed out that the federal monitoring process, being continuous, could never result in closure.

Reports were presented regarding programs for both school-aged and preschool children. Each report was several hundred pages long. After the meeting, several parent representatives remarked that they saw little connection between the activities conducted through the federal monitoring and discernible improvements in the educational services offered to their children. The best that can be said of the self-study is that it allows parents and special educators to voice their concerns. However, there is little reason to suspect that this unfocused airing of grievances is likely to produce substantive improvements in special education. More likely, because the state officials who led the self-study procedure were diverted from their responsibilities to monitor and support local education agencies (LEAs), the federal monitoring program is likely to result in decreased attention to the problems faced by children and youths with disabilities, their families, and the schools that serve them.

The Practice of Special Education . . .

IEPs

As originally conceived, IEPs were to be a flexible tool for creating specialized programs responsive to student needs as well as parental and school concerns. However, Virginia practice emphasizes *pro forma* compliance with IEPs in order to protect educators from administrative and legal actions. A typical IEP form offers 45 boxes for committees to check off before they even begin to describe the student's own education program. Rather than a flexible pedagogical tool, the IEP is often a ritualized document. As one special education administrator said, "Of course, all of our special ed students have IEPs. But how relevant are [the IEPs] to what our teachers are doing on a day-to-day basis? Not very."

Parents are not alone in their dissatisfaction. Teachers often complain that IEPs do little but absorb time and repeat platitudes. . . .

IEPs have historically reflected a given student's particular instructional regimen, rather than provided a road map for helping that child accomplish the general education goals promulgated by the school or state. A result is that they are often written with little input from general education teachers and scant regard for the standards of general education programs. . . .

The 1997 amendments required that general education teachers be included in IEP meetings and that IEPs yield "meaningful access to the general education curriculum." Unfortunately, both changes appear to hold only limited promise. So long as special education policy is driven by rights and legalisms, inserting general education teachers into IEP planning sessions is unlikely to produce significant changes in practice. As for "meaningful access to the general education curriculum," the phrase is so nebulous as to serve no real purpose, while creating yet one more interpretive minefield for school personnel.

The trouble with most efforts to improve IEPs is that they fail to address the contradiction at the heart of the process. On the one hand, professional educators are charged with designing flexible programs that respond to the needs of each student with disabilities. On the other hand, these plans are devised and implemented in a context shaped by compliance-based rules and marked by legal peril. The result is that IEPs cease to be useful pedagogical tools.

Discipline Policy

The IDEA requires the development of distinct disciplinary policies for students with disabilities. Some of these distinctions make sense. It is unreasonable to discipline a wheelchair-bound student for failing to stand during the national anthem. The IDEA prevents schools from punishing students in such situations (although we see no evidence that Virginia schools, left to their own judgment, would engage in such practices). The IDEA requires a "zero reject" model that extends special education services to *all* students with disabilities. Under this logic, schools may not interrupt or withhold services for any such students save for infractions involving guns or possession of drugs. Such interruption of services has been deemed to violate the IDEA's procedural safeguards....

IDEA regulation of discipline may serve a legitimate purpose. It is well established that students with disabilities are frequently "over-punished" for behavior infractions. Many parents of children with disabilities report that their children feel singled out by school officials for behavior that rarely leads to sanctions for other students....

Unfortunately, the IDEA also has a number of undesirable disciplinary consequences. School officials must determine the extent to which an act of misbehavior results from a disability. Judgments regarding the motivation of a specific act have eluded philosophers and psychologists through the ages, yet are required by the IDEA. Such deliberations are bound to yield variable results, even as they consume substantial time. Effective disciplinary procedures require that acts and consequences be closely linked in time and consistent over time if they are to have the desired effect. The IDEA's procedural mandates make such practices doubly difficult when the child has any sort of disability.

Despite the frequent voicing of such concerns, the IDEA constraints do not actually result in many disciplinary measures being challenged or over-turned in Virginia.... Still, the fear of such a challenge reportedly causes many teachers and administrators to shy away from punishing students with disabilities for infractions for which others would be disciplined.... The perception in Virginia that the IDEA creates a class of students licensed to "terrorize schools and teachers" undermines public trust in school safety and support for special education.

State Education Standards

... Much special education practice draws heavily on the philosophy of progressive education, emphasizing notions of personal relevance more heavily than traditional academic skills and knowledge.... The IDEA's ethos of individualized instruction is at odds with systems of standards-based accountability that seek to improve education by requiring all students to perform at a measurably high level on a specified set of objectives.

In the past, this conflict was often accommodated by exempting special education students from standardized assessments. In the 1990s, however, special educators began to assert that such policies caused disabled students to be denied effective and equitable instruction. Consequently, the 1997 IDEA amendments mandated that students with disabilities be included in testing programs to the maximum feasible extent. As a result, students with special needs now participate in Virginia's SOL [Standards of Learning] testing regime.

This change places schools and districts in an awkward position, as the state simultaneously asks them to raise test results and to include students who have shown historically poor performances on standardized assessments. The IDEA requires educators to take greater responsibility for the achievement of students with disabilities. However, the law can also encourage educators to look for loopholes to relax the standards for students who are unlikely to fare well on high-stakes assessments. An example of this tendency was the SSEAC recommendation in early 2000 that the state extend the category of "developmental disabilities" up to the federal maximum age of nine so that more students would be afforded special accommodations on the SOL tests. The nature of this request suggests the fundamental tension between special education provisions and the push toward high uniform standards....

Perhaps the central dilemma for states pursuing high-stakes accountability is how best to serve those students with mild disabilities who find attaining acceptable levels of performance a daunting challenge. On the one hand, it is sensible to hold these students and their teachers to the same high level of expectations to which we hold others. On the other hand, these students may find assessments frustrating or insurmountable and may drop out of school altogether. This bifurcation is partly a function of the Virginia SOL's virtually exclusive focus on academic preparation. Although this emphasis is understandable, it leads to de-emphasis of programs such as vocational education and the arts that can provide other forms of useful instruction and skill-based learning for students with mild or moderate disabilities.

Conclusion

Surveying the six dimensions of policy and practice in which special education poses significant challenges, we can see that the key problems have much in common. FAPE and LRE demand that educators abide by open-ended and ill-defined directives, even as the court-enforced right of a select group of children to "free and appropriate education" prohibits measured decisions regarding the allocation of resources. The monitoring of special education relies upon documentation and paper trails, requiring much time and effort and forcing educators to base program decisions upon procedures rather than determinations of efficiency or effectiveness. IEPs intended as flexible instruments of learning have evolved into written records of compliance with formal requirements. In the area of school discipline, protections afforded to special education students have caused educators to look askance upon these children and have made it more difficult to enforce clear and uniform standards in schools. And in jurisdictions such as Virginia, which have moved to a standards-based curriculum and a results-based accountability system, the question arises of how to track the progress of disabled students and whether they will be treated as part of the reformed education system or (reminiscent of pre-IDEA discrimination) as a separate educational world.

Reformers have sought to tackle one or another of these issues in isolation, acting in the belief that incremental policy shifts could remedy the particular problem. For example, the 1997 IDEA reforms sought to emphasize outcomes by requiring schools to test all students and enhancing schools' ability to discipline disabled students who misbehave. Such efforts have not worked very well, however, because they fail to recognize that the enumerated problems are symptomatic of a deeper tension at the heart of the federal-state relationship.

In sum, special education policy today is unwieldy, exasperating, and ripe for rethinking. Congress has demanded that states and schools provide certain services, but it has refused to pay their costs. States are obliged to deliver special education, yet lack substantive control over its objectives and policy design and the nature and shape of its services. But Washington does not actually run the program, either. Instead it tells states, albeit in ambiguous terms, what they must do, no matter whether these requirements are in the best interests of children, schools, or the larger education enterprise. Whatever the cost of compliance, states and districts are obliged to pay it, regardless of the effect on other children, programs, and priorities. The result is a hybrid reminiscent of the "push-me, pull-you" that accompanied Dr. Doolittle in Hugh Lofting's legendary children's tales. Like that mythical two-headed creature, the special education system is constantly tugged in opposite directions. To compel state cooperation with its directives, Washington relies upon a rights-based regimen of mandated procedures and voluminous records, enforced by the specter of judicial power. Yet because states and districts end up paying most of the bill for special education, Congress is hesitant to order the provision of particular services or to demand specific results. The consequence is that educators must interpret vague federal directives while operating under the shadow of legal threat.

Arguably, this produces the worst of two very different policy regimes. If special education were an outright federal program, like the National Park Service, the Weather Bureau, or Social Security, Washington would run it directly, in uniform fashion, with all bills being paid via Congressional appropriation. If it were a state program, Congress might contribute to its costs but states would determine how best to run it. Today, however, it is neither, and the result is not working very well.

These are two obvious solutions. The first is for Congress to pay for the special education services that it wishes to provide disabled children. The second is for Washington explicitly to decentralize special education, granting substantive authority to states, districts, and schools.

Either remedy, of course, would bring its own new problems. Full federal funding, for example, may encourage local overspending. Similarly, decentralization raises the likelihood that substantial variation will occur between states.

Yet these problems are likely to be less vexing than those we now face and apt to be more amenable to solution. The intergovernmental confusion would diminish. Those setting policy would be directly in charge of those delivering services. And a shift away from today's emphasis on rights and procedures will increase flexibility and foster innovations responsive to the distinctive needs of individual students, the judgments of expert educators, the preferences of parents, and the priorities of communities. This, we believe, would be good for children. And that, we believe, is the main point.

POSTSCRIPT

Will More Federal Oversight Result in Better Special Education?

A frequently heard comment is that IDEA is the "full employment for attorneys" act. Sometimes it feels that way. There is a long distance between the dream of helping all children learn and the reality of legal time deadlines, shifting interpretations, and confusing terminology.

In writing *Back to School on Civil Rights,* from which the NCD's selection was excerpted, the authors interviewed 14 parents from nine states, each of whom trusted that their children would receive an appropriate education in the least restrictive environment. Each shared the disillusionment and distrust that resulted from finding their rights sidestepped or ignored. The NCD found substantiation in their review of monitoring activities. Without increased federal attention to legal detail and requirements, the authors worry that schools will continue to avoid meeting the requirements of the laws. In the full report, the NCD expresses dismay that education reform efforts and budgetary cutbacks have siphoned away state funds that could have been used for compliance monitoring. They urge restoration of this money so that no more ground (or time) is lost.

In sharp contrast, Hess and Brigham assert that much ground has been too easily surrendered because districts fear costly litigation that might find them out of bureaucratic compliance with special education laws. The impact of individual challenges to school performance provides the protection that a global state audit could not—perhaps preventing educators from selecting effective practices that could benefit the whole school. Unfortunately, according to the authors, the confusing tangle of regulations often prevents schools from focusing on the more appropriate target of accountability for the progress of all children.

IDEA97 made a shift from compliance to accountability, requiring that all students have access to the general curriculum and can participate in the large-scale testing that is part of education reform. Regretting a lost opportunity, Wolf and Hassel (Finn, Rotheram, & Hokanson, 2001) argue that this change has succeeded only in adding another layer of bureaucratic responsibilities while reducing none.

Providing the perspective of attorneys who have represented both parents and schools, Lanigan et al. (Fordham, 2001) see the situation this way:

> Special education staff members in the public schools devote their professional lives to educating children with disabilities, are truly dedicated to the endeavor, and genuinely want to provide appropriate special education and related services to the students they are charged with educating. Yet school

176

resources are not unlimited, budget pressures are real, and the IDEA allows districts to take program costs into account only so long as they still are meeting the FAPE requirement. This is the fundamental source of school district conflict with parents.

Parents (and other guardians) who devote their lives to raising children with disabilities genuinely want to make sure that their children receive at least appropriate special education and related services. In truth, however, what these parents really want—indeed what all parents want—is an education that will allow their children to maximize their potential. The IDEA does not require this. This is the fundamental source of parents' conflict with school officials.

Does monitoring of complex federal regulations waste time and resources that could be devoted to the education of children? Do these very regulations protect the rights of children with disabilities to an equitable education? Can two well-meaning people interpret the law in two different ways yet both care deeply about the children they share? If so, how can they resolve their differences? How do your local educators view the controversy? What do they do now because of oversight? What would they do better if there were closer scrutiny? What would they do if no one checked to see if they were complying—would students with disabilities benefit from creative new programs, or would options be foreclosed because no one was watching?

ISSUE 8

Should One-on-One Nursing Care Be Part of Special Education?

YES: John Paul Stevens, from Majority Opinion, *Cedar Rapids Community School District v. Garret F.*, U.S. Supreme Court (March 3, 1999)

NO: Clarence Thomas, from Dissenting Opinion, *Cedar Rapids Community School District v. Garret F.*, U.S. Supreme Court (March 3, 1999)

ISSUE SUMMARY

YES: U.S. Supreme Court justice John Paul Stevens, writing for the majority of the Court, affirms the "bright line test," establishing that school districts are required by IDEA to provide one-on-one nursing services and any other health-related services that can be delivered by individuals other than a licensed physician.

NO: U.S. Supreme Court justice Clarence Thomas, representing the dissenting minority opinion, asserts that continuous one-on-one nursing services for disabled children are indeed medical and, as such, beyond the scope of congressional intent in IDEA. He concludes that such services are not the responsibility of special education programs within school districts.

Recognizing that some children need more than traditional educational services, IDEA directs schools to provide "related services" necessary to enable a child with a disability to access the special education program designed by the school team (IDEA, Section 300.24). Like the program, these must be provided at no cost. Related services include speech, occupational and physical therapy, and transportation. School health services and "medical services for diagnostic or evaluation purposes" are also mentioned in IDEA, though not medical procedures or treatment.

Court cases about related services began almost as soon as IDEA was passed. The first to reach the Supreme Court questioned whether a sign language interpreter was a required related service for a child with a hearing impairment (*Board of Education v. Rowley,* 1982). The Court determined that this service was not required because it felt that the child was making effective school progress with the operative special education program.

Concurrent with *Rowley*, the first medically related cases were moving through the courts. The landmark case was *Irving Independent School District v. Tatro* (1984), in which the Supreme Court required school personnel to perform clean intermittent catheterization, a procedure used to empty a child's bladder, so that she could remain in school and benefit from special education services. Although the school district felt that this procedure crossed the line into medical services, the Supreme Court established its own "bright line": If a procedure could be performed by a trained, supervised individual, it fell within the realm of the school's responsibilities. The Court acknowledged, however, that there are likely some medically related services that are too financially burdensome or complicated to be included.

Following *Tatro*, court decisions split into two lines of reasoning. Initially, lower courts adopted the "burden" and "complexity" elements of the decision, finding some medical services (tracheostomy care and cardiopulmonary resuscitation, for example) to be beyond the professional and financial responsibility of schools. About 10 years later, courts emphasized the "bright line" standard, finding that cost and complexity should not pose a barrier to access to education.

The issue crystallized with Garret Frey, a high school student who had been paralyzed since childhood. Academically successful in school, Garret required continuous medical support in order to attend. Having exhausted available personal funds, and believing that the services were well within the capacity of trained staff, Garret's parents turned to the school district. However, the district believed that the bright line standard should be overridden in this case by overall consideration of cost, complexity, time, and amount of services required, as well as liability for improper services.

In *Cedar Rapids Community School District v. Garret F.*, the Supreme Court voted 7–2 in favor of the bright line standard. The majority and dissenting opinions are reprinted in the following selections. Writing for the majority, Justice John Paul Stevens finds the continuous nursing services required by Garret to be well within the confines of school health services, noting that current federal law does not permit districts to consider the total cost or complexity of medically related assistance.

Justice Clarence Thomas, writing for the dissenting minority, holds that the services required by Garret—indeed, those discussed in *Tatro*—are medical and clearly outside the boundaries of school responsibility as written in IDEA. The minority opinion identifies financial and professional limits to the extent of a school's responsibility as well.

As you read these Supreme Court opinions, ask yourself these questions: What is the difference between medicine and education? Should there be a limit to a school's responsibilities to provide access? Where do you draw the line?

 **YES**

Majority Opinion

Cedar Rapids Community School District *v.* Garret F.

Justice Stevens delivered the opinion of the Court.

The Individuals with Disabilities Education Act (IDEA), 84 Stat. 175, as amended, was enacted, in part, "to assure that all children with disabilities have available to them... a free appropriate public education which emphasizes special education and related services designed to meet their unique needs." 20 U.S.C. § 1400(c). Consistent with this purpose, the IDEA authorizes federal financial assistance to States that agree to provide disabled children with special education and "related services." See §§1401(a)(18), 1412(1). The question presented in this case is whether the definition of "related services" in §1401(a)(17)[1] requires a public school district in a participating State to provide a ventilator-dependent student with certain nursing services during school hours.

I

Respondent Garret F. is a friendly, creative, and intelligent young man. When Garret was four years old, his spinal column was severed in a motorcycle accident. Though paralyzed from the neck down, his mental capacities were unaffected. He is able to speak, to control his motorized wheelchair through use of a puff and suck straw, and to operate a computer with a device that responds to head movements. Garret is currently a student in the Cedar Rapids Community School District (District), he attends regular classes in a typical school program, and his academic performance has been a success. Garret is, however, ventilator dependent,[2] and therefore requires a responsible individual nearby to attend to certain physical needs while he is in school.[3]

During Garret's early years at school his family provided for his physical care during the school day. When he was in kindergarten, his 18-year-old aunt attended him; in the next four years, his family used settlement proceeds they received after the accident, their insurance, and other resources to employ a licensed practical nurse. In 1993, Garret's mother requested the District to accept

From *Cedar Rapids Community School District v. Garret F.*, 119 S. Ct. 992 (1999).

financial responsibility for the health care services that Garret requires during the school day. The District denied the request, believing that it was not legally obligated to provide continuous one-on-one nursing services.

Relying on both the IDEA and Iowa law, Garret's mother requested a hearing before the Iowa Department of Education. An Administrative Law Judge (ALJ) received extensive evidence concerning Garret's special needs, the District's treatment of other disabled students, and the assistance provided to other ventilator-dependent children in other parts of the country. In his 47-page report, the ALJ found that the District has about 17,500 students, of whom approximately 2,200 need some form of special education or special services. Although Garret is the only ventilator-dependent student in the District, most of the health care services that he needs are already provided for some other students.[4] "The primary difference between Garret's situation and that of other students is his dependency on his ventilator for life support." App. to Pet. for Cert. 28a. The ALJ noted that the parties disagreed over the training or licensure required for the care and supervision of such students, and that those providing such care in other parts of the country ranged from nonlicensed personnel to registered nurses. However, the District did not contend that only a licensed physician could provide the services in question.

The ALJ explained that federal law requires that children with a variety of health impairments be provided with "special education and related services" when their disabilities adversely affect their academic performance, and that such children should be educated to the maximum extent appropriate with children who are not disabled. In addition, the ALJ explained that applicable federal regulations distinguish between "school health services," which are provided by a "qualified school nurse or other qualified person," and "medical services," which are provided by a licensed physician. See 34 CFR §§300.16(a), (b)(4), (b)(11) (1998). The District must provide the former, but need not provide the latter (except, of course, those "medical services" that are for diagnostic or evaluation purposes, §1401(a)(17)). According to the ALJ, the distinction in the regulations does not just depend on "the title of the person providing the service"; instead, the "medical services" exclusion is limited to services that are "in the special training, knowledge, and judgment of a physician to carry out." App. to Pet. for Cert. 51a. The ALJ thus concluded that the IDEA required the District to bear financial responsibility for all of the services in dispute, including continuous nursing services.[5]

The District challenged the ALJ's decision in Federal District Court, but that Court approved the ALJ's IDEA ruling and granted summary judgment against the District. *Id.,* at 9a, 15a. The Court of Appeals affirmed. 106 F.3d 822 (CA8 1997). It noted that, as a recipient of federal funds under the IDEA, Iowa has a statutory duty to provide all disabled children a "free appropriate public education," which includes "related services." See *id.,* at 824. The Court of Appeals read our opinion in *Irving Independent School Dist. v. Tatro,* 468 U.S. 883 (1984), to provide a two-step analysis of the "related services" definition in §1401(a)(17)—asking first, whether the requested services are included within the phrase "supportive services"; and second, whether the services are excluded as "medical services." 106 F.3d, at 824–825. The Court of Appeals succinctly answered both questions in Garret's favor. The Court found the first step plainly satisfied, since Garret cannot attend school unless the requested services are available during the school day. *Id.,* at 825. As to the second step, the Court reasoned that *Tatro* "established a bright-line test: the services of a physician (other than for diagnostic and evaluation purposes) are subject to the medical services exclusion, but services that can be provided in the school setting by a nurse or qualified layperson are not." *Ibid.*

In its petition for certiorari, the District challenged only the second step of the Court of Appeals' analysis. The District pointed out that some federal courts have not asked whether the requested health services must be delivered by a physician, but instead have applied a multi-factor test that considers, generally speaking, the nature and extent of the services at issue. See, *e.g., Neely* v. *Rutherford County School,* 68 F.3d 965, 972–973 (CA6 1995), cert. denied, 517 U.S. 1134 (1996); *Detsel* v. *Board of Ed. of Auburn Enlarged City School Dist.,* 820 F.2d 587, 588 (CA2) (*per curiam*), cert. denied, 484 U.S. 981 (1987). We granted the District's petition to resolve this conflict. 523 U.S. __ (1998).

II

The District contends that §1401(a)(17) does not require it to provide Garret with "continuous one-on-one nursing services" during the school day, even though Garret cannot remain in school without such care. Brief for Petitioner 10. However, the IDEA's definition of "related services," our decision in *Irving Independent School Dist.* v. *Tatro,* 468 U.S. 883 (1984), and the overall statutory scheme all support the decision of the Court of Appeals.

The text of the "related services" definition, see n. 1, *supra,* broadly encompasses those supportive services that "may be required to assist a child with a disability to benefit from special education." As we have already noted, the District does not challenge the Court of Appeals' conclusion that the in-school services at issue are within the covered category of "supportive services." As a general matter, services that enable a disabled child to remain in school during the day provide the student with "the meaningful access to education that Congress envisioned." *Tatro,* 468 U.S., at 891 (" 'Congress sought primarily to make public education available to handicapped children' and 'to make such access meaningful' " (quoting *Board of Ed. of Hendrick Hudson Central School Dist., Westchester Cty.* v. *Rowley,* 458 U.S. 176, 192 (1982)).

This general definition of "related services" is illuminated by a parenthetical phrase listing examples of particular services that are included within the statute's coverage. §1401(a)(17). "Medical services" are enumerated in this list, but such services are limited to those that are "for diagnostic and evaluation purposes." *Ibid.* The statute does not contain a more specific definition of the "medical services" that are excepted from the coverage of §1401(a)(17).

The scope of the "medical services" exclusion is not a matter of first impression in this Court. In *Tatro* we concluded that the Secretary of Education had reasonably determined that the term "medical services" referred only to services that must be performed by a physician, and not to school health services. 468 U.S., at 892–894. Accordingly, we held that a specific form of health care (clean intermittent catheterization) that is often, though not always, performed by a nurse is not an excluded medical service. We referenced the likely cost of the services and the competence of school staff as justifications for drawing a line between physician and other services, *ibid.*, but our endorsement of that line was unmistakable.[6] It is thus settled that the phrase "medical services" in §1401(a)(17) does not embrace all forms of care that might loosely be described as "medical" in other contexts, such as a claim for an income tax deduction. See 26 U.S.C. § 213(d)(1) (1994 ed. and Supp. II) (defining "medical care").

The District does not ask us to define the term so broadly. Indeed, the District does not argue that any of the items of care that Garret needs, considered individually, could be excluded from the scope of §1401(a)(17).[7] It could not make such an argument, considering that one of the services Garret needs (catheterization) was at issue in *Tatro,* and the others may be provided competently by a school nurse or other trained personnel. See App. to Pet. for Cert. 15a, 52a. As the ALJ concluded, most of the requested services are already provided by the District to other students, and the in-school care necessitated by Garret's ventilator dependency does not demand the training, knowledge, and judgment of a licensed physician. *Id.,* at 51a–52a. While more extensive, the in-school services Garret needs are no more "medical" than was the care sought in *Tatro.*

Instead, the District points to the combined and continuous character of the required care, and proposes a test under which the outcome in any particular case would "depend upon a series of factors, such as [1] whether the care is continuous or intermittent, [2] whether existing school health personnel can provide the service, [3] the cost of the service, and [4] the potential consequences if the service is not properly performed." Brief for Petitioner 11; see also *id.,* at 34–35.

The District's multi-factor test is not supported by any recognized source of legal authority. The proposed factors can be found in neither the text of the statute nor the regulations that we upheld in *Tatro.* Moreover, the District offers no explanation why these characteristics make one service any more "medical" than another. The continuous character of certain services associated with Garret's ventilator dependency has no apparent relationship to "medical" services, much less a relationship of equivalence. Continuous services may be more costly and may require additional school personnel, but they are not thereby more "medical." Whatever its imperfections, a rule that limits the medical services exemption to physician services is unquestionably a reasonable and generally workable interpretation of the statute. Absent an elaboration of the statutory terms plainly more convincing than that which we reviewed in *Tatro,* there is no good reason to depart from settled law.[8]

Finally, the District raises broader concerns about the financial burden that it must bear to provide the services that Garret needs to stay in school. The problem for the District in providing these services is not that its staff cannot be trained to deliver them; the problem, the District contends, is that the existing school health staff cannot meet all of their responsibilities and provide for Garret at the same time.[9] Through its multi-factor test, the District seeks to establish a kind of undue-burden exemption primarily based on the cost of the requested services. The first two factors can be seen as examples of cost-based distinctions: intermittent care is often less expensive than continuous care, and the use of existing personnel is cheaper than hiring additional employees. The third factor—the cost of the service—would then encompass the first two. The relevance of the fourth factor is likewise related to cost because extra care may be necessary if potential consequences are especially serious.

The District may have legitimate financial concerns, but our role in this dispute is to interpret existing law. Defining "related services" in a manner that *accommodates* the cost concerns Congress may have had, cf. *Tatro,* 468 U.S., at 892, is altogether different from using cost *itself* as the definition. Given that §1401(a)(17) does not employ cost in its definition of "related services" or excluded "medical services," accepting the District's cost-based standard as the sole test for determining the scope of the provision would require us to engage in judicial lawmaking without any guidance from Congress. It would also create some tension with the purposes of the IDEA. The statute may not require public schools to maximize the potential of disabled students commensurate with the opportunities provided to other children, see *Rowley,* 458 U.S., at 200; and the potential financial burdens imposed on participating States may be relevant to arriving at a sensible construction of the IDEA, see *Tatro,* 468 U.S., at 892. But Congress intended "to open the door of public education" to all qualified children and "require[d] participating States to educate handicapped children with nonhandicapped children whenever possible." *Rowley,* 458 U.S., at 192, 202; see *id.,* at 179–181; see also *Honig* v. *Doe,* 484 U.S. 305, 310–311, 324 (1988); §§1412(1), (2)(C), (5)(B).[10]

This case is about whether meaningful access to the public schools will be assured, not the level of education that a school must finance once access is attained. It is undisputed that the services at issue must be provided if Garret is to remain in school. Under the statute, our precedent, and the purposes of the IDEA, the District must fund such "related services" in order to help guarantee that students like Garret are integrated into the public schools.

The judgment of the Court of Appeals is accordingly

Affirmed.

Notes

1. "The term 'related services' means transportation, and such developmental, corrective, and other supportive services (including speech pathology and audiology, psychological services, physical and occupational therapy, recreation, including therapeutic recreation, social work services, counseling services, including rehabilitation counseling, and medical services, except that such medical services shall be for diagnostic and evaluation purposes only) as may be required to assist a child with a disability to benefit from special education, and includes the early identification and assessment of disabling conditions in children." 20 U.S.C. § 1401(a)(17). Originally, the statute was enacted without a definition of "related services." See Education of the Handicapped Act, 84 Stat. 175. In 1975, Congress added the definition at issue in this case. Education for All Handicapped Children Act of 1975, §4(a)(4), 89 Stat. 775. Aside from nonsubstantive changes and

added examples of included services, see, *e.g.*, Individuals with Disabilities Education Act Amendments of 1997, §101, 111 Stat. 45; Individuals with Disabilities Education Act Amendments of 1991, §25(a)(1)(B), 105 Stat. 605; Education of the Handicapped Act Amendments of 1990, §101(c), 104 Stat. 1103, the relevant language in §1401(a)(17) has not been amended since 1975. All references to the IDEA herein are to the 1994 version as codified in Title 20 of the United States Code—the version of the statute in effect when this dispute arose.

2. In his report in this case, the Administrative Law Judge explained that "[b]eing ventilator dependent means that [Garret] breathes only with external aids, usually an electric ventilator, and occasionally by someone else's manual pumping of an air bag attached to his tracheotomy tube when the ventilator is being maintained. This later procedure is called ambu bagging." App. to Pet. for Cert. 19a.

3. "He needs assistance with urinary bladder catheterization once a day, the suctioning of his tracheotomy tube as needed, but at least once every six hours, with food and drink at lunchtime, in getting into a reclining position for five minutes of each hour, and ambu bagging occasionally as needed when the ventilator is checked for proper functioning. He also needs assistance from someone familiar with his ventilator in the event there is a malfunction or electrical problem, and someone who can perform emergency procedures in the event he experiences autonomic hyperreflexia. Autonomic hyperreflexia is an uncontrolled visceral reaction to anxiety or a full bladder. Blood pressure increases, heart rate increases, and flushing and sweating may occur. Garret has not experienced autonomic hyperreflexia frequently in recent years, and it has usually been alleviated by catheterization. He has not ever experienced autonomic hyperreflexia at school. Garret is capable of communicating his needs orally or in another fashion so long as he has not been rendered unable to do so by an extended lack of oxygen." *Id.*, at 20a.

4. "Included are such services as care for students who need urinary catheterization, food and drink, oxygen supplement positioning, and suctioning." *Id.*, at 28a; see also *id.*, at 53a.

5. In addition, the ALJ's opinion contains a thorough discussion of "other tests and criteria" pressed by the District, *id.*, at 52a, including the burden on the District and the cost of providing assistance to Garret. Although the ALJ found no legal authority for establishing a cost-based test for determining what related services are required by the statute, he went on to reject the District's arguments on the merits. See *id.*, at 42a–53a. We do not reach the issue here, but the ALJ also found that Garret's in-school needs must be met by the District under an Iowa statute as well as the IDEA. *Id.*, at 54a–55a.

6. "The regulations define 'related services' for handicapped children to include 'school health services,' 34 CFR § 300.13(a) (1983), which are defined in turn as 'services provided by a qualified school nurse or other qualified person,' §300.13(b)(10). 'Medical services' are defined as 'services provided by a licensed physician.' §300.13(b)(4). Thus, the Secretary has [reasonably] determined that the services of a school nurse otherwise qualifying as a 'related service' are not subject to exclusion as a 'medical service,' but that the services of a physician are excludable as such.

   ... "By limiting the 'medical services' exclusion to the services of a physician or hospital, both far more expensive, the Secretary has given a permissible construction to the provision." 468 U.S., at 892–893 (emphasis added) (footnote omitted); see also *id.*, at 894 ("[T]he regulations state that school nursing services must be provided only if they can be performed by a nurse or other qualified person, not if they must be performed by a physician").

   Based on certain policy letters issued by the Department of Education, it seems that the Secretary's post-*Tatro* view of the statute has not been entirely clear. *E.g.*, App. to Pet. for Cert. 64a. We may assume that the Secretary has authority under the IDEA to adopt regulations that define the "medical services" exclusion by more explicitly taking into account the nature and extent of the requested services; and the Secretary surely has the authority to enumerate the services that are, and are not, fairly included within the scope of §1407(a)(17). But the Secretary has done neither; and, in this Court, she advocates affirming the judgment of the Court of Appeals. Brief for United States as *Amicus Curiae;* see also *Auer* v. *Robbins,* 519 U.S. 452, 462 (1997) (an agency's views as *amicus curiae* may be entitled to deference). We obviously have no authority to rewrite the regulations, and we see no sufficient reason to revise *Tatro,* either.

7. See Tr. of Oral Arg. 4–5, 12.

8. At oral argument, the District suggested that we first consider the nature of the requested service (either "medical" or not); then, if the service is "medical," apply the multi-factor test to determine whether the service is an excluded physician service or an included school nursing service under the Secretary of Education's regulations. See Tr. of Oral Arg. 7, 13–14. Not only does this approach provide no additional guidance for identifying "medical" services, it is also disconnected from both the statutory text and the regulations we upheld in *Irving Independent School Dist.* v. *Tatro* 468 U.S. 883 (1984). "Medical" services are generally *excluded* from the statute, and the regulations elaborate on that statutory term. No authority cited by the District requires an additional inquiry if the requested service is both "related" and non-"medical." Even if §1401(a)(17) demanded an additional step, the factors proposed by the District are hardly more useful in identifying "nursing" services than they are in identifying "medical" services; and the District cannot limit educational access simply by pointing to the limitations of existing staff. As we noted in *Tatro,* the IDEA requires schools to hire specially trained personnel to meet disabled student needs. *Id.,* at 893.

9. See Tr. of Oral Arg. 4–5, 13; Brief for Petitioner 6–7, 9. The District, however, will not necessarily need to hire an additional employee to meet Garret's needs. The District already employs a one-on-one teacher associate (TA) who assists Garret during the school day. See App. to Pet. for Cert. 26a–27a. At one time, Garret's TA was a licensed practical nurse (LPN). In light of the state Board of Nursing's recent ruling that the District's registered nurses may decide to delegate Garret's care to an LPN, see Brief for United States as *Amicus Curiae* 9–10 (filed Apr. 22, 1998), the dissent's future-cost estimate is speculative. See App. to Pet. for Cert. 28a, 58a–60a (if the District could assign Garret's care to a TA who is also an LPN, there would be "a minimum of additional expense").

10. The dissent's approach, which seems to be even broader than the District's, is unconvincing. The dissent's rejection of our unanimous decision in *Tatro* comes 15 years too late, see *Patterson* v. *McLean Credit Union,* 491 U.S. 164, 172–173 (1989) (*stare decisis* has "special force" in statutory interpretation), and it offers nothing constructive in its place. Aside from rejecting a "provider-specific approach," the dissent cites unrelated statutes and offers a circular definition of "medical services." *Post,* at 3–4 (" 'services' that are 'medical' in 'nature' "). Moreover, the dissent's approach apparently would exclude most ordinary school nursing services of the kind routinely provided to nondisabled children; that anomalous result is not easily attributable to congressional intent. See *Tatro,* 468 U.S., at 893. In a later discussion the dissent does offer a specific proposal: that we now interpret (or rewrite) the Secretary's regulations so that school districts need only provide disabled children with "health-related services that school nurses can perform as part of their normal duties." *Post,* at 7. The District does not dispute that its nurses "can perform" the requested services, so the dissent's objection is that District nurses would not be performing their "normal duties" if they met Garret's needs. That is, the District would need an "additional employee." *Post,* at 8. This proposal is functionally similar to a proposed regulation—ultimately withdrawn— that would have replaced the "school health services" provision. See 47 Fed. Reg.

33838, 33854 (1982) (the statute and regulations may not be read to affect legal obligations to make available to handicapped children services, including school health services, made available to nonhandicapped children). The dissent's suggestion is unacceptable for several reasons. Most important, such revisions of the regulations are better left to the Secretary, and an additional staffing need is generally not a sufficient objection to the requirements of §1401(a)(17). See n. 8, *supra.*

Clarence Thomas

NO

Dissenting Opinion of Clarence Thomas

Justice Thomas, with whom Justice Kennedy joins, dissenting.

The majority, relying heavily on our decision in *Irving Independent School Dist.* v. *Tatro,* 468 U.S. 883 (1984), concludes that the Individuals with Disabilities Education Act (IDEA), 20 U.S.C. § 1400 *et seq.,* requires a public school district to fund continuous, one-on-one nursing care for disabled children. Because *Tatro* cannot be squared with the text of IDEA, the Court should not adhere to it in this case. Even assuming that *Tatro* was correct in the first instance, the majority's extension of it is unwarranted and ignores the constitutionally mandated rules of construction applicable to legislation enacted pursuant to Congress' spending power.

I

As the majority recounts, *ante,* at 1, IDEA authorizes the provision of federal financial assistance to States that agree to provide, *inter alia,* "special education and related services" for disabled children. §1401(a)(18). In *Tatro, supra,* we held that this provision of IDEA required a school district to provide clean intermittent catheterization to a disabled child several times a day. In so holding, we relied on Department of Education regulations, which we concluded had reasonably interpreted IDEA's definition of "related services"[1] to require school districts in participating States to provide "school nursing services" (of which we assumed catheterization was a subcategory) but not "services of a physician." *Id.,* at 892–893. This holding is contrary to the plain text of IDEA and its reliance on the Department of Education's regulations was misplaced.

A

Before we consider whether deference to an agency regulation is appropriate, "we first ask whether Congress has 'directly spoken to the precise question at issue. If the intent of Congress is clear, that is the end of the matter; for the court, as well as the agency, must give effect to the unambiguously expressed intent of Congress.'" *National Credit Union Admin.* v. *First Nat. Bank & Trust Co.,*

From *Cedar Rapids Community School District v. Garret F.,* 119 S. Ct. 992 (1999).

522 U.S. 479, 499–500 (1998) (quoting *Chevron U.S.A. Inc.* v. *Natural Resources Defense Council, Inc.,* 467 U.S. 837, 842–843 (1984)).

Unfortunately, the Court in *Tatro* failed to consider this necessary antecedent question before turning to the Department of Education's regulations implementing IDEA's related services provision. The Court instead began "with the regulations of the Department of Education, which," it said, "are entitled to deference." *Tatro, supra,* at 891–892. The Court need not have looked beyond the text of IDEA, which expressly indicates that school districts are not required to provide medical services, except for diagnostic and evaluation purposes. 20 U.S.C. § 1401(a)(17). The majority asserts that *Tatro* precludes reading the term "medical services" to include "all forms of care that might loosely be described as 'medical.'" *Ante,* at 8. The majority does not explain, however, why "services" that are "medical" in nature are not "medical services." Not only is the definition that the majority rejects consistent with other uses of the term in federal law,[2] it also avoids the anomalous result of holding that the services at issue in *Tatro* (as well as in this case), while not "medical services," would nonetheless qualify as medical care for federal income tax purposes. *Ante,* at 8.

The primary problem with *Tatro,* and the majority's reliance on it today, is that the Court focused on the provider of the services rather than the services themselves. We do not typically think that automotive services are limited to those provided by a mechanic, for example. Rather, anything done to repair or service a car, no matter who does the work, is thought to fall into that category. Similarly, the term "food service" is not generally thought to be limited to work performed by a chef. The term "medical" similarly does not support *Tatro*'s provider-specific approach, but encompasses services that are "of, *relating to, or concerned with* physicians *or* the practice of medicine." See Webster's Third New International Dictionary 1402 (1986) (emphasis added); see also *id.,* at 1551 (defining "nurse" as "a person skilled in caring for and waiting on the infirm, the injured, or the sick; *specif:* one esp. trained to carry out such duties under the supervision of a physician").

IDEA's structure and purpose reinforce this textual interpretation. Congress enacted IDEA to increase the *educational* opportunities available to disabled children, not to provide medical care for them. See 20 U.S.C. § 1400(c) ("It is the purpose of this chapter to assure that all children with disabilities have . . . a free appropriate public education"); see also §1412 ("In order to qualify for assistance . . . a State shall demonstrate . . . [that it] has in effect a policy that assures all children with disabilities the right to a free appropriate public education"); *Board of Ed. of Hendrick Hudson Central School Dist., Westchester Cty.* v. *Rowley,* 458 U.S. 176, 179 (1982) ("The Act represents an ambitious federal effort to promote the education of handicapped children"). As such, where Congress decided to require a supportive service—including speech pathology, occupational therapy, and audiology—that appears "medical" in nature, it took care to do so explicitly. See §1401(a)(17). Congress specified these services precisely because it recognized that they would otherwise fall under the broad "medical services" exclusion. Indeed, when it crafted the definition of related services, Congress could have, but chose not to, include "nursing services" in this list.

B

Tatro was wrongly decided even if the phrase "medical services" was subject to multiple constructions, and therefore, deference to any reasonable Department of Education regulation was appropriate. The Department of Education has never promulgated regulations defining the scope of IDEA's "medical services" exclusion. One year before *Tatro* was decided, the Secretary of Education issued proposed regulations that defined excluded medical services as "services relating to the practice of medicine." 47 Fed. Reg. 33838 (1982). These regulations, which represent the Department's only attempt to define the disputed term, were never adopted. Instead, "[t]he regulations actually define only those 'medical services' that are owed to handicapped children," *Tatro,* 468 U.S., at 892, n. 10) (emphasis in original), not those that *are not*. Now, as when *Tatro* was decided, the regulations require districts to provide services performed " 'by a licensed physician to determine a child's medically related handicapping condition which results in the child's need for special education and related services.' " *Ibid.* (quoting 34 CFR § 300.13(b)(4) (1983), recodified and amended as 34 CFR § 300.16(b)(4) (1998).

Extrapolating from this regulation, the *Tatro* Court presumed that this meant "that 'medical services' not owed under the statute are those 'services by a licensed physician' that serve other purposes." *Tatro, supra,* at 892, n. 10 (emphasis deleted). The Court, therefore, did not defer to the regulation itself, but rather relied on an inference drawn from it to speculate about how a regulation might read if the Department of Education promulgated one. Deference in those circumstances is impermissible. We cannot defer to a regulation that does not exist.[3]

II

Assuming that *Tatro* was correctly decided in the first instance, it does not control the outcome of this case. Because IDEA was enacted pursuant to Congress' spending power, *Rowley, supra,* at 190, n. 11, our analysis of the statute in this case is governed by special rules of construction. We have repeatedly emphasized that, when Congress places conditions on the receipt of federal funds, "it must do so unambiguously." *Pennhurst State School and Hospital* v. *Halderman,* 451 U.S. 1, 17 (1981). See also *Rowley, supra,* at 190, n. 11; *South Dakota* v. *Dole,* 483 U.S. 203, 207 (1987); *New York* v. *United States,* 505 U.S. 144, 158 (1992). This is because a law that "condition[s] an offer of federal funding on a promise by the recipient . . . amounts essentially to a contract between the Government and the recipient of funds." *Gebser* v. *Lago Vista Independent School Dist.,* 524 U.S. 274, 276 (1998). As such, "[t]he legitimacy of Congress' power to legislate under the spending power . . . rests on whether the State voluntarily and knowingly accepts the terms of the 'contract.' There can, of course, be no knowing acceptance if a State is unaware of the conditions or is unable to ascertain what is expected of it." *Pennhurst, supra,* at 17 (citations omitted). It follows that we must interpret Spending Clause legislation narrowly, in order to avoid saddling the States with obligations that they did not anticipate.

The majority's approach in this case turns this Spending Clause presumption on its head. We have held that, in enacting IDEA, Congress wished to require "States to educate handicapped children with nonhandicapped children whenever possible," *Rowley,* 458 U.S., at 202. Congress, however, also took steps to limit the fiscal burdens that States must bear in attempting to achieve this laudable goal. These steps include requiring States to provide an education that is only "appropriate" rather that requiring them to maximize the potential of disabled students, see 20 U.S.C. § 1400(c); *Rowley, supra,* at 200, recognizing that integration into the public school environment is not always possible, see §1412(5), and clarifying that, with a few exceptions, public schools need not provide "medical services" for disabled students, §§1401(a)(17) and (18).

For this reason, we have previously recognized that Congress did not intend to "impos[e] upon the States a burden of unspecified proportions and weight" in enacting IDEA. *Rowley, supra,* at 176, n. 11. These federalism concerns require us to interpret IDEA's related services provision, consistent with *Tatro,* as follows: Department of Education regulations require districts to provide disabled children with health-related services that school nurses can perform as part of their normal duties. This reading of *Tatro,* although less broad than the majority's, is equally plausible and certainly more consistent with our obligation to interpret Spending Clause legislation narrowly. Before concluding that the district was required to provide clean intermittent catheterization for Amber Tatro, we observed that school nurses in the district were authorized to perform services that were "difficult to distinguish from the provision of [clean intermittent catheterization] to the handicapped." *Tatro,* 468 U.S., at 893. We concluded that "[i]t would be strange indeed if Congress, in attempting to extend special services to handicapped children, were unwilling to guarantee them services of a kind that are routinely provided to the nonhandicapped." *Id.,* at 893–894.

Unlike clean intermittent catheterization, however, a school nurse cannot provide the services that respondent requires, see *ante,* at 3, n. 3, and continue to perform her normal duties. To the contrary, because respondent requires continuous, one-on-one care throughout the entire school day, all agree that the district must hire an additional employee to attend solely to respondent. This will cost a minimum of $18,000 per year. Although the majority recognizes this fact, it nonetheless concludes that the "more extensive" nature of the services that respondent needs is irrelevant to the question whether those services fall under the medical services exclusion. *Ante,* at 9. This approach disregards the constitutionally mandated principles of construction applicable to Spending Clause legislation and blindsides unwary States with fiscal obligations that they could not have anticipated.

⚬◈⚬

For the foregoing reasons, I respectfully dissent.

Notes

1. The Act currently defines "related services" as "transportation and such developmental, corrective, and other supportive services (including speech pathology and audiology, psychological services, physical and occupational therapy, recreation, including therapeutic recreation, social work services, counseling services, including rehabilitation counseling, and medical services, *except that such medical services shall be for diagnostic and evaluation purposes only*) as may be required to assist a child with a disability to benefit from special education...." 20 U.S.C. § 1401(a)(17) (emphasis added).

2. See, *e.g.*, 38 U.S.C. § 1701(6) ("The term 'medical services' includes, in addition to medical examination, treatment and rehabilitative services... surgical services, dental services,... optometric and podiatric services,... preventive health services,... [and] such consultation, professional counseling, training, and mental health services as are necessary in connection with the treatment"); §101(28) ("The term 'nursing home care' means the accommodation of convalescents... who require nursing care and related medical services"); 26 U.S.C. § 213(d)(1) ("The term 'medical care' means amounts paid—... for the diagnosis, cure, mitigation, treatment, or prevention of disease").

3. Nor do I think that it is appropriate to defer to the Department of Education's litigating position in this case. The agency has had ample opportunity to address this problem but has failed to do so in a formal regulation. Instead, it has maintained conflicting positions about whether the services at issue in this case are required by IDEA. See *ante,* at 7–8, n. 6. Under these circumstances, we should not assume that the litigating position reflects the "agency's fair and considered judgment." *Auer* v. *Robbins,* 519 U.S. 452, 462 (1997).

POSTSCRIPT

Should One-on-One Nursing Care Be Part of Special Education?

As with most complex legislation, the implementation of IDEA has been defined through court decisions. Garret's case—and others like it—highlight the complexity involved in designing education that includes all learners.

All members of the Supreme Court agreed that Garret's services were costly and complicated. The majority found that these factors do not matter, almost requesting a renovation of IDEA to be more specific about limits in this area. In short, while it did not seem very happy about the decision, the majority felt that it was the only choice under the current law. The bright line may not be the best line, but it is clear and easy to apply. Now it is clear that schools have no choice.

The minority contends that *Garret* and *Tatro* have crossed a boundary that was very clear in IDEA. Schools cannot fulfill their educational mission when their energies are focused on medical care. If Congress had meant to include daily medical attention, it would have said so. IDEA limits medical services to diagnosis and evaluation, argues the minority. Continuous care does not fall within that limit.

Despite the clear connections to health-related conditions, parental medical insurance is not a resource for schools. Because families of children with significant disabilities can easily exceed lifetime limits on coverage or be placed in financial risk categories with costly premiums, courts have upheld exclusionary clauses that prohibit insurance coverage for services or equipment that the insured is entitled to under IDEA (Katsiyannis and Yell, *Exceptional Children*, 2000).

As more children come to school in a fragile condition—and as the procedures to support them become more complex—district personnel must be prepared to deliver emergency care, sometimes in life-threatening situations. The consequences of not reacting fast enough or with sufficient wisdom and skill raise fears of liability among educators. To date, this issue has not been tried in the courts, which have determined that concerns about consequences should not prohibit implementation of accommodations and services by individuals who have been adequately trained.

As medical science continues to advance, will schools soon be required to provide even more extensive and expensive medical services? Is this what IDEA meant? Should the federal law be rewritten to refocus human and financial resources on education and to delegate medical responsibilities to other agencies? Can the line be drawn more clearly in a different location, or will any change simply spawn more debate? Should there be any line at all?

Center for Law and Education

This Web site is operated by the Center for Law and Education, which is based in Washington, D.C., and Boston, Massachusetts. It is a source for information about legal access issues for students with disabilities, with a special focus on those who have the added challenge of low income. This site has numerous links to current legal issues, upcoming changes in regulation, and hot issues such as curriculum access, discipline, and testing.

http://www.cleweb.org

Institute on Disability/UAP

This site details the actions of the Institute on Disability/University Affiliated Program, located at the University of New Hampshire in Durham, New Hampshire. The institute has a wide scope of activities designed to promote active and effective inclusion of individuals with disabilities in school and work settings.

http://www.iod.unh.edu

National Association of the Deaf

The National Association of the Deaf (NAD) is a nonprofit organization dedicated to advocacy for individuals who are deaf or hard of hearing. This site provides extensive information and links regarding the array of issues pertinent to those who are Deaf and those who are deaf/hard of hearing.

http://nad.org

Circle of Inclusion

This Web site, funded by the U.S. Office of Special Education Programs, is targeted to providing information and resources about the effective practices of inclusive educational programs for children from birth through age eight. Links to additional resources and videoclips can be found on the home page.

http://www.circleofinclusion.org

National Resource Center for Paraprofessionals in Education and Related Services

The National Resource Center for Paraprofessionals addresses questions of policy and practice regarding the work done by paraprofessionals. Bibliography entries on paraprofessionals, articles, and research updates enhance knowledge about this growing group of educators.

http://www.nrcpara.org

PART 2

Inclusion

*A**fter talking with educators, parents, and aspiring teachers for years, I am convinced that the definition of* inclusion *is infinitely variable. It is a term so widely used that some may think it synonymous with special education. The practice of balancing a free appropriate public education (FAPE) and the least restrictive environment (LRE) is delicate. Inclusive programming is not easily accomplished, and inclusionary programs are not strategies for saving money. Like all good education, inclusion re-quires careful attention to individuals. Awareness of the dimensions of the debate keeps everyone's eyes on the best interests of each child.*

- Does Inclusion Work?

- Does Full Inclusion Deliver a Good Education?

- Are Residential Schools the Least Restrictive Environment for Deaf Children?

- Should Students With Disabilities Be Exempt From Standards-Based Curricula?

- Are the Least Trained Teaching Our Most Needy Children?

ISSUE 9

Does Inclusion Work?

YES: Dorothy Kerzner Lipsky and Alan Gartner, from "Taking Inclusion Into the Future," *Educational Leadership* (October 1998)

NO: Daniel P. Hallahan, from "We Need More Intensive Instruction," *LD Online,* http://www.ldonline.org/first_person/hallahan.html (June 30, 2001)

ISSUE SUMMARY

YES: Dorothy Kerzner Lipsky, director of the National Center on Educational Restructuring and Inclusion at the City University of New York, and professor of educational psychology Alan Gartner emphasize that IDEA97 supports inclusion as the best way to educate students with disabilities and discuss the ingredients that contribute to successful inclusionary practices.

NO: Daniel P. Hallahan, a professor of education at the University of Virginia in Charlottesville, fears that students with disabilities will lose access to necessary, specially designed instruction in the inclusionary rush to return them to the very classrooms in which they experienced failure.

In 1986 Madeline Will, then–assistant secretary of education, launched the Regular Education Initiative (*Exceptional Children,* 1986). While acknowledging that the first 10 years of mandated special education had provided opportunities for many children, Will decried the separate nature of special education. She challenged general education administrators to take responsibility for the education of students with mild to moderate disabilities and to accept "the general applicability of special education techniques beyond the confines of the special education class." In words that could have been spoken last week, Will predicted that less-segregated programming would "prepare all children to identify, analyze and resolve problems as they arise; to increase their ability to cope in a flexible manner with change... and to enter the community as informed and educated citizens who are capable of living and working as independent and productive adults."

Information from the *Annual Reports to Congress* indicates that the percentage of children with disabilities increased consistently and substantially from 1988 to 1995, especially students identified as having learning disabilities, health or orthopedic impairments, or communications disorders. In general, these students are considered to have mild disabilities, and the services and supports that they need are not viewed as intense.

The impact of these disabilities is deceptive, however. Although children with mild disabilities might look, think, and behave more like their nondisabled peers than students with severe disabilities, they encounter significant challenges mastering the basic building blocks of reading, writing, and math. Educators and researchers labor mightily to identify specialized teaching methods to overcome the hurdles posed by nimble minds that are stymied by tasks that others learn easily.

As special education developed, many children with mild disabilities received their specially designed instruction in small self-contained rooms, with little connection to their age-mates. Alternatively, some children would be enrolled in typical classes but "pulled out" of class to receive help from a specialist. School days focused on intensive instruction and remediation. The goal was to help students conquer the basic skills so that they could return to their "regular" classes. While this remediation occurred, students often missed the curriculum and activities of the general classroom. Two separate educational systems existed; Will proposed that they merge, sharing responsibility for the education of all children.

In the following selection, Dorothy Kerzner Lipsky and Alan Gartner support that merger and review the elements of IDEA97 that will propel schools to make the structural changes necessary to create inclusive environments. The authors assert that combining the classroom teacher's curriculum knowledge with the special educator's ability to individualize instruction increases options for all children. Such collaboration will eliminate the need to make a choice between remediation and curriculum.

In the second selection, Daniel P. Hallahan contends that inclusion represents a step backward in time—one that ignores research findings about the effectiveness of specially designed instruction. Instead of combining expertise to create a whole larger than the sum of the parts, Hallahan fears that inclusionary collaboration dilutes the effectiveness of both educational environments, helping no one and widening the educational gap between children with mild disabilities and their grade-level peers.

As you read these selections, ask yourself whether inclusionary programs for students with mild disabilities are doorways to expanded learning or barriers preventing access to critical remediation.

**Dorothy Kerzner Lipsky
and Alan Gartner**

 **YES**

Taking Inclusion Into the Future

T o improve education for children with disabilities, we cannot address special education by itself. Rather, we must look toward educational restructuring —changing the nature and practice of education in general, not just education called "special." The reauthorized Individuals with Disabilities Education Act (IDEA) reflects these needs and propels them further.

Until 1975, with the passage of the Education of All Handicapped Children Act, children with disabilities were not ensured what was a right of their nondisabled siblings and peers, the right to attend public schools. The 1975 law granted a "free appropriate public education" to all children, regardless of the nature or severity of their handicap. In the two decades since then, the U.S. public education system has provided students with that access, an achievement unparalleled anywhere in the world. As such, it both marks what schools can do and provides a basis for what still needs to be done—educational outcomes of high quality for all students.

Special Education, Both Separate and Unequal

Too often in the past, providing access meant that students with disabilities were served in separate special education classes and programs—despite the 1975 law's "least restrictive environment" (LRE) mandate. This mandate required that students with disabilities be educated to the maximum extent with children who were not disabled, and that students with disabilities be removed from regular classes only when they could not be educated in a regular setting with supplementary aids and support services. After more than two decades, the most recent data from the U.S. Department of Education reports that 55 percent of children with disabilities, ages 6 through 21, are not fully included in regular classes. This, despite the fact that more than 71 percent of the five million students with disabilities, ages 6 through 21, served through IDEA in the 1995–96 school year had the least severe impairments—learning disabilities (51 percent) and speech or language impairments (20 percent) *(U.S. Department of Education, 1997, Tables II-6).*

Throughout the 1980s and into the current decade, the experience of students with disabilities, their parents, and their teachers is that a dual system of

From Dorothy Kerzner Lipsky and Alan Gartner, "Taking Inclusion Into the Future," *Educational Leadership*, vol. 56, no. 2 (October 1998). Copyright © 1998 by The Association for Supervision and Curriculum Development. Reprinted by permission. References omitted.

education fails all students, primarily those with disabilities, in terms of student learning, drop-out rates, graduation rates, participation in postsecondary education and training, and community living (see Lipsky & Gartner, 1997). The most recent federal study reports that the graduation rate for students with disabilities was 57 percent, as compared with 76 percent for students without disabilities. *(U.S. Department of Education,* 1997, p. IV-11).

Longitudinal studies and research findings confirmed the experience of students, parents, and teachers that the separate system was flawed and unequal; this led to many championing a new inclusive design. This model holds to several principles: students are more alike than different; with effective educational practices, schools can educate well and together a wide range of students with better outcomes for all; and separation is costly, a civil rights violation, and a cause for limited outcomes for students with disabilities.

IDEA 1997

Similar beliefs motivated the administration and Congress to reauthorize the federal law. Culminating a two-year process, the reauthorized IDEA emphasizes two major principles: The education of students with disabilities should produce outcomes akin to those expected for students in general, and students with disabilities should be educated with their nondisabled peers. These features are expressed in the law's "findings" section, its implementation provisions, and the funding provisions as they concern inclusive education. Although the reauthorization does not mention "inclusive education" (nor had previous laws), one might think of IDEA 1997 as the *I*nclusion *D*evelopment and *E*xpansion *A*ct.

Findings: Congress asserted that the education of students with disabilities would be more effective by "having high expectations for students and ensuring their success in the general curriculum...."; "[ensuring] that special education can become a service for such children rather than a place where they are sent...."; and "providing incentives for the whole-school approaches...." The House and Senate Committee reports that accompany the law highlight the primary purpose of the new Act: to go beyond access to the schools and to secure for every child an education that actually yields successful educational results.

Implementation: Two sets of requirements will have direct consequences for students: student evaluation requirements and instruction and assessment requirements. In determining a student's classification and special needs, schools must consider whether factors other than disability will affect the student's performance. Specifically, the law states that a student may not be identified as disabled if the determining factor is inadequacy of instruction in reading or math. In other words, if the failure lies in the school's services, then the remedy is not labeling the student but fixing the school's program.

IDEA consistently reinforces the expectation that a student with a disability will be educated in the general education environment. For example, if a student is or may be participating in the general education program, the individual education program (IEP) team must include a general education teacher. If the child is currently in a general education classroom, the classroom teacher is to be a member of the IEP team. This brings to the IEP process someone familiar with the general education curriculum, which will be the basis of the student's program. And since the IEP meeting is supposed to be a decision-making event in which parents also participate, a school might be vulnerable to a legal challenge if it fails to include a general education teacher.

Further, should the school system propose that a child with a disability not participate with nondisabled students in academic, extracurricular, or nonacademic activities, it must justify such nonparticipation. In other words, supplemental aids and support services in the general education environment and in the curriculum should be considered the norm; schools must justify and explain exclusion in any of these areas. Only then may they consider other placements.

Schools must develop performance goals drawn from general classroom students for all students with disabilities. They then must develop performance indicators to assess achievement of these goals, with necessary adaptations and modifications. The school's and district's public reports must incorporate the results of performance. This is a requirement for all schools and covers all students.

Funding: States must change their funding formulas for supporting local school districts by removing incentives for placing students in more (rather than less) restrictive environments. This will require changes in all but a handful of states. Additionally, the previous provision that IDEA funds may not be used to benefit nondisabled students has been rescinded. Further, given that general education teachers will have a major role in providing services to students with disabilities, IDEA personnel-preparation funds may be used to train them. Indeed, in language accompanying the appropriations bills, Congress has emphasized that the substantial new funds must be used for such activities.

Implementing Inclusive Education Programs

In the implementation of the new federal mandate, a growing body of experience can guide practice. Over a two-year period, the National Center on Educational Restructuring and Inclusion (NCERI) surveyed school districts identified by each chief state school officer as implementing inclusive education programs *(NCERI, 1994, 1995)*. The reports from nearly 1,000 school districts provide a basis for understanding the factors necessary for successful implementation. These are congruent with the findings of a Working Forum on Inclusive Schools, convened by 10 national organizations *(Council for Exceptional Children, 1995)* and reported in an Association for Supervision and Curriculum Development publication (Thousand & Villa, 1995).

The NCERI study identified seven factors for the successful implementation of inclusive education:

1. *Visionary leadership.* This leadership can come from many sources, including school superintendents, building administrators, teachers, parents, school board members, disability advocates, and universities. Whatever the initial impetus for inclusive education programs, all stakeholders must ultimately take responsibility for the outcome.

2. *Collaboration.* The process of inclusive education involves three types of collaboration: between general and special educators, between classroom practitioners and providers of related services, and between those involved in student evaluation and program development (that is, the IEP team) and classroom practitioners. Each group needs time for collaboration.

3. *Refocused use of assessment.* Schools must replace the traditional screening for separate special education programs with more authentic assessment that addresses student strengths as well as needs and that provides useful guidance for classroom practitioners. Schools must develop and use adapted methods to assess student knowledge. They must question the use of traditional measures of potential (such as IQ tests) and opt for curriculum-based assessment.

4. *Support for staff and students.* School staff must have time to work together and have effective professional development programs. Staff development should be sensitive to the needs of adult learners and involve more than one-shot experiences. Support for students should include the full panoply of supplemental aids and services that the law mandates, such as curriculum modifications; alternative instructional strategies; adapted assessment measures; and procedures, technology, and roles for paraprofessionals and other support personnel.

5. *Appropriate funding levels and formulas.* Data from school districts about special education funding are limited and difficult to compare. School districts reporting in the *National Study* (NCERI, 1994, 1995) indicate that although there are initial start-up costs for planning and professional development activities, a unitary system over time is not more expensive than separate special education. Funds that follow the student with special needs into the general education environment can provide preventive services for some students and enhanced learning opportunities for others, thereby making inclusive education no more costly over time. However, districts that continue to operate under a dual system will be more costly.

6. *Parental involvement.* Because parental involvement is essential, schools report creative approaches to make parents an integral part of the school community. This goes well beyond the procedural due process requirements of the law. For example, in New York City's Community School District 22, pairs of general and special education parents have been instructed about the basis of inclusive education and its benefits for all students.

7. *Effective program models, curriculum adaptations, and instructional practices.* There is no single model of inclusion. Most common is the pairing of a general and a special education teacher to work together in an inclusive classroom with general and special education students. At one middle school, a special education teacher and his or her class become part of the team. In other settings, a special education teacher serves as a consultant to several general education teachers, in whose classes students with disabilities are included. Increasingly, districts are seeking teachers who are dual licensed and, thus, can themselves teach inclusive classrooms.

Special education teachers often report their lack of knowledge about the general education curriculum, whereas general education teachers often report their lack of knowledge about individualizing instruction. However, after a year of collaboration, both report greater knowledge and comfort in these areas. They use many of the same instructional strategies in the inclusive education classroom that are effective for students in general classrooms. These include cooperative learning, hands-on learning, peer and cross-age tutoring and support models, instruction based on students' multiple intelligences, classroom technology, and paraprofessionals and classroom assistants (not "Velcroed" to the individual child but serving the whole class).

As Congress pointed out in the reauthorized IDEA, special education should be understood as a service, not a place. Thus, a student (labeled either special or general education) may receive services in a variety of settings or groups. Though not a legal term, inclusion is best expressed in the student who is on the regular register, attends homeroom with her or his peers, participates equally in all school activities, receives instruction suited to her or his needs, is held to the school's common standards, and receives the same report card as other students. As a New York City Public Schools superintendent stated, "Inclusion is about 'ownership.' They are all our students."

The Future of Inclusive Education

As Edmonds (1979) declared two decades ago concerning the education of minority students, we know how to provide effective education at the school level, but we have yet to do so on a districtwide basis. So, too, with inclusive education. We have numerous pilot programs and, increasingly, whole-school approaches for inclusion. However, inclusion as yet remains largely a separate initiative, parallel to, rather than integrated within, broad school reforms. Some of the national reforms, especially Slavin's Success for All, Levin's Accelerated Schools, Sizer's Coalition of Essential Schools, Comer's School Development, and Wang's Community for Learning, incorporate inclusive models (Wang, Haertel, & Walberg, 1998).

Beyond these efforts, other factors are conducive to the expansion of inclusive education. They include the success of inclusive education programs; the now firm legal mandate to educate students with disabilities with their nondisabled peers, especially the requirement that their performance be included in school and district performance reports; public concern for the costs of separate programs that do not serve students with disabilities well; and the growing insistence from parents not only that their children with disabilities be served in the public schools, but also that their children's education be of high quality, preparing them to participate as full and contributing members of an inclusive society. These changes need to occur in more than just school. Commensurate changes must occur in the universities, in the workplace, and in the community.

Inclusion goes beyond returning students who have been in separate placements to the general education classroom. It incorporates an end to labeling students and shunting them out of the regular classroom to obtain needed services. It responds to Slavin's call for "neverstreaming" by establishing a refashioned mainstream, a restructured and unified school system that serves all students together.

Daniel P. Hallahan  **NO**

We Need More Intensive Instruction

I would like to sketch out a few of my major concerns related to the field of special education, generally, and to learning disabilities, in particular. Although I don't view myself as a whiner by nature, I was surprised at just how many concerns flashed through my mind as I set about preparing for this article. I really do think that special education, and especially learning disabilities, is in trouble. And I guess, if I had to pinpoint the one thing that pervades most of my concerns, it would be that the field has lost its instructional momentum. Or as my respected colleague, Doug Fuchs, remarked at a recent meeting, the field has lost its instructional intensity.

What do I mean by instructional momentum or instructional intensity? Back in the early 1980s the field had a focus on instructional issues and methodology. Researchers were focused on testing interventions for students. And special education teachers were actually teaching students with learning disabilities—in small groups, in large groups, or individually.

In the past 10 years or so, however, researchers and practitioners, alike, have been pulled away from this concentration on instruction. Any focus on instruction has been lost to a seeming obsession with where instruction takes place. Starting with Madeline Will's call in 1986 (Will, 1986) for a regular education initiative, to the call for the total annihilation of special education by the full inclusionists, up to the present-day love affair with collaborative teaching and the general education curriculum, we have lost our resolve to teach students with learning disabilities to read better, do math better, attend-to-task better, and/or interact with their peers better.

Researchers have been diverted from pursuing topics related to instruction in order to try to put out brush fires set by those who would gut the continuum of placements in favor of full inclusion. Teachers have been forced into hastily conceived models of inclusion and collaborative teaching. And those of us in teacher education have all too often caved in to pressures from the marketplace to prepare teachers certified to teach students from two or three different categories of disability as well as general education students. On top of this, we're expected to prepare novice preservice teachers to be ready to teach collaboratively with general education colleagues, some of whom have several years of teaching experience.

From Daniel P. Hallahan, "We Need More Intensive Instruction," *LD Online,* http://www.ldonline.org/first_person/hallahan.html (June 30, 2001). Copyright © 2001 by Daniel P. Hallahan. Reprinted by permission of *LD Online* and the author. References omitted.

Please don't get me wrong. Collaborative teaching can work. I'm sure many [such teachers] have engaged in some very successful collaborative teaching arrangements. But I'm also sure [they] recognize that, when it does work, it's because of a very special relationship [they] forged with [their] general education colleague—a relationship that research shows is not easily established and maintained. Collaborative teaching can be a very effective model under the right circumstances for some students—maybe even many students—but not for all students. In a collaborative model, what happens to those students who require intensive instruction? Who provides it? My fear is that the current emphasis on collaboration leads teachers away from actual teaching. They are spending their time consulting with general education teachers rather than teaching. Or, at best, they are teaching, but the effects of their instruction are diminished because it's spread over large numbers of students, some of whom are not learning disabled.

A recent study by Budah, Schumaker, and Deshler (1997) is important here. This is one of the few well controlled studies of collaborative teaching. In a secondary setting, they found that both teachers (the general education and special education teacher) spent over half their time engaged in non-instructional behaviors. Furthermore, they spent less than 10% of their time presenting content. Not surprisingly, they also found that the outcome measures for the students with learning disabilities were very disappointing.

Also, don't get me wrong on another point—it is important that students with learning disabilities have access to the general education curriculum. A very legitimate criticism of the resource room model of the 1980s is that far too often the special education teacher and his or her students had no idea what was transpiring in the general education classroom. I fear, however, that folks are going to translate the 1997 IDEA [Individuals with Disabilities Education Act] emphasis on the general education classroom to mean exclusive placement in general education classrooms. Why can't students with learning disabilities learn the general education curriculum with the help of special educators in special education settings? Furthermore, let's not forget that failure in the general education curriculum is what got many of these students into special education in the first place. Just maybe there's something wrong with the general education curriculum. Access to the general education curriculum is great, but how about access to instruction?

I have to wonder if there isn't a connection between the current zeitgeist and the tremendous teacher attrition problem in special education. The irony is that learning disabilities teachers are working harder than ever, but they're spending less and less time actually teaching. Special education teachers have lost their identity as teachers. Instead, they find themselves in a limbo-like state somewhere between special and general education. In fact, their strongest identity with special education is probably linked to the IEP [individual education program]. And with the new IDEA Amendments, the paperwork associated with that document is only going to increase. In short, special education teachers often find themselves being glorified aides and paper-pushers.

Perhaps one of the major reasons we're in the mess we're in is because people don't take learning disabilities seriously enough. It's almost as if they view it as a minor inconvenience rather than the life-long serious condition [we] know it can be, and often is. This carefree attitude toward learning disabilities, coupled with the mantra of reformers, "all children can learn," ends up short-changing students with learning disabilities. Sure, all children can learn, but they have to be instructed first. Sure, all children can learn, but not to the same degree and not with the same facility. At the core of special education are the ideas that some children are able to learn better than others and that some children will find learning some things virtually impossible. That's why we have special education. It's the erosion of these core beliefs that many reformers would like to see happen—reformers who assert that students with learning disabilities can be served in general education classrooms, with, at most, a little consultation from special educators.

I'd like to end by referring to Martha Minow's (1985) idea of the "dilemma of difference." She wrote a chapter on bilingual education, in which she talked about the dilemma one faces by either ignoring or recognizing differences in children. To recognize that some children are different, carries the risk of labeling and stigmatizing them. However, to ignore differences runs the risk of neglecting student's instructional needs. It's unfortunate that so many are opting to ignore the differences. It seems to me that ignoring differences is a totally unsatisfactory solution to the dilemma. A better course is to admit that the dilemma of difference doesn't have a completely satisfactory solution. In lieu of a perfect solution, we need to recognize, not ignore, the differences students with learning disabilities exhibit. We need to find ways to diminish these differences. And the way to do this, I think, is through intensive instruction. If we ignore differences, the children won't learn plus they'll be stigmatized anyway because of their learning problems. But if we recognize differences and actually do something about them through intensive instruction, the children will at least learn.

POSTSCRIPT

Does Inclusion Work?

Debates about inclusion often take place in hearing rooms and courts, with schools and parents supporting their preferred programs. The direction of preference is not at all predictable. Schools sometimes advocate for services delivered in the regular education classroom rather than intensive specialized programs. At other times, the same schools may favor a more restrictive, separate program. Some parents feel that the regular education classroom holds the key to generalized learning and growth. Others feel that a private school focuses on direct and intensive programming that will ensure success for their children. It is likely that the position held is governed by direct experience with school programs. One's position is also affected by the individual child.

As might be expected, legal decisions regarding inclusive programming have also varied in outcome, although there is a guiding decision point. In light of the language of "least restrictive environment," the courts place the burden on the party seeking a more restrictive program to prove that it is most beneficial to the child (McCarthy, *Educational Horizons,* 1998). To prevail, this party must make a solid argument demonstrating that genuine efforts to support education in the mainstream have not resulted in school progress.

The efforts to support inclusion are significant. Lipsky and Gartner discuss factors that are critical to successful programs, ranging from leadership to financial and professional support. Students, teachers, and parents, they say, will not be helped by programs that are mandated by administration directives to unprepared faculty or by programs that are understaffed. Also, school and district administrators who support and value inclusion must help teachers and parents solve the most difficult problems.

Energies for successful inclusion are so substantial that Hallahan wonders if they will overburden special education faculty, who he feels are already buried beneath required paperwork. When more time is devoted to meetings and collaboration, less is available for direct contact with students who are crying out for professional expertise.

Hallahan's concerns about the effectiveness of inclusion programs are echoed by Baker and Zigmond (*Journal of Special Education,* 1995), whose extensive study of five schools found numerous examples of admirably adapted assignments for whole classes but few situations in which the education was specially designed and delivered to meet the specific educational needs of students with disabilities within those classes.

How do the schools that you know address inclusion? What factors do they consider when making decisions to balance classroom participation and intensive remediation? How are inclusion efforts supported? What do teachers, parents, and students say about the compromises that have been struck?

ISSUE 10

Does Full Inclusion Deliver a Good Education?

YES: Susan Shapiro-Barnard et al., from *Petroglyphs: The Writing on the Wall* (Institute on Disability/UAP, 1996)

NO: Gary M. Chesley and Paul D. Calaluce, Jr., from "The Deception of Inclusion," *Mental Retardation* (December 1997)

ISSUE SUMMARY

YES: Susan Shapiro-Barnard and her colleagues in the Institute on Disability at the University of New Hampshire affirm the positive outcomes of full inclusion at the high school level for students with significant cognitive disabilities.

NO: Public school administrators Gary M. Chesley and Paul D. Calaluce, Jr., express their concern that full inclusion of students with significant cognitive disabilities does not provide appropriate preparation for successful life following school.

$\mathbf{A}$sk a group of people about the definition of *inclusion* and they will usually come up with a statement like, "All children being educated in the same school." Ask again, "Do you mean *all* children?" The reply is likely to be a bit less certain: "Well, maybe not *all*." Probe a bit further and someone is likely to admit (with a bit of trepidation) that inclusion should mean "all students except..." The words that follow might vary, but usually there are exceptions for students with severe cognitive challenges—those who have mental retardation or those who have disabilities in multiple areas and require complex and broad levels of support in order to communicate, move, and learn. So inclusion, for many people, does not really include *all* children.

Proponents of full inclusion would have a very different answer. They would say—and mean—all children being educated in the same school. Full inclusion advocates insist that all children, regardless of level of need, have a moral and legal right to attend their home school, be enrolled in a general education class, and receive all necessary supports within that class. In a full inclusion environment, students do not need to fit into the school; the school needs to adapt to all students. This means that services are brought to the child; children are not sent out (or away) because what they need is not available.

Those who oppose full inclusion cite the difficulties of adapting instruction, meeting student needs, and acquiring needed supports. Accustomed to a traditional academic curriculum for some students and a vocational, life skills–based curriculum for others, they ask how the needs of both can be met.

The challenge of full inclusion is perhaps greatest for high schools, which focus on distinct academic disciplines and college hopes. Communication among high school teachers is complicated by the increased number of people who interact with each student and the large numbers of students taught by each educator. The specialization and concentration of high schools has become even more intense with the advent of high-stakes testing, causing some to wonder if the needs of every child can be met within a typical classroom.

Susan Shapiro-Barnard, Carol Tashie, Jill Martin, Joanne Malloy, Mary Schuh, Jim Piet, Stephen Lichtenstein, and Jan Nisbet have worked with numerous high schools across New Hampshire, overcoming long-held assumptions about possibilities and individual potential. In the following selection, the authors look beyond what they "used to think" and reflect on the accomplishments of students with disabilities and fully inclusive high school programs.

In the second selection, Gary M. Chesley and Paul D. Calaluce, Jr., advise caution, noting that the solutions and suggestions of full inclusion proponents are complex, time consuming, and challenging. They express concern that full inclusion of students with significant disabilities—especially at the high school level—might appeal to everyone's sense of fairness and goodness but result in precious little time spent on the skills and knowledge that are essential for adult success.

As you read these selections, ask yourself, Is it educationally reasonable to expect the general education classroom to meet the needs of every student? And can a student be truly included in the adult world if that process does not begin in school?

Petroglyphs: The Writing on the Wall

Although inclusive education has taken a strong hold in schools throughout the country, high school students with disabilities still face the real and frightening possibility of segregation. We used to accept this. We used to think that high schools could not embody both excellence and equity. But we now know better. By challenging existing beliefs and practices, [we] advocate... change. Change that disturbs the universe of special education. Change that goes beyond a revelation to become part of a revolution. Change that is more than a nodding of the head.

Frederick Douglas once wrote, "People who advocate freedom, yet deprecate agitation, are people who want crops without plowing the ground." It's time to turn the soil. Douglas continued, "Without struggle, there is no progress." [We] honor... the struggle in all of us. The struggle to embrace our old thinking for a moment, learn from it, and then push it aside. With confidence. For the writing is on the wall.

We used to think students with disabilities couldn't learn academics in regular high school classes. That functional-daily-living-skills were more important than reading and writing and math. That cooking skills were more important than knowledge. So we taught students to read safety words while their peers were reading books. We took students to the bowling alley while their classmates studied physics. We equated not being able to read Shakespeare, with not being able to appreciate it. Not being able to raise your hand in class, with having nothing to say.

We now know seven of the most dangerous words in our vocabulary are "she won't get anything out of it." We now know students with disabilities can learn academic skills. And that it's advantageous to do so. We now know literacy is probably the most functional skill in our society. And there is great value in knowledge. We now know about the "least dangerous assumption." So when we aren't sure whether or not a student understands, we must assume that she does. We now know the high price of assuming she does not.

We used to think if a student wasn't able to open a biology book and answer the questions on page seventy-two, that the student would be better off in a special education classroom. But then we learned about the importance of inclusion. And so, when the teacher said turn to page seventy-two, we no

From Susan Shapiro-Barnard, Carol Tashie, Jill Martin, Joanne Malloy, Mary Schuh, Jim Piet, Stephen Lichtenstein, and Jan Nisbet, *Petroglyphs: The Writing on the Wall* (Institute on Disability/UAP, 1996). Copyright © 1996 by The Institute on Disability/UAP, University of New Hampshire. Reprinted by permission.

longer asked that student to leave. Instead, we handed her something else to do—something "on her level." And we called on a special education teacher to create it. And we called on a paraprofessional to implement it. But the student never got called on, because the biology teacher didn't know what the student was doing.

We now know we can do better. That it is possible for students with disabilities to learn from the regular education curriculum. That the barrier to this happening isn't the student's ability, but often it is our own. We know "no man is an island," but without modifications and supports, sometimes students with disabilities in regular classrooms can be. We now know the difference between alternative and modified. That "being in" isn't the same thing as "being with." And that ultimately we need to stop talking about curriculum modification and start talking about inclusive curriculum design.

We used to think students with disabilities didn't need guidance counselors. Or lockers, or notebooks, or an excuse for being late to class. We used to think students with disabilities couldn't be sent to the principal's office. Didn't need transcripts. Couldn't make the team. When students needed to practice communication skills we sent them to the speech room—we forgot about the cafeteria. When students got sick, the special education teacher called home—we forgot about the school nurse. And when classmates were getting homework assignments, we forgot to give students with disabilities anything at all.

We now know about natural supports. And that "only as special as necessary" are words to live by. We now know about the people, places, and things that support all high school students. So instead of "checking in" each morning to the special education room, students check into homeroom. Instead of aides being assigned to students, instructional assistants are assigned to classrooms. And instead of IEP [individual education program] progress notes, all students get report cards. We now know that including students without natural supports just moves the self-contained classroom into regular education. It only changes the place where supports are provided. Not the way. Not the who. Not the how.

We used to think making a bed, change for a dollar, and a grilled cheese sandwich were important skills for students with disabilities to learn during high school. That achieving these skills would lead to a full—and fulfilling—life. Of course, we had heard about inclusion. Of course, we had heard stories of students learning academics, gaining friendships, and trying out for the school play. It sounded great. It sounded wonderful. But it sounded like something was missing. When did these students learn functional skills?

We now know when—and how—students with disabilities can learn functional skills during a typical high school day. We now know money skills can be taught in math class, the cafeteria, and the school store. That cooking can be learned in culinary arts. And let's face it, just how important is "bed-making" anyway? At the same time, we realize these things are not enough. That learning to work in a group, solve a problem, and ask for help are essential skills for all people in the real world. At home. Around town. On the job. And these things are taught in regular education classes. Everyday. To all students.

We used to think it was a good idea for students with disabilities to spend a portion of their day out in the community separated from their peers. We used to think they needed "the exposure." We used to think when students left school in the middle of the day, they didn't really miss anything. And if it's true actions speak louder than words, then it can be said we thought going to the mall was more important than going to class. It's as if we thought once a student had the skills to eat in a restaurant, buy a bus ticket, and cross the street, something magical would happen. We used to think only students with disabilities needed to learn in the community. But then students without disabilities began leaving school during the day. And we wondered what they were doing.

We now know community-based instruction is not the same as community service. Job shadowing isn't an internship. And walking the mall is walking the mall. We now know that community-based-instruction is rooted in the notion that—in the name of skill acquisition—it's okay to separate students with disabilities from their peers. (Didn't we used to call that segregation?) We still recognize that some skills need to be learned outside of the school building. But we now know this can happen at times when all students are out of school. For there are still too many students who can eat in a restaurant but have no one to eat with. Too many students who are buying vowels instead of bus tickets.

We used to think being included from seven-thirty until two was enough. That a full day of classes equaled a full life. We thought if students were well supported during the school day, we had done our job. Yes, there were stories of students sitting in front of the television everyday after school. Yes, parents asked for ideas, names, and activities. And yes, we were concerned. But what could we do? After-school was not our responsibility. Surely there was an agency that could help.

We now know life does not end after the last bell. That all students need to be supported to have full after-school lives. That clubs, sports, teams, and just "hanging out" matter as much as classes. And sure, we still struggle to get students the right after-school supports. In the right places. At the right times. And it's not always easy to find that ride home. And we still worry about the limits of our responsibility. But we're talking about people's lives, so can we really just say, "It's not my job"?

We used to think friendships for students with disabilities couldn't happen. That it was too hard. That the only way to get people involved was to pay them. We used to think peer support was friendship. And that it was okay if the aide was the student's "best friend." We used to think having people say "hello" in the hallways was enough. And that we were working on friendship if socialization goals were written on the IEP. As if maintaining eye contact could fill a Saturday night.

We now know we were right about friendships being hard work, but wrong to think they couldn't happen. We now acknowledge what we should have known all along—students absolutely must share time and space. There is no other way. We have learned this from students who tell us they are lonely. We have learned this from parents who would trade all of their child's therapy units for a single phone call. And, as hard as it is to hear, we have learned this from classmates who tell us that adults often stand in the way—literally—of real friendships happening. Their advice: take a step back, don't force it, trust us.

We used to think high school students with disabilities needed to learn prevocational skills. That sorting forks from spoons, nuts from bolts, and red from yellow would lead to gainful employment. But how many jobs are there sorting nuts and bolts? We used to tell students they had plenty of jobs to choose from. (As if working with food, cleaning supplies, and plants was choice enough.) And that they needed job coaches by their sides. Because employers didn't have the training. Or the time. We used to think going to work was more important than going to class. That a student couldn't learn job skills in school. And that filling a soda machine was more important than geography.

We now know the best kind of job training for any student is a wall-rounded education. That students with disabilities shouldn't have to choose between classes and work. That real jobs happen after and beyond school. And involve a paycheck at the end of the week. We now know the best person to teach the job is a person who knows the job—a co-worker. Because the job coach has never worked in a bank, or a record store, or a law office. We now know that being on time, working with others, and organizing materials are skills for work as well as school. That they can be learned in regular classes. And that prevocational training only gets a student ready to get ready to get ready to get ready . . .

We used to think students with disabilities didn't need to graduate. We used to think that getting a diploma didn't matter. Caps, gowns, photographs, and graduation parties—well, those things just weren't very important. And not only did we believe that students shouldn't graduate, we thought students should come back to school after their senior year. And the year after that. And sometimes even longer. It was an entitlement, so we did it. And afterwards, students went through the graduation ceremony with a class they didn't know. We used to think that made sense.

We now know graduation is one of the only remaining "rites of passage" for most young people in our country. And that it does matter. We learned this when a high school "graduate" had to get his GED [general equivalency diploma] in order to go to college. We learned this when a student confessed it was embarrassing to be a third year senior. We learned this when the bus stopped coming the day after a student's 21st birthday. We now know that students with disabilities should graduate. That some students may need continued school district support. And that we have both the power and the responsibility to figure out a way for one not to cancel out the other. Students cannot be held hostage to policy that lags behind practice.

We used to think we needed to make schools better. We still think that, and we probably always will. But we used to think schools could get better without being better for all students. That when we improved education for students without disabilities, we had improved education. We used to think ninety percent of the student population was the whole school. Or close enough. And though we never dared to say it aloud, we secretly questioned whether it was even possible to design a school that met the needs of all students. Therefore, it wasn't even our goal.

We now know equity and excellence are both possible. That they are partners when educational reform is meaningful, sustainable, and real. In fact, without equity there can be no true excellence. We now know we need to include everyone in school reform. Parents. Students. With and without disabilities. But we also know we can't wait for schools to be perfect before students with disabilities are included. (Can a school be perfect if not everyone belongs?) We now understand inclusion is not a guarantee for a flawless education—it's an assurance of a typical one. Isn't that only fair?

We used to think getting a student "into" a job was supporting her to plan for her future. That aptitude tests and vocational assessments would tell us everything we needed to know. And if the student wasn't successful, well, we did our best. But we forgot to ask students what they wanted to study. We forgot to ask students where they wanted to work. And sometimes we even forgot to ask students to attend and direct the meetings where all of these decisions were being made.

We now know that nobody has the right to plan somebody else's future. So we've stopped telling students what they should be. We've stopped telling students what they can't be. And we have started listening to what students want to be. We now know work is just one of many options for a new high school graduate. That college is a possibility for everyone. That passions and interests are just as important as skills and abilities. And "being realistic" often results in shattered dreams.

We used to think disabilities were bigger than people. That students' days were best filled with what someone said they couldn't-wouldn't-shouldn't do. So we pulled students out of English class to do physical therapy. Out of math to work on speech. Out of lunch to learn social skills in a restaurant. And although it's difficult to admit, we often believed that a student with disabilities was in need of repair. So if we could remediate the disability, we could help the student learn more. Live more. Become a better person.

We now know students with disabilities are not broken. That unlike automobiles, people don't need to be fixed. We now see past a student's label and learn the student's name. Past the IQ score to find the student's talent. We now know people are people. (Scary to think that this is something new.) And so we talk with students, not about them. We work with students, not on them. We plan with students, not for them. We follow, not lead. Ask, not tell. Respect, not change.

We used to think inclusion was a good idea for little kids, but it couldn't work in high school.

That professionals wouldn't make it work.

That high school students would be too cruel.

We now know high school inclusion can happen.

Is happening.

And continues to get better.

(The end, or maybe just the beginning.)

NO

Gary M. Chesley and
Paul D. Calaluce, Jr.

The Deception of Inclusion

Our national obsession with the inclusion of special education students into the mainstream is analogous to the description of a liberals as an individual who frantically throws 200 feet of rope to a drowning swimmer struggling only 100 feet from the shore. This liberal throws the rope in the conviction that he is saving another. Then he scampers frantically down the beach, seeking other souls to save, before he pulls the original dying victim to safety. His good intentions are misguided and provide us with a lesson about how schools treat individuals with disabilities.

Today, far too many special needs children are drowning. They are being short-changed in the name of socialization. We ar truly reliving the myth of the "Emperor's New Clothes." Everyone is afraid to state the obvious. Full inclusion for all is a myth that exists in the hearts of its supporters—those who have lost sight of practical reality. Harsh words perhaps, but they express a sentiment that needs to be addressed so that we may best prepare students with disabilities to become successful participants in our society. Once again the educational pendulum has taken a good idea to the extreme.

Inclusionists argue that children with disabilities make the greater gains when they are completely educated, *included,* in general education classes. Although there is a good deal of evidence that supports the argument that social gains can be made by students with disabilities in full inclusionary programs, the professional literature is devoid of documentation in support of the argument that full inclusionary programs improve the cognitive development of students with disabilities.

Inclusionists also contend that through cooperative planning, students with disabilities receive lessons that are modified to meet their specific needs while remaining fully involved in general education classes. On the surface this contention seems instructionally plausible and the politically correct philosophical stance for a school system to take. For those of us who walk through the halls of our nation's schools, it is clear that this strategy is flawed for several fundamental reasons.

The instructional coordination required in many of these cases sets up situations where the left hand cannot know what the right hand is doing. It is extremely difficult for a principal to provide all of the staff generally involved

From Gary M. Chesley and Paul D. Calaluce, Jr., "The Deception of Inclusion," *Mental Retardation* (December 1997). Copyright © 1997 by The American Association on Mental Retardation. Reprinted by permission of *Mental Retardation* and the authors; permission conveyed through Copyright Clearance Center, Inc. References omitted.

in supporting a fully mainstreamed child with the time necessary to adjust and to enhance curricular experiences for one child. As a result, too much planning is done "on the fly" and without a timely effort to assess the value of the modifications. In reality, many students with disabilities go through their educational career with a paraprofessional assisting them in class after class. Recently, a parent complained that her son, who had severe handicaps, had received less than an A in his English class. She contended that the boy's B+ was a result of the paraprofessional not following completely the classroom teacher's direction. What is the student actually learning in such a case, and does anyone really care?

Equally problematic is the general education curriculum's lack of focus on functional and vocational skills. Curricular demands as early as first grade do not match the educational needs of many students with disabilities. Even with an infinite amount of planning, the educational interests of some students with disabilities cannot be met through modifications to the general education curriculum. Meanwhile, the performance of special education students on state-mandated performance instruments, such Connecticut's CAPT (Connecticut Academic Performance Test), are a siren call for many to criticize the overall performance of our schools. These results, in reality, indicate the need for more aggressive and intensive remediation for our lowest achievers. Sufficient remediation is not likely to occur when a special needs student is fully included with peers who are zooming ahead academically.

Many students who have handicaps graduate from high school without the skills required to be successful in the adult world. These skills cannot, and should not, be the main focus of the general education curriculum. Classroom modifications are becoming so intrusive that many special needs students are, in the end, responsible for just a small sampling of the curriculum requirements that their peers take for granted; and this is precisely where the educational establishment is blinded at the sight of the emperor's new clothes. Too often, we feel warm and fuzzy at the mere presence of a child with disabilities mainstreamed in a regular classroom. Mom and Dad are pacified and "a program is in place"; but warm and fuzzy does not necessarily translate into academic results. When headlines scream out that high school graduates do not demonstrate basic academic skills, it is too often the special education students who are not making the grade. These young people have not acquired the cognitive skills needed to be competitive in our society nor the functional and vocational skills required for independent living. Parents tend to accept this reality only when their child is approaching graduation and the safety net of public education is about to be removed. Recently, the parents of a child who has been totally included for his entire school career petitioned a school district for an out-of-state residential placement for the student's senior year. When asked why they were requesting a program diametrically opposed to that for which they had advocated throughout the previous 10 years, their stunning response was that the child (in the end) was not prepared for the adult world.

Another fundamental requirement of a full inclusionary program is the commitment of a regular education teacher with the expertise and the perseverance to modify instruction appropriately for one, two, three or more students in a single classroom setting. In theory, all teachers provide differentiated instruction that recognizes learning styles and modalities appropriate to all students. Teaching that recognizes the needs of learners who have disabilities is sound instruction for all children. That is the theory we all know. In reality, even our best trained and most willing teachers have difficulty meeting the diverse needs of their heterogeneously grouped classes, let alone the special requirements of students with moderate to severe disabilities. "*I have twenty-five children in my second-grade class, and you can't expect me to take on more students with special needs,*" has become the oft-heard plea in school after school. This sentiment carries some grain of truth to even the most hard-core supporters of inclusion and clearly illustrates one of the legitimate road blocks to a full inclusionary program. It is inconceivable to imagine a third-grade teacher being asked to focus on entire curriculum on life skills and functional academics. Yet, it is precisely this type of program that is required by many students with severe disabilities. Yasutake and Lerner (1996) reported that 41.9% of regular educators feel that inclusion is not workable, regardless of the level of support provided, with only 4.6% responding very positively about the academic results of inclusion.

It is very disconcerting to attend a Planning and Placement Team meeting where loving parents insist that all services recommended for their child be implemented within the regular classroom. Services, such as speech and occupational therapy, are tightly focused and require a special approach and setting to maximize their effectiveness. These services, and others like them, are not delivered productively in the general education classroom. It is also common practice for independent evaluators, experts from the world outside the public schools, to recommend individual one-to-one instruction to remediate learning and language difficulties; however, these services too belong as a supplement to regular instruction.

In addition, parental demands for inclusion are often unrealistic, and at times absurd. Recently, the parent of a student with almost total intellectual and language impairment insisted that her son be included in a high school French class. Other parents of a child with multiple disabilities, including mental retardation and chronic health problems, demanded that she attend a week-long outdoor nature excursion while hooked to a life support device rather than the alternative educational experience planned for general education students not participating. The parent was making this demand on purely philosophical grounds, dismissing the fact that the field trip would be dangerous and educationally incomprehensible to the student.

Today's public schools are a microcosm of the communities that they serve. We have the opportunity to use a public school experience to teach children with disabilities the many cognitive and social skills needed for assimilation into the community. The socialization gains are important but need to be placed within a valid educational context. Proponents of inclusion assume that through mainstreaming skills will be assimilated as they are taught in the regular classroom. A better solution is to work intensively on skill development and remediation first in a more intensive setting, with the goal being to mainstream children incrementally when they can best benefit from being included. Students with disabilities should be educated to the maximum extent possible with peers who do not have disabilities, but they should not be asked to sacrifice cognitive and vocational preparation for social interaction.

The original guiding philosophy of P. L. 94-142 acknowledged that students with disabilities require individually designed educational plans that offer the child a blend of specialized instruction in different settings. A continuum of service options and integrated social experiences in mainstream classes was the vision in this legislation. We should return to that philosophy. Local schools should develop a practical litmus test that guides the placement of children with disabilities. Issues such as planning time, the preparation and commitment of teachers, the acceptance of the child's peer group, how and where services are best delivered, and a clear identification of targeted skills should guide the placement process. Quite simply, we need to ask whether the classroom teacher can achieve the best academic results for the identified child.

Teachers and parents of special education students must look carefully and forthrightly at the real needs of our children and recommend the programs and learning environments that will best prepare them for academic as well as social success as adults. We must remove the emperor's cloak of inclusion and substitute it with a warm woolen coat, one that will provide the practical academic foundation to serve children well for years to come.

POSTSCRIPT

Does Full Inclusion Deliver a Good Education?

In some schools, "fully included" children sit isolated in the back of general education classrooms, their education addressed by a stream of specialists with whom they work individually or in small groups. Interaction with the rest of the class is limited. This arrangement offers the worst of both options—the student with disabilities receives a separate education in a way that prominently advertises his difference. He is a class of one.

Increasing numbers of schools—particularly at the elementary level—are discovering creative ways of addressing the academic needs of a wider range of students in general education classrooms. Supportive adults become functional classroom members rather than appendages. Extensive summer workshops foster faculty communication about universally designed educational practices. And differentiated instruction—so much the rage in general education —embraces all children, especially in these days of high content standards.

Shapiro-Barnard and her colleagues invite educators to make the "least dangerous assumption" and expect academic ability rather than assume limitations based on a disability. They see an opportunity to develop a world of social justice for all within a fully inclusive school environment that makes few assumptions about students except that each can excel in all areas. The theme of social justice is echoed by Gerrard (*Equity and Excellence,* 1994), who maintains that the entire inclusion debate is moot because students with disabilities have already "won" the right to be included through IDEA.

Chesley and Calaluce believe in individual potential but are doubtful that the potential of each child can be reached in today's general education classroom. They argue that the ability to provide numerous services, supports, and modifications within a finite school day stretches the capability of a system. Such a stretch limits educational opportunities for students who need to develop specialized skills.

Macmillan, Gresham, and Forness (*Behavioral Disorders,* 1996) argue that full inclusion creates an ideological debate in which the "where" of education takes precedence over the "what" of education. Rather than saying that one location or approach applies equally to every student, the authors advise readers to be open to multiple options to meet divergent needs at different life stages.

As fully included students move to highly academic secondary schools, will instructional practices change? Does full inclusion tear down barriers constructed by a needlessly protective educational system? Or does full inclusion focus on a dream of belonging at the cost of the acquisition of needed life skills with trained educators?

ISSUE 11

Are Residential Schools the Least Restrictive Environment for Deaf Children?

YES: Harlan Lane, Robert Hoffmeister, and Ben Bahan, from *A Journey Into the Deaf-World* (DawnSignPress, 1996)

NO: Tom Bertling, from *A Child Sacrificed to the Deaf Culture* (Kodiak Media Group, 1994)

ISSUE SUMMARY

YES: Harlan Lane, a faculty member at Northeastern University; Robert Hoffmeister, director of the Deaf Studies Program at Boston University; and Ben Bahan, a deaf scholar in American Sign Language linguistics, value residential schools as rich cultural resources that enable Deaf children to participate fully in the educational experience.

NO: Tom Bertling, who acquired a severe hearing loss at age 5 and attended a residential school for the deaf after third grade, favors the use of sign language in social situations but views residential schools as segregated enclaves designed to preserve the Deaf culture rather than to develop adults who can contribute fully to society.

Hearing Impairment—Impairment in hearing, whether permanent or fluctuating, that adversely affects a child's educational performance but that is not included under deafness in this section

Deafness—A hearing impairment so severe that the child is impaired in processing linguistic information through hearing, with or without amplification, that adversely affects a child's educational performance.

— IDEA 97

The term *hard of hearing* includes individuals whose hearing acuity is not equal to that identified as "normal." Most individuals covered by this definition can perceive some conversation with a hearing aid, although it might not be sufficient for school learning. The term *deafness* is reserved for a more restricted range of hearing. Although an aid might increase sensitivity to some sounds, clear access to conversation is not possible.

Apart from medical descriptions of deafness lives the powerful cultural discussion of Deafness (capital letter intended). In deference to the authors of the following selection, the term will be capitalized here as it is in their writing. The Deaf believe that they are linguistically different, not disabled. Members of the Deaf culture maintain that they have not "lost" anything but, instead, belong to a unique group with its own language, traditions, and social life. Some people who are deaf do not join the Deaf culture. Others who are very much a part of the Deaf culture may hear.

Several visual languages, codes, and signing systems have been part of the education of deaf individuals. These include idiosyncratic signs, developed at home; oralism (emphasizing the development and use of speech without signing); and fingerspelling of English words and total communication (combining pantomime, drawing, fingerspelling, and oral language). Several formal systems of signed language also exist, which differentially represent the word order and practices of spoken English. Each of these methods has its supporters. The language of the Deaf culture is American Sign Language (ASL).

With its own grammar and syntax, ASL is not a translation of spoken English but its own language, fully developed and complex (as detailed in the works of Stokoe, Bellugi, and Klima). Emphasis on ASL as the natural language of the Deaf has increased in the last 30 years.

Residential schools for the deaf have been an established element of life for Deaf children. While lessons are presented either in ASL or spoken English, the Deaf child is surrounded by others who "speak the same language." Dorm life is a pivotal component, a rich environment within which to convey culture and develop lifetime friendships. However, IDEA and the inclusion movement challenge the existence of residential schools, asking if they truly offer the least restrictive environment to deaf children.

In the following selection, Harlan Lane, Robert Hoffmeister, and Ben Bahan argue that residential schools for the Deaf, while appearing to be very restrictive for deaf children, actually provide a freer educational environment, with role models who use the natural language of the children to create strong cultural bonds and to enhance self-esteem. In contrast, they see public school programs as isolating in terms of language, social interaction, and exposure to role models.

Although his mother is involved in the Deaf culture and he is fluent in ASL, Tom Bertling considers the Deaf culture a social invention, which he does not embrace. In the second selection, Bertling shares the feelings of isolation he experienced after moving to a residential school for the deaf. He decries the limited expectations of the residential school, maintaining that he lost more than he gained by his attendance.

Harlan Lane, Robert Hoffmeister,
and Ben Bahan

Educational Placement and
the Deaf Child

What if you were a child and you had to go to a school where you didn't understand the teacher in your classroom? At the very least, your access to the subject matter would be limited, dependent on what you could learn from texts.

But what if you couldn't read very well either? What if you were thirteen before you were able to understand print, and even then your comprehension was extremely limited? What if, on entering junior high school, you were reading at the third-grade level, which is the situation for the typical Deaf child? ...

Suppose you were unable to understand even your peers, so that your only meaningful interactions at school took place between you and one other adult, your interpreter or teacher, who "filtered" all information from the environment for you. What would you learn then? How would your psychological and social development proceed? How could your teacher evaluate your progress?

... [Y]oung Deaf children often face educational environments like this. We will examine some of the forces that place these obstacles in the way of their education: the hearing parents' natural desire to have their children schooled close to home; the small numbers of Deaf children; the higher academic quality of many local schools compared to specialized programs; and especially, the dominant educational philosophy, which views Deaf children as children with a disability and has a single solution for virtually all categories of children with disabilities—inclusion in mainstream schools and programs. ...

Deaf Education and the Law

... Under IDEA [Individuals with Disabilities Education Act], the Federal government became responsible for defining "appropriate education" for children with disabilities, and it proceeded to issue guidelines specifying a range of acceptable placement options. At the time the law was passed, many children with disabilities, in particular those with mental retardation, lived in separate residential facilities, where they frequently received poor educational and social training. IDEA was intended in part to ensure that such separate facilities, often referred to as "institutions," would be the last place a state or a public school

From Harlan Lane, Robert Hoffmeister, and Ben Bahan, *A Journey Into the Deaf-World* (DawnSign-Press, 1996). Copyright © 1996 by Harlan Lane, Robert Hoffmeister, and Ben Bahan. Reprinted by permission of DawnSignPress. Notes omitted.

district would choose to send a child with a disability. To this end, the act specified that every such child was entitled to an education in the "least restrictive environment" (LRE) possible; thus, the range of acceptable placements for the child became a hierarchy in which residential facilities ranked at the bottom. In fact, according to the strictest interpretation of the principle of the LRE by the Office of Special Education and Rehabilitation Services of the federal Department of Education (OSERS), the preferred locale of educational services for the child with a disability is the neighborhood school, and the child should be placed in as close proximity as possible to his or her peers without disabilities, which in the case of the Deaf would be hearing children in a regular classroom.

The problem for the Deaf was, and still is, twofold. First, under the LRE principle as interpreted by OSERS, the residential schools for the Deaf, which are a core element in the very identity of many members of the DEAF–WORLD, and where the Deaf children of hearing parents may encounter peers and adults fluent in ASL [American Sign Language] for the first time, are referred to as "institutions" and hence positioned at the bottom of the placement hierarchy. Second, most Deaf children require the use of a unique, visual language, which is the language neither of instruction nor of conversation in the preferred setting for the education of most children with disabilities, that is, regular public schools. Thus, the laws that were created to protect those with disabilities carry with them conflicts for the Deaf child and, often, for the Deaf adult who wishes to obtain a quality education. These conflicts are grounded in the issues of language and culture that mark the interface between the DEAF–WORLD and the hearing world....

Placement Options

... Determining the educational placements where Deaf students will be most successful is becoming a very complex business. Increasingly, special-education professionals desire inclusion of the Deaf child with an interpreter in a regular classroom in the midst of hearing pupils. Many hearing parents may be reluctant to accept a school where signing is used. Professionals in audiology and related medical fields continue to push for an emphasis on speech; if the child has had cochlear implant surgery, the hospital team and the parents may insist on special classes for Deaf children where primarily spoken language is used. In some settings, the content of the curriculum may be simplified to make it accessible, and teaching staff may be isolated from the latest developments in pedagogical practice. In others, a Deaf child may have no peers with whom he or she can communicate.

For 150 years, separate facilities, either residential schools or, in large cities, day schools, were the main setting for the education of the Deaf. Since the 1960s, various forms of what is called generically *mainstreaming* have been encouraged, ranging from the self-contained day class within a regular public school (with interaction, if any, with hearing students limited to activities outside the academic program), to *full inclusion* of the Deaf in hearing classrooms. More recently, ... there has been a strong push for inclusion, with (or without) the provision of signed language interpreters and other support services like resource rooms and itinerant teachers.

In the following pages we will look at these options largely in terms of three factors parents should consider in determining where and how to obtain the highest quality education for their Deaf child. These factors are the language of instruction; the academic quality of the program, including the subjects offered and the level of instruction; and the degree of social interaction.

... [R]esidential schools for the Deaf—large, centrally located schools providing education from preschool through high school (and, in some cases, adult education)—were at one time the center of the DEAF–WORLD. However, ... starting in the 1860s, ... oralists took control of the residential schools in the U.S. and abroad, virtually eradicating the influence of the DEAF–WORLD. From then on, the teaching staff and administrators were hearing, instruction in almost all schools was oral throughout the elementary years, and the Deaf staff were relegated to nonacademic posts with less influence on academic achievement, posts such as dormitory supervisor, coach, shop instructor, and custodian.

As a result of these changes, the students acquired much of their information and, unless they had been born into the DEAF–WORLD, all of their language, from other Deaf students or the after-school staff. The elementary and middle-school academic personnel especially did not know ASL and therefore could not communicate effectively with their students. Since the students' success was measured by what they knew in English, but most had great difficulty learning English (or much else) through oral instruction, the level of accomplishment was low, both as measured, and in fact. The result was drastically lowered expectations and, in consequence, the drastic lowering of curriculum content. The advent of the special education laws and the change from strictly oral instruction to the combined use of signs from ASL and speech in the 1960s improved matters somewhat, but one of the major drawbacks of the residential schools remains to this day. That is the low expectations they have for many of their students, and the low quality and limited variety of their academic offerings.

Residential schools typically are divided into a lower school, a middle school, and an upper school—designations that may signal the low expectations of the staff. The upper school will include students of high-school age but may well not offer high-school-level instruction. At each grade level, the curriculum that many residential schools offer is much less demanding than that offered to hearing students at the same grade level in most regular public schools, and materials are created or adapted to match the low reading levels of the students. Isolated and insular, the schools find it difficult to incorporate new educational strategies into the curriculum, and they even tend to lose sight of what hearing students of a given age are expected to know.

These are admittedly generalizations; happily, there are residential schools that have changed and that challenge many students appropriately. However, a consequence of the situation generally is that residential school graduates tend not to enroll in college, nor are they prepared to do so. Most students are encouraged to pursue vocational training in high school, with courses in printing, computer data entry, or auto body repair, rather than pre-college courses.... Sometimes ... the residential schools collaborate with local vocational centers and high schools for hearing students to permit the Deaf students to attend classes.

If, however, most residential schools are below par academically, they do have a great advantage for the average Deaf student: as they always have, they do an excellent job of socialization. There are several reasons for this. For one, since all the children in the school are Deaf, participation in extracurricular functions, such as school government, sports, or dramatic performances, is not dependent on the level of speech one may have, or on the use of an interpreter, as it is in non-residential programs. Moreover, because all their students are Deaf, some hearing teachers in residential schools become proficient in some form of signed communication (though usually not ASL) and are therefore able to converse with students and with Deaf staff to a much greater extent than their counterparts in general education. Children in residential schools can thus participate in every aspect of their schooling beginning very early in their academic careers.

The most important advantage of the residential schools in this regard is the large number of Deaf staff who traditionally work in them (residential schools are the largest single employer of educated Deaf adults). Although some Deaf staff are teachers, most, as we have noted, are employed in non-educational activities as dorm counselors, groundskeepers and cooks—all the many functions besides teaching that make a boarding school work. These people are able to communicate fluently and efficiently with the Deaf students. In addition, like Deaf parents, they tend to have high expectations for Deaf children. . . .

In fact, nowhere other than the residential school, is the Deaf child likely to come into contact with so many Deaf role models, including not only Deaf staff, but older Deaf students and alumni as well. The latter, with whom the residential schools maintain strong ties, support their schools as centers where the Deaf may meet, hold workshops and become involved with students. It is through these contacts that Deaf children, especially Deaf children of hearing parents, may begin to understand that there is a Deaf society, a Deaf culture—a DEAF-WORLD—where they may feel at home. They also have the opportunity to learn a great deal from a Deaf perspective about how to function as a Deaf person in the hearing world.

As a result of all this, most students graduate from the residential schools with healthy self-esteem. Integrated into the DEAF-WORLD by virtue of their attendance at the school, especially if they were residents, they have many friends and are able to take advantage of the DEAF-WORLD's sophisticated networks as they begin their adult lives. . . .

Before the 1960s almost eighty percent of the Deaf children in the U.S. attended residential schools. Today only about thirty percent do. This sharp reversal is mostly a result of the push of the mainstreaming and inclusion movements, coupled with the expansion of interpreter training programs, which have changed the way residential facilities operate. When Deaf students get older, some tend to move to mainstream settings to take advantage of the wider course offerings available in regular high schools. And as enrollments decline, funding becomes a more and more serious problem. Not only does the hearing world consider the mainstream to be the most inclusive and positive educational setting (the Least Restrictive Environment) for all students with disabilities, among whom the Deaf are included, but also the desire of state legislatures to minimize state expenditures on residential schools reinforces the bias in favor of the mainstream placement.

By contrast, the DEAF–WORLD considers the residential school, one of its core institutions, to be the most inclusive and the best placement (the Least Restrictive Environment) for Deaf students....

[M]any students, typically fifty to seventy percent of the school population, commute daily even to the residential schools, which effectively also makes them function as day schools.

Since the commuting time for students is limited to an hour each way by law, separate day schools are located in urban areas and tend to serve inner-city populations. Many have large minority populations and their students may also come from immigrant families, where English is a second language. As a result, the day schools must be concerned not only with the problems of the education of Deaf children per se, but with the functioning of the Deaf child within a multicultural framework.

Day schools have the disadvantages of many of the residential schools, without their advantages. That is, generally the teaching staff is hearing, and because of difficulties in communication and low expectations, the curriculum is severely degraded. There is no large number of Deaf non-teaching staff with whom the students may associate after school. If there are Deaf staff members, they tend to be aides in classrooms. Because they leave for home after classes, younger pupils at day schools also seldom come into contact with the older students.... The lack of Deaf role models means that the child attending such schools often does not discover the DEAF–WORLD until much later in life.... [I]dentity crises can be severe. As in the residential schools, pressure is now being exerted by individuals in the local DEAF–WORLD where the day school is situated, and by local and state associations of the Deaf, to see that more Deaf teachers are hired....

Least Restrictive Environment and Inclusion

By definition, *least restrictive environment* means the most appropriate educational placement for the child, the setting in which the child's capacities may be developed to the greatest possible extent. We have noted ... that the hearing world in general, and special educators who are not familiar with the DEAF–WORLD in particular, tend to see the full integration of the Deaf child into the hearing classroom as providing the least restrictive environment for the education of that child. The DEAF–WORLD clearly sees things differently....

The Paradox of Inclusion

... Advocates of full inclusion for children with disabilities seek to make the educational system keep the promise that mainstreaming in special self-contained classes failed to keep, namely real integration in school—education of children with disabilities alongside children who have none. And for many children with disabilities, special classes are indeed not necessary, though for others, such as some children with multiple severe handicaps, they are. But from the perspective of the DEAF–WORLD, full inclusion is a disaster. . . .

So, what is the Least Restrictive Environment for [Deaf] children . . . ? For one thing, it seems to change between elementary and high school. Many Deaf students who have been in putatively integrated and even in self-contained settings for their elementary years, and who may have the academic skills to go to a hearing high school, may opt to attend a residential school so that they can have some social interaction with their peers. On the other hand, those Deaf students who have been in attendance in a residential school may well feel competent and secure enough to enter into a regular hearing high school because they have the social development and peer network to make the experience meaningful, as well as the language skills (English and ASL) to function well in the regular classroom, where the academic level is generally higher than in residential or day programs for the Deaf.

The education of the Deaf student in any setting is a problem. The overall dropout rate of Deaf high schoolers has been estimated at twenty-nine percent. One in every five Deaf students who "graduate" does not meet the academic requirements for a diploma and leaves with a certificate instead. Thus only half the Deaf students who enter high school graduate with a diploma. The lowest dropout rates are found in the residential schools, seventeen to twenty-three percent. For Deaf students who are placed in integrated settings in regular high schools, the dropout rate is thirty-seven percent. If a Deaf student is placed in a self-contained program and is not integrated into the school's regular classes, the dropout rate almost doubles to fifty-four percent (recall that many of these programs will not have any Deaf teachers or contact with the DEAF–WORLD). Different kinds of Deaf students go into different kinds of programs, so the dropout rate reflects both the kinds of students and the type of programming. In all types of programs, if a Deaf student has disabilities, such as a putative learning or behavior disorder or blindness, the dropout rate is fifty-seven percent, and if the Deaf student is Hispanic, the rate is thirty-six percent. Thirty-three percent of Deaf females drop out of high school.

In general, the Least Restrictive Environment for Deaf students is probably the one that allows the freest and fullest communication with teacher and peers, which is a prerequisite to academic progress and psychological and social development. For the vast majority of Deaf students, enjoying the communication conditions that their hearing counterparts take for granted requires teachers and peers fluent in a visual/manual language—ASL in most of North America. That requirement, combined with the small numbers of children who are Deaf, favors specialized educational programs with significant numbers of Deaf children. If we further seek not to restrict the Deaf student in participation in extra-curricular activities and in exposure to pertinent role models, the LRE is the residential school.

In concluding in favor of the residential schools, we must acknowledge the pain that hearing parents (but, significantly, not Deaf parents) feel at the prospect of sending their young child to a boarding school. We Americans like to keep our children close to home. The hearing parents must wonder, too, whether an institution can give their children the attention and care they need. It should be reassuring that Deaf parents who have attended such schools and know what they have to offer are grateful to *their* parents for having sent them there, and they do likewise with their own children if Deaf, even though they are in some ways in a better position than hearing parents to provide at home what the Deaf child requires. The sense of shared language and culture at these schools and the presence of healthy, happy and smart Deaf children is a counterpoise to the regimentation and anonymity that can arise in boarding schools. We have repeatedly cited drawbacks in the residential schools, but many of those drawbacks can be corrected and are being corrected in the most progressive schools today. Teachers have better training and higher expectations, and curricula are being enhanced. Meanwhile the residential schools' traditional strengths, such as better communication, more Deaf role models, and opportunities for personal growth, are being reinforced. . . .

Deaf children should receive what we desire for hearing children as well: an education delivered in their best language. Anything less is not equal educational opportunity. Since their best language is different from that of their hearing peers, their education needs to be conducted separately, at least in part.

A Childhood's End

The first year at the deaf school, I was ten years old in the fourth grade. My first class of the day was leather shop. The classroom was at the far end of the institution grounds facing one of the main streets through town. I spent much time in the storage room looking out the window at the activity across the street. There were businesses plus a public elementary school much like the one I had gone to before being sent here.

The street became a symbol of the stark reality of where I was and the "outside world" to which I had once belonged. I would watch the grade school kids walk to school in the playful and happy manner I had done myself once upon a time. I have never felt as sad as I did watching the world go on without me.

As the months went by, I found it easier to fight back the tears as I looked out the storeroom window, but forever etched in my mind are those dark dreary November mornings that my childhood came to an end.

A few months earlier, on the first morning of the new school year at the state deaf school, all the children gathered in the auditorium for assignment to teachers and classes. The names of the students were called in sign language; then assigned to a teacher and reported to class.

Not having any knowledge of sign language, I sat through the whole process, not knowing if my name was called, not to mention the bewilderment of not being sure of what was going on and what might eventually happen to me. On top of all that, I was dealing with a sense of abandonment for being sent here. I felt I was being punished for not hearing better when I was in the public school.

After nearly everybody had finally dispersed did somebody show concern for me. I was made to wait in a foyer for quite a while until there was enough finger pointing done at me and a flurry of conversations in sign language giving me the impression of their being mystified about what to do with me.

Then somebody led me from the intermediate school building and started to walk me to a different building where the first through third grades were taught. I would have entered fifth grade had I remained in public school and now here I was being led to the primary school.

From Tom Bertling, *A Child Sacrificed to the Deaf Culture* (Kodiak Media Group, 1994). Copyright © 1994 by Tom Bertling. Reprinted by permission of Kodiak Media Group.

I remember vividly wondering what I might have done wrong to be headed toward this fate. Was it because I did not see my name being finger-spelled out? Did I look at somebody wrong? I did not know the proper way for a deaf person to behave and remember thinking that I must have done something wrong.

The walk to the school building seemed to take years. With an unexplained ominous future looming ahead, I was reliving what was a happy childhood prior to being sent here. All the scenes were replaying as I walked. It seemed slowly what was my life was now becoming someone else's. Although I did not know it at the time, for the rest of my time at this deaf school things felt somewhat as one would describe being transcendental. I would from then on be present but mentally distanced as a way to cope.

I was told to sit in a chair in the hall outside the administration office apparently used for disciplinary purposes. Drawing stares and mockery by ignorant students unaware of my plight, I became embarrassed and angry for not knowing what was happening to me.

I dared not ask anybody for fear of making another mistake. I felt hurt over the loss of my old life and was disturbed by not knowing what I had done, resulting in being placed in this deaf school.

It was after lunch before the primary school principal led me to my new classroom and told me it was the second grade as I entered the room. As I took my seat after the hearing teacher pointed to a chair, I noticed that the other children were about my age as the teacher resumed writing on the blackboard. After getting over the initial shock of a new setting, I came to realize what my new teacher was teaching that day.

The teacher had written on the blackboard a list of colors such as gold, gray and silver and a few others. Another list had names of common animals. The lesson for the day was "difficult colors." We were to look at pictures she showed us and write down the appropriate color and name of animal.

Disbelief and confusion reigned in my head. I would have been in the fifth grade had I not been sent here. I knew the names of all the astronauts who have flown in space and today, here I was, being taught new colors I learned years ago.

The transformation was nearly complete. What did I do that was so bad to end up being sent here? I remember thinking I should have tried harder to hear when I was in public school and maybe I would not be here. I was heartbroken as I looked out the second floor window glancing at the tall chain-link fencing that ran far as I could see. The thought of running away slipped away when I remembered I lived 200 miles away and felt as if I had done something so bad that my Mom and Dad did not want me anymore. The realization set in, my world had come to an end, and I had nowhere to go.

I was to remain in that 2nd grade class for a few weeks before I was moved up into the fourth grade. By then the damage had been done. Apparently, the deaf school had the practice of placing a new student in a class with his age group. Perhaps making an adjustment later in the school year instead of evaluation by testing and utilizing placement exams. Nobody bothered to tell me what was going on and I did not feel that it was safe to ask. I already felt enough harm had been dealt me without asking for more.

Perhaps I was a bit spoiled. At the public school my teachers were always asking me if I understood what was going on. I had special speech classes and teachers concerned with my education. I never felt left out or mystified at what was happening to me. But here at this deaf school, I was just another deaf kid. No speech classes anymore. Nobody cared.

My first week on the campus ended up being a lesson in restrictions. Seems like since I first walked, I always rode some sort of a bicycle. It was part of my life and all my friends from the public school went everywhere with them. But, here at this school of 350 students, bikes were banned. The only bikes to be seen were the ones ridden across the street by kids not penalized for being deaf.

Reality continued to set in. I wasn't going anywhere anymore. My whole world was being shrunk into a closely controlled and monitored situation where decisions I once used to make were now being made for me.

Personal radios and television sets were not allowed in the dormitory. There was one small set in the "sitting room" that was usually on something the dorm staff wanted to watch and the volume low not to "disturb" the hearing staff. In the "sitting room" were enough chairs for all the boys on the floor. If the boys were not in their bedrooms, they were expected to be in the "sitting room." Except for school, mealtimes and supervised extracurricular activities, my life was now confined to this area. The only alternative to watching television, (this being before widespread closed-captioning) was a stack of decades-old obsolete magazines donated to the school. Nothing which a ten-year-old boy would find of interest. By the end of the year I had read them all several times anyway.

Personal items or toys that could not be shared with everybody were rounded up and locked away. I could see that the dorm staff were going to select all my activities outside of school hours, and individualism, which was my nature, was not going to be allowed. Outside world contact barely existed. "Warehousing kids" accurately describes the conditions.

My whole life prior to coming to this place, I had never once considered myself "deaf." I always knew that I had a hearing loss and needed to wear a hearing aid, but I took it in stride much the same way other people need to wear glasses. I considered myself the same as everybody else and the term "deaf" never applied to me.

I remember staring at deaf children who were using sign language before being sent to this institution and thinking it was good that I wasn't "deaf."

But now here I was, dumped together with "them," confined to the school grounds, segregated from the mainstream world, forced to learn sign language and live in a dormitory with strangers, separated from my Mom, Dad, brothers and childhood friends, placed in demeaning classes never being able to do what normal people do. No more bike rides, no more building forts, no more watching space launches. And now I was also "deaf."

I was born with normal hearing. I was about three years old when my hearing started to deteriorate. By age 5, I had an 85 to 95 db hearing loss in both ears. Fortunately, I had already developed language and speech skills before my hearing loss arrested further development.

Before entering pre-school I was fitted with a hearing aid. Although I clearly remember hating it, I eventually ended up wearing it nearly all the time. Being deprived of a sense was not to my liking, so the bulky electronic device was tolerated.

Although my Mom had hearing loss similar to mine, and knew sign language, (along with her parents and numerous other relatives) our family communicated by voice only and I never learned sign language until the first day at the deaf school. My Dad had normal hearing and had one brother who was also hard-of-hearing and two others with normal hearing.

At the public school I attended, I had an hour a day with a speech therapist. Along with extra concern for me by my first and second grade teachers in the public school, the use of amplification at an early age, and the exclusive use of voice communication at home contributed to my having a normal language development in spite of a very severe hearing loss.

My childhood prior to coming to the deaf school was filled with happiness and fun. The days were full of adventures and challenges. I had future plans and dreams. My hearing disability barely existed. There was not anything I could not do, it seemed. Life was good to me.

My first grade teacher and especially my second grade teacher in the public school had genuine concern for their students. If any of their students were to fail later in life, it certainly was not anything that happened in their early school years. The biggest impact was the introduction of music into my life. The teacher, for the first hour of class every morning would play the piano and sing childhood songs and contemporary hits of the day, placing an importance on class participation.

By the time I was in the third and fourth grade at the public school, extracurricular activities started to have an impact in the way of social skills and a diversified education. There was Cubs Scouts, roller skating and swimming lessons. At school, band instrument music lessons, papier mache projects, and even though I hated it, square dancing came into play. Once, a select few of us with a strong interest in music were chosen to learn Christmas songs in order to go caroling at senior citizen centers during the Christmas season. I remember a visitor came to school once for the purpose of teaching us to sing a certain Christmas song in German.

The rest of my times were spent with my neighborhood friends. One of my friends and classmate at school and I always had numerous construction projects going on. By the time I was in the fourth grade at the public school, we had built a fort in my friend's backyard, one behind the back fence at my house, another up in a tree that our parents did not know too much about and a fourth we started to build with scraps from a subdivision under development. My Dad tore that one down after it started to get taller than all the new houses going up around it.

Other times, we would be on our bikes riding to areas farther and farther away from our houses. For eight-year-olds, the sense of discovery and curiosity overwhelmed the danger we might face from our parents for exceeding the boundary of the "immediate neighborhood."

One of our discoveries was Trouble Lake. In deep woods near our neighborhood, only a few kids and supposedly, no parents knew of its existence. Tales of snakes and other water creatures kept most kids away. The trail to the lake resembled the Amazon rain forest to an eight-year-old. Things crawled and slithered along the trail.

We built a raft and went on imaginary expeditions, and when the lake froze over during the winter, we pretended to conquer Alaska. Our creature-fearing friends were left behind.

Once, during a heavy snowstorm, we were checking out the lake and my little brother ended up in water up to his waist. I do not remember the excuse I gave my parents, but it must have been good because I did not have to mention Trouble Lake, named after the trouble you would be in if your parents found out you were there.

On occasion, we would go with my Mom to visit her culturally-deaf friends. In one instance, we visited a deaf couple who had a deaf son attending a "special" school for the deaf in another part of the state. Their son came home once every few weeks for the weekend and it would be my first time meeting him.

He did not have any speech ability and I did not know sign language. The hearing aid that was helping me overcome a hearing loss was of no use in this circumstance. I thought how glad I was to not be like him and never once thought I was "deaf" like him.

It was in instances like this that parents of deaf children had seeds sown by members of the deaf culture encouraging them to send their child to a state residential school for the deaf and convincing them of its being the best possible option for their deaf child.

This culturally-deaf couple were eager to bring another deaf child whom they did not even know into their culture regardless of the consequences, which if in error, would be difficult to reverse. This is typical of leaders and members of the deaf culture trying to preserve their culture. I had no idea they were conspiring to send me to this deaf school.

During the summer before entering the deaf school in the fall, I was still unaware of the changes that lay in store for me. Part of the summer was spent at my grandparents' house across the country. Days were spent building yet more forts, swimming, watching lightning from the evening thunder storms and catching fireflies.

Late at night I'd go down into the basement and listen to the transistor radio my grandpa gave me. I would hold it to my ear and would be fascinated how clear I could hear things and the variety of the medium.

Little did I know a cruel trick was being played on me. In a few weeks that radio would be the only thing

I would have left from my childhood and my only connection to the world I would be taken from.

POSTSCRIPT

Are Residential Schools the Least Restrictive Environment for Deaf Children?

Deaf linguists Padden and Humphries (*Deaf in America: Voices From a Culture,* 1988) describe the richness of the Deaf culture: the dramatic range of storytelling and the National Theatre of the Deaf; the active community life of Deaf clubs; and the prevalence of Deaf sports, including the Deaf World Games, which have been held since 1924 and which now feature more than 4,500 athletes from 75 countries in the summer and about 400 athletes from 20 countries in the winter. Could these exist without the links that are forged in residential schools? Should the culture that supports their existence be underwritten by special education?

In the remaining chapters of the book from which his selection was taken, and in his other writings, Bertling expands his position that separate education is not in the best interests of the deaf, who he feels really should be part of the national culture. While acknowledging that sign language is sensible for social interaction, he maintains that deaf individuals must master English in order to maximize learning and to participate fully in society. Focusing on the narrow range of deaf experiences, says Bertling, severely limits a child's horizons and wastes time that could be spent becoming more proficient in written English and academic learning.

Lane, Hoffmeister, and Bahan, in the balance of the book from which their selection was taken (and in their other writings), emphasize the profound isolation that a Deaf person experiences in the hearing world. The authors cite higher dropout rates of Deaf children enrolled in hearing schools to bolster the benefits of early exposure to ASL and the residential school as truly effective education, opening the door for a Deaf child to develop complex language, thought, and social relationships that lead to productive adulthood.

Despite their opposing positions on the value of residential schools, both sides agree that academic expectations for deaf children are too low, regardless of the setting. Not surprisingly, their solutions differ. Bertling would increase exposure to written and spoken English. Lane, Hoffmeister, and Bahan would hire more speakers of ASL to respond to increasing academic standards.

Citing research evidence that use of ASL from birth provides language access resulting in "normal and successful language acquisition," which serves as the foundation for literacy and learning, Drasgow (*Exceptional Children,* 1998) supports increased use of ASL, despite the fact that there is no parallel written form of the language. The challenge for the field, according to Drasgow, is to identify the most successful ways in which written language can be acquired.

A third position, which supports Deafness as a linguistic entity, is Deaf-BilingualBicultural (DBiBi), in which ASL is introduced as early as possible, matching the critical period of language learning. Early education focuses on teaching ASL and Deaf culture. Written English is later taught as a second language. Spoken English can be taught, but it is not emphasized. This model more closely resembles that of bilingual education, which uses a child's first language and culture to support the development of a second language. This option has the highest level of applicability for children whose parents are fluent speakers of ASL—but will it work for children whose parents use spoken English as their first language?

What is the balance between least restrictive environment (LRE) and free appropriate public education (FAPE) for students who are deaf? Does a residential, ASL-based education enable a deaf child to take advantage of the critical period of language acquisition, or does it waste time that could be spent learning English and gaining access to the printed word? What will be the future for Deaf individuals in a world that focuses on high-stakes testing? Will residential schools for the Deaf increase academic expectations and outcomes? Can the high academic standards of the public school somehow be blended with the cultural connections of Deaf culture to create the best possible outcome? What is the most inclusive?

ISSUE 12

Should Students With Disabilities Be Exempt From Standards-Based Curricula?

YES: Rex Knowles and Trudy Knowles, from "Accountability for What?" *Phi Delta Kappan* (January 2001)

NO: Jerry Jesness, from "You Have Your Teacher's Permission to Be Ignorant," *Education Week* (November 8, 2000)

ISSUE SUMMARY

YES: Rex Knowles, a retired college professor, and Trudy Knowles, an assistant professor of elementary education, argue that federal mandates for all students to master the same curriculum fail to consider students' individual differences and needs.

NO: Jerry Jesness, a special education teacher, stresses that students who complete school without learning the basics will be ill-equipped to succeed as adults and that any program that avoids teaching these essentials fails to address the long-term needs of students.

In 49 of the 50 U.S. states, "standards-based education" is the watchword. Curriculum expectations are changing. The range and dimension of these expectations differ widely across the country. Some states are designing high-level academic programs to meet world-class standards. Others have embraced literacy standards that measure the basic skills that students will need to be successful in the world of work. Some states have designed their standards to apply to all students. Others have formulated separate sets of standards for students with severe disabilities. Still others do not expect their standards to apply to all students with disabilities.

Individual education program (IEP) expectations are changing as well. Eligibility for special education has always hinged on the disability's adverse impact on classroom academic performance, but once a student entered special education, the IEP frequently *became* the curriculum, seldom referencing classroom content. IDEA97 altered this pattern with its stipulation that students with disabilities must have access to the general curriculum and that IEPs must focus on ways in which this access can be facilitated.

As might be expected, this shift in special education has required some major alterations. Historically, special education programs have focused on goals that include academics but sometimes go beyond them to the types of skills that students will need to succeed independently in the workplace. For some students with significant disabilities, this has meant a heavy focus on communication and community-based application of a more limited range of academic skills. IDEA97 mandates a closer connection with the learning that happens in more typically academic programs.

In the following selection Rex Knowles and Trudy Knowles assert that individual differences warrant differences in instruction—sometimes different curricula. They contend that society bestows too much reverence on the mastery of reading, which is a supreme struggle for some children with disabilities and not terribly relevant to many rewarding jobs. Forcing the same curriculum on everyone means that some children learn to hate school, feel like failures, and do not gain the competence that they could bring to adult life.

In the second selection, Jerry Jesness maintains that holding all students to a high-level curriculum may help children overcome some struggles to reach greater heights. Warning that lowered expectations can lead students into a false sense of competence, Jesness cautions that educators should not confuse difficulty learning with an inability to learn or the need for the same skills for lifelong success as nondisabled children.

As you read these selections, consider these questions: How much struggling is detrimental to a child's self-confidence, and when does hard work lead to success and personal accomplishment? How would you decide whether or not to stop driving for mastery of the skill of reading (or math, or any other academic subject) and shift to teaching skills that are more related to the expected workplace? When would you make this decision? What would the student say about this change now? In 20 years? What options would this open or close?

Do your state standards include students with disabilities, or are there separate, less-academic standards for students covered by special education? How was your state's decision made, and how does it impact the education of all students? How does your state's curriculum affect your reaction to this issue?

 **YES**

Accountability for What?

America instituted public education and compulsory attendance partly to save its children from exploitation. We wanted all children to be freed from the demands of sweatshops and farm labor that filled the days of 10-year-olds.

What started as a noble attempt to save children from forced labor has ended up as a daily sentence to a six- to seven-hour prison from which they have no escape. We refuse to let them leave if they feel bad; we regiment their hearing, speaking, seeing, walking, eating, arrival, departure, and bowel movements. We even tell them when they have to wear a coat.

Child abuse is a very strong term, and it rightly makes us angry. That much is clear. But our schools practice child abuse every day. That is also clear.

Every day we ask children to do what they can't do, at least at the moment we ask them. And then we grade them, as if they were eggs. "You're grade A." "You're grade B." "You're rotten." We shame them, and we embarrass them.

We could tell many stories. One lovely, considerate, and gentle 11-year-old girl studied for four hours for a spelling test. The next day she took the test and failed. According to the girl, when her teacher handed back the papers, she said to her, within earshot of the rest of the class, "You're lazy. If you'd put in any time at all on your work, you would get an A. You're just lazy! We're not going to let you hold this class back."

That young girl spells quite well orally. She is helpful and responsible around the home. She is well liked by her peers and adored by her younger brother and sister. She is bright beyond her years. And she is absolutely terrorized by school. She has a perceptual-motor problem. Writing is just not her thing. The internal details regarding the figures she draws and the words she writes get mixed up. While these facts were carefully explained to the teacher, she continued—either from ignorance or cruelty—to insult the girl. That's child abuse. And it's not an isolated incident.

A bright young man with attention deficit disorder and a severe organizational deficit consistently posted failing grades on major assignments because he couldn't seem to keep all the materials together that he needed to hand in. When it was suggested that the teacher help the student set up a system for keeping track of materials, the response was, "He's going to have to figure out how to get by in the real world sometime. Might as well do it now." The young

From Rex Knowles and Trudy Knowles, "Accountability for What?" *Phi Delta Kappan* (January 2001). Copyright © 2001 by Phi Delta Kappa International. Reprinted by permission of *Phi Delta Kappan* and Trudy Knowles.

man continued to fail until his severe depression resulted in his being taken out of school and put in a homebound tutoring program.

We think it's time to start yelling. We have been treating our children badly for a long time now. With the new emphasis on "accountability," the abuse will only multiply. "The word in education is accountability," according to one state commissioner of education—a view no doubt shared by many of his peers. That is a worrisome sentiment. The easy acceptance of the statement by parents and teachers is even more worrisome.

If the word meant that teachers are to be accountable for the respect they show to children, we would rejoice. If it meant that teachers are to be accountable for helping students to find joy in learning and to become lifelong contributors to their society, we would rejoice. If it meant that teachers are to be accountable for ensuring that all children are successful and that those teachers will be required to find the means to guide students and to assess students in multiple ways, we would rejoice.

But "accountability" in today's discussions of education means that teachers will be held accountable for how well their students read and for what they score on achievement tests. Everyone in the class will be performing above average—or else. Teachers' salaries and promotions will depend on their ability to bring children up to grade-level norms.

Even the most naive statistician knows that half of all people who take a norm-referenced test will be below average. That's what average means. Statistical accountability automatically makes some children "leftovers." It is not true that any good teacher can teach any child to read at grade level, any more than any good physical education teacher can teach any child to be an above-average baseball player.

Reading and throwing a baseball are skills. If you're not a Greg Maddux or a Pedro Martinez, reading is probably a more important skill, but a skill it remains. Why do we make this particular skill the sine qua non of education?

Through training, almost anyone can improve his or her skills, but individual differences will remain. Some children will always be terrible baseball players (often to their shame), and some children will always be terrible readers (always to their shame). To base the notion of the "good teacher" on such "objective measurements" as test scores is to create teachers who teach not for creativity, fun, imagination, freedom, exuberance, and the love of learning, but rather for test results. And teaching merely to get test results not only deprives students of the opportunity to think, question, reason, or disagree, it also informs 50% of the group that they are below average and tells 10% that they are just no good at all!

If teachers are to be held accountable, will those students who are below average in reading be pushed, mauled, and remediated? Shouldn't we instead tinker with the regular education regimen and get on with the process of educating the child? But that's not what we do. Instead, we say, "If a child doesn't learn to read, we can't teach him anything." So we make him spend extra time working on this particular skill. If another child can't get the assigned reading in one hour, should we make her spend two? We take children with eyes that won't focus, fingers that won't cooperate, sensory pathways that won't coordinate, association areas that won't associate, neurons that don't fire appropriately, connections that aren't connected, brains that won't attend, and we say, "Sorry, but you must read anyway. And if you don't read, you're educationally and vocationally shot. (And I don't get my raise.)" The combination of school and homework is for some students far more arduous than the 19th-century sweatshops.

Parents sometimes get angry at brutish physical education teachers who shame children who can't throw a ball because they aren't physically coordinated to do so. In enlightened schools, we even excuse some children from physical education. But we do nothing about teachers who shame children who can't read because they aren't physically coordinated to do so. And we never excuse them from reading. Instead, we pile on more. It's about accountability, after all.

Our emphasis on accountability fails to take into consideration the single clear fact of life: *children are different.* It is the only psychological truth accepted by all psychologists. Children are different. Certainly educators know this to be true. Howard Gardner has been espousing the idea of multiple intelligences for years. Teacher educators have been teaching it for years. Why, then, do federal and state mandates for accountability result in what teachers know will never work: a foolish emphasis on sameness—same classes, same books, same chronological age in the classroom, same program, same assignments, same tests, same curriculum, same instruction?

The tremendous variation in children is not abnormal, but squeezing them into a common learning mold is. In our emphasis on accountability, we operate as though individual differences *don't* exist. That's just plain stupid. But we also operate as though differences *shouldn't* exist, and that's just plain cruel.

The child with low reading ability is not diseased. That child is different in a very normal way, and if you shove a book into his or her hand, you are limiting that child's education.

There has been no essential change in schooling in more than a hundred years—except in the number of inmates being schooled. We still think students can learn only through the sacred tool of reading. We still act as if a child learns more under conditions of stress and seem to believe that the more stress, the more learning. We still think that children ought to be punished if they aren't the same as the rest and that differences—in responses, attitudes, movements—are deviant, disabling, and disturbing. We still teach children that, unless they are successful in school, they are losers. And we still hold teachers accountable for the failure of children to read.

Many school systems are guilty of child abuse, dehumanizing children, and teaching them that they are an educational waste. When children are having trouble with reading, they learn that they are not okay and that school is not where they belong.

Check the dropouts. Many of them were diagnosed with learning disabilities. A great many have attention deficits. They became problem children—hyperactive, demanding attention, disruptive, aggressive, truant. They didn't really drop out by choice. They were forced out of school. In fact, they are not learning disabled; the schools are teaching disabled.

Why is it that we insist on calling a child "learning disabled" if he has difficulty reading, but we don't label a child "disabled" if she can't compose a song? Educators have set up altars to reading. They worship at its shrine and intone the doctrine "Outside of reading, there is no salvation." And if the child can't read, there are the stocks, the pillories, solitary confinement—all the torture devices.

A graduate student who teaches in a high school for students with language learning disabilities recently asked for help with some strategies for teaching *Huckleberry Finn*. She said she was having a hard time getting students to appreciate or understand the story. While thinking about strategies she could use, it suddenly became clear that perhaps there was really no point in trying to get these students to appreciate classic literature. They are a group of students who will rarely, if ever, pick up a novel to read for pleasure.

A student who recently graduated from college with a 3.7 grade-point average told us that she had to read 32 novels in high school. For her it was a painful, tearful, agonizing experience. She has never picked up a book to read for pleasure, because for her there is no pleasure in reading.

Let's be honest. Is the skill of reading classic literature that important? For students to become successful citizens, it is certainly helpful to have a command of the written word. But do we need to expose all students to courses in fiction and literature as ninth-graders, in poetry and drama as 10th-graders, in American literature and folklore as 11th-graders, and in British literature as 12th-graders? Can you pick out the slow readers and the nonreaders as you walk down the street? Does a person who hears well, remembers adequately, and works in a nonwriting or nonreading vocation (which includes most) suffer greatly from a reading disability? Only until commencement day, if there is one. The disability disappears as soon as such a student leaves school. Why should school be such an agony? Who declared that reading was so important?

Art can be viewed and created without reading. Concerts can be heard and instruments played. History can come in the form of videos, movies, photographs, and plays. Social studies and current events flow from the television sets. Films, videos, cassette tapes, records, pictures, demonstrations, and the spoken word are all available as ways of learning. And yet where do we force education to abide? In the textbook. In the written word. Imagine a book designed to show students how to assemble an engine. Then imagine a written test to see if the students have learned how to assemble an engine. Then imagine having your car fixed by a student who had passed the test but had never worked on an engine.

We "do" physical education. Why can't we "do" art and music and history and science and math? If there are good readers around, let them review the literature as their contribution. Why must everyone do so? The library is not necessarily the center of the educational process. And if learning by reading is torturous, arduous, even impossible, let's forget the reading. Give every child every opportunity to learn to read, but let's not make failure to acquire this skill mean failure in virtually all school learning. If the skill of reading makes each day a torment, makes the child feel devalued, and interferes with the acquisition of knowledge, then away with it! Let's put reading in its rightful place and get on with the learning process.

The "three R's" of reading, 'riting, and 'rithmetic are the marks of an educational elite, excellent hallmarks for what schools were meant to do a hundred years ago. We are appealing for a new way of looking at schooling, for more recognition of individual differences, for more concern for true democracy, and for fewer objective tests.

Accountability? Sure. But accountability for what? Let's make teachers accountable only for their humane treatment of children. Let's make them accountable not for how well their children test in the three R's, but for how well they function in the three "L's": living without fear or shame, loving themselves and others, and learning about this wonderful world at their own speed and in their own way.

You Have Your Teacher's Permission to Be Ignorant

I once read a cheery story about a caring teacher who helped her failing students by shortening their assignments. "Don't worry," the teacher assured a crying child as she handed him a shortened list of spelling words, "I will give you an assignment at which you can succeed." The implication was that the teacher, by crossing some words off of a list, "gave" the student success. We teachers are familiar with this line of thought. It is almost a rite of passage for first-year teachers to be called into their principals' offices to be chastised after releasing their first round of grades. "If you want to fail these children," the principal begins, as if the teacher is issuing failing grades for her own pleasure. "We want these children to succeed," the teacher is told. "We don't want them to experience failure."

We teachers remember with pain, laughter, or both, the in-service sessions in which we learned to empathize with our students, to feel their pain. At one such session, a presenter gave several commands in rapid succession. "Fold your paper in nine equal parts," he commanded, and rapidly added: "Draw a tetrahedron in the upper left corner. Write the name of the capital of Outer Mongolia in the square directly above the lower left-hand corner. Write the square root of 386 rounded to the nearest whole number in the square closest to the center. Put down your pencils! Why aren't you finished?" he shouted in feigned anger.

At another workshop, participants were asked to write while viewing their hands and writing in a mirror. At another, participants were asked to assemble jigsaw puzzles which, in reality, contained mismatched pieces. The moral of these sessions was always that it hurts to fail; therefore, give the kids tasks that they can perform with relative ease. Success is good and failure is bad, so let us give our students the former.

It is truly absurd to suggest that teachers are so powerful that we can somehow grant and withhold success with mere strokes of our pens. Sixty-nine percent represents failure, 70 percent represents success, and 90 percent represents honor. So, according to this way of thinking, a teacher can bring students success or honor by simply simplifying the assignments or by devising an excuse to tack on a few extra points.

From Jerry Jesness,"You Have Your Teacher's Permission to Be Ignorant," *Education Week*, vol. 20, no. 10 (November 8, 2000). Copyright © 2000 by Editorial Projects in Education. Reprinted by permission of *Education Week* and the author.

It is a linguistic fluke that the word "fail" means both to lack success and to score below a set standard. Real success is based on what the student knows, not on what a teacher ordains. If a 1st grade student learns to read, he has succeeded. A classmate who did not learn to read has failed, even if the teacher declares him a success by giving him a passing grade. A well-read, knowledgeable recent high school graduate has the tools for success. In fact, so does a well-read, knowledgeable dropout. A barely literate graduate armed only with an undeserved diploma and a transcript filled with inflated grades is, however, going to have problems. Only knowledge is power.

Some of the greatest frustrations that we teachers feel result from conflicting expectations placed on us. On the one hand, we are expected to honestly evaluate our students' knowledge, skills, and progress. On the other, we are expected to assure that all, or at least most, "succeed," even if we have to fabricate that success by watering down the material or inflating the grades. Teachers are expected to both follow a curriculum and to manipulate that curriculum so that all students at least enjoy the illusion of success.

Low standards, particularly for students who have known little else, can actually make a teacher look good. Feel-good activities and mind-numbing busywork can be very effective classroom-management techniques. While challenging assignments may motivate students who have come to expect them, students who have never been pushed are likely to react to such assignments by misbehaving. Veteran teachers will tell you that some of their best teaching may have appeared to be their worst. The student who refuses to open his literature textbook in August, yet somehow develops a love for reading by the following May, or one who quivers with anger or frustration while attempting new algorithms, yet becomes enthusiastic about math after mastering them, should warm our hearts.

Many competent readers had to be dragged, screaming and kicking, through their first novels, and many top math students once had to have the multiplication tables drilled into them. Helen Keller first reacted to Anne Sullivan's finger-spelling lessons by screaming, kicking, and biting. Unpleasant confrontations, however, may result in poor evaluations from administrators or complaints from parents. Smiling faces and busy fingers make for the best public relations.

⚜

[Recently] a journalist for a Houston newspaper visited an inner-city high school and observed some classes. He wrote disparagingly of an English teacher whose 11th grade students were performing dismally on a test covering a Shakespeare play, but praised an algebra teacher who captured his students' attention by using games of chance to teach them about probability. What's wrong with this picture? Probability is not a part of algebra. While I do not know the teachers in question and therefore cannot judge their abilities, it is clear that the English teacher was, however unsuccessfully, covering high-school-level literature, while the algebra teacher had abandoned his assigned subject and replaced it with basic math.

I recently had a conversation with a probationary teacher who had just been told that her contract would not be renewed. I was quite impressed by both her general knowledge and her knowledge of the subject she taught. She explained to me that, despite the fact that most of her 11th graders came to her reading at only a 4th or 5th grade level, she had managed to lead them through Rudolfo Anaya's *Bless Me Ultima,* a novel appropriate for students who can at least read at a high school level. She had also managed to coax research papers from most of them. Earlier this year, she had been called into her principal's office and asked to "adjust" some of her student's grades. She was also asked to apologize to the parents of some discontented students. She refused to do either, and she is now looking for another job. She refused to give her students permission to be ignorant, so now she will pay the price.

While most teachers who give their students permission to know less than their peers do so by turning a blind eye to their failures, we special education teachers put that permission in writing. Each year, we meet with an administrator, a student's parents, and others responsible for the student's education to discuss his or her individual educational program, or IEP. At these meetings, we set the student's educational goals for the year.

I never cease to be awed by this responsibility. It is not that it is wrong to hold those of lesser skills and abilities to a lower standard. We certainly should not, for example, demand that Down's syndrome children perform differential calculus. Nor should we require illiterate children to analyze great works of literature. Still, the responsibility of determining the standard to which a child should be held is an awesome one.

⋅⟨◉⟩⋅

It is easy to succumb to the temptation to teach special-needs children at their comfort levels. The system allows and often encourages us to do so. This, however, is rarely in the child's best interest.

My school once had a 4th grade child come from a neighboring district unable to subtract or to write in cursive handwriting. Although her IEP included only the most rudimentary literacy and math skills, the girl seemed to be fairly bright, so we wrote her new IEP near her grade level. After some pushing and prodding, she mastered her basics and is now comfortably working with regular 4th grade material. Another 4th grader was reduced to tears several times in the process of learning long division, a procedure he eventually mastered. It is fortunate that I was not observed during some of those students' more difficult moments in my class.

There is nothing more heart-wrenching than a special-needs child in tears, but there is nothing more heartwarming than the smile of a child for whom schoolwork has ceased to be a mystery.

We teachers should imagine ourselves as swimming instructors whose charges will someday be thrown out of a boat half a mile from shore. If we certify that a nonswimming student is a competent swimmer, he will still sink like a stone when thrown from the boat.

   In like manner, a graduate who lacks real academic skills, who has only the trappings of scholarly success, will have a difficult time swimming in the real world. Failure is failure, with or without our permission.

POSTSCRIPT

Should Students With Disabilities Be Exempt From Standards-Based Curricula?

$\mathbf{M}$ore exacting standards—for teachers, students and schools—are here. There is no changing this reality. Yet how should this reality impact students with disabilities?

Vohs, Landau, and Romano, the authors of the *PEER Information Brief* "Raising Standards of Learning" (1999), acknowledge that while state standards range from broad to specific, all share the common goal of raising expectations —from which all students can benefit. The report concedes that it is certainly easier to include all students in broad, literacy-based frameworks, but it also states that, with appropriate support, all students can participate at some level of the new standards.

Although Knowles and Knowles might be more at ease with standards that stress basic literacy, they are still concerned that some students will be unnecessarily hurt by the rigor of today's new expectations. They find that the short-term misery and struggle of learning specific skills deprives children of the ability to feel empowered to develop life skills at which they really are competent.

Lanford and Carey (*Remedial and Special Education,* 2000) maintain that since most students with disabilities spend most of their time in general education classes, they should work within the same curriculum. However, the authors also indicate that a total academic curriculum may not be appropriate for all students with disabilities, whose programs should be clearly stated in their IEPs.

Jesness would counsel teachers and parents not to stray from the standard curriculum too easily, lest opportunities for success be lost. Yet Jesness acknowledges that high expectations do not mean the same expectations for everyone. The challenge is in knowing how to balance the curriculum and individual needs.

Since educational standards are decided on a state-by-state basis, the involvement of students with disabilities will likely be determined that way as well, guided by the mandates of IDEA97. Yet that very strategy brings a number of questions to mind: Does what you learn depend on where you live? If so, will parents of children with disabilities move to locations where the specific needs of their children are best met? Is there a core curriculum that everyone needs to learn? For students with complex needs, does a vocational course of study limit horizons, provide time on task for relevant skills, or offer opportunities for creative connection with academic frameworks?

ISSUE 13

Are the Least Trained Teaching Our Most Needy Children?

YES: Michael F. Giangreco et al., from "Helping or Hovering? Effects of Instructional Assistant Proximity on Students With Disabilities," *Exceptional Children* (Fall 1997)

NO: Susan Unok Marks, Carl Schrader, and Mark Levine, from "Paraeducator Experiences in Inclusive Settings: Helping, Hovering, or Holding Their Own?" *Exceptional Children* (Spring 1999)

ISSUE SUMMARY

YES: Michael F. Giangreco, a research associate professor specializing in inclusive education, and his colleagues assert that untrained teacher assistants spend too much time closely attached to individual students, often hindering the involvement of certified teachers and nondisabled peers.

NO: Susan Unok Marks, Carl Schrader, and Mark Levine, of the Behavioral Counseling and Research Center in San Rafael, California, find that professionally trained classroom teachers are often less prepared than some assistants to work with children in inclusive settings and that, unprepared to supervise assistants, they use this lack of knowledge to avoid teaching children with disabilities.

Teacher assistant, paraprofessional, teacher's aide, inclusion aide, special education paraeducator; whatever the title, every district has many dedicated, hard-working people who support children in inclusive classroom settings. What do we know about what they do? And what do *they* know about what *they* do?

Teacher assistants first appeared in U.S. schools in the 1950s to address the teacher shortage that arose as baby boom children came of age. Their first roles were clerical, helping the classroom teacher with routines such as copying, maintaining bulletin boards, and taking attendance. By 1965 there were about 10,000 teacher assistants in U.S. schools. Tasks and responsibilities remained clear: the aide helped; the teacher taught.

In the full flower of the inclusion movement, as well as the special education teacher shortage, there are now over 500,000 teacher assistants in schools across America. More than half of them work with children who have disabilities, frequently spending all day with a single child who is enrolled in a general education classroom.

While paralegals and paramedics have clearly delineated job responsibilities separating their roles from those of the professionals whom they assist, such is not the case with paraeducators (French and Pickett, *Teacher Education and Special Education,* 1997). Few states require specific qualifications for paraprofessionals. Many districts have a single job description (if that) covering individuals who help with the cafeteria and the lunchroom as well as those who assist with medical procedures, support children with severe behavior problems, assist in separate classrooms, or work as inclusion supports.

Michael F. Giangreco, Susan W. Edelman, Tracy Evans Luiselli, and Stephanie Z. C. MacFarland devote much of their time to designing and supporting inclusive educational programs to maximize student participation. In the following selection, they supplement the comments of teachers, therapists, parents, and paraprofessionals with their own observations of the assistants' activities. Parents and teachers want paraprofessionals in the general classrooms so that students with significant disabilities can be adequately supported. Unfortunately, say Giangreco et al., by their close physical presence assistants often prevent active inclusion, frequently hovering over their charges rather than encouraging involvement and natural supports. Training for the assistants rarely occurs—most frequently they learn from each other. The result, according to the authors and the people they interviewed, is that the paraprofessional assumes full responsibility for teaching the child—and is the least trained to do so.

Susan Unok Marks, Carl Schrader, and Mark Levine collaborate closely with school staff to design positive behavioral support plans for students with challenging behaviors. Their interviews with a number of paraprofessionals, which they discuss in the second selection, echoed many of the same themes found by Giangreco et al. Assistants say that they willingly assume significant responsibilities, including the role of "expert." The difference is that Marks et al. found the assistants, in fact, to be the experts. Most of the classroom teachers did not attend training or know the inclusion students well enough to feel comfortable taking charge of instruction. In fact, according to Marks et al., the teachers are the least trained, and they are not teaching the children.

As you read these selections, you will hear the voices of the people who are most closely connected to children whose needs require extra assistance. These voices convey commitment as well as concern. Who *is* teaching the neediest students? Are they prepared to do so? Are teachers delegating responsibilities to support personnel fairly, or have teachers abdicated their own responsibility to teach a wide range of children?

Michael F. Giangreco et al.  **YES**

Helping or Hovering?

$\mathbf{A}$s students with disabilities increasingly are placed in general education schools and classes, the use of instructional assistants has greatly expanded. Recent national figures estimate that over 500,000 instructional assistants are employed in public schools, and increases are anticipated in the coming years. Although their changing roles and responsibilities have gained recent attention, the proliferation of instructional assistants in public schools often has outpaced conceptualization of team roles and responsibilities, as well as training and supervision needs of instructional assistants. Nowhere is this more evident than in schools where students with severe or multiple disabilities are included in general education classrooms.

In our work in public schools, we have noticed intructional assistants playing increasingly prominent roles in the education of students with disabilities. With pressure from parents, who want to ensure that their children are adequately supported, and general educators, who want to make sure they and their students are adequately supported, the use of special education instructional assistants has become a primary mechanism to implement more inclusive schooling practices. Although we have been encouraged by situations where students with disabilities have been provided with previously unavailable educational opportunities, we are concerned that some current approaches to providing instructional assistant support might be counterproductive....

The purpose of this study was to... [highlight] some of the key issues we observed in general education classrooms where students with disabilities were supported by instructional assistants. The nature of these findings holds important implications for evaluating how we use, train, and supervise instructional assistants so that their work can be supportive of valued educational outcomes for students with disabilities and their peers without disabilities in general education classrooms....

One of the most prominent findings that emerged from the [our observations] was that instructional assistants were in close proximity to the students with disabilities on an ongoing basis. This was evidenced by (a) the instructional assistant maintaining physical contact with the student (e.g., shoulder, back, arms, hands) or the student's wheelchair; (b) the instructional assistant sitting in a chair immediately next to the child; (c) the student sitting in the

From Michael F. Giangreco, Susan W. Edelman, Tracy Evans Luiselli, and Stephanie Z. C. MacFarland, "Helping or Hovering? Effects of Instructional Assistant Proximity on Students With Disabilities," *Exceptional Children*, vol. 64, no. 1 (Fall 1997). Copyright © 1997 by The Council for Exceptional Children. Reprinted by permission. References omitted.

instructional assistant's lap when classmates were seated on the floor; and (d) the instructional assistant accompanying the student with disabilities to virtually every place the student went within the classroom, school building, and grounds.

Although study participants indicated that some level of close proximity between students with disabilities and instructional assistants was desirable and sometimes essential (e.g., tactile signing, instructional interactions, health management), they also recognized that unnecessary and excessive adult proximity was not always necessary and could be detrimental to students. As one mother who had observed her son's classroom stated:

> At calendar time in the morning she (instructional assistant) doesn't have to be right by his side. She could kind of walk away. She doesn't have to be part of his wheelchair. That's what it feels like. I just think that he could break away a little bit (from the instructional assistant) if he were included more into all the activities with the regular classroom teacher.

A speech/language pathologist from the same team independently stated, "I think there is some unnecessary mothering or hovering going on."

... [Eight] subthemes pertaining to proximity between instructional assistants and students with disabilities... are presented in the following sections.

Interference With Ownership and Responsibility by General Educators

Most of the classroom teachers in this sample did not describe their role as including responsibility for educating the student with disabilities who was placed in their class. Team members reported that the proximity and availability of the instructional assistants created a readily accessible opportunity for professional staff to avoid assuming responsibility and ownership for the education of students with disabilities placed in general education classrooms.

Different expectations regarding the role of the classroom teacher was a point of conflict within many of the teams. As one related services provider stated, "She (the classroom teacher) doesn't take on direct instruction (of the students with disabilities). In fact, ... she stated at meetings that she doesn't see that as her role. And I disagree with that. I mean she is a teacher."

Although special educators and related services providers were involved in each case, almost universally it was the instructional assistants who were given the responsibility and ownership for educating the students with disabilities. Teachers were observed having limited interactions with the student with disabilities, proportionally less than those with other class members. Involvement by the teachers that did occur most often was limited to greetings, farewells, and occasional praise. Instructional interactions occurred less frequently (e.g., being called on to answer a question in class). A special educator summed up the need for clarification sought by many educational team members when she said, "What should the classroom teacher's role be? Even in our most successful situations we don't have a lot of classroom teachers who are saying, 'I have teaching responsibility for this kid.'" Most teams we observed had not confronted this issue. "We haven't as a team come out and said, 'All right, what is the role of the classroom teacher in teaching this child?'"

Data consistently indicated that it was the instructional assistants, not the professional staff, who were making and implementing virtually all of the day-to-day curricular and instructional decisions. One speech pathologist said, "[We (the team) have talked about this many times. We have our most seriously challenging students with instructional assistants." A special educator explained, "The reality is that the instructional assistants are the teachers. Though I'm not comfortable with them having to make as many instructional decisions." An experienced instructional assistant explained, "I never get that kind of information (about instruction related issues and planning). I just wing it!"

The instructional assistants demonstrated unfettered autonomy in their actions throughout the day as evidenced by entering, leaving, and changing teacher-directed whole class activities whenever they chose with no evidence of consulting the teacher. As one instructional assistant said, "We do not do a lot of what the class does. I do what I think he can do." She justified her role as decision maker by saying, "I am the one that works with him all day long." Instructional assistants reported becoming increasingly comfortable with their role as the primary instructor for the student with disabilities, as one stated, "[We are] the only people who really feel comfortable with Holly."

The instructional assistants in this study reported that they received mostly on-the-job training from other instructional assistants by talking with each other and job shadowing so that patterns of interaction by instructional assistants were passed on. Inservice training that a small number received typically was conducted in groups that included only other instructional assistants. Ironically, experienced professionals who said things like, "We do not have the training to work with these high needs kids" turned over the education of their most challenging students to instructional assistants, many of whom were high school educated, had no previous classroom experience, and had minimal training. As one special educator acknowledged, from a logical perspective, "It doesn't make sense."

In one site where an instructional assistant was not present, the classroom teacher, with support from special educators and related services providers, successfully assumed the primary role for instructing the student with disabilities. She directed his instructional program, spent time teaching him within groups and individually, used sign language to communicate with him, and included him in all class activities. This teacher stated, "You know the teacher needs to be the one who makes the decisions a lot because she is working with Mark (student with disabilities) and she knows Mark and knows which areas he needs help in." A special educator in this site acknowledged that not every aspect of this student's individualized education program (IEP) requires significant support and that some aspects of the IEP, "left to the regular educator would be just fine." The specialist for the deaf-blind on this team said, "I think a lot of it (the teacher's success with the students with disabilities) is that she has high expectations for Mark. She does not do for him; instead she shows him how to do things. She considers him very much part of the class."

Separation From Classmates

Instructional assistants were regularly observed separating the student with disabilities from the class group. For example, when it was time to go to a special area class (e.g., art, music, physical education) one instructional assistant consistently left class a couple minutes before the rest of the class to wheel the student with disabilities to the specialty classroom.

Even when the students were basically stationary, such as seated on a rug to hear a story, the instructional assistant often physically separated the student with disabilities from the group by positioning him on the fringe of the group (e.g., the farthest away from the teacher). Instructional assistants reported that their positioning of the student allowed them to leave the activity whenever they chose.

Sometimes separation from the class occurred during circumstances where the match between class activity and the student's individual needs appeared highly compatible. For example, Annie entered the classroom during an individual writing time. As the instructional assistant began an adapted writing activity using large chart paper and markers, a second instructional assistant approached her and said, "She can do this writing just as easily in the other room as here." With that prompt, the instructional assistants separated Annie from the class without consultation with, or resistance from, the classroom teacher.

Dependence on Adults

Instructional assistants in close proximity to students with disabilities were observed prompting most every behavior exhibited by the students in this study (e.g., using writing implements, using gestures, following instructions, using materials). There was little evidence of fading prompts to decrease dependence and encourage students to respond to other people (e.g., school staff, peers) and more naturally occurring cues (e.g., the presence of certain toys or school supplies). Alternatively, an instructional assistant who was cognizant of Helen's dependence on her, encouraged her to do things for herself through redirection, especially when the student sought unneeded assistance with tasks such as dressing and grooming.

An example of dependence on adults was observed on the school playground during recess. The student with disabilities was being shadowed on a large wooden play structure by an instructional assistant. The student was capably crossing a wooden bridge where safety was not a concern. The student charged toward the bridge, letting go of her assistant's hand. A few steps onto the bridge she stopped abruptly and quietly turned back toward the instructional assistant who was only a foot behind her. The instructional assistant smiled, saying, "You know me. I stick right with you." The student reached back and took the instructional assistant's hand instead of crossing the short span of the playground bridge on her own. Sometimes the school system's dependence on instructional assistants was so strong that when the instructional assistants were absent, the family was asked to keep the child home from school or the mother was asked to be the substitute instructional assistant.

Sometimes the school system's dependence on instructional assistants was so strong that when the instructional assistants were absent, the family was asked to keep the child home from school or the mother was asked to be the substitute instructional assistant.

Impact on Peer Interactions

Data indicated that close proximity of instructional assistants had an impact on interactions between students with disabilities and their classroom peers. As one special educator shared:

> Sometimes I think it inhibits her relationship with her peers because a lot is done for Holly and Holly doesn't have the opportunity to interact with her peers because there is always somebody hovering over her, showing her what to do or doing things for her. I'd like to get the instructional assistant away from Holly a little bit more so that peers will have a chance to get in there and work more with Holly.

A classroom teacher offered her perspectives on how instructional assistants might be used differently.

> I would definitely prefer having a paraprofessional assigned to the classroom and then just as necessary to have her work with a child (with special educational needs) when there is a specific activity, but not exclusively to work with just that child. I think it is important for two reasons. One is that you don't want to give the child any extra stigma that is associated with a special education label. Second is that it is more healthy for the paraprofessional to work with other children so that he or she doesn't get burned out with working with just one child all the time.

Interference with peer interactions did not occur in all cases. Some team members said that if the instructional assistant was well liked by the other children it had a positive impact on the student with disabilities' access to peers. As a physical therapist described, "I have also seen it (proximity of instructional assistants) be very, very positive, in that the instructional assistant is really well liked and has done a lot to establish wonderful friendships for the student."

Conversely, if the instructional assistant was not well liked it had a corresponding negative impact. Sometimes the close proximity students had with instructional assistants led peers to perceive them as a package deal. As one mother cautiously shared, "I don't know if I should say this or not, but a lot of it was that kids didn't like the aide, so they would stay away from Annie for that reason."

When teachers assigned students to student-directed pairs or small groups, instructional assistants were often observed dominating the group's interactions. In some cases, the involvement of the instructional assistant was so omnipresent that children without disabilities simply left the group with the instructional assistant and joined a different group with only classmates, no adults. In other cases when students without disabilities initiated interactions, they were rebuffed by the instructional assistant. Ronny (a student without disabilities) asked the instructional assistant, "Do you want me to help Jamie?"

She answered, "No, not yet." Ronny was never asked back to assist his class-mate. At other times instructional assistants interrupted initiations made by peers. For example, in a physical education class, Michael went over to Jaime and began to run with him in his wheelchair to participate in the activity. The instructional assistant interrupted this interaction saying to Michael, "If you want to run, I'll push Jaime." After a hesitant pause, Michael reluctantly gave way to the instructional assistant. At times, prolonged close adult proximity adversely affected peer involvement even when the instructional assistant was not present. As one special educator shared:

> We've tried (reducing adult proximity)... like in the lunchroom. Like putting Maria or any of the other students (with disabilities) in the lunch-room and then backing off a little bit. But I think that it (close adult proximity) has been done for so long, that the peers have stayed away for so long, that they are just kind of hesitant to jump right in and do anything.

When the instructional assistant was not in close proximity to the student with disabilities, peers were more likely to fill the space the instructional assistant had vacated. The following example is typical of what we observed.

> As the instructional assistant leaves momentarily to get some materials, Mal-lory (student without disabilities) walks over to Elena (student with disabili-ties). She puts her hand gently on her shoulder and calmly says "easy hands" in response to Elena being a bit rough with her book. Elena turns to look at Mallory and then makes some vocalizations and moves her hands as Mallory talks to her about her book. As the instructional assistant starts to return, Mallory stops talking with Elena and returns to her seat.

Limitations on Receiving Competent Instruction

Observations and interviews indicated that students in this study participated in classroom activities that typically were not planned by trained professional staff. While several team members praised the work of instructional assistants in their "caregiving duties" (e.g., feeding, dressing), they expressed concerns about their role as assistants of instruction.

Many classroom teachers expected capabilities and performance from in-structional assistants that were potentially unrealistic. As one teacher explained, "My problem is that I will be teaching a class and my expectations are that the paraprofessional will get the gist of what I am doing and glean some kernel out of it that can be used right then on the spot." Making such on-the-spot decisions requires a depth of instructional knowledge and skill that many para-professionals and professionals do not possess.

When instructional assistants are assigned to a task, many of them say they feel compelled to go through the motions of an activity even when it seems apparent to them that their efforts are not being effective. As one in-structional assistant explained, "Sometimes it gets discouraging because he is asleep, but I try. I just feel like I'm baby-sitting. I don't feel like I'm doing what I am supposed to be doing." This instructional assistant was observed repeat-edly continuing to speak to the student and presenting activity-related objects, even though it was obvious that the student was asleep. In other cases, instructional assistants would both ask and answer questions posed to students with disabilities. "Would you like to paint the turkey?" (after a 1 sec pause with no observable response) "You would!", then the activity would begin.

Loss of Personal Control

When students have significant communication, motor, and/or sensory difficulties, it can be a challenge for students to advocate for themselves, express their preferences, or at times to reject the decisions of the adults who control most aspects of their personal daily functions at school (e.g., eating, toileting, mobility, selection of leisure activities, choice of friends with whom to spend time). A vision specialist put it succinctly when she pointed out the limited opportunities for choices provided to students with disabilities who "can't verbalize and say 'stop talking to me like that' or can't run away." Instructional assistants frequently made such choices for the student under their supervision. In cases where student communication is unclear, we are left to wonder if the decisions are those the student would make. As one parent wondered, "I think it would be intimidating for me if I was a kid. Just being watched over all the time."

The following examples from our observations, presented as questions, highlight the kinds of decisions made every day that represent a loss of personal control by the students:

- Did Mary really want her cheeseburger dipped in applesauce before she ate each bite?
- Did James really need to be excused from the fun activities in the gymnasium early to have his diapers changed?
- Did James really want to stay inside during recess because it was too cold outside?

Loss of Gender Identity by Students With Disabilities

In cases where the instructional assistant and the student were the opposite gender we observed some interactions that suggested the gender of the student with disabilities was secondary to the gender of the instructional assistant. For example, the gender of the instructional assistant superseded that of the student with disabilities in a physical education class. The teacher divided the class into two groups for warm-up activities. The girls were directed to take five laps around the gym and the boys were directed to do jumping-jacks. As the physical education teacher said, "OK. Let's go!", the female instructional assistant grabbed James' wheelchair and began running around the gym with him along with all the other girls. When the activity was switched, she assisted him in moving his arms to partially participate in jumping-jacks, again with the girls.

Interference With Instruction of Other Students

Students without disabilities did not seem to be distracted much by idiosyncratic behaviors of their classmate with disabilities (e.g., coughing, vocalizations, stereotyped body movements) or common classroom sounds and movements (e.g., small group discussions, questions being asked of the teacher, talk among classmates, computers, pencil sharpener being used, doors and drawers being opened and closed). However, in some cases instructional assistant behaviors were observed to cause distraction during large group lessons taught by the teacher. During these times, if the instructional assistant began doing a different activity with the student with disabilities in the midst of the teacher's large group activity (e.g., reading a story, playing a game, using manipulative materials), those students without disabilities closest to the instructional assistant turned their attention away from the teacher and toward the instructional assistant.

Discussion

Although many team members acknowledged that instructional assistants can and do play an important role in educating children with disabilities, our interviews and observations identified a series of concerns regarding their proximity to the students they are assigned to support.... [A]ny generalization to other situations should be approached cautiously, especially considering the modest number of sites, the limited geographic distribution of sites, and their homogeneity in terms of serving students with multiple disabilities in general education classrooms.

... Too often students with disabilities are placed in general education classrooms without clear expectations established among the team members regarding which professional staff will plan, implement, monitor, evaluate, and adjust instruction. This absence of clarity helps create an environment in which the instructional assistant directs a student's educational program and maintains excessive proximity with the student. We believe this occurs not because instructional assistants seize control, but rather because instructional assistants are the people in the most subordinate position in the school hierarchy. When supervisory personnel (e.g., classroom teachers, special educators) engaged in limited planning and implementation of instruction for the student with disabilities, the responsibility fell to the assistants. These observations highlight that some decisions about the use of instructional assistants are not necessarily rational, but rather may be driven by teachers' (a) fear of difference or change, (b) adherence to customary routines, (c) a reluctance to add another substantial task to what many perceive as an already extensive set of responsibilities, or (d) lack of knowledge and/or support for teaching the student with disabilities. Instructional assistants can play a valuable educational role in assisting the teaching faculty, but generally we believe it is inappropriate and inadvisable to have instructional assistants serve in the capacity of "teacher."

Although awareness... is an important first step in addressing... potential hazards, teachers and instructional assistants may need specific training in basic instructional methods designed to fade assistance and encourage students to respond to natural cues.... Otherwise adults may inadvertently be strengthening the student's cue and prompt dependence. To some extent, many students are initially dependent on cues and supports from the adults who teach them. This starting point needs to change so that adults are increasingly aware of fading their supports to allow students greater autonomy. While capable learners can often overcome less than stellar teaching approaches, those students with more significant learning difficulties often require more precise planning and instruction in our efforts to help them learn. We believe that this problem is not an issue of placement location, since these same problems can exist in special education classes.... We suggest that the classroom involvement of instructional assistants must be compatible within the context of the broader plan for the classroom that is developed and implemented by the classroom team for the benefit of all the students.

Conclusions and Implications for Practice

The findings of this study demonstrate that there are a number of areas of concern regarding the roles of instructional assistants who support the education of students with disabilities in general education settings. The following is a list of considerations for future policy development, school-based practices, training, and research.

- School districts need to rethink their policies on hiring instructional assistants for individual students. We suggest that alternatives be explored that include hiring assistants for the classroom rather than an individual student. This would allow general and special education teachers to distribute instructional assistants' time and job responsibilities more equitably to benefit a variety of students, both with and without disabilities.
- School staff and families need to reach agreement on when students need the close proximity of an adult, when that proximity can be appropriately provided through natural supports such as classmates, and when to appropriately withdraw supports that require close proximity.
- School staff and community members (e.g., classroom teachers, special educators, parents) need awareness training on the effects and potential harm to children caused by excessive adult proximity....
- School teams need to explicitly clarify the role of the classroom teacher as the instructional leader in the classroom including their roles and responsibilities as the teacher for their students with disabilities. It is the classroom teacher's role to direct the activities of the classroom, including the activities of instructional assistants in their charge.
- School staff (e.g., classroom teachers, instructional assistants) should be afforded training in basic instructional procedures that facilitate learning by students with special educational needs in the context of typical classroom activities. Additionally, training should specifically include approaches related to decreasing dependence and fading

prompts often associated with excessive and prolonged proximity of adults.

- Students with disabilities need to be physically, programmatically, and interactionally included in classroom activities that have been planned by a qualified teacher in conjunction with support staff as needed (e.g., special educators, related services providers). Such changes in practice should decrease problems associated with students with disabilities being isolated within the classroom.
- Instructional assistants should be provided with competency-based training that includes ongoing, classroom-based supervision by the teacher.
- Instructional assistants should have opportunities for input into instructional planning based on their knowledge of the student, but the ultimate accountability for planning, implementing, monitoring, and adjusting instruction should rest with the professional staff, just as it does for all other students without disabilities.
- Use of instructional assistants in general education classrooms must increasingly be done in ways that consider the unique educational needs of all students in the class, rather than just those with disabilities.

... [A]ssigning an instructional assistant to a student with special educational needs in a general education class, though intended to be helpful, may sometimes result in problems associated with excessive, prolonged adult proximity. In questioning the current use of instructional assistants, we are not suggesting that instructional assistants not be used or that the field revert to historically ineffective ways of educating students with disabilities (e.g., special education classes, special education schools). We are suggesting that our future policy development, training, and research focus on different configurations of service delivery that provide needed supports in general education classrooms, yet avoid the inherent problems associated with our current practices. Undoubtedly, these service provision variations will necessarily need to be individualized and flexible to account for the diverse variations in students, teachers, schools, and communities across our country. We hope that by raising the issues presented in this study, we can extend the national discussion on practices to support students with varying characteristics in general education classrooms and take corresponding actions that will be educationally credible, financially responsible—helping, not hovering!

Susan Unok Marks, Carl Schrader,
and Mark Levine

 **NO**

Paraeducator Experiences in Inclusive Settings

Increasing parental demands to place children in least restrictive environments have resulted in school districts being faced with providing inclusion experiences for students with a range of disabilities. However, the option to place a special education student in an inclusive setting is typically limited by many factors, including the (a) student's academic and social functioning level, (b) presence and severity of challenging behaviors, (c) willingness of the general education classroom teacher, and (d) availability of resources within a particular school. Even so, as the benefits of inclusion, particularly in the social areas, have become highlighted, parents have increasingly asserted that regardless of their child's functioning level, willingness of teachers, or current availability of resources, the best educational environment for their child is the inclusive setting.

A growing number of parents are impatient with waiting for schools to undergo the types of systemic changes necessary for creating inclusion programs.... In other words, although the literature on inclusive practices continues to highlight the limitations of the general education setting in meeting the needs of students with disabilities, particularly for students with challenging behaviors, many parents are not willing to wait for a "right time," a time when all the issues that plague placement in inclusive settings and that are often the focus of heated discussions are completely resolved. From the parents' perspective, a *reasonably good* inclusion program today is preferable to a *perfect* inclusion program tomorrow. These parents appear to concur with Keith Storey, who notes "physical integration is a necessary first step for other forms of integration."

One type of support that general education teachers have identified as essential for placing special education students in their classrooms has been extra classroom support. As a result, many school districts, in an effort to meet both the needs of the teachers and the inclusion students, have hired paraeducators....

From Susan Unok Marks, Carl Schrader, and Mark Levine, "Paraeducator Experiences in Inclusive Settings: Helping, Hovering, or Holding Their Own?" *Exceptional Children*, vol. 65, no. 3 (Spring 1999). Copyright © 1999 by The Council for Exceptional Children. Reprinted by permission. References omitted.

Purpose of the Study

In order to better understand the experiences of paraeducators working with inclusion students, the first author conducted a series of interviews. Our purpose in this article is to highlight the primary themes related to how paraeducators assumed their roles and responsibilities and the dilemmas they faced while providing educational and behavioral supports for inclusion students. . . .

Results

Paraeducators [who were interviewed] assumed a range of job responsibilities, such as providing instruction in academic and social skills; making curricular modifications; managing student behaviors; and developing working relationships with others. What is striking about how paraeducators negotiated their roles and responsibilities is that many of them appeared to assume the primary burden of success for the inclusion students. This involved assuming primary responsibility for both academic and behavioral needs in order to ensure that students would be successful (e.g., would remain in the inclusive setting, would be accepted by the teacher). Paraeducators, however, expressed that it was more appropriate for the classroom teacher to assume these primary responsibilities. Why then did these paraeducators take on so much of the responsibility, which inadvertently downplayed the role of the classroom teacher? . . .

Not Being a "Bother" to the Teacher

In supporting an inclusion student, paraeducators were very concerned with building a positive working relationship with the teacher to whom they were assigned. As one paraeducator noted, "If I had to look at a single factor that made the largest difference in my job, it's the teacher that I'm placed with." The primacy of this aspect of the job also appeared to perpetuate paraeducators assuming primary responsibility for the inclusion student. This was reflected in how paraeducators attempted to ensure that the teacher was not "burdened" by the inclusion student. In other words, they wanted to ensure that the experience of having an inclusion student would be a positive one for the teacher. Further, most of the paraeducators felt that their own success would be defined by how well the teacher accepted the inclusion student.

Concern for building a positive working relationship with the teacher and concern for ensuring positive teacher responses towards them and the inclusion student resulted in paraeducators assuming primary responsibility for managing student behaviors. For many, this role was viewed as an explicit feature of their job responsibilities. For example, as one paraeducator put it, "My job . . . was to make sure the child was calm and safe enough that the person whose job it is to educate him can do that." However, the challenge of managing student behaviors within an inclusive setting created a level of stress and frustration for many of the paraeducators. One paraeducator expressed a sense of responsibility for making sure that the student's behavior did not disrupt the classroom or "disturb the teacher":

> It felt like a lot of pressure [being in the inclusive setting] because I ... didn't want her [the inclusion student] to disturb the others and I didn't want her to disturb the teacher. So I felt responsible for every single little sound she made.

Another paraeducator also expressed the importance of maintaining a sense of control with managing behaviors:

> When I went into this experience, I was expecting a child who just needed academic support and adaptations, and it was really all behavioral ... but [I was] just trying to maintain a calm demeanor around him, when really I was very frustrated and a lot of times, very unsure of what to do.

Even when student behaviors were managed for a period of time, events in a student's life (e.g., home circumstances, medication changes) could result in increased problem behaviors. These "episodes" were at times difficult to manage, and one paraeducator talked about a period of time when his student who was having changes in medication levels, "was having around three tantrums a day, and ... it was so draining." Another paraeducator described a similar period of time as "just riding through that storm."

It is clear that these paraeducators felt the primary responsibility for directly handling almost all of the behaviors that would arise. At times this meant explaining the probable reasons for the challenging behaviors to the teachers in order to help them understand the influence of environmental variables, as well as to support the teacher in not taking challenging behaviors personally. At other times, this meant intervening before the classroom teacher would have to:

> I would address a behavior as it arose, before it got to a point where she'd [the teacher] notice it, and so there wasn't an opportunity for her to set a lot of limits with him, because ... I never let it get to that point.

This paraeducator felt it was important not to involve the teacher in managing the student's behavior. Another paraeducator concurred:

> When he [the student] had control, the teacher ... would usually be the first person to [intervene].... Sometimes she would even have him sit in a chair. That was her way of disciplining him ... and when he was in control of himself, he really did very well in those situations ... And, again, if it was a day when he had no control ... I would usually pull him from that activity right away, and do something else. She didn't know him well enough to know real well if it was a day he had control over what he was doing.

Meeting Students' Immediate Academic Needs

Addressing the immediate and daily academic needs of the inclusion student was an equally challenging role for most of the paraeducators. In fact, more than half of the paraeducators identified this as a primary area of support in their job responsibilities. These responsibilities included designing and making adaptations to the curriculum, and in many ways, functioning as the student's primary teacher. Many of the paraeducators assumed tutoring roles (working with their students, one-on-one) for some part of the school day, particularly if the student was not able to "keep up with what the teacher was teaching." One paraeducator felt the biggest challenge was to help his student "keep up academically." Another described her role as "taking what is being taught and making it appropriate for [the student]."

Paraeducators noted that they felt it was the responsibility of the teacher to manage the curriculum; however, they also expressed that this rarely occurred:

> What happens is that they [teachers] leave it up to the aide to do a lot of the work.... But for the most part, the teachers are the ones to create the curriculum for the child, and modify it. And that takes time.... It usually takes a lot of modifications so the child can participate more in the class.... And it was left for me to initiate, and they would say, "Oh, that sounds like a great idea" ... And I would end up doing it, and trying it.

Another paraeducator expressed that no one seemed to want to take responsibility for creating the student's curriculum, and "it just got to the point where it was just easier to do it than to keep asking people to do it." This same paraeducator noted how one of the teachers had been a special education teacher, but didn't have the time to adapt the curriculum. Others echoed this issue of teachers not having enough time or energy for developing and adapting the curriculum for students with disabilities. Another paraeducator further expressed how the teacher with whom she worked was even apologetic about how little attention and time had been given to curricular adaptations due to being busy with other teaching responsibilities.

One paraeducator also noted how it was up to him to ask for ideas and that teachers were generally open to this; however, paraeducators felt it was up to them to ask for ideas only when he or she felt "at a loss":

> The teachers I've been able to work with have been really open—receptive to everything about the program. I think I can walk up to a teacher and ask them what they're doing in class and then sometimes if I'm just at a loss, they'll give me some ideas on some alterations I can make to the curriculum whether it's simplifying it, or altering it in some way... but I don't do that very often, probably only about once a month.

For the most part, paraeducators found themselves in situations in which waiting for teachers and other professionals to make curricular and teaching decisions was not feasible. Consequently, faced with the need to provide daily academic activities and to make "on-the-spot" modifications to the classroom activities, paraeducators found themselves assuming primary responsibility for day-to-day educational decisions.

Being the "Hub" and the "Expert"

One interesting subtheme that emerged was how paraeducators were placed in the role of being a "hub," or being the liaison between all the various individuals involved in the inclusion student's school life. As one paraeducator put it, "Frankie is a child with more resources available to him than any child I've ever met." Intricately tied to this role of being the hub was being in a position in which they needed to be able to incorporate a range of suggestions and recommendations made by school team members.

On the other hand, many of the paraeducators felt that their daily close contact with the inclusion student made them an expert on the needs of the student with whom they worked. This feeling of being the expert was reflected in how the paraeducators assumed primary responsibility for managing student behaviors and for the day-to-day academic and teaching roles. For example, one paraeducator noted how the teacher didn't know the student well enough to know if it was a day in which the student "had control over what he was doing... and I got to know him so well that I could tell pretty quickly in a day what kind of shape he was in and if he had control." Further, most of the paraeducators had received training throughout the year on positive behavioral support strategies, resulting in them actually having more knowledge about behavioral support plans and strategies than the classroom teacher. One paraeducator expressed the dilemma of being an expert, yet being in the position of implementing the various suggestions made by others:

> I felt like... I was very much the hub, with the spokes coming in.... Sometimes I felt like it was hard to be the liaison, or the hub, the person who was the closest, but with the least to say.... It was just a frustrating situation to be in, as an assistant without the degree that gives me the right to say, "Well, my expertise tells me that this is the case."

Being in their unique position of working closely with the student, their job entailed negotiating, mediating, interpreting, and translating the various suggestions presented to them by various members of the school team. One paraeducator described this process as requiring her to at times "blend" the various orientations and suggestions presented to her. This often proved challenging, particularly when the goals and expectations presented by a range of professionals and parents appeared to conflict.

Paraeducators also talked about their unique position in working with parents of inclusion students. Some found this challenging, while others found the experience rewarding. However, it was also noted that by virtue of their positions, parents often approached the paraeducators for ongoing information as well as making educational suggestions regarding what they wanted their child to learn. For example, one of the paraeducators started developing strategies for teaching the inclusion student how to count money, at the request of the parent. This tendency for parents to communicate through the paraeducator also appeared to contribute to the paraeducator feeling like they were the hub, or the liaison between parents and school personnel and between school service providers as well.

"Representing Inclusion": Advocacy and Feelings About Inclusion

Sometimes being the hub or the expert included representing the student and the idea of inclusion to the rest of the school community. As one paraeducator reflected:

> It really matters so much, the . . . personality of the assistant, because you're the one . . . you represent him. I represent Chris at work, to the other staff members. (All names are pseudonyms.) I represent the project of full inclusion. And it's not always a popular project; it's not a popular thing to start. And, just how well I get along with the staff members, I think, really mattered.

This sense of responsibility seemed to include the feeling that how well the special education student actually did in the inclusive setting would be a direct reflection on how school personnel would view the paraeducator. Again, the success of the inclusion placement was assumed by many of the paraeducators. Being in a position in which this success appeared to be highly personalized, paraeducators expressed sensitivity to how the school in general responded to the inclusion student as well as the general concept of inclusion. For one student who required significant academic modifications, the paraeducator noted how the responses from the school as a whole had been "mixed."

> What I get from a lot of people is that they don't really see that Cory is intelligent. They see the disability. They don't see beyond it. It's a weekly event that somebody will sit down and say, "Well, you know, how can you expect her to learn to read and write," or "I don't understand why the parents want her to learn to read or write." And it's a lot of education, talking to people about the student, "Well, you know she is very capable, she learns at a slower rate because of her disability, but she is quite capable of functioning as a normal student." With the adaptations, of course.

One paraeducator also noted the "reputation" of the student with whom she worked. To some extent, many of the paraeducators felt that their students were fairly "high profile" in that most students and faculty in a school knew of their students.

> Absolutely everyone knows his name. In the beginning it was hard, because literally, he would be tantrumming in the middle of the hall, he'd be screaming. . . . I mean, everybody knew he was there. And there were a lot of people who just avoided the situation. . . . And you know, many people would say to me at the end of the day, "You know, I don't know how you do it." I had one teacher who said to me, "Well at least you're the only person who can see some good in him."

In another case, the paraeducator talked about how the school personnel's perception of the inclusion student actually influenced how they felt about her as a paraeducator:

> Each teacher has their own personality, just like we all do... and everyone has their opinion of what special ed is... And some of them have very much different attitudes about what my role is. So, I get the sloughed-off opinions... it's like what they think of him [the student] gets sloughed off on to me.

Another paraeducator noted that the school personnel did not appear to be supportive of inclusion for her student, which she found surprising since this particular student had been at the same school for most of her 5 years of schooling. This paraeducator described this lack of support by talking about not feeling accepted herself:

> I have never felt very accepted in that school, personally. Or, you know, just the talk I've heard that they didn't agree. And still today, they think that Wendy should be in a special day class and she doesn't belong in a regular classroom.

As can be seen from these quotes, many of the paraeducators found themselves in an advocacy role, one in which it was their responsibility to work towards general acceptance of the inclusion student, or to "represent" the student in a way that would support that acceptance. This responsibility included educating others about the student as well as educating others to the idea of inclusion. Being in a position in which they had a close understanding of the special education student, and oftentimes feeling that they were the only ones in the school who knew the student, resulted in what many of the paraeducators described as a feeling of isolation and loneliness in their daily work. For example, one of the paraeducators noted the importance of positive communication between teachers and the paraeducators, "because sometimes the job can get down and lonely." This theme was also expressed by another paraeducator, who felt she was the only one in the school who truly understood the student's disability (autism):

> I'm on an island, basically; we're alone... just Paul and me out there. Nobody else knows anything about his disability.... People don't have the experience, the resource teacher didn't have experience, the teacher.... I don't think anybody at my school knows anybody else with autism.

Not having others in the school with whom to share ideas about the particular inclusion student further contributed to this feeling of being on an island:

> [The biggest challenge was] the isolation of the work itself. Being isolated, feeling like an island, as far as in the environment I was working in.... I felt sometimes that, although the kids in the classroom were very supportive, we were sort of on an island.... Even in the special ed environment, you have other aides and other teachers you can discuss things and pass by them.

In a more positive light, one paraeducator described her role as one of "interpreter" for the inclusion student:

> My attention and my care goes to one student; and in the life of that student;
> I interact with all the adults that he interacts with.... And then to speak to
> the teachers, to be an advocate for my student, to be in the middle of the
> adult world and his world makes me a kind of interpreter for my student.

Discussion

... [T]he picture that emerges from interviews with paraeducators is that inclusion students, although generally accepted, are not necessarily included in the overall curriculum planning for the class as a whole. In other words, most of the teachers appeared to act as "hosts." Without the presence of the paraeducator, the educational benefits for the inclusion student would have been extremely minimal. On the other hand, it might be possible that because the paraeducator assumed this role, teachers never really felt the need to make these types of adaptations....

[It] appears that some of the responsibilities, although "accepted" by the teachers and paraeducators, could not be viewed as ideally "acceptable" for supporting inclusive practices. Paraeducators feeling responsible for the success of inclusion students might be viewed as an acceptable role; however, assuming sole responsibility rather than a shared one with the classroom teacher cannot be viewed as acceptable. This shared responsibility, although difficult to create, is the missing ingredient in the inclusive practices reported in this study, resulting in too many of the paraeducators "holding their own." ...

Ongoing Collaborative Meetings for Sharing Expertise Areas

Bringing together all the team members of a special education student's program takes considerable effort and time. Yet, ... it is an extremely important component. Certainly, more collaborative meetings in which the expertise of the teachers (from both special and general education) and the expertise of the paraeducator are utilized needs to be promoted. In this way, paraeducators and teachers can share their expertise: paraeducators on student information and teachers on educational and curricular decision-making strategies. In addition, classroom teachers can begin to develop expertise around the inclusion student, instead of the paraeducator being the sole holder of this knowledge. Paraeducators, in turn, can begin to provide more effective and educationally beneficial learning strategies for the student, rather than making on-the-spot activity decisions which may meet the immediate objective of engaging the student, but may not have sufficient long-term educational benefits.

These ongoing and regular discussions between teachers and paraeducators need to also include defining the teacher's and the paraeducator's roles and responsibilities. As Giangreco et al. also concluded, "school teams need to explicitly clarify the role of the classroom teacher as the instructional leader in the classroom including their roles and responsibilities as the teacher for the students with disabilities." As part of school team discussions, it is important to broach the issue of allowing paraeducators to take some risks, to begin to shift their attention to the class as a whole and to encourage teachers to take a more active role with the inclusion student. Interestingly, paraeducators reported that many of the inclusion students who were close to grade level, regardless of severity of problem behaviors, for the most part were able to be more independent as the year progressed. In other words, as the student's behaviors became increasingly managed, the classroom teacher was gradually able to assume primary responsibility for the student. However, for those students needing instructional adaptations, paraeducators continued to play a prominent role. This would indicate that assuming primary responsibility for providing curricular modifications and adaptations may present more significant and ongoing challenges for classroom teachers.

Including "fading plans" is another important strategy for clarifying the roles and responsibilities of the paraeducators and classroom teachers. Through this process, the goal of having the paraeducator shift attention to the whole classroom rather than just focusing on the inclusion student is made explicit and increases accountability for keeping this general goal at the forefront. For example, beginning with "low-risk" times, we have been successful in gradually increasing the paraeducator's proximity levels from the inclusion student. However, we have found that this process also needs to include natural supports (e.g., teacher reminders, peer supports, written instructions) in order to replace the support levels that were previously provided by the paraeducator.

Training for Paraeducators, Teachers, and Other School Personnel

Further training for paraeducators, teachers, and school personnel is absolutely necessary. Teachers in particular may not feel comfortable with, nor have many of them had training in, positive behavioral support strategies or in curricular modifications for special education students. Providing sufficient release time and opportunities to learn these important strategies will be essential if teachers are to assume greater responsibility for inclusion students with challenging behaviors. If teachers feel they lack this knowledge, they will most likely continue to defer this responsibility to the paraeducator, especially if that paraeducator has specific training in that area. Ironically, in our own practice, we offer training to the paraeducators, but classroom teachers do not typically attend these training sessions due to time constraints. Unfortunately, providing training to paraeducators, although very much needed..., can increase the possibility that teachers leave the paraeducators to manage on their own.... [S]imply providing consultation and training to paraeducators is not sufficient and may inadvertently perpetuate paraeducators assuming an unbalanced (and in our view, unacceptable) responsibility for inclusion students. Therefore, it is critical that classroom teachers be provided with this training as well. Further, ... it is important for teachers to be provided training on how to supervise paraprofessionals, especially in how to coordinate instructional efforts to better meet the needs of inclusion students.

For the paraeducators, there is a need for training regarding the goals of inclusive practices and their roles in that process. This training needs to include examining what inclusion is and how to work as a team member, including working with and communicating with parents. In other words, we may need to redefine what successful inclusive practices look like, from a vision where inclusion students are simply maintained in general education classrooms and teachers respond in generally positive ways towards the inclusion student, to one in which the inclusion student is supported in his or her membership in the classroom.

Paraeducators will also need ongoing support and supervision by a special educator assigned to overseeing the inclusion student's educational needs. Too often, in our experience, special educators assigned to this role have high caseloads, resulting in extremely limited time for the level of ongoing support that is necessary for daily academic and curricular modifications. Again, in the absence of such resources, paraeducators will likely continue to assume roles that others more qualified should assume.

POSTSCRIPT

Are the Least Trained Teaching Our Most Needy Children?

According to Giangreco et al., hiring an assistant is viewed as supporting inclusion. Yet that very support seems to isolate, rather than involve, the child. Does an untrained person have the ability to support an educational program?

Marks, Schrader, and Levine state that parents and teachers think that hiring an assistant provides a "good enough" level of inclusion until a more perfect model can be implemented. If teachers are not skilled in inclusive practices or in the supervision of paraprofessionals, how will the high standards of the general curriculum ever reach the child with disabilities?

Litigation has established paraprofessionals as supports that might be necessary for a child to have access to a free and appropriate education (Katsiyannis, Hodge, and Lanford, *Remedial and Special Education,* 2000). The key word here is *supports.* The same legal cases have determined that paraprofessionals who lack appropriate training may not directly provide special education services and may assist only if supervised by certified professionals.

One point of view is that aides need training to be of assistance to teachers (Johnson, Lasater, and Fitzgerald, *Journal of Staff Development,* 1997). Specifically, aides should learn to observe and record student performance using data collection strategies ranging from anecdotal reports to structured records of the frequency, duration, and intensity of target behavior. Skills in behavioral and instructional strategies, such as modeling, shaping, prompting, cuing, reinforcing, questioning, and providing feedback, would help teachers gain information about the response of the inclusion children to educational challenges. The most difficult challenge, helping students become more independent—physically, socially, and academically—requires particular attention. These specialized skills, along with an established support system, will increase the skills of assistants and help both students and teachers focus on instruction.

On the other hand, French (*Teaching Exceptional Children,* 1999) finds that teachers are rarely prepared to share instructional activities and are uncomfortable supervising adults—competencies that should be directly addressed in order to keep the teacher connected with students as more people join the educational team. Educational responsibilities should be shared, not ceded to an assistant. Teacher training needs to incorporate skills as direction-giver, monitor, coach, and support person as well as instructor of students with varied needs.

A third viewpoint argues against assigning paraprofessionals full time to individual students, striving instead for cross-training to decrease both stress and dependency and to rotate tasks (Rea, *Quinlan's Special Education Law Bulletin*, 2001). In addition to building a ready corps of substitutes in case a paraprofessional is absent or leaves the job, such a practice also creates a group of individuals who share concerns and responsibilities rather than bearing them alone. Complementing the option of assigning assistants to classes rather than to students, this strategy provides individual assistance when necessary but is flexible enough to encourage independence and natural supports.

Is it possible that, as educators have tried to include more children, general education teachers have come to believe that the aides know better than they how to teach children with significant disabilities? Is it possible that administrators, parents, and special education teachers assume that general education teachers will know how to use the services of paraprofessionals to assist their teaching? Have paraprofessionals been caught in the middle—without the training but with the responsibility?

271

On the Internet ...

Children and Adults with Attention-Deficit/Hyperactivity Disorder

Children and Adults with Attention-Deficit/Hyperactivity Disorder (CHADD), founded in 1987 by families seeking information about this disorder, is now a national organization linked to a variety of activities. The CHADD Web site contains extensive information on ADHD and ADD and is helpful to anyone who wants to learn more about these conditions.

http://www.chadd.org

Facilitated Communication Institute

This site is based at the Facilitated Communication Institute at Syracuse University. The organization and its site serve as a source for sharing information on facilitated communication, training opportunities, and individual experiences.

http://soeweb.syr.edu/thefci/

National Center on Educational Outcomes

The National Center on Educational Outcomes (NCEO), based at the University of Minnesota, is a primary research site for the participation of students with disabilities in large-scale high-stakes testing. This Web site contains current information on the status of testing in all states as well as information on the way in which students with disabilities participate. Resources include numerous NCEO publications.

http://www.coled.umn.edu/nceo/

LD OnLine

A service of the Learning Project at WETA (FM) in Washington, D.C., LD OnLine is supported by numerous foundations. Oriented toward parents and children, this Web site provides a range of information, personal stories, home-schooling ideas, and resources for children, parents, and teachers who are interested in learning disabilities.

http://www.ldonline.org

Scientific American Feature Article: Attention-Deficit Hyperactivity Disorder

Over time, *Scientific American* has explored numerous issues regarding disabilities, especially those suggesting that their basis lies in neurological functioning. This article explores ADHD. The site has links to related articles, and it also contains a search function that accesses other *Scientific American* articles.

http://www.sciam.com/1998/0998issue/0998barkley.html

PART 3

Issues About Disabilities

*E*arlier sections of this book focused on global issues regarding the education of children with disabilities. Apart from these issues of law, policy, and practice exist controversial issues about the reality of particular disabilities and the efficacy of unique methodologies. The fervent desire of parents and educators to help children nurtures the development of approaches that promise success. The challenge of evaluating new ways of thinking will be with us so long as there are children who need extra support in order to learn.

- Are Learning Disabilities a Myth?

- Is Attention Deficit Hyperactivity Disorder Real?

- Are We Turning Too Easily to Medication to Address the Needs of Our Children?

- Should Parents Choose Cochlear Implants for Their Deaf Children?

- Do Students With Disabilities Benefit From Participating in High-Stakes Testing?

ISSUE 14

Are Learning Disabilities a Myth?

YES: G. E. Zuriff, from "The Myths of Learning Disabilities: The Social Construction of a Disorder," *Public Affairs Quarterly* (October 1996)

NO: Michael M. Gerber, from "An Appreciation of Learning Disabilities: The Value of Blue–Green Algae," *Exceptionality* (March 2000)

ISSUE SUMMARY

YES: G. E. Zuriff, a professor of psychology at Wheaton College, challenges the differentiation between children who are diagnosed as learning disabled and those who are found to be slow learners, asserting that all children struggling in school deserve assistance. He questions the tests and assessment strategies that are used to determine the diagnosis of learning disabilities (LD), holding that LD is based on false comparisons to individuals with brain damage.

NO: Michael M. Gerber, a professor in the Graduate School of Education at the University of California, Santa Barbara, acknowledges that all the answers about LD have not yet been found, but he maintains that much has been learned in the process of exploring the unique learning characteristics of individuals who learn some subjects with ease and struggle mightily over others.

Specific learning disabilities:

A disorder in one or more of the basic psychological processes involved in understanding or in using language, spoken or written, that may manifest itself in an imperfect ability to listen, think, speak, read, write, spell, or to do mathematical calculations, including conditions such as perceptual disabilities, brain injury, minimal brain dysfunction, dyslexia, and developmental aphasia. This does not include learning problems that are primarily the result of visual, hearing or motor disabilities, of mental retardation, of emotional disturbance, or of environmental, cultural, or economic disadvantage.

— IDEA97

Have you ever met a student who seems to be very capable in many ways —can communicate, compute, and reason well—but who simply cannot read well? Or one who is proficient in all academic areas except in composing a coherent narrative? The puzzle is that the student seems so competent, except in one specific area. Motivation, family support, and good teaching have all been present, but learning in this one area still lags behind success in other areas.

Curiosity and frustration about this type of student have been the source of discussion for the last century. In 1963 Samuel Kirk formalized thinking into a condition he termed "learning disabilities." And education has never been the same since.

With the advent of special education law, educators, parents, and attorneys have argued over the shape and meaning of learning disabilities, a disability that seems to be defined mostly by what it is not. The federal definition cited above describes a disability that is most apparent while learning academic subjects, is likely the result of some neurological difference, and occurs in a child who appears to have the background and capability to learn easily.

G. E. Zuriff doubts the basis for the definition of learning disabilities because the existence of specific neurological damage cannot be routinely documented and assessment is based on questionable strategies and shifting definitions. In the following selection, he challenges the differentiation between children diagnosed as LD and those who are thought to be slow learners, insisting that all struggling learners deserve assistance without resorting to questionable labels that are based on false comparisons to individuals with observable brain damage.

In the second selection, Michael M. Gerber finds merit and valuable knowledge in the 40-year investigation of the phenomenon called "learning disabilities." Gerber maintains that there is no doubt that investigation in this area probes a specific type of disability rather than a generalized learning struggle. Linking learning disabilities studies to those spawned by the discovery of different colored algae or a new animal species, Gerber discusses what the field has learned—as well as what has yet to be learned—about a very particular way of learning.

As you read these selections, decide whether you think that the definition of learning disabilities ought to include all children who struggle with school or whether learning disabilities is a real condition that will become more definable with additional research.

G. E. Zuriff

 **YES**

The Myths of Learning Disabilities

If the reports are to be believed, our children are in the grip of a cognitive epidemic. Nearly two-and-a-half million U.S. school children are currently diagnosed with learning disabilities (LD), an increase of roughly 150% in fifteen years. In Massachusetts, for example, 17% of schoolchildren have LD. Between 1988 and 1994, the number of students entering college with LD increased 142%. Of all disabled children, 52% are LD, up from 24% in 1976. My purposes in this paper are to: (1) provide an historical understanding of the LD concept; (2) raise serious objections to the conceptual and empirical bases of the LD concept; and (3) show that LD is a socially constructed disorder (i.e. one created to serve social needs) rather than a medically or scientifically based one.

The LD concept was introduced in the 60s to describe children of normal cognitive capacity who nevertheless had trouble learning in school because of assumed neurological dysfunctions. These LD children were thought to have problems in the *psychological processes* needed for academic success, not in their basic intelligence. They therefore could be helped by instruction in the deficient psychological processes.

Educators and parents of LD children soon founded several national organizations to inform the public and advocate for the learning disabled. The Learning Disabilities Association of America, the largest, now has over 60,000 members in 775 chapters. In addition, a new industry emerged to diagnose, treat, and lobby for LD persons and to consult to businesses, colleges, and government.

Eventually this LD lobby brought pressure to bear on state and Federal governments. Their major victory came in 1975 with the signing of a Federal law mandating that all children, regardless of disability, are entitled to a free and appropriate public education. To support this entitlement, the Federal government provides funds to local educational programs based on the number of participating students. Now known as the Individuals with Disabilities Education Act (IDEA), this act mandates that schools must provide all disabled students, . . . free services, diagnosis, an individualized education plan, and special education specifically designed for their disability.

Congress also passed Section 504 of the Rehabilitation Act of 1973 and the Americans with Disabilities Act of 1990 (ADA). These laws protect the civil

From G. E. Zuriff, "The Myths of Learning Disabilities: The Social Construction of a Disorder," *Public Affairs Quarterly*, vol. 10, no. 4 (October 1996). Copyright © 1996 by *Public Affairs Quarterly*. Reprinted by permission.

rights of individuals with disabilities in employment, public accommodations, transportation, and government services. Under these laws, LD is considered on a par with physical disabilities. Not only is discrimination outlawed, but businesses, public facilities, and universities must make "reasonable" accommodations for persons with disabilities. For example, colleges are required to modify any degree requirement, examination format, or admission standard that discriminates against LD students. Similarly, for employers of a LD individual, these accommodations may include special computers, aides to read material to the employee, or reassignment of certain tasks to other employees.

Thus a diagnosis of LD carries profound implications throughout life. But along with the LD child (let us call her Jennifer), there are other students having academic problems. Labelled "slow learners" rather than LD, they are seen as possessing low intelligence, and their poor performance is therefore to be expected. The slow learner (call him Scott) is not considered disabled and is thus ineligible for the benefits and protections afforded Jennifer. The difference between Jennifer and Scott is supposedly best captured in the fact that Scott does poorly in nearly all his classes, as would be expected of someone with low cognitive ability, while Jennifer does quite well in many classes, and fails only a few, suggesting that she is basically intelligent and would excel in school but for her specific brain dysfunction.

One might assume that with the billions spent under IDEA and ADA, and with the millions of Americans deeply affected by these laws, there is a clear definition of LD and good reasons why Jennifer is said to have it but not Scott. Yet a careful conceptual examination of LD shows that many of our commonly held assumptions are only myths and that the LD concept is seriously flawed.

The first myth of LD is that Jennifer and Scott must be treated differently because Jennifer, but not Scott, is known to have a brain dysfunction. Contrary to this widely held belief, however, of all the millions diagnosed with LD, few have had a brain examination showing anything wrong. In nearly all LD cases, the diagnosis is based on observations of academic work and performance on psychological tests. Brain dysfunction is inferred by a process of elimination— if no other cause for Jennifer's unexpected school performance is discovered, the conclusion is that a neurological condition must be responsible. In Scott's case, however, because he is merely a slow learner and his poor performance is expected, there is nothing to explain and no brain dysfunction need be inferred. Nevertheless, the fact remains that we still do not know the biological basis for either Jennifer's or Scott's school difficulties.

To understand this myth's hold on the LD movement, we must understand its history. In pioneering research at the end of the 19th century, early neurologists studied the often strange symptoms of individuals who survived traumatic head injuries. In some cases, the patients returned to near cognitive normalcy with a few peculiar exceptions in language. For example, a brain-damaged patient might speak and understand English quite well but have lost the capacity to read. These patients could see and hear the letters; their problem was that they could not make sense of specific language information.

Eventually, similarities were noted between these patients and uninjured school children who were normal in nearly every respect but who had specific deficits in language skills. Some showed good intelligence in many subjects but had serious difficulties in reading, writing, or verbal expression. From these observations, early neurologists constructed a critical but deeply flawed syllogism: If people with known brain damage (i.e. head injured patients) show certain cognitive symptoms (i.e. specific language deficits) but are otherwise normal, then children who show the same cognitive symptoms and are also otherwise normal, must have similar brain damage from other causes.

Thus began a long and tortuous history of attempts to find the specific brain dysfunction responsible for LD. As each theory has proven wrong, others have arisen to take its place. The belief in a neurological cause has proven irresistible and remains a central tenet of the LD movement.

To see the weakness of the syllogism, consider another analogy. One morning my car does not start. My neighbor tells me that when his car failed to start, he discovered worn spark plugs. I then reason: His car and mine have similar symptoms (i.e. problems starting); since the reason for his car's symptoms is worn spark plugs, my car also must have worn spark plugs. We immediately recognize the logical flaws. My car might not be starting for a variety of reasons (e.g., no gas, weak battery); a similarity of symptoms does not necessarily entail a similarity of causes. In the same way, the children and the brain-injured patients may have similar symptoms for very different reasons. Furthermore, in the case of my car, we have ample evidence that with increased use, plugs do get worn and fail to start the car. With children, we have no evidence whatsoever that the kind of brain damage caused by a head injury can also occur in a child with no head injuries.

Besides its tenuous logic, the brain dysfunction myth is questionable on other grounds. It assumes that LD children suffer with a brain dysfunction, but slow learners do not. According to the myth, Scott's brain is normal; it is just functioning inefficiently—there are fast normal brains and slow normal brains. Why should we accept this myth? When it comes to math and reading, Scott and Jennifer both function very poorly. We have no evidence that in these subjects, their brains are operating differently. Even if we do someday find differences in functioning, if neither brain is doing well in these areas, why call one brain "dysfunctional" and the other just "slow?" After all, cognitive capacities are all based somewhere in the nervous system, and both Jennifer's and Scott's problems are ultimately to be traced to the brain.

To be sure, modern neuroscientists using anatomical techniques and magnetic resonance imaging scans have found abnormalities in the brains of a very small number of dyslexic children. However, the brains of these LD children are judged abnormal only in comparison to those of normal children. No study to date has compared the brains of LD children to those of slow learners. Were such comparisons to be made, we may well find that Scott and Jennifer share common abnormalities in the brain areas associated with math and reading but they differ markedly in other areas. Or we may find that Jennifer and Scott exhibit no brain similarities, and that their brains differ from normal brains in different ways. In this latter case, we still have no rationale for considering only the deviations in Jennifer's brain to be "dysfunctions."

The only known difference between Jennifer and Scott is that Scott has difficulties in all his subjects while Jennifer has difficulties in only some. Clearly, we should reject the myth of brain dysfunction and either admit that Scott's consistently poor academic performance is equally the result of brain dysfunctions, or admit that Jennifer's uneven school performance is the result of normal variations among normal brains.

If Jennifer and Scott are not distinguished by brain examination, how is LD identified for Federal grants and special accommodations? According to a 1976 U.S. Office of Education definition, LD involves a "severe discrepancy between achievement and intellectual ability" in one or more of 8 specified areas, including listening and reading comprehension, and mathematical calculation. Although this formulation was later dropped by the Office, it was adopted by many states to interpret the vague language of IDEA. This definition fits the image of Jennifer as a bright child whose brain disorder manifests itself in the discrepancy between how well she should be performing based on her intelligence and her actual poor achievement. Scott on the other hand, is not LD because he shows no discrepancy; as a slow learner, his low performance is appropriate to his overall low intelligence.

Diagnosis is thus a two-step procedure. Children are given I.Q. tests to measure intelligence as well as a series of standardized achievement tests to assess academic achievement. Any student showing at least a normal score on the I.Q. test but a significantly lower score on one of the achievement tests is diagnosed with LD. For example, Jennifer may score an I.Q. of 103, indicating that she is of above average intelligence, while Scott may have scored only a below-average 89. Yet, both may score a poor 85 on reading achievement. Because only Jennifer shows a "severe discrepancy," she alone is diagnosed as LD.

Plainly, every discrepancy definition must specify "normal intelligence." For some states the cut-off point is an I.Q. of 90 and for others, 85. Thus, in some states, Scott would not qualify for LD benefits, regardless of how low his achievement scores are because they would be considered the expected result of his below normal intelligence. He also is not eligible for special education as mentally retarded because mental retardation requires an even lower I.Q., as low as 70 in many states. He remains stuck in the grey area of "slow learner"— an I.Q. too high for mental retardation status, but too low for LD.

That children identified as LD through these discrepancy definitions are qualitatively different from slow learners is a second myth of LD. Discrepancy definitions are riddled by problems. First, although I.Q. tests have proven to be good predictors of a variety of adult achievements, they do not measure the full range of intellectual potential. There are many kinds of intelligences, and I.Q. measures only a narrow range of these, particularly those dealing with abstraction and analysis.

A second problem is that, whether or not I.Q. tests are biased, the fact is that African-Americans have an average I.Q. test score of 85, 15 points below the average score of whites. This means that if a LD definition specifies 85 as the lower limit for normal intelligence, then half the African-American population will automatically be excluded from qualifying for LD benefits, regardless of their academic difficulties, as compared to only 15% of whites. This use of I.Q.

tests in LD diagnosis probably accounts for the fact that although under IDEA, whites and blacks receive special education at comparable rates, only 44% of those blacks qualify as LD as compared to 52% of the whites.

Problems with achievement tests are even more serious. Although the number of achievement tests generated by educators has proliferated, among the nearly 100 tests currently available, very few have been rigorously studied and proven their validity. Even fewer are scaled adequately for adults and for college level skills.

Another questionable assumption of the discrepancy model is that performance in school should be consistent with I.Q. score, and discrepancies therefore reflect something amiss. Yet, we all know of scientific whizzes in math and physics who are not very good at writing; as well as brilliant literary critics who are lost when they see mathematical symbols. The fact is that we lack good data on how frequently discrepancies occur within our population. Indications are that discrepancies are normally distributed, just as cognitive abilities are. An unusually large discrepancy is thus no more a symptom of a disorder than is an unusually low achievement unaccompanied by a discrepancy.

The discrepancy model also assumes that I.Q. and achievement tests, although correlated, measure different things. This is why Jennifer can be viewed as having high intelligence but low math achievement. However, it is well known that achievement problems, especially deficiencies in reading and language listening, can depress I.Q. scores, and this depressing effect increases with grade level. Ironically, because of his reading problems, Scott will thus have an increasingly difficult time scoring in the "normal range" of I.Q. to qualify as LD. The alleged independence of I.Q. and achievement tests is further undermined by the fact that thinking or reasoning is often included among the achievement skills included in LD definitions. Yet, reasoning and thinking are the very core of intellectual aptitude, and it seems philosophically odd that there can be a severe discrepancy between intelligence and reasoning.

The discrepancy model further assumes that the low intelligence of slow learners fully accounts for their academic failings. However, recent research has shown that many children with low I.Q.s may do quite well in reading. In fact, among children with reading problems, I.Q. score is not a good predictor of the degree of reading impairment. This research thus overturns the assumption that Scott's reading deficiencies are a direct result of his low I.Q.

Because of these problems with the discrepancy model, many researchers recommend abandoning it. However, because of the discrepancy myth's strong hold, they have replaced the aptitude/achievement discrepancy formula with yet another discrepancy formulation. This new discrepancy is not between aptitude and achievement, but among the achievements themselves. This "intra-skill definition" still works against Scott. Since his performance is consistently low in all academic skills and not "specific," he does not show the required intra-skill discrepancy, and he still will not qualify as LD. To be sure, this newer definition avoids the objections to I.Q. tests, but it leaves all the problems associated with invalid achievement tests, the vagueness and arbitrariness of a cut-off point for a "significant discrepancy," the high probability of "false positives" due to multiple testing, and inconsistencies in diagnostic criteria.

These problems suggest a third myth—that LD is a well defined disorder. In a 1985 survey of leaders in the study of LD, 59% reported that the most critical problem facing the field was in finding an accepted definition for LD. In 1991, an entire issue of *Learning Disability Quarterly* was devoted to articles on defining LD. The confusion continues today. Although the 1977 Department of Education definitions are regarded as obsolete and unscientific, they still determine eligibility for Federal funds, and are therefore the most widely used. Because they are vague, they have been differently interpreted by the various states. In addition, many states have their own definitions for state laws. Complicating matters more, researchers, educators, administrators, and organizations have their own, sometimes contradictory, definitions. At the bottom of this chain of abstraction are the specialists who ultimately decide which students receive special education for LD. Studies have shown that their decisions are often not only inconsistent with one another but also inconsistent with the diagnostic criteria they think they are following.

Under ADA, the situation is yet more confusing. The law does not specify assessment methods, diagnostic criteria, or who is authorized to diagnose LD. For example, the University of Georgia found that 54% of applicants claiming LD did not meet the University's eligibility criteria, and similarly, the New York State Board of Law Examiners disqualifies most applicants for special accommodations on the bar exam. Yet, in both situations, most applicants provided documentation supporting their claims and had previously been granted special accommodations for LD. The myth that LD is a well defined psychological disorder is thus undermined by controversy and uncertainty over diagnostic criteria....

Even if discrepancy definitions can be made precise and conceptually coherent, it is yet only another myth that they distinguish among low achieving students in any meaningful way. One popular myth is that LD students have trouble hearing, seeing, or "processing" verbal materials. For example, they supposedly see letters out of sequence or reversed. Our mythical picture is that Jennifer can read perfectly well, but when she looks at a page, the letters are distorted, making reading difficult. Accordingly, in the 70s, treatment for LD students was not specialized instruction in the skills troublesome to them but rather "off-task process training," that is, training to improve their presumed perceptual/motor deficiencies. LD students trained on exercise mats, trampolines, and other non-academic skills.

Eventually, however, research showed that process training does not improve cognitive skills, academic performance, or even the processes they were designed to improve. Yet, the myth stubbornly refuses to die. For example, among individuals requesting special accommodations on the New York State Bar Exam on the basis of LD, the most commonly cited supporting clinical evidence is some sort of visual processing deficit.

Too often, a diagnosis of a problem in "processing" information is misunderstood to mean that the individual has a sensory problem. In fact, the term "processing," borrowed from computer jargon, is simply a technical sounding word referring to any cognitive activity such as understanding, learning, and interpreting. To say that someone has a deficit in processing a specific kind of information is to say merely that person has problems learning, understanding, remembering, or using that kind of information. In those cases in which LD individuals are shown to have processing deficits, for example, in phonological processing (i.e. the ability to hear sounds precisely and associate them with written letters), these deficits are no different from those of slow learners having comparable academic problems. Reversals do not occur more often in dyslexics than in slow learners having comparable reading problems, nor do reversals account for most of the reading problems in dyslexics. In numerous studies comparing children with discrepancies to children having comparable school problems but no discrepancies (i.e. "slow learners"), it is nearly always found that the two groups are virtually indistinguishable in the nature of their learning problems.

The most pernicious myth of LD is that individuals diagnosed with LD on the basis of a discrepancy require special kinds of education while slow learners do not. Yet, careful research shows that both LD students and slow learners benefit from the very same kind of special education and have the same prognosis. In fact, many of the instructional techniques now recommended for LD children were first used successfully with slow learners. This instruction focuses, not surprisingly, directly on the academic skills troubling the pupil rather than on some assumed perceptual process deficit. Direct instruction is self-paced and intensive, with the child moving on to the next level of difficulty only after the prerequisite level is highly mastered. Although both Scott and Jennifer will benefit from this special education, only Jennifer will receive it because only she has the discrepancy requisite for the LD label and funding.

The remedy for this unconscionable situation is simple enough and has been advocated by several leading researchers for years. *All* students having serious trouble in school are learning disabled in certain ways and should be given appropriate remedial instruction, regardless of whether they show discrepancies. All the dollars spent each year on LD diagnoses can be better spent on improving the education of all children failing in school. Determining which children are in need of remedial instruction can most simply and efficiently be carried out by the regular teacher. An additional assessment by an educational specialist could screen for emotional problems, inadequate prior instruction, or sensory impairments and map each child's particular problem areas. Most importantly, we can skip the costly step of determining if the student is LD or simply a slow learner, and immediately provide the appropriate remedial instruction.

Why has this solution been resisted for so long? The more fundamental question is why is the field of learning disabilities in such a conceptual mess? With the passage of IDEA and the Rehabilitation Act, LD became an entitlement, and a LD diagnosis became the admission ticket to that entitlement. With a LD diagnosis, a parent can guarantee a child improved educational opportunities through high school, Federal funds to support that education, special accommodations in college and employment, and Supplemental Security Income, if needed.

Once a LD diagnosis became an entitlement ticket, its definition ceased to be a matter of objective research. Instead, definitions were subject to the forces of politics, court decisions, ideology, government regulations, racial conflicts, special interest lobbying, and school budgets. Although many serious scholars in the LD field have long rejected discrepancy formulae for defining LD, their opinions have little effect compared to these societal currents. LD has become a socially constructed disorder, formulated largely by political and social interests.

For parents, the clear incentive is to acquire the entitlement ticket. Those with money and skills in operating the system can use their resources to maneuver through the bureaucracy to obtain the ticket. Educators fear that wealthy parents worried about getting their children into good colleges are seeking the LD designation to give their children an advantage. For example, the number of graduating high school students who request an untimed Scholastic Assessment Test on the basis of LD has more than doubled in five years. Many of these students had never before claimed LD. In the words of one anonymous special education director quoted in the *Boston Globe*, "It's been hard to stem the tide of people wanting untimed testing. If you have the money, you can go to any hospital in Boston and find a disability."

The incentives for public schools are not different. For every child the school identifies as LD, it receives government money. Schools and teachers can blame neurological dysfunctions, rather than school programs, for school failures. Every child moved out of the regular classroom and into special education means a smaller class for the teacher, a higher average score for the school on standardized tests, and one fewer problem child for the teacher. Conversely, for the nearly 100,000 LD special education teachers funded under IDEA, every LD student assigned to them represents further job security. Similarly, for the legions of LD test producers, evaluators, and consultants, the more LD candidates, the more they can sell their goods and services.

Colleges face similar incentives. For the past decade, colleges, especially those heavily dependent on tuition revenues, have faced the serious problem of a dwindling source of students. Many schools have responded by recruiting non-traditional students, for example older students and foreigners. Another source of non-traditional students is the more than 65,000 LD students graduating from high school annually. Good support services and accommodations for LD students thus become effective marketing tools targeting a rapidly growing clientele. Twenty years ago these students could not have met college admission standards, often set by faculty. Today however, as required by law, colleges can bypass traditional admission standards and take into account an applicant's LD.

With this powerful convergence of interests to expand LD entitlement eligibility, it is not surprising that the number of persons diagnosed with LD has exploded. In recent years, the annual increases in the number of disabled students under IDEA is almost totally attributable to the growth in the number of LD children. The Office of Special Education Programs is currently investigating the causes for this continued growth, but given the incentives operating, the causes should not be hard to find.

Why then not simply drop discrepancy diagnoses and give all children educational programs matched to their strengths and weaknesses? Again, the answer seems to be political. Under the status quo, local, state, and Federal governments must provide extra money for LD special education only for those who somehow manage to obtain a LD diagnosis, while slow learners, above the level of mental retardation, remain in the less expensive regular classroom. Were special education to be made available to all who could benefit, costs would skyrocket. Any suggestion to expand LD eligibility is therefore resisted by the fiscal pressures operating on politicians. In fact, the Federal government, already struggling with the growth in LD numbers under current definitions, has imposed a cap of 12% on the percentage of the public school population in each state that it will fund.

Ironically, another source of resistance against expansion of LD eligibility consists of LD organizations. These groups correctly recognize that were slow learners to be provided LD special education, it is unlikely that funding will increase in proportion to the resulting dramatic increase in eligibility. Consequently, the quality of services now available to LD students would have to be diluted, a result they oppose. This lifeboat attitude says, in effect, that for fear of jeopardizing our own benefits, we oppose adding others to the boat, even though they will benefit and even though we boarded in questionable ways.

The alternative, of course, is to advocate for *all* children experiencing school problems. Of all our national goals, an optimal education for all children must surely be of high priority. LD will not cease to exist with an expansion of eligibility. There will still be children with severe academic problems, but not all of them will show discrepancies. Yet, all of them will benefit from the same special education, and all deserve it. Until further research shows otherwise, we should drop the myths of LD, and meet the individual needs of each child.

NO

Michael M. Gerber

An Appreciation of Learning Disabilities

I begin by stating two nontrivial presuppositions. Both stem from professional experience as well as from at least one possible interpretation of extant literature. First, learning disabilities (LDs) exist. That is, I believe that LD has a material (i.e., neurological) as well as a psychological and social basis in reality. Second, it is clear to me that many children and youth benefit substantially from special education they receive after being classified as having a LD.

I acknowledge immediately that these propositions are subject to intense debate. Better scholars than I have argued these matters relentlessly, and I hasten to declare that I am in possession of no dramatically new or more persuasive data. In fact, I will simply assert that there exists no adequate empirical basis for resolving most of the matters of importance, sometimes because of limitations in theory and methodology, but sometimes because advocates and critics talk at cross-purposes. Opponents can generate alarming stories pointing to disappointment, inadequacy, or alleged harm as a consequence of particular students being identified as learning disabled. However, one could just as easily present case histories or testimonials supporting the perceived good that has followed for particular children and families from having LD as a recognized disability providing special education eligibility. Reasonable people can and do disagree about these matters. It is clear that advocates as well as critics, policy makers as well as academics, and parents as well as teachers have failed to come to meaningful, lasting consensus about something as basic as a definition of LD. In addition, critics from both ends of the political spectrum have found reasons to be rabidly unhappy about the policies and practices and, indeed, even the concept of LD. On the right, LD is a suspicious kind of excuse for insufficient ability or effort by children and their parents. On the left, LD is a weapon of discrimination being used to consign students who are, for a variety of unjust reasons, to a diminished educational opportunity on the way to a degraded social status.

There is little point and certainly no advance to merely repeat here a quarter century of such contentious and by now tedious polemic about either the existence or benefits of LD. Either at this point in time one believes the body of evidence is sufficient to support presuppositions of *existence* and *benefits,* or one does not. However, so interwoven are the purposes of investigation into LD that

From Michael M. Gerber, "An Appreciation of Learning Disabilities: The Value of Blue-Green Algae," *Exceptionality*, vol. 8, no. 1 (March 2000). Copyright © 1999–2000 by Lawrence Erlbaum Associates, Inc. Reprinted by permission of Lawrence Erlbaum Associates, Inc., and the author. References omitted.

even among those devoted to nonpolitical debate, a fundamental misunderstanding of *scientific* as opposed to *social* classification (i.e., labeling) continues. The former is necessary, even critical, for the advancement of knowledge, and the latter is necessary for the implementation of public policy, especially policy meant to guide decisions about allocation of scarce resources. It would be convenient if these two purposes of classification perfectly converged. For many reasons, they do not. How school professionals decide to identify and classify students with learning disabilities continues to be a question deserving intensive investigation, but that question will not be my concern here.

In light of chronic criticism and impassioned attack, is there anything good we might find in LD? What could be good about this situation? In this article, I will concentrate on what benefits arise from *scientific,* as differentiated from the *sociopolitical* or *educational,* construction of LD. I will argue that the chronic turmoil surrounding LD concepts, policies, and practices, albeit discomforting, is natural, necessary, and has produced a clearly beneficial intellectual vitality in special education, specifically, and thinking about individual differences more generally. Taking this broader view, the continuing scientific debate ultimately has served and will serve a good purpose even if unambiguous benefits in practice are not apparent.

Specifically, active debate over concepts, policies, and practices of LD produces benefits by creating, attracting, and focusing intellectual (as well as material) resources in a universe of problems that, although complex, tangled, ambiguous, even poorly defined, are nonetheless real and important to those who engage over them.

Back to Basics

From the previous, it may seem as if in the absence of new facts I have taken refuge in a broader, more speculative, philosophical and historical perspective. Perhaps that is true. If so, it is because there may be value periodically in taking this perspective. Specifically, there may be value in focusing, for the moment, away from disputed facts to the fact of dispute itself. A pause for some reflection might be warranted. What history brought us to this point in time? Why does the attempt to conceptualize LD represent, in itself, a significant intellectual advance? ... I will argue that LD classification unleashed a still beneficial search for better understanding of individual differences. It has done this by generating thoughtful consideration of the multiple factors likely to be related to LD, rejection of factors once thought to be importantly related to LD, invention and creation of new tools for both investigation and intervention, and the beginning of new, more complex hypotheses about its development and expression in school contexts. ...

LD as Search Engine

Before the specific terms, *learning disability,* came into use, researchers had already begun to look more deeply and find within group differences in disabilities previously thought to be unitary, distinct, or pervasive. A natural by-product of this process of differentiation was conjecture not only that existing disability classifications had probable subtypes but also that variations in existing types might really be different disabilities.

Professional folklore and a little formal history hold that the use of the specific terms, learning disability, began in 1963 when Samuel Kirk suggested them in remarks made at an advocacy convention... called to create a new, unified, national advocacy organization for children thought to have been victims of brain-injury and perceptual or neurological disabilities, but not mental retardation. After Kirk's address, those assembled voted to create the Association for Children with Learning Disabilities (now the Learning Disabilities Association). A year later, Kirk presented his idea to friends and colleagues at an annual meeting of the Council for Exceptional Children.

On the shallowest level, adoption of terms like learning disability requires at least tentative consensus that the terms use language acceptable for communicating about a phenomenon of common interest. More deeply, though, negotiation over terms and their definitions is the cognitive equivalent of building a search engine for seeking relevant data from a universe of potential information. When practitioners and advocates achieved a broad consensus on the terms, learning disability, a wave of intellectual effort was marshaled in search of what it all meant....

Scientific Versus Policy Construction

From the start, researchers have understood the conflict between the scientific and policy constructions of LD. For many years, many have argued for an uncoupling of the two purposes so that schools can go about their business of giving additional help to those students who need it, and science, presumably, can go about its business of understanding why some of these students experience such difficulty in the first place. It has proved very near impossible to do this. However, even if public policy supported identification of students only on the basis of their demonstrated learning problems, we would still need to differentiate among those in need, if only for reasons of economic efficiency.

Despite the confounding interweaving of purposes, the research community, in laboratory and in the field, has attempted to sort out what knowledge about individual differences and learning can be gained from study of LD. Like much early work in complex fields, we have been better at documenting what LD is not rather than what it is. There is nothing unusual about this. A scientific orientation and method is fundamentally analytical. That is, like Michelangelo's search for the statue inside of the block of marble, scientists chip away from a phenomenon those variables that are not critical to defining it. Although occasionally we are just left with a pile of chips, this remains the best approach we know for understanding what difference human differences make.

This is not merely artful avoidance of the question, it is very much the question at stake in trying to understand differences. Most taxonomies in biology have been built by observations that seek to discriminate between and within species. The first chore in such effort—an effort that, in the case of biology, has taken hundreds, if not thousands, of years—is to find and record those observations that might be used to reliably discriminate one living thing from another. We pursue such a laborious effort not because the differences are "out there" to be discovered but rather because the effort to make distinctions is itself a cognitive tool for developing coherent understanding about the world around us. Attempts to distinguish some learners as learning disabled serves the same cognitive purpose. It must be recalled that the modern study of LD is less than 40 years old, somewhat more than one working lifetime. A little perspective on the productivity of our effort thus far is therefore in order.

Learning What It Is Not

In this relatively short span of time, research has yielded persuasive evidence that whatever a LD may be, it is not, at least in any simple way, brain damage, brain dysfunction, perceptual defect, sensory defect, sensory integration failure, vitamin or mineral deficiency, perceptual or sensory process deficit, food allergy, any specific subtest profile, verbal-performance IQ discrepancy, "garden variety" poor reading, low scores on any test, or arbitrary school nominations.

Despite a sense of urgency induced by families, teachers, and policymakers to arrive at final answers, patience and perspective is, nevertheless, required. Considering the inherent complexity of a cognitive phenomenon that develops along with the children who exhibit it and that expresses itself most frequently in social and political contexts that frustrate experimental method, we have seen a substantial record of achievement for a 40-year investment of effort by relatively few, modestly funded research efforts using often inadequate methodological and conceptual tools. Further, what is invisible in this record is the capacity-building by-products of sustained investigation of LD....

Despite lack of definitive answers, this 40-year effort has nonetheless yielded powerful and still promising avenues of thought and investigation.... Research based on information processing strategies, for example, have isolated factors of language, attention, and memory and how these interfere with acquisition and performance of basic skills as well as broader comprehension and problem solving across a range of subjects in the curriculum. Similarly, explorations of the components of successful strategy acquisition and training have generated useful techniques and insights that marry elements of instructional communications, behavior, cognitive processes, and subject-matter knowledge in sophisticated ways that we could not have envisioned 40 years ago.... We have learned more about the complexity of classroom learning and curriculum, in general, and moved away from the "magic bullet" of pharmaceutical, psychological, behavioral, or perceptual–motor explanations and interventions. In all of this, there is cause to be proud rather than apologetic. Certainly, many would like concrete, reliable methods and techniques that could be easily and cheaply taught to and implemented by teachers, but these 40 years of exploration may have wrought their greatest benefit by teaching us that the problem is just not that simple....

Lessons From Lucy

We rarely surrender our assumptions gracefully. More frequently, we dig in tenaciously, and debate can become ferocious. When Donald Johanssen discovered a hominid fossil in Afar, Ethiopia, a major debate broke out among paleoanthropologists over whether the specimen represented an *Australeopithicus africanus* or, as Johanssen believed, a new species, *Australeopithicus afarensis*. The arguments were technical but represent a general and fundamental problem of classification, one of knowing when to separate naturally varying phenomena to fit a preconceived taxonomy and when a taxonomy must be rebuilt. In principle, special educators confront the same problem when they attempt to determine a student's category of disability.

The debate over Lucy (the name Johanssen gave to his fossil) represented more than a disagreement about the fossil's observable anatomical features. There was no debate, in fact, that Lucy was an "ape" (Australeopithicus) rather than a "human" (Homo). Rather the dispute was over her species. At the level of anatomy, was she a member of a species whose central tendency for size was different from *africanus,* or was she simply an atypically small member in the normal distribution of *africanus* individual variations? . . .

The debate over Lucy's species is instructive for those disturbed by the seeming inability to reliably identify LD. When LD was first unearthed, had we found a new, heretofore, undetected class of disability or a natural variation in differences among "normal," nondisabled children? It is a trick question because the answer depends on some judgment about whether observed differences make any difference in how we understand the relation between cognitive characteristics of children and their likelihood of academic success under specified instructional arrangements. It was not measurement but rather how to interpret measurements that formed the center of the debate about Lucy's fossilized remains.

The anthropologists' dispute over Lucy reminds us that beneath disagreements about facts lie deeper questions that often have no easy answers or, in some cases, prompt questions not yet asked. In retrospect, the sometimes heated debate about Lucy's identity prompted new critical thought that, ultimately, has been beneficial. The lesson for special education is that the honest attempt to fit "facts" into a received taxonomy eventually clarifies and often changes underlying theory. Another striking example of the intellectual productivity generated by the attempt to fit observations into existing taxonomies is the case of blue-green algae.

Lessons From Blue–Green Algae

The modern two-part classification system of living things (i.e., genus name followed by species name) used for Lucy and other hominid fossils was designed by Linnaeus several hundred years ago. It attempted to group specimens by levels of (usually, morphological) similarity. It provided an ordered way for biologists to observe and describe specimens and, therefore, facilitated scholarly communication and expansion of knowledge. It also provided a rational framework for expecting and searching for new genera, species, and families of living things. However, it was not perfect. It represented a creationist theory, implicitly assuming that the apparent categorical orderliness among living things had been produced simultaneously by a rational and orderly divine plan.

As new species were collected around the globe and discovered in the fascinating new worlds uncovered by microscopy, they tended not to fit satisfactorily into the received taxonomical scheme. In general, the world looked to be divided among the kingdom of plants and the kingdom of animals with respective branches into ever finer, but clearly related, subdivisions. When scientists first described blue-green algae, the characteristics of these monocellular, sometimes colonial, organisms simply resisted comfortable assignment in the existing taxonomy of living things. However, the impact on biology of the problem created by blue-green algae and related microscopic organisms was tremendous. The "facts" presented by blue-green algae not only necessitated expansion of the taxonomical structure of living things to consider new "kingdoms," it also forced reconsideration of what underlying, invisible dynamic created such variation in living things.

Observing or measuring more carefully were not sufficient to resolve the matter. Science needed a new, more powerful theory of how all organisms relate to one another. That theory was evolution and its internal dynamic, natural selection. That is, one could understand the apparently confusing morphology of organisms like blue-green algae if one could imagine how another unseen organizing dynamic, an evolutionary dynamic, also ran through the taxonomy of species. Armed with this new explanation, the *Archaea,* the new Kingdom to which blue-green algae belonged, were understandable. They were structurally more primitive because they branched from the tree of life much earlier in the course of geological time.

LD is the blue-green algae of human learner differences.

Lessons From LD

Is the medical taxonomy of human beings divided neatly into the "normal" and the "abnormal"? Is the psychosocial taxonomy similarly divided into the "able" and "disabled"? Protest if you like, but until the advent of LD, most were content to believe in a world somewhat like this. There were, of course, "species" of disabled, differentiated by category of disabling condition (e.g., mental, emotional, sensorial, and orthopedic). If you could not see, you were blind. If you could not hear, you were deaf. If you could not learn, you were mentally deficient. How, in this neat worldview, could we accommodate such a thing as a LD? These students could see but not read words, could hear but made errors as if they sometimes did not, and could do most things associated with normal intelligence but yet mysteriously displayed enormous difficulty learning academic skills. It made no sense.

Try as we might, we cannot fit them comfortably into our received taxonomies, and we cannot reasonably deny that they exist. If we stopped teachers from picking them out, would they go away? Not likely. In 1973, we stopped teachers from nominating students with IQs between 75 and 85, simply removed the categorical label that once defined these students, simply defined educable mental or familial retardation out of existence. Did these students or their difficulties in learning go away?

Identifying LD did more than launch a search for useful and valid information about variations in human beings as they relate to academic and life success. The more difficult it was to create this new taxon of disability, the more the received taxonomy describing able and disabled began to unravel. It became clear we needed better understanding of intelligence beyond IQ as its indicator. We needed to understand more about how cognitive capacities and functions, like attention, memory, and metacognition, subserve learning and performing in academic domains. We needed to learn more about the nature of these domains. For example, we needed better componential analyses of the specific cognitive operations that permit word decoding and prose comprehension. The detailed experiments and analyses required for reading were needed in all other suspect domains as well, and so a literature was developed that investigated other aspects of language development and use, writing, mathematics, content study, and social cognition. Investigative tools needed to be invented.

In LD research, interventions have served double duty as conceptual tools. Fashioning tools (e.g., mnemonics, self-regulation or performance-monitoring, and varieties of cognitive–behavioral strategy training) are as important to overall progress as using tools for targeted interventions. We have learned that to investigate LD fully requires active effort to promote learning. Thus, the effort and effect are related. It has been a valuable lesson to understand that LD expresses itself most dramatically in the moment of instruction as opposed to in subtest profiles.

... How can a child be intellectually normal and yet fail to learn basic academic skills? That question alone has pushed us to look deeper than we might have otherwise. Now, it may have brought us to two, far more complex aspects of individual learner differences.

First, LD develops along with the child. That is, it cannot be easily shown to be a "condition" that resides in a child and expresses itself exactly the same way at each and every moment across a life's span. Is there, then, a developmental dynamic underlying the taxonomy of human differences as there is an evolutionary dynamic underlying the taxonomy of living things? If so, we step into moving water every time we observe a child. We need to better understand the implications of small starting differences in the development of complex behaviors....

Second, during development, children interact with an environment, an environment that purposively begins overt instruction long before formal schooling. Is variation induced by instruction a kind of experimental noise that keeps us from seeing the truth of LD? Or, is the developmental dynamic even more complex than proposed in the previous paragraph? Development, like evolution, unfolds by a combination of internal and external influences, and we may not fully understand how subtly variations in the learner as well as those in the learning environment shape both current achievement and cumulative ability to successfully engage in formal academic learning. Demonstration that schools identify problem learners with markedly different characteristics than those proposed by formal models... too often has led to premature conclusion that the models must be right and the schools wrong. When we look closer, however, the issue is far from clear, but certainly the notion that LD only expresses within-organism characteristics and not more complex transaction of organism and environment can be seriously questioned. That is, does the instructional environment, while imposing constraints, impose a "test" of academic learning that can usefully supplement other means for measuring difference? Some work indicates that this is possible and, under a broader theory of learner differences, even necessary for understanding LD....

Summary

In this article, I have argued that the advent of a classification for LD may have embroiled researchers, parents, practitioners, and policymakers in tedious debate about not only its benefits but also its very existence. My position is that the debate itself has been an incalculable benefit. It has unleashed 40 years of scholarly interest and effort. That effort, in turn, has debunked bromides, generated valuable new methods and techniques, research capacities, and several promising insights. It has called into question our entire understanding of intelligence, learning, and disability. It has shaken a simplistic, received taxonomy of human learning differences to its root and readied us for more complex theory, measurement, and research. These are not small or inconsequential intellectual achievements and, despite impatience to improve the practical lives of real children, continuing on this path is likely to yield still greater rewards.

POSTSCRIPT

Are Learning Disabilities a Myth?

More than half of all the children who receive special education services have been identified as having a specific learning disability. The rapid increase in this category has raised more than a few eyebrows. How could this disability appear so suddenly? And how could so many problems exist in children who seem to be so capable?

In 1995 Jon Westling, then-provost of Boston University, publicly denounced the existence of learning disabilities and other "boutique diagnoses." Boston University's legal challenges to the special education accommodations claimed by students who asserted the existence of learning disabilities are explored by Shalit (*The New Republic,* 1997), who broadens the discussion with descriptions of several legal cases regarding the impact of learning disabilities on all levels of education.

Lyons (*The Future for Children,* 1996) asserts that the term *learning disabilities* is too broad to be helpful and that confusion about definitions, assessment, diagnostic standards, and instruction would diminish if each type of learning disability (listening, speaking, reading, computing, and reasoning) were addressed separately.

While many people think that the looseness of the LD determiners causes too many children to be "dumped" into this category of questionable disability, Zuriff wants to take advantage of the nonspecificity to include more children. Ideally, he says, schools would more appropriately address the needs of a wider range of students without resorting to questionable assessment and labeling practices. Zuriff, however, is not optimistic that his ideal will become reality, maintaining that the entitlements and funding that come with LD encourage people to continue to seek this diagnosis.

One example of the ongoing, lively discussion of this topic can be found in the 1998 thematic issue of *The Learning Disabilities Quarterly,* which explores the range of views about learning disabilities. In it, Kavale, Forness, MacMillan, and Gresham assert that a learning disability is definitely not the same as low overall achievement. The authors maintain that the definition has become unclear over time because political and social forces have ensured that children are incorrectly diagnosed.

A number of responses follow Kavale et. al., including one by Sleeter, a former learning disabilities teacher who doubts the existence of learning disabilities primarily because she did not see results from specifically designed instructional methodologies. Looking at the field from the perspective of critical race theory, she wonders (like Zuriff) whether or not schools are really designed to serve the needs of all children.

ISSUE 15

Is Attention Deficit Hyperactivity Disorder Real?

YES: Edward M. Hallowell, from "What I've Learned From ADD," *Psychology Today* (May/June 1997)

NO: Thomas Armstrong, from "ADD: Does It Really Exist?" *Phi Delta Kappan* (February 1996)

ISSUE SUMMARY

YES: Edward M. Hallowell, director of a clinic that specializes in the diagnosis and treatment of attention deficit hyperactivity disorder (ADHD), discusses how he utilized his own diagnosis of ADHD to change the direction of his life and those of his clients, becoming more knowledgeable about brain functioning and implementing strategies that enhance daily life.

NO: Thomas Armstrong, an author and speaker specializing in learning and human development, is troubled by the fact that schools, doctors, and society have embraced ADHD as a real disorder. He raises questions about the reality of ADHD, the soundness of the diagnostic tools, and the motivation that leads society to create and believe in ADHD.

Attention deficit hyperactivity disorder, or ADHD, describes someone who cannot stop moving, has difficulty concentrating, and is distracted by what happens around him or her. Without the H (hyperactivity), ADD refers to someone who can sit relatively still but has difficulty concentrating and is likely distracted by internal thoughts and events. Although ADD and ADHD refer to variations of the same condition, ADHD will be used here to refer to both. Here are the official diagnostic criteria for ADHD:

    A. Either (1) or (2):

            1. Six (or more) of the following symptoms of inattention have persisted for at least six months to a degree that is maladaptive and inconsistent with developmental level: often fails to give close attention to details or makes careless mistakes;

often has difficulty sustaining attention in tasks or play; often does not seem to listen when spoken to directly; often does not follow through on instructions and fails to finish chores or duties (not due to oppositional behavior or failure to understand); often has difficulty organizing tasks and activities; often avoids, dislikes, or is reluctant to engage in tasks that require sustained mental effort; often loses things necessary for tasks or activities; often forgetful.

2. Six (or more) of the following symptoms of hyperactivity-impulsivity have persisted for at least six months to a degree that is maladaptive and inconsistent with developmental level: often fidgets with hands or feet or squirms in seat; often leaves seat unacceptably; often runs about or climbs excessively when inappropriate (in adolescents or adults, may feel restless); often has difficulty playing quietly; often talks excessively; often blurts out answers before questions are completed; often has difficulty awaiting turn; often interrupts or intrudes on others.

B. Some symptoms present before age 7
C. Present in two or more settings
D. Clear evidence of clinically significant impairment
E. Symptoms are not due to another disorder

— Adapted from *DSM-IV-TR,* 2000

ADHD is one of the fastest-rising medical/behavioral conditions known. It is likely the topic of at least one article in at least one of the magazines on the rack at your supermarket's checkout counter. Although it is a medical condition, ADHD is frequently considered by parents and teachers when a child seems to have difficulty in school.

The authors of the following selections are prolific writers about ADHD. They are widely read and frequently quoted in newspaper and magazine articles. However, their opinions are poles apart. Which one is right? Or can they both be right?

In the first selection, Edward M. Hallowell argues that ADHD is a real neurological disorder and is more than a periodic focusing problem. He maintains that his study of this disorder offered him a radical new understanding of the human brain, of his patients, and of himself, which he has used to help others deal with this condition and its lifelong effects.

In the second selection, Thomas Armstrong discusses his observations of a young man and wonders whether ADHD truly exists as a disorder or whether the condition called ADHD is really a set of sporadic behaviors that exist when there are difficulties between an individual and the environment.

As you read these selections, ask yourself how often you have wondered if you or someone you know has ADHD. Is it possible for us to concentrate fully all the time, or is there a real biological disorder that deserves attention? How can we tell the difference?

Edward M. Hallowell

 **YES**

What I've Learned From ADD

When I discovered, in 1981, that I had attention deficit disorder (ADD), it was one of the great "Aha!" experiences of my life. Suddenly so many seemingly disparate parts of my personality made sense—the impatience, distractibility, restlessness, amazing ability to procrastinate, and extraordinarily brief attention span (here-one-moment-gone-the-next), not to mention the high bursts of energy and creativity and an indefinable, zany sense of life.

It was a pivotal moment for me, but the repercussions have been more powerful and wide-ranging than I could have imagined 16 years ago. Coming to understand ADD has been like stepping through a porthole into a wider world, expanding my view of my patients, friends, and family. I now know that many personality traits and psychological problems have a genuine basis in biology —not just ADD, but also depression, learning disorders, anxiety, panic attacks, and even shyness.

That insight has been tremendously freeing, for myself and my patients, and it has also led the mental health field to novel, effective treatments for brain disorders. I use the word "brain" intentionally, to emphasize that in many ways our personality is hardwired. Yet just as important is the fact that biology is only part of the story. We're all born with a set of genes, but how those genes get expressed depends largely on life experience and the way our environment interacts with our biology. If we understand this, we can "manage" our brains more deftly, using methods that range from medicine to lifestyle changes. Diagnosing and treating ADD—in my own life and those of hundreds of patients— has shown me just how remarkable these interventions can be. I have seen more than a few teetering marriages right themselves when the couple understood it was ADD, not bad character, causing their troubles. I have also seen many careers that had been languishing in the bin labeled "underachiever" suddenly take off after diagnosis and treatment of ADD. Scores of students have been able to rescue their academic careers after diagnosis and treatment. It is a powerful diagnosis: powerfully destructive when missed and powerfully constructive when correctly picked up.

ADD has taught me to look at people differently. These days, when I meet someone I often ask myself the question, "What kind of brain does he have?" as a way of trying to understand the person. I've learned that brains differ

From Edward M. Hallowell, "What I've Learned From ADD," *Psychology Today*, vol. 30, no. 3 (May/June 1997). Copyright © 1997 by Sussex Publishers, Inc. Reprinted by permission of *Psychology Today*.

tremendously from person to person, and that some of the most interesting and productive people around have "funny" (i.e., highly idiosyncratic) brains. There is no normal, standard brain, any more than there is a normal, standard automobile, dress, or human face. Our old distinctions of "smart" and "stupid" don't even begin to describe the variety of differences in human brains; indeed, these distinctions trample over those differences.

Today we know more than ever about the brain—but in learning more we have realized how little we actually know. With sophisticated brain scans that map the activity of networks of neurons we can peer inside the once impenetrable armor of our skulls and learn just how brains act when they are seeing, thinking, remembering, and even malfunctioning. And yet the vast territory of the brain still stretches out before us uncharted, like the sixteenth-century maps of the New World we used to see in our fifth-grade history books. Although we are coining new terms all the time (like emotional intelligence or post-traumatic stress disorder or even attention deficit disorder), although we are discovering new neurotransmitters and brain peptides that reveal new connections and networks within the brain, and although we are revising or throwing out old theories as new ones leap into our screens, any honest discussion of mental life must begin with the confession, "There's so much we still don't know."

Disorder and Metaphor?

What do these philosophical flights of fancy have to do with ADD and me? A few years ago ADD burst upon the American scene the way psychiatric disorders sometimes do, emerging as a riveting new metaphor for our cultural milieu. In the 1930s we embraced neurasthenia; in the '50s W. H. Auden coined the term "the age of anxiety"; in the '70s Christopher Lasch dubbed us the "culture of narcissism." Now, in the '90s, ADD has emerged as a symbol of American life.... This may explain why *Driven to Distraction* and *Answers to Distraction*, two books I wrote a few years ago with Harvard psychiatrist John Ratey, M.D., found a surprisingly wide and vocal audience.

At the same time, there has been some misunderstanding because of the sudden popularity of ADD. Scientists rightly get upset when they see extravagant claims being made that studies cannot justify—claims, for instance, that up to 25 percent of our population suffers from ADD. (The true number is probably around 5 percent.) And ordinary people are annoyed because they feel this diagnosis has become a catchall excuse—clothed in neurological, scientific language—for any inappropriate behavior. ADD can seem to undercut our country's deep belief in the work ethic. "Why didn't you do your homework?" *"Because I have ADD."* "Why are you late?" *"Because I have ADD."* "Why haven't you paid your income tax in five years?" *"Because I have ADD."* "Why are you so obnoxious?" *"Because I have ADD."* But, in fact, once ADD is properly diagnosed and treated, the opposite happens: The sufferer is able to take responsibility more effectively and becomes more productive and patient. The student who always forgot his homework and was constantly penalized for doing so is able to remember his homework—after his ADD is treated. The same is true for the adult in the workplace, who, once his ADD is treated, is finally able to finish the project he has so "irresponsibly" neglected, or the academician who is at last able to complete her Ph.D. dissertation.

So what is this condition, and where has it been all these centuries? Is it just another fad, or is there some scientific basis to ADD?

ADD is not a new disorder, although it has not been clearly understood until recent years, and its definition will become even more refined as we learn more about it. Right now, we are like blind men describing an elephant. The elephant is there—this vast collection of people with varying attentional strengths and vulnerabilities. However, generating a definitive description, diagnostic workup, and treatment plan with replicable research findings still poses a challenge. As long ago as the 1940s, the term "minimal brain damage syndrome" was used to describe symptoms similar to what we now call ADD. Today, the standard manual of the mental health field, the DSM-IV, defines ADD as a syndrome of involuntary distractibility—a restless, constant wandering of the crucial beam of energy we call attention. That trait is the hallmark of this disorder. More specifically, the syndrome must include six or more symptoms of either inattention or hyperactivity and impulsivity—the latter variant is known as attention deficit disorder with hyperactivity, or ADHD. . . .

To define a disorder solely in terms of attention is a true leap forward, since for centuries nobody paid any attention to attention. Attention was viewed as a choice, and if your mind wandered, you were simply allowing it to do so. Symptoms of ADD—not unlike those of depression, mania, or anxiety disorders—were considered deep and moral flaws.

When people ask me where ADD has been all these years, I respond that it has been in classrooms and offices and homes all over the world, right under our noses all along, only it has been called by different names: laziness, stupidity, rottenness, and worthlessness. For decades children with ADD have been shamed, beaten, punished, and humiliated. They have been told they suffered from a deficit not of attention but of motivation and effort. That approach fails as miserably as trying to beat nearsightedness out of a child—and the damage carries over into adulthood.

It's All in Your Head

The evidence that ADD has a biological basis has mounted over the last 20 years. First, and most moving, there is the clinical evidence from the records of millions of patients who have met the diagnostic criteria and who have benefited spectacularly from standard treatment. These are human stories of salvaged lives. The fact that certain medications predictably relieve target symptoms of ADD means that these symptoms have roots in the physical world.

I recall watching an eighth grader named Noah receive a reward for "Most Improved" at graduation. This boy's mother had been told by an expert that Noah was so severely "disturbed" that she should look into residential placement. He was often in trouble at school. From my first meeting with Noah I was struck by his kindness and tenacity; no expert had understood that he suffered from ADD, as well as mild cerebral palsy. Like many ADDers he was intuitive, warm, and empathic. After coaching, teacher involvement, extra structure, and the medication Ritalin, Noah improved steadily, from the moment of diagnosis in sixth grade until graduation from eighth. As I watched him walk up to receive his award, awkward but proud, shake the hand of the principal, then turn and flash us all a grin, I felt inside a gigantic, "YES!" *Yes* for the triumph of this boy, *yes* for the triumph of knowledge and determination over misunderstanding, *yes* for all the children who in the future will not have to suffer. Standing in the back of the gym, leaning against the wall, I cried some of the happiest tears I've ever shed.

There is also intriguing biological evidence for the existence of ADD. One seems to inherit a susceptibility to this disorder, which appears to cluster in families just as manic-depression and other mental illnesses do. Though no scientist has been able to isolate a single causative gene in any mental disorder—and, in fact, we are coming to understand that a complex interaction of genes, neurotransmitters, hormones, and the environment comes into play in mental illness—there is solid evidence that vulnerability can be passed down through generations. One particularly careful, recent review in *The Journal of The American Academy of Child and Adolescent Psychiatry* supported the heritability of ADD based upon family and twin-adoption studies and analysis of gene inheritance.

Evidence of ADD may even show up in specific areas of the brain. In 1990, Alan Zametkin, M.D., a psychiatrist at the National Institute of Mental Health (NIMH), reported startling findings about the ADD brain in the *New England Journal of Medicine*. Zametkin measured sugar metabolism—a major indicator of brain activity—in the brains of 30 adults who had a childhood history of ADD, along with 30 normal individuals. PET scans (positron emission tomography) allowed Zametkin to determine just how much sugar each participant's brain was absorbing, and in what regions. Sufferers of ADD absorbed less sugar in the areas of the brain that regulate impulse control, attention, and mood. Another study, by NIMH researcher David Hauser, M.D., linked ADD to a rare thyroid condition called generalized resistance to thyroid hormone (GRTH). Seventy percent of individuals with GRTH suffer from ADD—an extraordinarily high correlation. Finally, recent brain scan studies have revealed both anatomical and functional differences in the brains of individuals with ADD—slight but real differences in the size of the corpus callosum (which serves as the switchboard that connects the two hemispheres of the brain), as well as differences in the size of the caudate nucleus, another switching station deep within the brain. These breakthrough studies lay the foundation for promising research, but much more work needs to be done before we may be able to use these findings to actually help us diagnose ADD. They simply point us in the direction of biology—and that pointer is powerful.

The Pivotal Movement

Nothing matters more in ADD than proper diagnosis. Even today this condition is so misunderstood that it is both missed and overdiagnosed. As the public's awareness of the disorder grows, more and more people represent themselves as experts in ADD. As one of my patients said to me, "ADD has become a growth industry." Not every self-proclaimed expert knows ADD from ABC. For instance, depression can cause someone to be distracted and inattentive (and in many cases depression and ADD even occur together). However, a constant pattern of ADD symptoms usually extends back to early childhood, while depression is usually episodic. Thyroid disease can also look very much like ADD, and only testing by a physician can rule this out. High IQ can also mask or delay the diagnosis of ADD.

If the proper care is taken, a diagnosis of ADD can be made with confidence and accuracy, even though there is no single proof-positive test. Like most disorders, ADD occurs on a wide spectrum. In severe cases an individual can barely function due to rampant disorganization or uncontrollable impulsivity, not to mention secondary symptoms such as low self-esteem or depression. Yet very mild cases of ADD can be barely noticeable, especially in a bright individual who has adapted well.

To me, the life history is the one, absolutely convincing "test," which is then supported by the criteria of the DSM-IV and by psychological testing. When someone tells me they've been called "space-shot," "daydreamer," and "out in left field" all their lives, I suspect they might have ADD. At our clinic in Concord, Massachusetts, we use an abbreviated neuropsychological battery that helps us confirm a diagnosis. The battery includes standard written tests that measure memory and logic, impulsivity, and ability to organize complex tasks. Score alone does not tell the whole story; the tester needs to watch the client to determine whether he or she becomes easily frustrated and distracted. We even include a simple motor test that measures how quickly a person can tap their finger. (Patients with ADD are very good at this; depressed patients are not.) Though these tests are helpful, they are by no means definitive. A very smart person without ADD may find these tests boring, and become distracted. On the other hand, one of the great ironies of this kind of testing is that three of the best non-medication treatments available for ADD—structure, motivation, and novelty—are actually built into the testing situation, and can temporarily camouflage ADD.

A diagnosis by itself can change a life. My own father suffered from manic-depression, and I used to wonder if I had inherited the same disorder. When I learned I had ADD, that fact alone made a huge difference to my life. Instead of thinking of myself as having a character flaw, a family legacy, or some potentially ominous "difference" between me and other people, I could see myself in terms of having a unique brain biology. This understanding freed me emotionally. In fact, I would much rather have ADD than not have it, since I love the positive qualities that go along with it—creativity, energy, and unpredictability. I have found tremendous support and goodwill in response to my acknowledging my own ADD and dyslexia. The only time talking about this diagnosis will get you in trouble is when you offer it as an excuse.

After a diagnosis of ADD, an individual and his or her family can understand and change behavior patterns that may have been a problem for many years. Treatment must be multifaceted, and includes:

• **Educating the individual** and his or her family, friends, and colleagues or schoolteachers about the disorder. Two of the largest national organizations providing this information are CHADD (Children and Adults with Attention Deficit Disorder; call (954) 587-3700) and ADDA (Attention Deficit Disorder Association; call (216) 350-9595).

• **Making lifestyle changes,** such as incorporating structure, exercise, mediation, and prayer into one's daily life. Structural approaches include using practical tools like lists, reminders, simple filing systems, appointment books, and strategically placed bulletin boards. These can help manage the inner chaos of the ADD life, but the structure should be simple. One patient of mine got so excited about the concept of structure he impulsively went out to Staples and spent several thousand dollars on complex organizing materials that he never used. An example of simple structure: I put my car keys in a basket next to my front door so that I do not have to start each day with a frantic search for them.

Exercise can help drain off anxiety and excess aggression. Regular meditation or prayer can help focus and relax the mind.

• **Coaching, therapy, and social training.** Often ADD sufferers complain that structure is boring. "If I could be structured, I wouldn't have ADD!" moaned one patient. A coach can be invaluable in helping people with ADD organize their life, and encouraging them to stay on track. If a psychotherapist is the coach, he or she needs to be actively involved in advising specific behavioral changes.

Therapy itself can help resolve old patterns of self-sabotage or low self-esteem, and may help couples address long-standing problems. For example, setting up a simple division of labor between partners can prevent numerous arguments. Social training can help those with ADD learn how to avoid social gaffes. And merely understanding the condition can promote more successful interactions.

• **Medication.** The medications used to treat ADD constitute one of the miracles of modern medicine. Drugs are beneficial in about 80 percent of ADDers, working like a pair of eyeglasses for the brain, enhancing and sharpening mental focus. Medications prescribed include stimulants like Ritalin or Dexedrine, tricyclic antidepressants like Tofranil and Elavil, and even some high-blood pressure medicines like Catapres.

All of these medications work by influencing levels of key neurotransmitters, particularly dopamine, epinephrine, and norepinephrine. It seems that the resulting change in neurotransmitter availability helps the brain inhibit extraneous stimuli—both internal and external. That allows the mind to focus more effectively. There is no standard dose; dosages can vary widely from person to person, independent of body size.

Ritalin, by far the most popular drug for the treatment of ADD, is safe and effective. Of course, Ritalin and other stimulants can be dangerous if used improperly. But Ritalin is not addictive. Nor is it a euphoric substance—people use drugs to get high, not to focus their minds. For example, you would not cite,

"I took Ritalin last night and read three books" as an example of getting high. Using stimulants to cram before exams, however, is as inadvisable as overdosing on coffee. Students do it, but they should be warned against it. Ritalin should only be taken under medical supervision and of course should not be sold, given away, or otherwise misused.

The diagnosis and treatment of ADD represent a triumph of science over human suffering—just one example of the many syndromes of the brain we are at last learning to address without scorn or hidden moral judgment. As we begin to bring mental suffering out of the stigmatized darkness it has inhabited for centuries and into the light of scientific understanding and effective treatment, we all have reason to rejoice.

Thomas Armstrong

ADD: Does It Really Exist?

Several years ago I worked for an organization that assisted teachers in using the arts in their classrooms. We were located in a large warehouse in Cambridge, Massachusetts, and several children from the surrounding lower-working-class neighborhood volunteered to help with routine jobs. I recall one child, Eddie, a 9-year-old African American youngster possessed of great vitality and energy, who was particularly valuable in helping out with many tasks. These jobs included going around the city with an adult supervisor, finding recycled materials that could be used by teachers in developing arts programs, and then organizing them and even field-testing them back at the headquarters. In the context of this arts organization, Eddie was a definite asset.

A few months after this experience, I became involved in a special program through Lesley College in Cambridge, where I was getting my master's degree in special education. This project involved studying special education programs designed to help students who were having problems learning or behaving in regular classrooms in several Boston-area school districts. During one visit to a Cambridge resource room, I unexpectedly ran into Eddie. Eddie was a real problem in this classroom. He couldn't stay in his seat, wandered around the room, talked out of turn, and basically made the teacher's life miserable. Eddie seemed like a fish out of water. In the context of this school's special education program, Eddie was anything but an asset. In retrospect, he appeared to fit the definition of a child with attention deficit disorder (ADD).

Over the past 15 years, ADD has grown from a malady known only to a few cognitive researchers and special educators into a national phenomenon. Books on the subject have flooded the marketplace, as have special assessments, learning programs, residential schools, parent advocacy groups, clinical services, and medications to treat the "disorder." (The production of Ritalin or methylphenidate hydrochloride—the most common medication used to treat ADD—has increased 450% in the past four years, according to the Drug Enforcement Agency.) The disorder has solid support as a discrete medical problem from the Department of Education, the American Psychiatric Association, and many other agencies.

I'm troubled by the speed with which both the public and the professional community have embraced ADD. Thinking back to my experience with Eddie

From Thomas Armstrong, "ADD: Does It Really Exist?" *Phi Delta Kappan*, vol. 77, no. 6 (February 1996). Copyright © 1996 by Thomas Armstrong. Reprinted by permission of the author. Notes omitted.

and the disparity that existed between Eddie in the arts organization and Eddie in the special education classroom, I wonder whether this "disorder" really exists *in* the child at all, or whether, more properly, it exists in the relationships that are present between the child and his or her environment. Unlike other medical disorders, such as diabetes or pneumonia, this is a disorder that pops up in one setting only to disappear in another. A physician mother of a child labeled ADD wrote to me not long ago about her frustration with this protean diagnosis: "I began pointing out to people that my child is capable of long periods of concentration when he is watching his favorite sci-fi video or examining the inner workings of a pin-tumbler lock. I notice that the next year's definition states that some kids with ADD are capable of normal attention in certain specific circumstances. Poof. A few thousand more kids instantly fall into the definition."

There is in fact substantial evidence to suggest that children labeled ADD do not show symptoms of this disorder in several different real-life contexts. First, up to 80% of them don't appear to be ADD when in the physician's office. They also seem to behave normally in other unfamiliar settings where there is a one-to-one interaction with an adult (and this is especially true when the adult happens to be their father). Second, they appear to be indistinguishable from so-called normals when they are in classrooms or other learning environments where children can choose their own learning activities and pace themselves through those experiences. Third, they seem to perform quite normally when they are *paid* to do specific activities designed to assess attention. Fourth, and perhaps most significant, children labeled ADD behave and attend quite normally when they are involved in activities that *interest* them, that are *novel* in some way, or that involve high levels of *stimulation*. Finally, as many as 70% of these children reach adulthood only to discover that the ADD has apparently just gone away.

It's understandable, then, that prevalence figures for ADD vary widely— far more widely than the 3% to 5% figure that popular books and articles use as a standard. As Russell Barkley points out in his classic work on attention deficits, *Attention Deficit Hyperactivity Disorder: A Handbook for Diagnosis and Treatment,* the 3% to 5% figure "hinges on how one chooses to define ADHD, the population studied, the geographic locale of the survey, and even the degree of agreement required among parents, teachers and professionals.... Estimates vary between 1[% and] 20%."

In fact, estimates fluctuate even more than Barkley suggests. In one epidemiological survey conducted in England, only two children out of 2,199 were diagnosed as hyperactive (.09%). Conversely, in Israel, 28% of children were rated by teachers as hyperactive. And in an earlier study conducted in the U.S., teachers rated 49.7% of boys as restless, 43.5% of boys as having a "short attention span," and 43.5% of boys as "inattentive to what others say."

The Rating Game

These wildly divergent statistics call into question the assessments used to decide who is diagnosed as having ADD and who is not. Among the most frequently used tools for this purpose are behavior rating scales. These are typically checklists consisting of items that relate to the child's attention and behavior at home or at school. In one widely used assessment, teachers are asked to rate the child on a scale from 1 (almost never) to 5 (almost always) with regard to behavioral statements such as: "Fidgety (hands always busy)," "Restless (squirms in seat)," and "Follows a sequence of instructions." The problem with these scales is that they depend on *subjective judgments* by teachers and parents who may have a deep, and often subconscious, emotional investment in the outcome. After all, a diagnosis of ADD may lead to medication to keep a child compliant at home or may result in special education placement in the school to relieve a regular classroom teacher of having to teach a troublesome child.

Moreover, since these behavior rating scales depend on opinion rather than fact, there are no objective criteria through which to decide *how much* a child is demonstrating symptoms of ADD. What is the difference in terms of hard data, for example, between a child who scores a 5 on being fidgety and a child who scores a 4? Do the scores mean that the first child is one point more fidgety than the second? Of course not. The idea of assigning a number to a behavior trait raises the additional problem, addressed above, of context. The child may be a 5 on "fidgetiness" in some contexts (during worksheet time, for example) and a 1 at other times (during recess, during motivating activities, and at other highly stimulating times of the day). Who is to decide what the final number should be based on? If a teacher places more importance on workbook learning than on hands-on activities, such as building with blocks, the rating may be biased toward academic tasks, yet such an assessment would hardly paint an accurate picture of the child's total experience in school, let alone in life.

It's not surprising, then, to discover that there is often disagreement among parents, teachers, and professionals using these behavior rating scales as to who exactly is hyperactive or ADD. In one study, parent, teacher, and physician groups were asked to identify hyperactive children in a sample of 5,000 elementary school children. Approximately 5% were considered hyperactive by at least one of the groups, while only 1% were considered hyperactive by all three groups. In another study using a well-known behavior rating scale, mothers and fathers agreed that their children were hyperactive only about 32% of the time, and the correspondence between parent and teacher ratings was even worse: they agreed only about 13% of the time.

These behavior rating scales implicitly ask parents and teachers to compare a potential ADD child's attention and behavior to those of a "normal" child. But this raises the question, What is normal behavior? Do normal children fidget? Of course they do. Do normal children have trouble paying attention? Yes, under certain circumstances. Then exactly when does normal fidgeting turn into ADD fidgeting, and when does normal difficulty paying attention become ADD difficulty?

These questions have not been adequately addressed by professionals in the field, yet they remain pressing issues that seriously undermine the legitimacy of these behavior rating scales. Curiously, with all the focus being placed on children who score at the high end of the hyperactivity and distractibility continuum, virtually no one in the field talks about children who must statistically exist at the opposite end of the spectrum: children who are too focused, too compliant, too still, or too *hypo*active. Why don't we have special classes, medications, and treatments for these children as well?

A Brave New World of Soulless Tests

Another ADD diagnostic tool is a test that assigns children special "continuous performance tasks" (CPTs). These tasks usually involve repetitious actions that require the examinee to remain alert and attentive throughout the test. The earliest versions of these tasks were developed to select candidates for radar operations during World War II. Their use with children in today's world is highly questionable. One of the most popular of the current CPT instruments is the Gordon Diagnostic System (GDS). This Orwellian device consists of a plastic box with a large button on the front and an electronic display above it that flashes a series of random digits. The child is told to press the button every time a "1" is followed by a "9." The box then records the number of "hits" and "misses" made by the child. More complex versions involving multiple digits are used with older children and adults.

Quite apart from the fact that this task bears no resemblance to anything else that children will ever do in their lives, the GDS creates an "objective" score that is taken as an important measure of a child's ability to attend. In reality, it tells us only how a child will perform when attending to a repetitive series of meaningless numbers on a soulless task. Yet ADD expert Russell Barkley writes, "[The GDS] is the only CPT that has enough available evidence... to be adopted for clinical practice." As a result, the GDS is used not only to diagnose ADD but also to determine and adjust medication doses in children with the label.

There is a broader difficulty with the use of *any* standardized assessment to identify children as having ADD. Most of the tests used (including behavior rating scales and continuous performance tasks) have attempted to be validated as indicators of ADD through a process that involves testing groups of children who have previously been labeled ADD and comparing their test results with those of groups of children who have been judged to be "normal." If the assessment shows that it can discriminate between these two groups to a significant degree, it is then touted as a valid indicator of ADD. However, one must ask how the initial group of ADD children originally came to be identified as ADD. The answer would have to be through an earlier test. And how do we know that the earlier test was a valid indicator of ADD? Because it was validated using two groups: ADD and normal. How do we know that *this* group of ADD children was in fact ADD? Through an even earlier test... and so on, ad infinitum. There is no Prime Mover in this chain of tests; no First Test for ADD that has been declared self-referential and infallible. Consequently, the validity of these tests must always remain in doubt.

In Search of a Deficit

Even if we admit that such tests *could* tell the difference between children labeled ADD and "normal" children, recent evidence suggests that there really aren't any significant differences between these two groups. Researchers at the Hospital for Sick Children in Toronto, for example, discovered that the performance of children who had been labeled ADD did not deteriorate over time on a continuous performance task any more than did that of a group of so-called normal children. They concluded that these "ADD children" did not appear to have a unique sustained attention deficit.

In another study, conducted at the University of Groningen in the Netherlands, children were presented with irrelevant information on a task to see if they would become distracted from their central focus, which involved identifying groups of dots (focusing on groups of four dots and ignoring groups of three or five dots) on a piece of paper. So-called hyperactive children did not become distracted any more than so-called normal children, leading the researchers to conclude that there did not seem to be a focused attention deficit in these children. Other studies have suggested that "ADD children" don't appear to have problems with short-term memory or with other factors that are important in paying attention. Where, then, is the attention deficit?

A Model of Machines and Disease

The ADD myth is essentially a *paradigm* or world view that has certain assumptions about human beings at its core. Unfortunately, the beliefs about human capacity addressed in the ADD paradigm are not terribly positive ones. It appears as if the ADD myth tacitly endorses the view that human beings function very much like machines. From this perspective, ADD represents something very much like a mechanical breakdown. This underlying belief shows up most clearly in the kinds of explanations that parents, teachers, and professionals give to children labeled ADD about their problems. In one book for children titled *Otto Learns About His Medicine,* a red car named Otto goes to a mechanic after experiencing difficulties in car school. The mechanic says to Otto, "Your motor does go too fast," and he recommends a special car medicine.

While attending a national conference on ADD, I heard experts share similar ways of explaining ADD to children, including comparisons to planes ("Your mind is like a big jet plane... you're having trouble in the cockpit"), a car radio ("You have trouble filtering out noise"), and television ("You're experiencing difficulty with the channel selector"). These simplistic metaphors seem to imply that human beings really aren't very complex organisms and that one simply needs to find the right wrench, use the proper gas, or tinker with the appropriate circuit box—and all will be well. They are also just a short hop away from more insulting mechanical metaphors ("Your elevator doesn't go all the way to the top floor").

The other feature that strikes me as being at the heart of the ADD myth is the focus on *disease* and *disability.* I was particularly struck by this mindset while attending a workshop with a leading authority on ADD who started out his lecture by saying that he would treat ADD as a medical disorder with its own etiology (causes), pathogenesis (development), clinical features (symptoms), and epidemiology (prevalence). Proponents of this view talk about the fact that there is "no cure" for ADD and that parents need to go through a "grieving process" once they receive a "diagnosis." ADD guru Russell Barkley commented in a recent address: "Although these children do not look physically disabled, they are neurologically handicapped nonetheless. . . . Remember, this is a disabled child." Absent from this perspective is any mention of a child's potential or other manifestations of health—traits that are crucial in helping a child achieve success in life. In fact, the literature on the strengths, talents, and abilities of children labeled ADD is almost nonexistent.

In Search of the ADD Brain

Naturally, in order to make the claim that ADD is a disease, there must be a medical or biological cause for it. Yet, as with everything else about ADD, no one is exactly sure what causes it. Possible biological causes that have been proposed include genetic factors, biochemical abnormalities (imbalances of such brain chemicals as serotonin, dopamine, and norepinephrine), neurological damage, lead poisoning, thyroid problems, prenatal exposure to various chemical agents, and delayed myelinization of the nerve pathways in the brain.

In its search for a physical cause, the ADD movement reached a milestone with the 1990 publication in the *New England Journal of Medicine* of a study by Alan Zametkin and his colleagues at the National Institute of Mental Health. This study appeared to link hyperactivity in adults with reduced metabolism of glucose (a prime energy source) in the premotor cortex and the superior prefrontal cortex—areas of the brain that are involved in the control of attention, planning, and motor activity. In other words, these areas of the brain were not working as hard as they should have been, according to Zametkin.

The media picked up on Zametkin's research and reported it nationally. ADD proponents latched on to this study as "proof" of the medical basis for ADD. Pictures depicting the spread of glucose through a "normal" brain compared to a "hyperactive" brain began showing up in CH.A.D.D. (Children and Adults with Attention Deficit Disorder) literature and at the organization's conventions and meetings. One ADD advocate seemed to speak for many in the ADD movement when she wrote: "In November 1990, parents of children with ADD heaved a collective sigh of relief when Dr. Alan Zametkin released a report that hyperactivity (which is closely linked to ADD) results from an insufficient rate of glucose metabolism in the brain. Finally, commented a supporter, we have an answer to skeptics who pass this off as bratty behavior caused by poor parenting."

What was *not* reported by the media or cheered by the ADD community was the study by Zametkin and others that came out three years later in the *Archives of General Psychiatry.* In an attempt to repeat the 1990 study with adolescents, the researchers found no significant differences between the brains of so-called hyperactive subjects and those of so-called normal subjects. And in retrospect, the results of the first study didn't look so good either. When the original 1990 study was controlled for sex (there were more men in the hyperactive group than in the control group), there was no significant difference between groups.

A recent critique of Zametkin's research by faculty members at the University of Nebraska also pointed out that the study did not make clear whether the lower glucose rates found in "hyperactive brains" were a cause or a result of attention problems. The critics pointed out that, if subjects were startled and then had their levels of adrenalin monitored, adrenalin levels would probably be quite high. We would not say, however, that these individuals had an adrenalin disorder. Rather, we'd look at the underlying conditions that led to abnormal adrenalin levels. Similarly, even if biochemical differences did exist in the so-called hyperactive brain, we ought to be looking at the nonbiological factors that could account for some of these differences, including stress, learning style, and temperament.

The Stigma of ADD

Unfortunately, there seems to be little desire in the professional community to engage in dialogue about the reality of attention deficit disorder; its presence on the American educational scene seems to be a fait accompli. This is regrettable, since ADD is a psychiatric disorder, and millions of children and adults run the risk of stigmatization from the application of this label.

In 1991, when such major educational organizations as the National Education Association (NEA), the National Association of School Psychologists (NASP), and the National Association for the Advancement of Colored People (NAACP) successfully opposed the authorization by Congress of ADD as a legally handicapping condition, NEA spokesperson Debra DeLee wrote, "Establishing a new category [ADD] based on behavioral characteristics alone, such as overactivity, impulsiveness, and inattentiveness, increases the likelihood of inappropriate labeling for racial, ethnic, and linguistic minority students." And Peg Dawson, former NASP president, pointed out, "We don't think that a proliferation of labels is the best way to address the ADD issue. It's in the best interest of all children that we stop creating categories of exclusion and start responding to the needs of individual children." ADD nevertheless continues to gain ground as the label du jour in American education. It's time to stop and take stock of this "disorder" and decide whether it really exists or is instead more a manifestation of society's need to *have* such a disorder.

POSTSCRIPT

Is Attention Deficit Hyperactivity Disorder Real?

Hallowell maintains that ADHD has always existed and can be tied to a number of personal qualities—some negative and some positive. He acknowledges that ADHD has been treated as a fad by many who do not use acceptable techniques and standards to make diagnoses.

Armstrong is not sure that there are any acceptable techniques and standards to make the diagnosis of ADHD, and he cites the results of several studies to support his contentions. He wonders why society wants the disorder to exist at all.

In 1996 the National Institute of Mental Health reprinted its informational booklet *Attention Deficit Hyperactivity Disorder,* which reviews research data that supports a genetic basis for ADHD. Cautioning that ADHD-like behaviors can result from underachievement in school, attention lapses due to epileptic seizures, hearing problems due to ear infections, or disruptive or unresponsive behavior caused by anxiety or depression, the authors emphasize the critical need for accurate, careful analysis of the events in a child's life as opposed to a quick assumption that ADHD is present.

Extensive information on ADHD is provided by Children and Adults with Attention-Deficit/Hyperactivity Disorder (CHADD), which maintains a very active Web site (http://www.chadd.org) containing numerous fact sheets, legislative updates, instructional and behavioral management strategies, and a newsletter, in addition to links to related sites.

Russell A. Barkley, a major researcher in the field of ADHD and the author of *Attention-Deficit Hyperactivity Disorder: A Handbook for Diagnosis and Treatment* (1998), presents a new view of this disorder in *ADHD and the Nature of Self-Control* (1997). Exploring the finding that people with ADHD can attend better when they receive reinforcement for doing so, Barkley hypothesizes that the nature of ADHD resides not within an inability to pay attention but in a disordered ability to control actions and to screen out unimportant thoughts. He also contends that people with this chronic disability do not readily understand the passage of time—they misjudge how long an action takes or how long they may take to react.

Several authors (among them Peter Breggin and Lawrence Diller) have written popular books questioning the reality and growth of interest in ADHD and the wisdom of using medication so freely with children.

Real or not, the existence of ADHD is firmly established in our society. Information about the behavior of ADHD children and its treatments is readily available. The scientific community has not identified a specific cause or universally effective treatments, and few experts believe that ADHD can be cured. Standard treatments include medication, behavioral supports, and counseling. Alternative treatments abound, including diet therapy, colored lenses, megavitamins, and chiropractic adjustment. To date, none of the latter have been supported by substantial research.

ADHD garnered much focused attention during the 1990 and 1997 reauthorization hearings for IDEA. Parents testified before Congress to include ADHD as a distinct disability that warranted specially designed instruction. Both times, the move failed; ADHD is currently included under the category "Health Impairment." Since it is so frequently addressed through medication, ADHD is often seen to warrant accommodations in the school setting only, rather than specially designed instruction provided through special education.

Has society lost the ability to tolerate anything other than total compliance and predictability, especially from little boys? Or is it just now becoming known that there are powerful biomedical conditions that affect our ability to attend, learn, and work? If ADHD is a real medical disorder, how much of a difference can schools make?

ISSUE 16

Are We Turning Too Easily to Medication to Address the Needs of Our Children?

YES: Lawrence H. Diller, from "The Run on Ritalin: Attention Deficit Disorder and Stimulant Treatment in the 1990s," *Hastings Center Report* (March–April 1996)

NO: Larry S. Goldman et al., from "Diagnosis and Treatment of Attention-Deficit/Hyperactivity Disorder in Children and Adolescents," *JAMA, The Journal of the American Medical Association* (April 8, 1998)

ISSUE SUMMARY

YES: Lawrence H. Diller, a pediatrician and family therapist, asserts that the use of stimulants on children has risen to epidemic proportions, occasioned by competitive social pressures for ever more effective functioning in school and at work.

NO: Larry S. Goldman, a faculty member of the Pritzker School of Medicine at the University of Chicago, and his colleagues review 20 years of medical literature regarding the diagnosis of attention deficit hyperactivity disorder and the use of stimulants. They conclude that the condition is not being overdiagnosed or misdiagnosed and that medications are not being overprescribed or overused.

The March 18, 1996, issue of *Newsweek* asked whether Ritalin is a miracle cure or a dangerous drug; four years later, an article in the April 24, 2000, issue stated, "Stimulants are still the most effective treatment for ADHD: The challenge is to use them wisely." Similarly, the cover story of the November 30, 1998, issue of *Time* addressed "The Age of Ritalin," including a discussion on the controversial antidepressant Prozac; by March 20, 2000, its "Families" section included "When Pills Make Sense," with the heading "Some parents turn too quickly to mood-altering drugs. But often medication is the right choice."

Most classes contain children who rely on medication, such as inhalers for asthma or EpiPens in case of bee sting. Most likely there is at least one child who takes some sort of medication for either issues of attention or depression. Or both.

An entire new field called *pediatric psychopharmacoepidemiology*—the study of the prevalence and patterns of psychiatric medication use among children—has developed, along with *The Journal of Child and Adolescent Psychopharmacology*. Although this field—and daily practice—covers much more than Ritalin, which is used to treat attention deficit hyperactivity disorder (ADHD), most of the questions around the use of medications and children do focus on the drugs that are designed to treat ADHD.

Russell A. Barkley (*ADHD: A Handbook for Diagnosis and Treatment*, 1998), cites research showing that 70–80 percent of children who are diagnosed with ADHD will require medication. Most patients respond to one of three stimulants, but some rely on antidepressants, and a small minority need antihypertensives.

Lawrence H. Diller is shocked by the 500 percent increase in the prescribed use of Ritalin in the mid-1990s. In the following selection, he argues that medication is an easy and fast answer for parents whose schedules do not permit them to spend time with their children; for doctors whose managed care responsibilities limit the amount of time they can spend with patients; for educators whose underfunded schools do not provide the resources to allow them to spend time with children; and for society, which demands faster, better performance from everyone.

In the second selection, Larry S. Goldman, Myron Genel, Rebecca J. Bezman, and Priscilla J. Slanetz acknowledge the increase in the use of medication but ascribe this rise to a shift in diagnostic criteria and the recognition that a useful intervention has been identified and is being used appropriately.

If a child has difficulty seeing the blackboard, it is easy to check to see if there are difficulties in visual acuity. If a child cannot see the board, glasses might help. The prescription written by a doctor is then filled, and learning can move forward.

Traditionally, when a child's behavior or learning raised questions for parents and teachers, educational testing was the way to learn about the child's learning style and capabilities. More and more frequently, questions about behavior and learning revolve around whether or not medication can help.

Medication is different from glasses. There are few side effects to wearing glasses; there might be many connected with medication. Yet both seem to be very effective if appropriately used.

As you read the following selections, ask yourself whether or not you would choose medication for yourself or your child in order to improve concentration or moderate behavior. Are the benefits and the potential long-term costs worth the risks? Or are the risks minimal, considering the overall improvement in quality of life?

Lawrence H. Diller

 **YES**

The Run on Ritalin

Stimulants were first reported as a pharmacologic treatment for children's behavioral problems in 1937. Methylphenidate, a derivative of piperidine, was synthesized in the 1940s and marketed as Ritalin in the 1960s. It is structurally related to the older drug still used for the treatment of hyperactivity, d-amphetamine. Their pharmacological actions are essentially the same.

Stimulant treatment for children became more common in the 1960s when its short-term benefits for what was then called hyperactivity were documented in controlled trials. In 1970 it was estimated that 150,000 children were taking stimulant medication in the U.S.

A furor over stimulants began in 1970. The reaction stemmed from an article in the popular press charging that 10 percent of the children in the Omaha school district in Nebraska were being medicated with Ritalin. While ultimately shown to contain inaccuracies, the article spurred other reports of "mind control" over children and led to congressional hearings about stimulants that same year. Numerous articles in newspapers and magazines and one book attacked Ritalin and the "myth" of the hyperactive child. Subsequently it was found that some of the criticism appeared to be led by supporters of the Scientology movement, who have consistently challenged mainstream psychiatry's use of psychoactive medications. Yet the negative publicity struck a nerve with the general public, which by the mid-1970s made it quite difficult to convince parents and teachers in many communities to attempt a trial of Ritalin.

The DEA [Drug Enforcement Agency] began monitoring the amounts of methlyphenidate and amphetamine produced in this country in 1971. Both became Schedule II controlled drugs partly in response to an epidemic of methylphenidate abuse occurring in Sweden and the illegal use of stimulants in this country. Estimates on the number of children using stimulants have varied widely. In 1980 it was estimated that from 270,000 to 541,000 elementary school children were receiving stimulants. In 1987 a national estimate of 750,000 children was made. Both estimates were guesses extrapolated from local surveys.

More precise than national estimates of children taking stimulants are the records of production quotas maintained by the DEA that show a steady

From Lawrence H. Diller, "The Run on Ritalin: Attention Deficit Disorder and Stimulant Treatment in the 1990s," *Hastings Center Report* (March–April 1996). Copyright © 1996 by The Hastings Center. Reprinted by permission of The Hastings Center and the author. References omitted.

output of approximately 1,700 kilograms of legal methylphenidate through the 1980s followed by a sharp increase in production in 1991. From 1990 through May 1995, the annual U.S. production of methylphenidate has increased by 500 percent to 10,410 kilograms, "an increase rarely seen for any other Schedule II Controlled Substance," according to the DEA. A national survey of physician's diagnoses and practices based upon data collected in 1993 found that of the 1.8 million persons receiving medication for Attention Deficit-Hyperactivity Disorder, 1.3 million were taking methylphenidate. A comparison of 1993 Ritalin production with the latest figures available for 1995 suggests that 2.6 million people currently are taking Ritalin, the vast majority of whom are children ages five through twelve.

Who is taking all of this Ritalin, and why? To get at the answers to these questions, we need to look at changes in professional and lay attitudes regarding psychoactive drugs, the brain, and children's behavior. Six hypotheses are suggested to explain the sudden increase in the demand for this drug.

Changes in Diagnostic Criteria

As more children's behavior is viewed as abnormal, more treatment is offered. The American Psychiatric Association distinguishes deviancy from normalcy in its *Diagnostic and Statistical Manual of Mental Disorders (DSM)*. With the introduction of the *DSM III* in 1980, mainstream psychiatry officially changed its view from a diagnosis of hyperactivity, highlighting physical movement, to one where problems with attention, Attention Deficit Disorder, were of primary concern. This change reflected research that suggested the primary problem for children was one of focus and distractibility. Hyperactivity, as a reflection of motoric impulsivity, was still important but not critical to the diagnosis. Thus, one could meet the criteria for ADD without being overly motorically active at all. The name of the condition was changed again in *DSM III-R* to Attention Deficit-Hyperactivity Disorder, and in *DSM-IV* separate subtypes of inattention and hyperactivity/impulsivity were restored.

There have been additional interpretative changes to the diagnosis. One need not demonstrate symptoms in every situation. Rather one need only display symptoms in at least two environments. Similarly one may concentrate satisfactorily at a number of tasks, perhaps even overfocus, yet still meet criteria for diagnosis if concentration and focus are problems for important tasks....

The changes in diagnostic criteria and interpretation have greatly broadened the group of children *and adults* who might qualify for the diagnosis. The line between children with "normal" variations of temperament, lively or spontaneous children who are sensitive to stimuli, and those who have a "disorder" has become increasingly blurred. The sine qua non for the diagnosis of hyperactivity in the mid-1970s was a demonstration of motoric overactivity and/or distractibility in nearly all settings including the doctor's office. Some children who may have benefited from identification and treatment were undoubtedly missed under these criteria, but this is less likely today. Now children who sit quietly and perform well in social situations or in one-on-one psychometric testing can still be candidates for the diagnosis and treatment of ADHD if their parents or teachers report poor performance in completing tasks at school or at home.

Prior to *DSM III*, etiologic factors were important in the diagnosis of psychiatric disorders. Since 1980 diagnosis has been descriptive, based primarily on observed behavior and self-report. While the multiaxial codings of the *DSM III* presumably account for medical factors and social stressors on the patient, less emphasis is placed on psychosocial influences, such as family, school, or work environments. In addition, the ascendancy of biological psychiatry, with its emphasis on the genetic and neurochemical factors directing behavior, implicitly diminishes the significance of development, learning disabilities, emotional status, family interaction, classroom size, and other environmental factors that may be relevant. Meeting ADHD criteria, which strictly speaking involves demonstrating a group of behaviors, has come to mean "having" ADHD, a neurological condition, such as Pervasive Developmental Disorder or Tourette Syndrome. Research purported to support a biological basis for ADHD, a brain scan of the cerebral cortex, or a survey of family epidemiology, cannot conclusively distinguish between biological or environmental etiologies.

Environmental factors can be seen either as contributing to the etiology or maintaining the symptomatic behavior. Indeed, a strongly stated case for neurological factors has been useful to counterbalance beliefs that such behaviors were attributable to lazy children and disorganized adults. However, if the symptoms of ADHD are to be viewed within the biopsychosocial model, calling ADHD a neurological disorder can mislead some into discounting psychosocial factors as unimportant.

The "Lean and Mean" '90s

As professional viewpoints have changed, so too have societal pressures and public attitudes toward attention and behavior problems in children and adults. Over the past two decades the pressure on children to perform has increased while support needed to help maximize performance has declined. Twenty-five years ago three- and four-year-old children were not expected to know the alphabet and numbers. Community programs like Head Start and television shows such as Sesame Street, while benefiting millions, have also led to expectations that children can learn at an earlier age. Yet over the concurrent past twenty years poverty rates for children, as a measure of their general well-being, have increased from 15 percent to 20 percent nationwide and children comprise 40 percent of all those who live in poverty.

More families are requiring two incomes to maintain their standard of living, and the increasing number of women in the workforce has led to large-scale preschool enrollment of children, requiring that younger children adhere to a more organized and less flexible social structure. Many children adapt easily to preschool and thrive in that group environment. Yet some children are not developmentally or socially ready for preacademic learning and a more demanding social structure. These children, had they stayed at home, would not be exposed to community scrutiny or come to the attention of teachers and physicians at an early age. At age three or four their behavior may qualify them for an ADHD diagnosis.

At the elementary school level, funding pressures on school systems have led to increased classroom sizes and higher student-to-teacher ratios. Also, more stringent criteria exist to qualify for special education services, which are often inadequately funded.

Similar conditions exist for high school and college students, especially in public education. The pressure to do well academically is immense. Inexorable pressures have developed to maintain a high grade point average in order to gain entry into a "good" college or graduate school.... Increasing attention through the use of medication may be seen as just another method to improve performance and results....

Pressures on Physicians and Educators

Physicians are also under pressure. Even before the managed care era, the time and economic constraints on the primary care physician were great. When presented with a potentially complex child behavioral problem, the physician may be attracted to the option of prescribing a medication rather than addressing the thornier and more time-consuming issues of emotions, family relationships, or school environment. Even with genuine concern for a multimodal evaluation and treatment plan, often little else is done on the primary care level.

Specialists, such as behavioral-developmental pediatricians and child psychiatrists, should be capable of spending more time and lending greater expertise to the resolution of the intricacies of the child, family, and school situation. These specialists are concerned, however, that the cost-containment measures of managed care will increasingly permit referrals only when medication is being considered for the child.

Increasing pupil-teacher ratios and diminishing special education services also have an effect. These conditions make it "easier" to medicate a child than to work with a dysfunctional family, decrease the size of the classroom, or augment funding for special education services. Because stimulants "work" more quickly, they are more attractive not only to families and physicians, but to managed care companies and financially strapped educational systems. It is unlikely that either would insist on medication in lieu of counseling or special education services, but neither would protest if medication allowed the child to function better without either service.

The Disability Issue

Society increasingly has interpreted performance problems as disease, which then become defined as a disability. People with defined disabilities cannot legally face discrimination and are entitled to the benefits of special services. The increasing numbers of children and adults who meet the broader ADHD criteria are beginning to have an impact in the classroom and workplace. Parents find the only way to get extra help for their children is to have them labeled with a disorder. The Individuals with Disabilities Education Act of 1990 and recent interpretations of Section 504 of the 1973 Rehabilitation Act have become broad and potent legal tools for families of children with ADHD seeking special services from their school districts....

Categorizing ADHD as a disability has created other dilemmas. Typically someone with a disability is provided special circumstances or allowances for optimal performance, for example, more time provided in a college entrance examination.... In the workplace more and more employers are being asked to make changes for their workers who are affected with ADHD. It is only a matter of time until an employer balks and a suit is filed. The trend is being followed closely by the business community....

The Culture of Prozac

Prozac (fluoxetine), the first of the serotonin reuptake inhibitors, went on the market in 1988. With its low side-effect profile compared to the earlier generation of antidepressants, it widened the range of individuals who might tolerate a psychotropic drug for depression and led to widespread popular debate on the subject. Peter Kramer's best-selling book, *Listening to Prozac,* reflected and further encouraged popular interest in the use of psychiatric medication to enhance mood and performance. The overall prevalence of antidepressant use in certain communities has quadrupled in a ten-year period. It has become much more acceptable to take a psychotropic medication. This new atmosphere has also increased acceptance of stimulant use for behavioral problems in children and attentional problems in adults.

The Role of Mass Media

The effects of mass media on the practice of medicine and concerns of patients are well documented. As TV news, talk shows, and print journalism have highlighted the use of psychotropic medication to cope with one's problems, a corresponding public interest in Ritalin and ADHD has developed. Personal and affecting testimonies of dramatic improvements after using Ritalin have been reported on national television broadcasts and many syndicated talk shows.... Prominent local and national news weeklies have made ADHD their cover stories.

In both the professional and lay media ADHD is routinely referred to as a neurological disorder. While most experts agree that generic-biochemical factors influence behavior to some degree, the general public tends to transform this view into a biological determinism in which only heredity and brain chemistry determine behavior rather than in interactions with the environment. This interpretation may be comforting to some perplexed and worried parents who feel responsible for their children's difficulties and help overburdened teachers gain assistance in teaching children with this "disability." Psychotherapeutic strategies can help "externalize" the disease as separate from the child. Yet when behavior is regarded as stemming from biological pathology, interventions like stimulant medication become more easily justified and emphasized, while others become less valued. Indeed, ADHD has become the somewhat dubious leading self-diagnosis as the "biological cause... for job failure, divorce, poor motivation, lack of success, and chronic mild depression."

Cosmetic Ritalin

"Cosmetic psychopharmacology," as Kramer puts it, is the elective use of medically prescribed drugs to enhance mood or improve behavior. Currently, it is considered medically and ethically justifiable to prescribe stimulants only when behavior meets criteria for a medical or psychiatric disorder. It is not known how much Ritalin currently is being prescribed for those on the indistinct line between "disease" and the general struggle for success. It is known, however, that Ritalin improves the focus and performance of those who do not meet ADHD criteria (normal, nonreferred children) and that the drug is prescribed for such use.

There remains no definitive "test" for ADHD. The ambiguities of the ADHD diagnosis were highlighted in a study on stimulant medication and primary care. Over one quarter of children diagnosed with ADHD by their physician failed to meet criteria for the diagnosis when the cases were compared to structured psychiatric interviews with the parents. The number of children who failed to meet criteria increased to half when compared to structured interviews with the children's teachers. While the overall number of children medicated was not seen as high by the investigators, they noted the nonspecificity of the behavioral symptoms in the children that responded to stimulants. Thus, the ADHD diagnosis was seen as a diagnostic cover, albeit inaccurate, for the use of stimulants in a range of behavioral and performance problems in children.

Questioning Ritalin

Stimulants can be used in an effective and sensible way, especially when other modalities of treatment for attentional problems are addressed concurrently. Undoubtedly many parents of children with ADHD and adults with ADHD feel Ritalin has been of immense benefit to their children or themselves. However, important questions remain unanswered and a pending request to decrease DEA controls on methylphenidate production and physician prescription practices makes them all the more urgent.

Ritalin's reemergence as a popular "fix" overlooks adverse side effects, a dearth of long-term studies, and a host of other ethical questions concerning unwitting coercion, fairness, informed consent, and potentially inadequate treatment of patients. Larger societal questions also should be asked: Should society use a biological fix to address problems that have roots in social and environmental factors? If it consistently does, how might society be affected?

If elective treatments are to warrant consideration, their side effects must be minimal. The short- and long-term physical side effects of Ritalin are generally considered minor on the basis of fifteen- to twenty-year follow-up studies involving children who took stimulants for several years up until early adolescence. The effects of continuous Ritalin use through adolescence and into adulthood have not, as yet, been studied. The drug's immediate side effects, brief appetite suppression and possible insomnia, are generally well tolerated by children. Some reports suggest Ritalin unmasks the tics of Tourette Syndrome, but this remains controversial. Long-term growth suppression has been attributed to Ritalin, but this effect can be minimized through the scheduling of drug "holidays."

Although one reason for the much greater use of Ritalin compared to amphetamine for ADHD has been the erroneous belief that it has less abuse potential, there exists a possibility of abusing Ritalin. The Swedish experience of the late 1960s and very recent examples of Ritalin abuse by teenagers in this country belie this myth of safety. However, there is little evidence of physical addiction to or abuse of Ritalin when used *appropriately* for ADHD. Despite the possibilities of abuse, Ritalin appears relatively safe from a strictly physical standpoint.

Evaluation of the emotional and psychological consequences of Ritalin use is more complex. There is still a strong cultural belief that it is better to cope by using one's inherent resources and interacting with people than by resorting to medication. This 'pharmacological Calvinism' may lead to feelings of inadequacy in the child who takes the drug, despite the physician's and family's view that Ritalin is necessary or benign. Teenagers, particularly sensitive about their identity, are especially vulnerable to issues of competence and biological integrity. These beliefs can be overcome, but remain a potential downside.

While physical addiction doesn't occur when Ritalin is used as prescribed for ADHD, psychological dependence is possible for the child, the family, the adolescent or adult. When queried, children attributed most of their success in a "vigilance" assignment to their own efforts rather than medication. It is family members and teachers who more often notice the child performing suboptimally and ask, "Did you take your pill today?" The question expresses an underlying message to the child about the drug's important contribution to performance and behavior, and ultimately, this message may undermine the child's confidence. This sense of dependency is highlighted when the medication is used "as necessary," in event-driven dosing, for example, when studying for an exam or attending a weekend family gathering. It is even possible that event-driven dosing may promote or exacerbate the often disorganized ADHD lifestyle by allowing the procrastinating individual to "catch up" at the last minute. The teenager and adult may also be tempted to stretch the normal wake-sleep cycle in order to achieve even greater performance, which could ultimately lead to an abuse pattern. The long-term consequences of self-administered stimulants by teenagers and adults for ADHD have not been studied to determine the likelihood of such a pattern developing. Thus, while achievements made under the influence of stimulants can enhance a sense of competence, self-esteem, and independence, the specter of psychological dependence, altered self-image, and potential abuse remains, especially in a society that paradoxically continues to be somewhat critical of psychotropic drugs while demanding greater performance.

Ritalin should be questioned further because no long-term studies prove its efficacy. Numerous reports show the stimulants to be of value in short-term memory and performance. In long-term studies benefits to children formally classified under the hyperactivity diagnosis have not been demonstrated. For children with ADHD without hyperactivity or for teenagers and adults there are *no* long-term studies of Ritalin's efficacy.

Long-term controlled studies are difficult to run and fund, and one can question the ethics of withholding a potentially effective treatment until there is more definitive proof of benefit. However, a single study in which children received Ritalin along with child-family counseling and special education services is the *only* research demonstrating long-term improvements. Most child behavior experts advocate a multimodal approach to treatment despite the lack of definitive evidence of improvement. In actual practice, though, the follow through for behavioral recommendations is poor. The multimodal model of treatment is also suggested for adults. Yet, here too, the emphasis in professional and lay articles is on the pharmacological interventions.

The increasing availability and use of Ritalin to enhance performance also raise questions of subtle coercion and fairness. As more children and adults use Ritalin to work more efficiently at school or in the office, will those who are also struggling to perform feel pressured to consider medication? Will there be an impetus to keep up with others, to compete for the good grade, bonus, or job promotion by whatever means necessary, medication or otherwise? Moreover, is it fair to use the same performance criteria for those who use Ritalin as for those who do not? In athletic competition, stimulants remain banned precisely because of fairness issues. Yet, recently, the case has been made that athletes with ADHD be allowed to compete while taking Ritalin because of their "handicap." Somehow viewing behavior as neurologically based makes it more acceptable to use medication.

Because many Ritalin users are children, issues concerning informed consent also arise. Although the treatment of undesired nonpathological conditions in adult medicine is not uncommon (for example, plastic surgery, topical minoxidil for baldness, estrogens for menopause, treatment for infertility, and contraceptives), elective therapies for children have been more controversial because it is the parents, not the children, who decide upon treatment. For example, growth hormone for constitutional short stature has been hotly debated. Who decides for whom in these cases? And how high should the standard be?

One last question concerns the tendency for genetic contributions and neurochemical influences on behavior to be understood deterministically by society, such as the media and the courts. Such an interpretation can have the effect of eclipsing other treatment options. Even "good" psychopharmacology decreases the need to scrutinize the child's social environment and may permit a poor situation to continue or grow worse. Should dysfunctional family patterns and overcrowded classrooms be tolerated just because Ritalin improves the child's behavior? An effort is underway to determine which combination of treatments is most effective. The National Institutes of Mental Health has funded a multisite ADHD study involving several thousand children, with the goal of comparing treatment efficacies with a variety of approaches and combinations. Yet in the absence of confirmed, effective long-term treatment for ADHD and the general recommendations for a multimodal approach, will medication-only treatment produce persistent problems later in a child's life?

Furthermore, this bioreductionistic interpretation of the neurobiological components of ADHD behavior attributes less power to free will and individual choice. Thus, the popular viewpoint of maladaptive behavior as disease conflicts with another historically strong cultural perspective: accountability and responsibility. This clash of views is likely to be resolved ultimately in the civil and criminal court systems and by the economic imperatives of the workplace. It is worth noting how recent court decisions on recovered memory of child sexual abuse are influencing psychiatric technique and practice and the frequency of diagnosis of multiple personality disorder. Similar court guidelines are likely to emerge for those on the borderline of an ADHD diagnosis.

Responses to the Epidemic

The main response to date over the epidemic of ADHD and the use of stimulants in America has been further efforts at informing professionals and the public about the "new" ADHD (without hyperactivity). For many physicians, psychologists, and educators, the identification of potential ADHD and consequent stimulant treatment are meeting an important need of the community. Further education about the benefits of diagnosis and stimulants is the present goal. Academic medicine remains primarily focused on substantiating a biological substrate for ADHD. A notable exception is a recent study on the effects of family stressors in the development of ADHD.

However, another view of ADHD diagnosis and the rise in stimulant use is far more sobering. As suggested earlier, the ADHD/stimulant phenomenon may reflect how the demands on children and families have increased as the social network supporting them has declined. The rise in the use of stimulants is alarming and signals an urgent need for American society to reevaluate its priorities.

On a clinical level, physicians treating children and adults may be locked into a "social trap." Though it may make sense to medicate individuals so they can function more effectively and competently within a certain environment, do doctors unwittingly permit and support a long-term collective negative outcome for the society? Are they unintentionally promoting an antihumanistic, competitive environment that demands performance at any cost? Should they more aggressively promote a general redistribution of society's resources to children and families? Some say there is no choice but to offer medication; it is not up to physicians to address society's ills. Peter Kramer in *Listening to Prozac* seems rather sanguine about a society that copes with newer, safer, improved psychopharmacologic agents. Whether individually beneficial or societally dangerous it behooves the physician to at least raise these questions about ADHD and stimulants with parents, teachers, and colleagues.

NO

Larry S. Goldman et al.

Diagnosis and Treatment of Attention-Deficit/Hyperactivity Disorder in Children and Adolescents

Attention-deficit/hyperactivity disorder (ADHD) is a common neuropsychiatric syndrome with onset in childhood, most commonly becoming apparent (and thus coming to medical attention) during the first few years of grade school. ADHD may be associated with a number of comorbid psychiatric conditions as well as with impaired academic performance and with both patient and family emotional distress. While it was previously thought that the disorder remitted before or during adolescence, it has become well established that many patients will have an illness course that persists well into adulthood. Pharmacological treatment, particularly with stimulant medication, is the most-studied aspect of management, although other forms of treatment (eg, behavior therapy, parent training) are important parts of good clinical care.

Despite an enormous body of research into this disorder, various aspects of ADHD have generated controversy over the years. Three features of ADHD in particular seem to have contributed to the controversy: (1) like most mental disorders, its diagnostic criteria involve patient history and behavioral assessment without the availability of laboratory or radiologic confirmation; (2) like many chronic illnesses of childhood, it has an early onset and extended course, thus requiring at times treatment of children and adolescents over many years; and (3) its treatment often includes stimulant medications that have abuse or diversion potential.

Debate has centered on the appropriate assessment and "labeling" of children: there have been allegations that the diagnosis is merely applied to control children who exhibit unwanted behaviors in the classroom or elsewhere and that medication is simply used to control such behavior. Along similar lines, concerns have been expressed about whether thorough enough evaluations are being performed by physicians prior to prescribing medication. Apart from diagnostic issues, concerns have been raised about young children taking medications for lengthy periods of time. In addition, some critics have complained that overemphasis on psychopharmacological treatment has led to neglect of other treatment modalities or served as a distraction from family problems or

From Larry S. Goldman, Myron Genel, Rebecca J. Bezman, and Priscilla J. Slanetz, "Diagnosis and Treatment of Attention-Deficit/Hyperactivity Disorder in Children and Adolescents," *JAMA, The Journal of the American Medical Association*, vol. 279, no. 14 (April 8, 1998). Copyright © 1998 by The American Medical Association. Reprinted by permission. References omitted.

school shortcomings. It should be stressed that these issues have been raised polemically or theoretically, rather than on the basis of particular scientific findings.

Another concern has been raised by the dramatic increase in methylphenidate (Ritalin) hydrochloride production and use in the United States in the past decade. This has raised questions about whether there has been a true increase in the prevalence of ADHD in this time period; a change in diagnostic criteria affecting practice; improved physician recognition of the disorder; a broadened spectrum of indications for use of stimulants; and an increase in stimulant abuse, diversion, and prescription for profit.

Debate over ADHD within the research and medical communities has been mild and mostly concerned with nuances in the diagnostic and treatment paradigms. By contrast, highly inflammatory public relations campaigns and pitched legal battles have been waged (particularly by groups such as the Church of Scientology) that seek to label the whole idea of ADHD as an illness a "myth" and to brand the use of stimulants in children as a form of "mind control." These efforts, which have been widely reported in the news media, have created a climate of fear among physicians, parents, and educators and have sown anxiety and confusion among the general public. It is thus most important to separate legitimate concerns raised by scientific studies from abstract, distorted, or mendacious information from other sources.

There are 6 main questions that underlie this professional and public concern and that this report will address by reviewing the pertinent research:

1. Is there an agreed-on set of diagnostic criteria for ADHD that reflects sufficient reliability and validity so as to delineate a clinically meaningful syndrome?
2. What is the epidemiology of ADHD, and how can the apparent disparities in prevalence in different populations be explained?
3. What is the course of the illness, and what are the adverse consequences of the illness that would justify treatment?
4. What constitutes optimal treatment for ADHD, and how do stimulants fit into it?
5. What are the adverse consequences of using stimulants, and in particular, what is known about the risks of abuse and diversion?
6. Are children being appropriately assessed and treated in clinical settings to ensure that diagnostic criteria are being used appropriately; ie, is there evidence of underdiagnosis, overdiagnosis, or misdiagnosis? . . .

Diagnosis of ADHD

. . . The *DSM-IV* [Diagnostic and Statistical Manual of Mental Disorders, Fourth Edition] criteria emphasize several factors:

The symptoms specified in the criteria must be present for at least 6 months, ensuring that persistent rather than transient symptoms will be included.

The symptoms must be "maladaptive and inconsistent with developmental level." This ensures that the symptoms are of sufficient severity to cause problems and that the child's age and neurodevelopment are considered in evaluating symptoms.

The symptoms must be present across 2 or more settings, ie, school problems alone do not meet criteria for the diagnosis.

The symptoms are not better explained by another disorder, such as mood disorder, psychosis, or pervasive developmental disorder (autism).

Taken as a whole, these criteria require an illness pattern that is enduring and has led to impairment. To make this diagnosis appropriately, the clinician must be familiar with normal development and behavior, gather information from several sources to evaluate the child's symptoms in different settings, and construct an appropriate differential diagnosis for the presenting complaints. This helps, for example, to distinguish children with ADHD from unaffected children whose parents or teachers are mislabeling normal behavior as pathological. The diagnostic criteria as used by appropriate examiners demonstrate high interrater reliability of individual items and of overall diagnosis.

A number of other psychiatric, medical, and neurologic disorders (eg, traumatic brain injury, epilepsy, depression) can lead to disturbances in attention and/or activity level. Thus, the diagnosis of "primary" ADHD is made when there is no evidence from the history, physical examination, or laboratory findings of another condition producing the clinical picture.

... [T]he overall approach to diagnosis may involve (1) a comprehensive interview with the child's adult caregivers; (2) a mental status examination of the child; (3) a medical evaluation for general health and neurologic status; (4) a cognitive assessment of ability and achievement; (5) use of ADHD-focused parent and teacher rating scales; and (6) school reports and other adjunctive evaluations if necessary (speech, language assessment, etc) depending on clinical findings. An evaluation can be performed by a clinician with the skills and knowledge to carry out those components....

Even with the use of carefully applied diagnostic criteria, there remains the issue of the validity of ADHD as a discrete condition. With regard to unitary etiology, many medical conditions (eg, heart failure, seizures) are syndromes representing a final common presentation of a number of pathophysiological disturbances. Thus, the absence of a single cause would be a weak argument against the validity of ADHD as a discrete syndrome. The familial, genetic, neuroanatomical, and neurophysiological studies are mounting evidence to date for postdictive validity. Findings with regard to concurrent validity are mixed: there is clearly a great deal of overlap between ADHD and a number of learning conditions and conduct disorder, among other conditions. The strongest evidence of validity has been for course prediction and treatment response. Overall, ADHD is one of the best-researched disorders in medicine, and the overall data on its validity are far more compelling than for any medical conditions.

Epidemiology of ADHD

A number of studies have examined the prevalence of ADHD in various populations. The patient sample used is critical because of variations in different settings: at least 10% of behavior problems seen in general pediatrics settings are due to ADHD, while children with ADHD make up to 50% of some child psychiatric populations. In general, most ADHD patients in the United States are cared for by pediatricians and family practitioners, while child psychiatrists, neurologists, and behavioral pediatricians tend to see refractory patients and those with significant comorbidity. Community studies have yielded prevalences between 1.7% and 16%, depending on the population and the diagnostic methods....

These results suggest that across fairly diverse populations (geographically, racially, socioeconomically) there exists a sizable percentage of school-aged children with ADHD. The evolution of criteria from *DSM-III* to *DSM-IV,* although based on a progressively larger empirical base, has broadened the case definition, so that more children appear to be affected. This is largely a function of the increased emphasis on attentional problems as opposed to a more narrow focus on hyperactivity in earlier diagnostic sets. As a result, girls have been diagnosed as having ADHD more frequently than they were in the past.

Illness Course and Comorbidity of ADHD

Longer-term follow-up studies of children with ADHD as well as "lookback" studies of symptomatic adults who can be retrospectively diagnosed as having had childhood ADHD show that there is symptomatic persistence into adulthood in many cases. On average, symptoms diminish by about 50% every 5 years between the ages of 10 and 25 years. Hyperactivity itself declines more quickly than impulsivity or inattentiveness.

A number of psychiatric conditions co-occur with ADHD. Between 10% and 20% of children with ADHD in both community and clinical samples have mood disorders, 20% have conduct disorders, and up to 40% may have oppositional defiant disorder. Bipolar disorder is being increasingly recognized. Only about 7% of those with ADHD have tics or Tourette syndrome, but 60% of those with Tourette syndrome have ADHD, raising questions about common etiologic mechanisms. Learning disorders (especially reading disorder) and subnormal intelligence also are increased in the total population of those with ADHD and vice versa. Overall, perhaps as many as 65% of children with ADHD will have 1 or more comorbid conditions, although their presence will not be recognized without appropriate questioning and evaluation. In general, when ADHD is untreated there is a gradual accumulation of adverse processes and events that increase the risk of serious psychopathology later in life. Whether this can be reversed by long-term treatment remains unknown.

The relationship between substance use disorders and ADHD is complex. Children with ADHD who do not have comorbid conditions have a risk of substance use disorders that is no different from children without ADHD up to the age of about 14 years. The risk of developing substance use disorders in those with ADHD is increased in adolescents, and the risk ratio increases further in adulthood, regardless of whether there is comorbidity. Persistence of ADHD symptoms and family history of both ADHD and substance use disorders are risk factors for their development. Highly potent risk factors are the presence of comorbid conduct disorder or bipolar disorder. There is debate about whether long-term treatment of ADHD may decrease the risk of subsequent development of substance use disorders....

Treatment of ADHD

Methylphenidate, created in 1955, now accounts for more than 90% of the stimulant use in ADHD in the United States. A racemic mixture of amphetamines (Adderall), dextroamphetamine sulfate (Dexedrine and others), and pemoline (Cylert) are also used. Methylphenidate is strongly favored by US physicians, perhaps because the overuse of amphetamines for treatment of obesity and their misuse in the 1960s gave that class of drugs a reputation as more problematic than methylphenidate.

There have been more than 170 studies involving more than 6000 school-aged children using stimulant medication for ADHD. The response rate for any single stimulant drug in ADHD is approximately 70%, and up to 90% of children will respond to at least 1 stimulant without major adverse events if drug titration is done carefully. A "response" in this context means a statistically or clinically significant reduction in hyperactivity or increase in attention as rated by parents, teachers, and/or research raters. There have been only about a half-dozen studies in adolescents.

Medications have been unequivocally shown (ie, by double-blind, placebo-controlled studies) to reduce core symptoms of hyperactivity, impulsivity, and inattentiveness. They improve classroom behavior and academic performance; diminish oppositional and aggressive behaviors; promote increased interaction with teachers, family, and others; and increase participation in leisure time activities. Finally, stimulants have demonstrated improvement in irritability, anxiety, and nail biting. A recent meta-analysis found that the effect of stimulants on behavior and cognition may be severalfold greater than the effects on academic achievement.

Contrary to earlier assertions, the response to stimulant medications in those with ADHD is not "paradoxical": the direction of changes in behavioral measures in those with ADHD, those with conditions other than ADHD (eg, learning disabilities, depression), and normal controls is the same. Thus, a favorable response to stimulants does not confirm a diagnosis of ADHD (nor, of course, does a nonresponse refute the diagnosis). A nonspecific performance-enhancing effect may mask other problems and delay use of other interventions.

In addition to their value in childhood and adult ADHD, methylphenidate and other stimulants may play a role in the treatment of other medical conditions, including narcolepsy, as a short-term treatment for depression in the medically ill, as potentiating agents with conventional antidepressants for major depressive disorder, as potentiating agents with opiates for pain control, and to reduce apathy in dementia and some other brain diseases. The number of patients receiving these drugs for these indications probably represents no more than a small percentage of all stimulant use in the United States.

For patients with ADHD who are intolerant of or unresponsive to stimulants, a number of other drugs have proven useful in clinical practice, including tricyclic antidepressants and bupropion hydrochloride, a newer antidepressant that blocks the reuptake of norepinephrine and dopamine. Serotonin-specific reuptake inhibitors have not been effective to date. Centrally acting α-blocking drugs (clonidine, guanfacine hydrochloride) have been helpful in some children, but data are still limited. Subsets of children seem to have some response to lithium carbonate. Neuroleptic medication is occasionally effective, but the risk of tardive dyskinesia makes this a problematic long-term approach. By contrast, some 20 studies have refuted the efficacy of dietary manipulations (eg, the Feingold diet) in ADHD.

It is important to emphasize that pharmacotherapy alone, while highly effective for short-term symptomatic improvement, has not yet been shown to improve the long-term outcome for any domain of functioning (classroom behavior, learning, impulsivity, etc). This may be a function of several factors: most studies have been carried out only for a short term, there may have been inadequate dosage titration to maximize the number of responders, and dose-response relationships may be different for different domains.

... [A] careful review of all review studies of stimulant use in children in 1993 ... found overwhelming evidence for temporary improvement of core symptoms (hyperactivity, inattention, and impulsivity) as well as the associated features of defiance, aggression, and negative social skills. On the other hand, changes that point toward longer-term improvement (eg, in academic outcome, antisocial behavior, or arrest rate) were not found, and only small effects were observed on learning and achievement.

Children should be reevaluated periodically while not taking medications to see if the medications are still appropriate and necessary.

Multimodal therapy, ie, integrating pharmacotherapy with a number of environmental, educational, psychotherapeutic, and school-based approaches, is a tailored approach that seems intuitively powerful, matching the child's particular problems to selections from a menu of focused treatment interventions. In a few studies, multimodal therapy has affected long-term results, although how applicable these findings are beyond research settings remains unclear. While three quarters of treatment review articles assert that multimodal therapy is superior to medication or psychosocial interventions separately, there is in fact little empirical evidence to support such a conclusion.

Nonmedication approaches include parent education; parent management training (contingency management in individual or group setting; this technique decreases disruptive behavior, increases parents' self-confidence, and decreases family stress); classroom environmental manipulations (special class, seating in class, etc); contingency management and daily report cards by teacher; individual psychotherapy for depression, anxiety, and low self-esteem; impulse and social skills control training; support groups such as Children and Adults With Attention Deficit Disorder and Attention Deficit Disorder Association for families; and summer treatment programs.

Some experts feel that stimulants alone may be adequate for cases of ADHD without comorbidity, but that additional treatments are necessary where there are co-occurring conditions. Behavioral therapy has not proved effective alone, although it has been when combined with pharmacotherapy. Since psychosocial treatments may be labor intensive and expensive, it is important to establish when and which treatments are indicated. A large multisite study is currently being carried out by the National Institute of Mental Health to clarify the role of multimodal treatment: carefully evaluated children will be randomized to receive standard community care, medication alone, psychosocial treatments alone, or multimodal therapy (medication and psychosocial treatments together).

A number of textbooks and many review articles are available to practitioners. The Academy of Child and Adolescent Psychiatry's practice parameters have recently been released. A recent American Academy of Pediatrics position paper emphasizes the need for careful evaluation and monitoring of children with ADHD, and it stresses that drugs be used as part of an overall care plan.

Adverse Effects of Stimulants

Adverse effects from stimulants are generally mild, short lived, and responsive to dosing or timing adjustments. The most common effects are insomnia, decreased appetite, stomach ache, headache, and jitteriness. Some children will exhibit motor tics while on stimulants: whether this reflects a true drug effect or an "unmasking" of a latent tic disorder is unknown. A small percentage of children experience cognitive impairment that responds to dosage reduction or drug cessation. Rare cases of psychosis have occurred. Pemoline has been infrequently associated with hepatic toxic effects, so periodic monitoring of liver enzymes is necessary.

Concerns had been raised about the effects of chronic stimulant ingestion on growth and development. It is unclear whether children's heights are affected by long-term use of these medications.

A great deal of concern has been raised by the DEA [Drug Enforcement Agency] and others about the potential for abuse or diversion of stimulant medication: production (and use) of methylphenidate in the United States has risen from less than 2000 kg in 1986 to 9000 kg in 1995, with a tripling between 1990 and 1995 alone. By contrast, amphetamine production rose from 400 to 1000 kg in the same period. More than 90% of US-produced methylphenidate is used in the United States.

The reasoning for the concern about possible overproduction of methylphenidate has been expressed as follows: Stimulants at times are abused by adolescents and adults; those with ADHD are at increased risk of developing a substance use disorder; methylphenidate and other stimulants may either become the drug abused by those with ADHD, or they may serve as a "gateway" to other drug use; and even if they do not abuse their medication themselves, children and adolescents with access to stimulants will be under pressure to divert their medication to those who will.

There is little disagreement that stimulants as a class have marked abuse potential, and their misuse can have severe adverse medical and social consequences. However, stimulants differ in their ability to induce euphoria and thus liability to abuse. Almost all of the reports of abuse of methylphenidate itself have been of polysubstance-abusing adults who have tried to solubilize the tablets and inject them (with disastrous results from talc granulomatosis in some cases). This last problem in particular led Sweden to withdraw methylphenidate from the market in that country entirely in 1968.

It is clear that there is a fair amount of use of stimulants by adolescents. The annual school survey of drug use conducted by the University of Michigan has shown an increase from 6.2% to 9.9% of eighth-graders reporting nonmedical stimulant use in the preceding year between 1991 and 1994. However, lifetime nonmedical methylphenidate use has remained essentially constant around 1% during the same period. Sixty percent of students who used any stimulants reported using them fewer than 6 times in their lifetime, and 80%, fewer than 20 times. Only 4% reported any injection use of stimulants. Thus, while nonmedical stimulant use may be somewhat more common among adolescents in recent years, little use is of methylphenidate itself, and the pattern of use for the vast majority appears to be experimental and not of the type (regular, heavy, injecting, etc) likely to lead to serious adverse consequences.

Drug Abuse Warning Network data on emergency department visit monitoring show a 6-fold increase between 1990 and 1995 in mentions of methylphenidate. A "mention" simply indicates that the patient listed the drug as one taken: it is not necessarily the drug leading to the emergency department visit, nor is there any medical confirmation. The rate of cocaine mentions, by contrast, is 40 to 50 times higher. The methylphenidate cases are overwhelmingly young women, not the population (ie, male adolescents) felt to be at highest risk for abusing prescription methylphenidate. The DEA has had reports of thefts of methylphenidate, street sales, drug rings, illegal importation from outside the United States, and illegal sales by health professionals. There have also been reports of theft of school supplies of methylphenidate.

On the other hand, abuse of methylphenidate by patients with ADHD or their family members has been reported rarely. Only 2 cases of methylphenidate abuse by adolescents with ADHD have been described, and only 2 cases of methylphenidate abuse by parents of children taking it for ADHD have been reported. While there is no way to know how many cases may have been unrecognized or unreported, such a minimal published experience is quite remarkable in light of the population exposed....

Current Practice

It is clear from the discussion of diagnostic assessment that ADHD simply cannot be diagnosed in a typical 15-minute primary care office visit.... Few data exist on actual practice habits in terms of what diagnostic criteria (if any) are used by clinicians, how they are applied, or exactly what a minimally satisfactory level of investigation entails.

A national survey of physicians found that 5.3% of elementary school children in pediatrics practices were diagnosed as having ADHD, and 4.2% were diagnosed by family practitioners. When explicit *DSM-III-R* [Diagnostic and Statistical Manual, Revised Third Edition] criteria were used, however, only 72% of those assigned a diagnosis of ADHD by their physicians would have received the diagnosis based on a structured interview. Only 53% of the physician diagnoses included teachers' reports. Eighty-eight percent of the physician-diagnosed children were prescribed methylphenidate, and 85% of the parents reported that the medication was helpful. Only 22% of the parents reported treatment with behavioral modification, and in 70% of those cases that modality was recommended by someone other than the treating physician. Eleven percent received counseling from the physician, and no parents queried judged it effective. The authors of this survey drew attention to the mismatch between physician diagnosis from a single source, often an unreliable one, and the use of stimulant medication. They also stressed the low rates of use of nonpharmacological treatment by their physician sample....

There is evidence to suggest that stimulants in ADHD populations are simply being used more broadly, for longer periods, and without interruptions in recent years than was done previously. Overall, there has been a 2.5-fold increase in the prevalence of child and adolescent methylphenidate treatment from 1990 to 1995, so that some 2.8% of US youth between the ages of 5 and 18 years were taking this medication in mid 1995. A recent national study found no evidence of overdiagnosis of ADHD or overprescription of methylphenidate.

... [F]rom 1990 to 1993 the number of patients diagnosed as having ADHD increased from 900 000 to 2 million, and the number of outpatient visits for the condition rose from 1.7 million to 4.2 million. The percentage of patients given methylphenidate remained around 70%. Thus, the amount of methylphenidate produced per 1 million patients increased from 1.98 g to 2.53 g, a 27% increase.

There are several important clinical reasons for the increased diagnosis and stimulant treatment of ADHD. These include increased public and physician awareness and acceptance of the condition; acceptance of a broader case definition as appropriate; greater knowledge of the illness course, justifying lengthier treatment (eg, of adolescents); fewer interruptions in treatment because of diminished concerns about growth retardation; and increased treatment of adults.

Finally, with regard to cross-national data, there is some consensus that most non-US clinicians are more likely to rely on older, more stringent diagnostic criteria, reserve the diagnosis for only the most obvious or severe cases, or even be reluctant to diagnose ADHD at all. Physicians from countries with strong psychoanalytic traditions may be particularly reluctant to use discrete diagnostic criteria at all. Physicians in the United Kingdom, for example, tend to use a *DSM-II* approach, so they place more emphasis on hyperactivity and therefore diagnose ADHD far less frequently than their US counterparts. When physicians in the United Kingdom are instructed in applying US criteria, however, they diagnose ADHD as often as their US counterparts do in US children. Thus, the apparent discrepancy is more a matter of case recognition than actual prevalence. Canadian physicians, who tend to use later *DSM* criteria, diagnose and treat children at rates similar to those seen in the United States.

Conclusions

1. ADHD is a childhood neuropsychiatric syndrome that has been studied thoroughly over the past 40 years. Available diagnostic criteria for ADHD are based on extensive empirical research and, if applied appropriately, lead to the diagnosis of a syndrome with high interrater reliability, good face validity, and high predictability of course and medication responsiveness. ADHD is one of the best-researched disorders in medicine, and the overall data on its validity are far more compelling than for most mental disorders and even for many medical conditions. Nonetheless, the pathophysiology of ADHD remains unknown, although a number of neurophysiological theories are under investigation. ADHD demonstrates a very high heritability.

2. The diagnostic criteria for ADHD are designed to be used by a clinician familiar with childhood development and behavioral disorders. Application of the diagnostic criteria requires time and effort to obtain a careful history from parents, teachers, and the child. As with almost all mental disorders, there is as yet no confirmatory genetic, radiologic, biochemical, neurophysiological, or neuropsychological test for ADHD, but such examinations may be helpful at times in evaluating presenting complaints suggestive of ADHD.

3. ADHD is associated with significant potential comorbidity and functional impairment, and its presence at any age increases the risk of behavioral and emotional problems at subsequent stages of life. It is thus a chronic illness with persistence common into adolescence and beyond.

4. Epidemiologic studies using standardized diagnostic criteria suggest that 3% to 6% of the school-aged population may have ADHD. A few studies have suggested a somewhat lower prevalence, but others, particularly those using newer, broader criteria, yield prevalences well above 6%. These studies have been conducted in a number of different countries and encompass a range of racial and socioeconomic backgrounds in the populations examined.

5. The percentage of US youth being treated for ADHD is at most at the lower end of this prevalence range. More cases of ADHD are being recognized and treated, and the duration of treatment is increasing. However, ADHD is also diagnosed inappropriately at times because of failure to do a thorough enough evaluation or to use established diagnostic criteria.

6. Pharmacotherapy, particularly stimulants, has been extensively studied. Medication alone generally provides significant short-term symptomatic and academic improvement, but response to stimulant medication is not specific to ADHD, and it is currently unknown whether long-term outcomes will be altered. The risk-benefit ratio of stimulant treatment in ADHD must be evaluated and monitored on an ongoing basis in each case, but in general is highly favorable.

7. Optimal treatment of ADHD involves an individualized plan based on any comorbidity as well as child and family preferences. This treatment generally will include pharmacotherapy (usually with stimulant medication) along

with adjunctive psychoeducation, behavioral therapy, environmental changes, and, at times, supportive psychotherapy of the child, the family, or both. Non-pharmacological treatment modalities are well accepted by parents and probably significantly underused in primary care settings.

8. There should be documentation in the medical record showing evidence that appropriate diagnostic criteria for ADHD have been met, that common comorbid conditions have been assessed, that there is a clear treatment plan, and that there is appropriate follow-up, including medication monitoring for efficacy, adverse effects, and ongoing need.

9. There is little evidence to suggest that stimulant abuse or diversion is currently a major problem, particularly among those with ADHD, although recent trends suggest that this could increase with the expanding production and use of stimulants. Clinicians need to be mindful of the risk of abuse and diversion: in addition to keeping careful records of medication prescribed, they may consider alternatives to stimulant use in patients at high risk (eg, patient or family members with substance use disorders or bipolar or conduct disorder co-occurrent in the patient).

POSTSCRIPT

Are We Turning Too Easily to Medication to Address the Needs of Our Children?

The arguments around the use of medication are powerful. Both sides in this debate hold that drugs can be the right answer to a problem. They disagree, however, on whether or not society is using the medications to create new problems.

Diller challenges the medical profession to break free of the "social trap" of using medication to support societal demands. He sees the consequence of continuing along the current path a life where much about human behavior becomes attributable to a disability that is out of the individual's control, except for the ingestion of a magic pill.

A darker view is predicated by Peter Breggin, the author of *Talking Back to Ritalin* (1998) and *Talking Back to Prozac* (1995). In addition to doubting the existence of many of the "disabilities" that are being identified, Breggin views children as the new market for drug companies that have saturated adult need. He warns that many of the prescribed drugs have not been adequately tested on children and also cautions against the "cloak of acceptability" that might come with Food and Drug Administration (FDA) approval. He worries that we may be heading toward a time when more children use these prescribed drugs than tobacco.

Sydney Walker (*The Hyperactivity Hoax: How to Stop Drugging Your Child and Find Real Medical Help,* 1998) suggests that, for today's system of managed care, a prescription for Ritalin is faster and easier than finding the real cause for distressing behavior. He expresses concern, however, that time spent on Ritalin (or similar medications) is time spent away from real treatment for a range of causes, including "medical disorders, lifestyle problems or just plain bad behavior."

Supporting the idea that people turn too quickly to Ritalin, Thomas Armstrong's book *ADD/ADHD Alternatives in the Classroom* (1999) offers a range of interventions, of which Ritalin may be one.

ISSUE 17

Should Parents Choose Cochlear Implants for Their Deaf Children?

YES: Thomas Balkany, Annelle V. Hodges, and Kenneth W. Goodman, from "Cochlear Implants for Young Children: Ethical Issues," in Warren Estabrooks, ed., *Cochlear Implants for Kids* (Alexander Graham Bell Association for the Deaf and Hard of Hearing, 1998)

NO: National Association of the Deaf, from "NAD Position Statement on Cochlear Implants," http://www.nad.org/info center/newsroom/positions/CochlearImplants.html (October 6, 2000)

ISSUE SUMMARY

YES: Thomas Balkany, Annelle V. Hodges, and Kenneth W. Goodman, of the University of Miami, argue that the Deaf community actively works to dissuade families from choosing cochlear implants for their children, preferring to have the decision made by Deaf individuals as a way to perpetuate the existence of a separate culture. The authors maintain that parents must decide whether or not their children receive cochlear implants, based on each child's best interest.

NO: The National Association of the Deaf (NAD), an education and advocacy organization committed to supporting the deaf and the hard of hearing, uses its updated position paper on cochlear implants to express concern that medical professionals will dissuade parents from considering the positive benefits of the Deaf community and choose, instead, a medical procedure that is not yet proven.

W hen a hearing family learns that their child is deaf, a sense of loss descends. They feel troubled, guilty, and desperate to "make things better." Teams of medical professionals and therapists arrive with interventions, remediation regimens, and hearing aids. The goal is to make the hearing problem go away—to "fix" the disability.

What would you do if your child was profoundly deaf and you thought a medical procedure could make hearing possible? Many parents jump at this chance when they learn of cochlear implants, a technology that, when it works correctly, can help people hear environmental sounds and conversation well enough for learning to occur. Who would not jump at the opportunity to help their child communicate more efficiently and learn through speech?

In reality, a lot of parents cringe instead of jump when they consider that their child, who can be fluent in American Sign Language (ASL), will lose his or her natural signed language and be unable to communicate and share the culture of her or his Deaf parents (capital "D" intended in reference to the culture of the Deaf). The cringing can become downright fear when they learn that this "medical miracle" might result in facial paralysis and no change in the child's hearing status. Families who belong to the Deaf community do not see themselves as disabled. The birth of a deaf child is greeted with joy and happiness—a celebration of a child with whom the family can freely communicate and share cultural values and traditions.

Cochlear implants replace a damaged cochlea (middle ear) with battery-powered technology to electronically stimulate the nerves that convey sound. Surgically inserted behind the ear, the device is connected to an external microphone and speech processor.

Implants, which were first approved for use in 1985, have caused a huge controversy between medical professionals and the Deaf community. Parents—especially those who are hearing and give birth to children who are deaf—find themselves in the middle of this debate. The choices they make—and the way their choices are made—pose a challenge to which schools must react.

In the following selection, Thomas Balkany, Annelle V. Hodges, and Kenneth W. Goodman examine the influences that parents face when deliberating cochlear implant surgery for their children and conclude that excessive force is being exerted by the Deaf community to influence parents away from a promising technological development. Although they acknowledge the value of Deaf culture, Balkany et al. maintain that parents should not be pressured by those whose agenda is to continue a way of life that they fear is threatened by technology.

In the second selection, the National Association of the Deaf asserts that the pressure comes from another direction and cautions parents not to be enchanted by a technology that has not been medically proven until they are advised by members of the Deaf community, who can speak for the quality of life without implants.

As you read these selections, consider the difficult choice for parents and the resultant educational impact. On whom should parents rely the most—doctors and therapists who are optimistic about the latest technology or Deaf individuals who live a rich life without hearing? Is a cochlear implant a safe choice for a child? Does it improve the child's educational chances? Does it result in isolation from the Deaf community?

Thomas Balkany, Annelle V. Hodges, and Kenneth W. Goodman

 **YES**

Cochlear Implants for Young Children: Ethical Issues

Ethics is the study of such concepts as goodness, duty, rightness, and obligation. In bioethics, these concepts are applied to practical problems raised in health care and biomedical research. Many of these problems arise along with the testing and adoption of new medical technologies. The second half of the 20th century has seen an extraordinary array of new and evolving technologies, ranging from organ transplantation and gene manipulation to life support systems and electronic medical records. This [selection] considers ethical controversy surrounding another technological development: cochlear implants for children, and is based in part on the authors' previous work in this area (Balkany, Hodges & Goodman, 1996).

Cochlear implants (CIs) represent an emerging technology that has the potential to change fundamentally the way people live. From the medical point of view, the CI is a safe and effective treatment for a severe disability—profound deafness. From the point of view of Deaf culture, however, it is unnecessary technology that is demeaning to deaf people's way of life (Lane, 1993). In the opinion of some Deaf activists, anything that prevents deafness or restores hearing to children who are deaf threatens Deaf society (Lane, 1993; Pollard, 1987). As a result of this perceived threat, there have been organized attempts to suppress CIs through the 1990s (Balkany, 1993).

It is essential to appreciate that Deaf society is dependent for perpetuation of itself on children who are deaf whose parents have normal hearing. Since 90 percent of children who are deaf are born to two hearing parents and 97 percent to at least one hearing parent, it is widely thought that if parents were given a safe and effective option to provide hearing to their child, many would choose to do so. If a large number of children who are deaf did not enter Deaf society, that society could be essentially changed. And because medical technology affects society, conflicts of an ethical nature may occur.

Members of mainstream society, or even the blind (who share with the deaf the inability to utilize one of humankind's dominant senses, but may not otherwise be similar), may have difficulties understanding opposition to providing a child who is deaf with the ability to hear. However, many in the Deaf

From Thomas Balkany, Annelle V. Hodges, and Kenneth W. Goodman, "Cochlear Implants for Young Children: Ethical Issues," in Warren Estabrooks, ed., *Cochlear Implants for Kids* (Alexander Graham Bell Association for the Deaf and Hard of Hearing, 1998). Copyright © 1998 by Warren Estabrooks. Reprinted by permission of The Alexander Graham Bell Association for the Deaf and Hard of Hearing. http://www.agbell.org. References omitted.

community see their way of life as emotionally fulfilling, promising, and independent without hearing (Balkany, 1993; Balkany & Hodges, 1995; Balkany, 1995). Some Deaf leaders also claim that the deaf are an oppressed linguistic minority and that any intervention to provide hearing to children who are deaf is inherently racist (Lane, 1993).

In the case of cochlear implants for children, the elements of conflict may be framed as issues that concern honesty, autonomy, beneficence, the best interests of the child, the needs of a linguistic minority to perpetuate itself, the cost of deafness to society, and acceptance of diversity.

Truthfulness

It is inherent that CI teams recommending implantation truthfully provide full information to parents as part of the process of obtaining informed consent. This includes not only describing the risks and benefits of the operation, but also ensuring that parents understand the limitations of the technology, the requirement for auditory (re)habilitation, as well as the options of joining Deaf society, communicating in American Sign Language (ASL), and avoiding "treatment" of deafness entirely.

Deaf culture is rich and diverse, and its members are bonded by ASL as well as by social and political organizations (Balkany, 1993; Lane, Hoffmeister, & Bahan, 1996). Deaf people attend parties, date, marry, have families, and raise children. In short, there are many positive aspects of life in the Deaf community, and they are best described to parents by a member of Deaf society.

Just as CI teams do with CIs, Deaf society proponents have an inherent responsibility to describe fully the positive as well as the negative aspects of life in Deaf society and to state their reasons for opposition to restoration of hearing. As in the informed-consent process for surgery, this discussion needs to be truthful and complete, allowing parents the autonomy to decide for themselves whether their child should receive a CI. Unfortunately, many members of Deaf society have been misinformed about CIs. One reason this has occurred is that the average graduate of a Deaf residential high school reads at a third- to fourth-grade level (Dolnick, 1993; Conrad, 1979) and is thus incapable of accessing moderately sophisticated published information in the lay media. Since there is no written form of ASL, many in the Deaf community rely on informal sources of information such as newsletters and storytellers at Deaf clubs. Deaf leaders and educators who, to a substantial degree, control this information, have misled the Deaf community in a highly successful effort to generate opposition to CIs (Balkany, 1995).

Examples of the misleading, pejorative picture of CIs painted by Deaf leaders include articles in Deaf culture newsletters:

> "I would be remiss not to equate cochlear implants with genocide." (Silver, 1992)

> "There is absolutely no question that our government has a hidden agenda for deaf children much akin to Nazi experiments on Holocaust victims." (Silver, 1992)

> "Using deaf children as 'lab rats' and medical guinea pigs is
> profoundly disturbing." (Roots, 1994)

Much more distressing, however, are inventions by respected colleagues designed to sway public opinion. Dr. Yerker Andersson, Professor and Chairman, Department of Deaf Studies at Gallaudet University and Emeritus President of the World Federation of the Deaf, published an article in the *World Federation of the Deaf News* in which he reported (without supporting reference) a surgeon who was "eager to use his skills on 17 Deaf individuals." According to Prof. Anderson, "Three died due to complications and one became mentally ill. The rest were failures" (Andersson, 1994). In fact, no deaths or cases of mental illness have been caused by CIs, and after hundreds of scientific papers and years of study, the U.S. Federal Drug Administration, medical oversight organizations, and even insurance carriers have concluded that CIs are safe and effective (Balkany, 1993). To say simply that Andersson was incorrect is to underestimate his scholarly abilities.

It is generally considered unethical to mislead people purposefully in order to persuade them to a point of view. The ethical principle violated by Andersson and others is autonomy as it relates to self-determination. People are deprived of their right to decide for themselves when they have been purposefully misled.

It is not surprising that, as a result of widespread misinformation, there is widespread misunderstanding. Many people who are deaf fervently believe that CIs are often fatal or severely damaging to children and they are therefore opposed to them.

The following are representative verbatim quotations from the future leaders of the Deaf community, college students at Gallaudet:

> "I read few articles about how cochlear implant. For deaf people died from cochlear implant. It was explained about how cochlear implant affected to brain damage."

> "I feel that cochlear implants are wrong because it makes the recipient a robot with wires sticking out of their head."

> "I may not aware of cochlear implant much but I do have a strong against it" (letters to the William House Cochlear Implant Study Group, a committee of the American Academy of Otolaryngology—Head and Neck Surgery, 1993; author's files).

Internal Inconsistency and Conflict of Interest

Other examples of failure to respect the value of truthfulness are seen in Deaf leaders' advocacy of mutually contradictory positions. For example, it is claimed that deafness is not a disability and, at the same time, that people who are deaf are entitled to disability benefits amounting to billions of dollars per year. Another is that CIs do not work and also that they work so well as to eliminate deafness (genocide). Consciously supporting both sides of mutually exclusive arguments in order to influence public opinion is not considered ethical behavior. Deaf advocates must decide whether to tell parents that the deaf or hard of hearing are independent or that the majority require disability (and other entitlement) benefits. They must decide whether it is ethical to say to parents that CIs don't work and to politicians that CIs work so well that they are genocidal.

Deaf activists who believe that their way of life is threatened by CIs may find themselves in conflict of interest. Barbara White, writing as an Associate Professor at Gallaudet [University], succinctly reveals this conflict of interest: "... the future of the deaf community is at stake. An entire subculture of America will no longer exist" (letters to the William House Cochlear Implant Study Group, a committee of the American Academy of Otolaryngology—Head and Neck Surgery, 1993; author's files). (Ear surgeons may be at similar risk for conflict of interest. It is estimated that CI surgery, however, constitutes less than one-tenth of one percent of the operations performed by otologists. A CI program, rather than generating income, actually costs a great deal to sustain by cost shifting and philanthropy.)

This potential conflict of interest among members of the Deaf community may operate to the disadvantage of individual children who are deaf. Australian physician Henley Harrison wrote, "The motive in opposing cochlear implants in children is self-interest rather than the children's welfare... it is the welfare of the children that should be borne in mind, not some other group" (Harrison 1991).

Ethical standards hold that Deaf advocates should reveal such conflicts of interest to parents who are considering the merits of life in Deaf society for their children. As a three-generation member of the Deaf community warns, "Parents should cast a cautious eye towards anyone wanting to sacrifice a deaf child towards preserving a culture (Bertling, 1994)"

In short, representatives of the Deaf community who wish to influence parents and the public must begin truthfully to reveal both the advantages and the disadvantages of life in Deaf society. Only in this way can parents make an informed decision regarding the best interests of their child.

Is Deafness a Disability?

Examination of the position that deafness constitutes neither a handicap nor a disability, but only an oppressed linguistic minority (Lane et al., 1996) is a central issue in the discourse about CIs for children. Deaf leaders surely understand that if deafness is not a disability, people who are deaf or hard of hearing must give up billions of dollars in public assistance that is intended for the disabled. In writing from the ethical perspective, Englehardt (1986) defines disability as the failure to achieve an expected state of function. Boorse (1975) more precisely defines disability as occurring (a) when a specific function is impaired, (b) there is reduced ability below typical efficiency, or (c) a limitation of functional ability occurs with reference to the patient's age or gender group.

It is clear that, in addition to its cultural definition, deafness fits the functional definition of a disability; but how does it compare with other disabilities? According to a California Department of Rehabilitation survey published in 1993, in which clients with all types of disabilities filled out self-assessment forms, deafness was associated with the lowest educational level, the lowest family income, the lowest percentage working, the lowest percentage in professional/technical jobs, and the poorest *self-assessment* of well-being (Harris, Anderson, & Novak, 1995). This study suggests that deafness is not only a disability, but that it may be among the most disabling of disabilities.

To deny that deafness is a disability, Deaf leaders must also deny its cost to society: $377,000 per child in K–12 residential Deaf school education (estimated $121.8 billion for educating all people who are deaf or hard of hearing at residential schools), $2.5 billion per year in lost workforce productivity, and more than $2 billion annually for the cost of equal access, Social Security Disability Income, Medicare, and other entitlements of the disabled (National Institutes of Health, 1992). As Tom Bertling, a third-generation member of Deaf culture, notes in his book, *A Child Sacrificed,* "Virtually every aspect of the deaf community is dependent on government support for the disabled" (Bertling, 1994).

Perhaps the greatest monetary cost to society of the disability of deafness is in education. It is estimated that the cost of kindergarten through 12th-grade education in Rhode Island is about $9,000 per hearing child. For children who are deaf who are mainstreamed in public schools, the cost jumps to $44,000 per child. If the same deaf students attend residential schools for the Deaf, the cost becomes $429,000 per child (Johnson, Mauk, Takeawa, Simon, et al., 1993).

At this high cost, what are the outcomes of current methods of, and approaches to, educating students who are deaf or hard of hearing? The average reading level of an adult who is deaf is at third or fourth grade (National Institutes of Health, 1992); further, when students who are deaf or hard of hearing finish high school, three of four cannot read a newspaper (Dolnick, 1993). In large part because of this low educational outcome, the deaf are too often unemployed or underemployed, resulting in a cost to society of $2.5 billion per year in lost wages (National Institutes of Health, 1992).

The Deaf community is well aware of the rights of the disabled under the Americans with Disabilities Act. As an example, a woman who was deaf sued a Maryland volunteer fire department because she was not selected to be a fire fighter (Strom, 1994). She was presumably unable to hear sirens, alarms, calls for help, or instructions for emergency action, and she could not express her own needs or instructions with sign language while holding a fire hose or climbing a ladder.

A controversial risk of deafness that is rarely discussed with parents is the prevalence of psychological disorders. Although the relationship has been confirmed by hundreds of independent investigators and scientific papers, the data on morbidity have been attributed by Deaf leaders both to poor parenting and to culturally/linguistically biased testing (Lane, 1993). Debate over the value of such data notwithstanding, ethical representatives of Deaf society must decide whether it is appropriate to discuss these studies with parents whom they are counseling about life in Deaf culture.

Another area that remains obscured from parents is much more difficult to approach delicately. Tom Bertling, in his second book, *No Dignity for Joshua*

(1997), describes in painful detail the ongoing problem with the physical, emotional, and sexual abuse that occurs, especially to the very young children, in residential Deaf schools. He feels that abuse is widespread, owing to a combination of low salaries paid to the nonprofessional members of the staff at state-run Deaf schools, a tendency among the Deaf community to conceal internal affairs, quasi-acceptance of such behavior within Deaf culture, and difficult communication between parents and their children who use ASL. Bertling's experiences are supported by scientific studies of over 480 abused children by Sullivan and colleagues (Sullivan, Brookhouser, Scanlan, Knutson, et al., 1991) showing a high incidence of sexual abuse in residential Deaf schools. On the basis of this awareness, several states are interceding to provide better supervision, especially for children who are deaf under the age of five years. (Bertling, 1994). Although similar problems may also occur at any residential school where poorly trained staff are underpaid, Deaf advocates must decide whether the ethical principle of truthfulness requires that parents be made aware of possible problems of sexual and other abuse at residential Deaf schools.

Deaf Leaders vs. Parents

Deaf activities hold conferences on the unseemly topic, "Who Owns the Deaf Child?" (Barringer, 1993). Their answer is that children who are deaf or hard of hearing are de facto members of the Deaf community and that hearing parents are obliged to "give up the child" (a phrase used by the Deaf) to be acculturated by Deaf society (Dolnick, 1993).

By this, Deaf activists mean that the usual values taught in families, including morals, ethics, religion, love, security, self-esteem, as well as language, should be taught by culturally Deaf adults who are not part of the child's family (Lane, 1993). This is process is termed *horizontal acculturation* (as opposed to *vertical acculturation,* in which these values are taught by parent to child, generation after generation). They claim that horizontal acculturation is best accomplished by removing the child from the home and placing him or her in a residential Deaf school (Lane, 1993).

Dr. Marina McIntire, director of ASL programs at Northeastern University, notes, "It has been argued that hearing parents have 'the right' to raise youngsters who are linguistically and culturally like themselves. We disagree" (letters to the William House Cochlear Implant Study Group, a committee of the American Academy of Otolaryngology–Head and Neck Surgery, 1993; author's files). Roz Rosen, president of the U.S. National Association of the Deaf in 1992, concurs: "Hearing parents are not qualified to decide about implants" (Coffey, 1992). In his book, *The Mask of Benevolence,* Dr. Harlan Lane states that parents cannot make decisions for their own child who is deaf because they don't "really know the patient" and are in a "conflict of interest with their own child." Lane has previously taken the position that a culturally Deaf adult who is not related to the child should be empowered to override the child's parents and make the decision as to whether a child should receive a CI (Lane, 1993).

This proposed intrusion into the American family is in direct conflict with Public Laws 94-142 and 99-4457, which ensure that children who are deaf are educated in the least restrictive environment (i.e., most like nonhandicapped children). These laws empower families of deaf children, and are directly opposed to horizontal acculturation (Gearhart, Wright, 1979; Katz, Marthis, & Merril, 1978).

Important Questions

Thus, two important questions arise regarding CIs for children: (1) Who should decide for the child? and (2) According to what standards should the decision be made?

The courts, as well as legal scholars and ethicists, concur that the rights and concerns of self-interest groups should be strictly excluded from decisions concerning the well-being of individual children (Buchanan & Brock, 1989). Interference from outside groups deprives families of their right to privacy. As Buchanan and Brock (1989) state in their book, *Deciding for Others: The Ethics of Surrogate Decision Making,* "the family must have great freedom from oversight, control and intrusion to make important decisions about the welfare of its children. Society should be reluctant to intercede in a family's decision." Parents exercise free informed consent on behalf of their children. "Others do not have the right to intervene in their . . . actions" (Englehardt, 1986).

In addition, "There must be a clear locus of authority or decision making will lack coherence, continuity and accountability" (Buchanan & Brock, 1989). Only the child's parents, or in their absence, a legal guardian who has authority for all aspects of the child's life, can provide such continuity and accountability. The suggestion that a culturally Deaf individual be appointed to decide whether a child should or should not receive a CI (or, for that matter, any other medical treatment or procedure) would violate the principle of a clear locus of authority because that individual would not have authority or responsibility for any aspect of the child's life.

However, parental rights to make health care decisions for children, while broad, are not unlimited. For instance, a decision to forgo treatment for a disability or other treatable disorder might appropriately be regarded as neglect. Nontheless, the exercise of a parent's judgment is rarely constrained, and only in extreme cases of neglect is parental judgment overridden.

Parents must bear the consequences and are financially responsible for decisions made about their children. Thus, only parents can decide for the child. But according to what principles should the choice be made?

Autonomy and Beneficence

Buchanan and Brock (1989) identify two underlying ethical values in making decisions for others: respect for self-determination (autonomy) and concern for well-being (beneficence).

In foreseeing the desire of special-interest groups such as Deaf society for influence, Engelhardt (1986) states, "This principle of autonomy provides moral grounding for public policies aimed at defending the innocent." In exercising autonomy for their children, parents act within the rights of their children, which include freedom of choice, respect for the individual, and free, informed consent to make decisions on behalf of their child. Engelhardt (1986) defines free choices, as "being unrestrained by prior commitments or justified authority, and being free from coercion."

Associated with the right to self-determination is the right to privacy. When Deaf activists attempt to impose their wishes on parents of deaf children and suggest that parents are in conflict of interest with their own children, that they are not aware of their own children's best interests, and that only culturally Deaf adults should be allowed to act as proxy decision makers on behalf of the deaf child (Lane, 1993), they ignore the family's right to privacy and self-determination and, in doing so, trample the family's autonomy.

The ethical value of beneficence also guides parents. In simplest terms, it involves a prudent effort to do good and avoid evil (Englehardt, 1986). Advocates of Deaf culture who claim that making CIs available to children who are deaf is tantamount to "genocide" for Deaf culture are more concerned with doing good and avoiding evil to their culture than honoring the value of beneficence as it applies to the child.

Beneficence also applies to the child's "right to an open future" (Buchanan & Brock, 1989). Children have clear interest in maintaining and developing functional abilities. The ability to hear not only has communicative value but also provides auditory enjoyment and is important to safety. Children who are deaf or hard of hearing also have an "opportunity interest" regarding preservation of opportunity for their future education, employment, and interpersonal relationships. Educational and employment expectations for culturally Deaf persons are unfortunately lower than those for hearing people (Balkany & Hodges, 1995; Dolnick, 1993). Since 99.8 percent of the population of the United States cannot communicate in ASL (Padden, 1987), opportunities for personal relationships (teachers, bus drivers, neighbors, friends) are highly restricted by primary or sole communication in ASL. Conversely, entering the hearing world may increase opportunity for education, employment, and personal relationships.

Standards for Making Surrogate Decisions

In addition to the two ethical values mentioned, there are three well-established standards for making surrogate decisions: advance directive, substituted judgment, and best interest. If an advance directive has been established by the patient, such as a living will or a specific nomination of surrogate, it should be meticulously followed. If none is available, a family member should make decisions on the basis of substituted judgment (using knowledge of the person, the surrogate does what he or she believes the person would do under the circumstances, if the person were competent). Neither of these first two standards applies to children. The third guiding standard, which does apply to children, is that of best interest. It is the parents' responsibility to make decisions according to their understanding of what is in the best interest of their child.

Diversity

A possible solution to the ethical conflict between the child's best interest and the needs of Deaf society to perpetuate itself lies in the well-established principle of social diversity. Efforts by Deaf leaders to keep the Deaf community pure, however, systematically exclude people who may be slightly different, for example, children who are deaf or hard of hearing and who have CIs. This demand for cultural purity, and the attendant exclusionary behavior, is generally not tolerated in advanced societies.

Diversity is a valued strength of modern society that requires open-mindedness and fairness. Whereas Deaf leaders rightfully insist that mainstream society accept Deaf persons, Deaf society itself systematically excludes children who are deaf or hard of hearing and who use CIs. As Bienvenue and Colonomos state, " ... implanted children can never be fully accepted within the Deaf community" (letters to the William House Cochlear Implant Study Group, a committee of the American Academy of Otolalryngology—Head and Neck Surgery, 1993; author's files). Lane (1993) agrees that if CI patients "turn to the deaf community for support, they experience discrimination." Donnel Ashmore states that "if a child shows 'signs of hearism' this will result in a hostile, silent reprimand" (Lane, 1993).

CI recipients in elementary schools have recently been taught a new sign for CIs by adult interpreters for the Deaf: the sign for "snake bite" made behind the ear. Such stigmatization is typical of societies that attempt to keep their ranks "pure" and avoid diversity.

Deaf advocates who oppose the diversity that children with CIs might bring seem to ignore the fact that the Deaf community is already diverse—socially, economically, educationally, and politically. Welcoming children who are deaf or hard of hearing and who are "different" (because they can use the CI to help them communicate) to be part of their community may enlarge and strengthen Deaf society.

Changing With the Times

Two recent strategic shifts in position have been notable in opposition to CIs: (a) in view of data showing remarkable hearing and language acquisition by children with CIs, some leaders have stopped emphasizing that CIs don't work and have begun to promote the notion that even if CIs restored hearing perfectly, they would be unacceptable (Lane, 1993); and (b) many Deaf leaders have retreated from their arguments that a representative of Deaf culture must decide whether a child receives a CI. They now agree that parents must be allowed that choice (Lane et al., 1996). It is hoped that others will follow this logic.

Another recent position adopted by some Deaf leaders is that cochlear implant professionals are in violation of United Nations conventions proscribing limitation of the growth of linguistic minorities. It would follow that since CIs work, they would limit the growth of the Deaf community (a linguistic minority): therefore, CIs are forbidden by the United Nations. This line of reasoning clearly establishes that these leaders are more concerned with the needs of their culture than with the best interests of deaf children.

In summary, the term deafness describes both an important, respected way of life and a disability. The ethical standard of truthfulness requires that representatives of Deaf society inform parents of both the positive and the negative qualities of life in Deaf society and that CI teams do the same regarding CIs.

The ethical values of autonomy and beneficence and the need for a single locus of authority in raising children determine that *parents* decide whether their child should receive a CI. The guiding standard for such a surrogate decision is best interest. Thus, parents must determine what is in the best interest of their child. The need of Deaf society to perpetuate itself has no bearing on that decision, although parents should consider the opinions and experiences of truthful Deaf adults.

The Deaf community should demand the same acceptance of diversity from itself that it does from mainstream society. There must be room for all who wish to join. Deaf society's goal of ethnic purity and its exercise of discriminatory exclusion of deaf children who have CIs countervail the norms of ethical behavior and weaken its moral position.

References

Andersson, Y. (1994). Do we want cochlear implants? *World Federation of the Deaf News, 1,* 3–4.

Balkany, T. (1993). A brief perspective on cochlear implants. *New England Journal of Medicine, 328,* 281–282.

Balkany, T. (1995). The rescuers, cochlear implants: Habilitation or genocide? *Advances in Otorhinolarynology, 50,* 4–8.

Balkany, T., & Hodges, A.V. (1995). Misleading the deaf community about cochlear implantation in children. *Annals of Otolaryngology, 104* (Suppl. 116), 148–149.

Balkany, T. Hodges, A.V., & Goodman, K.W. (1996) Ethics of cochlear implantation in young children. *Archives of Otolaryngology—Head & Neck Surgery, 114,* 748–755.

Barringer, F. (1993, May 16). Pride in a soundless world. *New York Times* (pp. 1, 14).

Bertling, T. (1994). *A child sacrificed to the deaf culture.* Wilsonville, OR: Kodiak Media Group.

Bertling, T. (1997). *No dignity for Joshua.* Wilsonville, OR; Kodiak Media Group.

Boorse, C. (1975). On the distinction between disease and illnesses. *Philosophy and Public Affairs, 5* 61.

Buchanan, A.E., & Brock, D.W. (1989). *Deciding for others. The ethics of surrogate decision making.* Cambridge, MA: Cambridge University Press.

Coffey, R. (1992). Caitlin's story on "60 Minutes." *The Biocultural Center News, 53,* 3.

Conrad, R. (1979). *The deaf school child: Language and cognitive function.* New York: Harper & Row.

Dolnick, E. (1993, September). Deafness as culture. *The Atlantic Monthly,* 37–53.

Englehardt, H.T. (1986). *The foundation of bioethics.* New York: Oxford University Press.

Gearhart, B.R. & Wright, W.S. (1979). *Organizations and administration of educational programs for exceptional children.* Springfield, IL: Charles C. Thomas.

Harris J.P., Anderson, J.P., and Novak R. (1995). An outcome study of cochlear implants in deaf patients. *Archives of Otolaryngology—Head & Neck Surgery, 121,* 398–404.

Harrison, H.C. (1991). Deafness in children. *Medical Journal of Australia, 154,* 11.

Johnson, J.L., Mauk, G.W., Takekawa, K.M., Simon, P.R., et al. (1993). Implementing a statewide system of services for infants with hearing disabilities. *Seminars in Hearing, 14,* 105–118.

Katz, L., Marthis, S.L., & Merril, E.C. (1978). *The deaf child in the public schools.* Danville, IL: Interstate Printers.

Lane, H. (1993). *The mask of benevolence.* New York: Vintage Books.

Lane, H. Hoffmeister, R., & Bahan, B. (1996). *A journey into the deaf world.* San Diego, CA: Dawn Sign Press.

National Institutes of Health Consensus Statement. (1992). *Early identification of hearing impairment in infants and young children, 11* (1), 1–12.

Padden, C.A. (1987). American Sign Language. In *Gallaudet encyclopedia of deaf people and deafness* (Vol. 3, pp. 43–53). Washington, DC: Gallaudet University Press.

Pollard, R.Q. (1987). Cross cultural ethics in the conduct of deafness research. *Rehabilitation Psychology, 37,* 87–99.

Roots, J. (1994). Deaf Canadian fighting back. *World Federation of the Deaf News,* 2–3.

Silver, A. (1992). Cochlear implant: Surefire prescription for long-term disaster. *TBC News, 53* 4–5.

Strom, K.E., (1994, February). Disability regulations review. *Hearing Review,* 12–14.

Sullivan, P.M., Brookhouser, P.E., Scanlan, J.M., Knutson, J.F., et al. (1991). Patterns of physical and sexual abuse of communicatively handicapped children. *Annals of Otology, Rhinology & Laryngology, 100,* 188–194.

NO

National Association of the Deaf

NAD Position Statement on Cochlear Implants

The NAD [National Association of the Deaf] recognizes that diversity within the deaf community itself, and within the deaf experience, has not been acknowledged or explained very clearly in the public forum. Deafness is diverse in its origin and history, in the adaptive responses made to it, and in the choices that deaf adults and parents of deaf children continue to make about the ever-increasing range of communication and assistive technology options. Diversity requires mutual respect for individual and/or group differences and choices.

The NAD welcomes all individuals regardless of race, religion, ethnic background, socioeconomic status, cultural orientation, mode of communication, preferred language use, hearing status, educational background, and use of technologies. The NAD also welcomes deaf, hard of hearing and hearing family members, educators, and other professionals serving deaf and hard of hearing children and adults.

The NAD subscribes to the wellness model upon which the physical and psychosocial integrity of deaf children and adults is based. The general public needs information about the lives of the vast majority of deaf and hard of hearing individuals who have achieved optimal adjustments in all phases of life, have well-integrated and healthy personalities, and have attained self-actualizing levels of functioning, all with or without the benefits of hearing aids, cochlear implants, and other assistive devices.

The NAD recognizes all technological advancements with the potential to foster, enhance, and improve the quality of life of all deaf and hard of hearing persons. During the past three decades, technological developments such as closed captioning, email and the Internet, two-way pagers, text telephones, telecommunications relay services, video interpreting services, visual alerting devices, vibro-tactile devices, hearing aids, amplification devices, audio loop and listening systems have had an important role in leveling the playing field. The role of the cochlear implant in this regard is evolving and will certainly change in the future. Cochlear implants are not appropriate for all deaf and hard of hearing children and adults. Cochlear implantation is a technology that represents a tool to be used in some forms of communication, and

From National Association of the Deaf, "NAD Position Statement on Cochlear Implants," http://www.nad.org/infocenter/newsroom/positions/CochlearImplants.html (October 6, 2000). Copyright © 2000 by NAD. Reprinted by permission of The National Association of the Deaf. http://www.nad.org.

not a cure for deafness. Cochlear implants provide sensitive hearing, but do not, by themselves, impart the ability to understand spoken language through listening alone. In addition, they do not guarantee the development of cognition or reduce the benefit of emphasis on parallel visual language and literacy development.

The NAD recognizes the rights of parents to make informed choices for their deaf and hard of hearing children, respects their choice to use cochlear implants and all other assistive devices, and strongly supports the development of the whole child and of language and literacy. Parents have the right to know about and understand the various options available, including all factors that might impact development. While there are some successes with implants, success stories should not be over-generalized to every individual.

Rationale

The focus of the 2000 NAD position statement on cochlear implants is on preserving and promoting the psychosocial integrity of deaf and hard of hearing children and adults. The adverse effects of inflammatory statements about the deaf population of this country must be addressed. Many within the medical profession continue to view deafness essentially as a disability and an abnormality and believe that deaf and hard of hearing individuals need to be "fixed" by cochlear implants. This pathological view must be challenged and corrected by greater exposure to and interaction with well-adjusted and successful deaf and hard of hearing individuals.

The media often describe deafness in a negative light, portraying deaf and hard of hearing children and adults as handicapped and second-class citizens in need of being "fixed" with cochlear implants. There is little or no portrayal of successful, well adjusted deaf and hard of hearing children and adults without implants. A major reason implantation and oral language training have been pursued so aggressively by the media, the medical profession, and parents is not simply because of the hoped-for benefits that come with being able to hear in a predominantly hearing society but more because of the perceived burdens associated with being deaf.

Because cochlear implant technology continues to evolve, to receive mainstream acceptance, and to be acknowledged as part of today's reality, it is urgent to be aware of and responsive to the historical treatment of deaf persons. This perspective makes it possible to provide more realistic guidelines for parents of deaf and hard of hearing children and for pre-lingually and post-lingually deafened adults.

Wellness Model

Many deaf and hard of hearing people straddle the "deaf and hearing worlds" and function successfully in both. There are many people with implants who use sign language and continue to be active members of the deaf community and who ascribe to deaf culture and heritage. There are many deaf and hard of hearing individuals, with and without implants, who are high-achieving professionals, talented in every imaginable career field. They, too, are successfully effective parents, raising well-adjusted deaf, hard of hearing and hearing children. As citizens, they continue to make contributions to improve the quality of life for society at large. Deaf and hard of hearing individuals throughout the ages have demonstrated psychological strength and social skills when surviving and overcoming society's misconceptions, prejudices, and discriminatory attitudes and behaviors, thus attesting to their resilience, intelligence, and integrity.

Given the general lack of awareness about the reality of the wellness model, the NAD strongly urges physicians, audiologists, and allied professionals to refer parents to qualified experts in deafness and to other appropriate resources so that parents can make fully informed decisions—that is, decisions that incorporate far more than just the medical-surgical. Such decisions involve language preferences and usage, educational placement and training opportunities, psychological and social development, and the use of technological devices and aids.

The Cochlear Implant

The most basic aspect of the cochlear implant is to help the user perceive sound, i.e., the sensation of sound that is transmitted past the damaged cochlea to the brain. In this strictly sensorineural manner, the implant works: the sensation of sound is delivered to the brain. The stated goal of the implant is for it to function as a tool to enable deaf children to develop language based on spoken communication.

Cochlear implants do not eliminate deafness. An implant is not a "cure" and an implanted individual is still deaf. Cochlear implants may destroy what remaining hearing an individual may have. Therefore, if the deaf or hard of hearing child or adult later prefers to use an external hearing aid, that choice may be removed.

Unlike post-lingually deafened children or adults who have had prior experience with sound comprehension, a pre-lingually deafened child or adult does not have the auditory foundation that makes learning a spoken language easy. The situation for those progressively deafened or suddenly deafened later in life is different. Although the implant's signals to the brain are less refined than those provided by an intact cochlea, an individual who is accustomed to receiving signals about sound can fill in certain gaps from memory. While the implant may work quite well for post-lingually deafened individuals, this result just cannot be generalized to pre-lingually deafened children for whom spoken language development is an arduous process, requiring long-term commitment by parents, educators, and support service providers, with no guarantee that the desired goal will be achieved.

Parents

Parents face challenges when their child is born deaf or becomes deaf. At least ninety percent of deaf and hard of hearing children are born to hearing parents who usually want their children to be like themselves, to understand sound, to use their voices and verbally express their thoughts through spoken language, and to hear the voices and spoken language of those around them.

However, language and communication are not the same as speech, nor should the ability to speak and/or hear be equated with intelligence, a sense of well-being and lifelong success. Communication and cognition are vital ingredients of every child's development, regardless of the mode in which it is expressed, i.e., visual or auditory.

Despite the pathological view of deafness held by many within the medical profession, parents would benefit by seeking out opportunities to meet and get to know successful deaf and hard of hearing children and adults who are fluent in sign language and English, both with and without implants. The NAD encourages parents and deaf adults to research other options besides implantation. If implantation is the option of choice, parents should obtain all information about the surgical procedure, surgical risks, post-surgical auditory and speech training requirements, and potential benefits and limitations so as to make informed decisions.

Cochlear implant surgery is a beginning, not an end. The surgery decision represents the beginning of a process that involves a long-term, and likely, life-long commitment to auditory training, rehabilitation, acquisition of spoken and visual language skills, follow-up, and possibly additional surgeries. Whatever choices parents make, the primary goal should be to focus on the "whole child" and early language development/literacy and cognitive development. The absence of visual language opportunities can result in developmental delays that can be extremely difficult to reverse. Since the first six years are critical for language acquisition and usage, concurrent acquisition of visual and written language skills should be stressed.

Further improvements to cochlear implant technology and greater experience with educating and supporting pre-lingually deafened children and adults may later result in better outcomes for both of these populations than are achieved at present. In the meantime, though, parents of deaf and hard of hearing children need to be aware that a decision to forego implantation for their children does not condemn their children to a world of meaningless silence. Regardless of whether or not a deaf or hard of hearing child receives an implant, the child will function within both the hearing and the deaf communities. For these reasons, parents of pre-lingually deaf children presently have a reasonable basis upon which to decline implantation for their child. Parents must feel comfortable with their decision, whether they choose implantation or not.

Once parents have arrived at a decision, they want their decision to be validated. They seek reassurances often solely from within the medical and professional hearing health care community. This is a serious and major concern to the NAD. By releasing this position statement, the NAD seeks to alert, educate, and inform parents about deafness and the deaf community.

Recommendations

The NAD hereby makes the following recommendations for action:

Professional Training

Medical professionals have historically been the first point of contact for parents of deaf children. Their expertise is valuable but is primarily limited only to their medical areas of expertise. They should not be viewed as, nor should they function as, experts with regard to larger issues such as the educational, psychological, social, and linguistic needs of the deaf child. Medical professionals may be experts regarding the mysteries of the inner ear, but they are not experts regarding the inner lives of deaf children and adults. Psychological, social, educational, cultural and communication aspects of deafness, including the wellness model, must be a significant part of every medical school curriculum, especially within the specialty of otolaryngology. In-service training programs should be implemented for all interdisciplinary staff at cochlear implant centers that would include guidance and counseling methods with parents of deaf children and adults considering cochlear implants. These training programs should be conducted by professional counselors who are trained, qualified, and competent to work and communicate with deaf and hard of hearing children and adults and their families.

Early Assessment of Hearing Aid Benefit

It is widely understood and accepted that a trial period of hearing aid use is necessary prior to cochlear implantation. Advanced digital hearing aids should be explored. The NAD encourages that this effort be earnest and of appropriate duration for adequate assessment by objective testing and skilled observation of behaviors and communication skills. This assessment is complicated by the child's lack of prior auditory experience, and inability to communicate what s/he is hearing. The length of this trial period will vary with the individual. Further research by the medical and educational communities regarding objective hearing assessment and hearing aid trials is strongly encouraged.

Cochlear Implant Team

Candidacy assessment and surgery must be performed in a medical setting that has a close working relationship with a team of professionals that will provide ongoing long-term support to implant recipients. To be a responsible implant center, caution must be taken when describing the potential benefits of implantation, including risks, limitations, and long-term implications. Parents of deaf children and adults must be assisted in developing realistic and appropriate expectations. Critical to both pediatric and adult cochlear implantation and the long-range medical, audiological, psychological, social, emotional, educational, and vocational adjustment is access to implant centers fully complemented by an interdisciplinary staff, including rehabilitation specialists, psychologists and counselors. Implant center personnel must also work with and involve deafness professionals in education and in the helping professions. It takes a coordinated team of specialists, parents, educators and counselors to raise an implanted child and to support an implanted adult over an extended period of time. The implant team is also morally obligated to recognize when the implant experience has been unsuccessful and provide alternate strategies for language training.

Habilitation

An essential component of the cochlear implant process is habilitation. Parents and professionals must make a long-term commitment to integrating listening strategies throughout the child's day at home and at school. It is important to recognize that a newly implanted child is unable to understand spoken language through listening alone. Therefore parents and professionals should continue to use sign language to ensure age-appropriate psychological, social, cognitive, and language development.

Insurance Coverage

The NAD recommends that medical insurance carriers also provide fair and equitable coverage for hearing aid devices and associated support services.

Media

Reporters, journalists, anchors and directors of newspapers, television networks and film are encouraged to research and prepare their material more carefully and without bias. There is a serious need for a more balanced approach to fact-finding and reporting.

Research

Longitudinal research is critically needed, including a more thorough analysis of those for whom the implant is not working. Future research should involve highly controlled, manufacturer-independent and unbiased research on the long-term outcomes of childhood implants on auditory and communicative development, academic and intellectual development and achievement, psychological, social and emotional adjustment, and interpersonal relationship functioning. Comparative research on children without implants receiving parallel support services should also be conducted, especially those for whom sign language is the primary form of communication. Research findings relative to children with and without cochlear implants in educated lay terms must be made available and disseminated to deaf individuals, to parents of implanted children, to those in the helping professions, and to those contemplating implants.

Parents

The NAD knows that parents love and care deeply about their deaf children. Since the decision to perform implant surgery on the deaf child is made for the child, it is necessary for parents to become educated about cochlear implants—the potential benefits, the risks, and all the issues that they entail. During this critical education process, parents have both the need and the right to receive unbiased information about the pros and cons of cochlear implants and related matters. The NAD knows that parents want to make informed decisions. Parents also would benefit by opportunities to interact with successful deaf and hard of hearing adults, as well as with parents of deaf and hard of hearing children.

Deafness is irreversible. Even with the implant and increased sound perception, the child is still deaf. Cochlear implants are not a cure for deafness. The most serious parental responsibility from the very beginning is total commitment to, and involvement with, their child's overall development and well-being. Throughout the developmental years, the deaf child—implanted or not, mainstreamed or not—should receive education in deaf studies, including deaf heritage, history of deafness and deaf people, particularly stories and accounts of deaf people who have succeeded in many areas of life.

Support Services

Parents must understand that, after suitability testing and the decision-making process, the actual surgical procedure is just the beginning—a prelude to a lifetime proposition for the child and years of commitment by the parents. Implanted children are still deaf and will continue to require educational, psychological, audiological assessment, auditory and speech training, and language support services for a long period of time. Services for families and children should be provided in a manner that is consistent with standards set by the Individuals with Disabilities Education Act (IDEA), with focus on the whole child and the family. It is imperative that psychological support be available, including counseling services. Such services are to be available throughout the child's developmental years, often until adulthood.

Visual Environment

The NAD has always and continues to support and endorse innovative educational programming for deaf children, implanted or not. Such programming should actively support the auditory and speech skills of children in a dynamic and interactive visual environment that utilizes sign language and English. In closing, the NAD asserts that diversity in communication modes and cultures is our inherent strength, and that mutual respect and cooperation between deaf, hard of hearing, and hearing individuals ultimately benefit us all.

POSTSCRIPT

Should Parents Choose Cochlear Implants for Their Deaf Children?

Approximately 95 percent of deaf individuals are born with little or no hearing and are referred to as *prelingually deaf*. People who lose their hearing—through accident, illness, or aging—after they have acquired language are referred to as *postlingually deaf*.

The NAD and Balkany, Hodges, and Goodman agree on many points. They agree that individuals who had hearing during the critical period for learning language benefit more from cochlear implants than do those who are prelingually deaf. They also acknowledge that parents are under pressure, they agree on the sources of the pressure, and they all hold that the ultimate choice made by the parents should be accepted and valued. The two sides diverge when they weigh the merits and motivations of those who try to influence parental choice. There is much support for each point of view.

Linda Benton (*Hearing Loss*, 1997) speaks of her personal decision as an adult to undergo cochlear implant surgery despite the objections of her family. Melissa Chaikof, in the Cochlear Implant Association publication *Contact* (2000), relates the experiences of a deaf family of four who are all using implants now. Although each story acknowledges the difficulty of their medical and cultural choices as well as the competing influences brought to bear by various groups, all report satisfaction with the results of their surgeries.

Acknowledging that their views might change if implants are perfected and additional research certifies their efficacy, Harlan Lane, Robert Hoffmeister, and Ben Bahan (*A Journey Into the Deaf-World*) caution that the unnecessary surgical risks of cochlear implants are significant. Identifying the clash of cultures, they contend that Deaf individuals see no reason to operate on a healthy child, and they say that the opinions of those in the Deaf culture should have equal (if not superior) weight to those of hearing parents who are uninformed about the options that are open to their children.

Shelli Delost and Sarah Lashley (http://www.drury.edu/ess/ irconf/DelostLashley.html) recognize that hearing parents have the best interests of their children in mind, but they hold that these parents focus too much on their own experiences and that only consultation and guidance by Deaf individuals will help them see the potential within their deaf children.

The complexities of cochlear implant decisions are portrayed strongly in the film *Sound and Fury,* which received a 2001 Academy Award nomination for Best Documentary Feature. Following an extended family through deliberations over whether or not to provide implants for two deaf children, this film has sparked much controversy as well as an online discussion (http://www.thirteen.org/soundandfury/cochlear/debate.html) between the executive directors of the National Association of the Deaf and the Alexander Graham Bell Association, which advocates the use of implants for suitable candidates.

IDEA97 places decision-making power in the hands of the parents for educational programs. The NAD is concerned that parents will listen exclusively to doctors and therapists. Balkany, Hodges, and Goodman are concerned that parents will be swayed by Deaf individuals with a personal interest.

Child-rearing decisions are never easy. Decisions about surgery are always full of tension and doubt. The cochlear implant choice illustrates the intersection of medicine, culture, and education, an encounter that is increasing in frequency as technology affects disabilities.

It is clear that many questions are yet to be answered. Until they are, should parents take the advice of medical strangers and risk surgery for the possibility of verbal communication or trust the opinions of cultural strangers that their child will flourish with a language and in a culture other than the one of her or his parents? Whom should parents trust? And what is the appropriate educational response—rehabilitative medical therapies or enrollment in separate schools for the Deaf?

ISSUE 18

Do Students With Disabilities Benefit From Participating in High-Stakes Testing?

YES: Martha L. Thurlow and David R. Johnson, from "High-Stakes Testing of Students With Disabilities," *Journal of Teacher Education* (September/October 2000)

NO: Pixie J. Holbrook, from "When Bad Things Happen to Good Children: A Special Educator's Views of MCAS," *Phi Delta Kappan* (June 2001)

ISSUE SUMMARY

YES: Martha L. Thurlow, director of the National Center on Educational Outcomes, and David R. Johnson, director of the Institute on Community Integration, both at the University of Minnesota, assert that high-stakes testing may hold many benefits for students with disabilities, especially if the tests are carefully designed and implemented.

NO: Pixie J. Holbrook, a special education teacher and consultant, maintains that high-stakes testing marks children with disabilities as worthless failures, ignores their accomplishments and positive attributes, and seriously limits their range of possibilities in adult life.

$\mathbf{F}$ind a state that has instituted new tests to measure educational progress and you will find controversy. Add the element of including all students with disabilities and the emotional pitch increases dramatically.

Historically, most students with disabilities have been excluded from formal districtwide and national tests. Sometimes people assumed that these children would not do well and acted to spare them stress. At other times schools were concerned that participation of students with disabilities would reduce overall test scores. In order to maximize results, some districts worked to classify low-performing students into special education so that their scores would not be counted. Once a student's scores did not count, less attention was paid to the curriculum content of that child's education. Special education and general education often pursued very different goals.

IDEA97 changed the playing field with its mandate that schools be held accountable for the academic performance of all students—even those with significant disabilities. Parents and educators now choose from a number of participation options. The majority of students with disabilities can take the tests along with other students. Other students with disabilities use accommodations that remove the barriers of their disabilities—like Braille for students who are blind. For the very small number of students who cannot demonstrate what they know and can do with accommodations, an alternative test option is possible. Whatever the choice, the school and district—and sometimes the student —are held accountable for test results.

In all states these tests are used for accountability purposes. In some cases the stakes are highest for districts, which are held responsible for student performance. In these states penalties exist for schools that do not achieve to expectations, but there are no direct consequences for students. In other states, the stakes are highest for individual students—the test must be passed in order to be promoted or to graduate.

In the following selection, Martha L. Thurlow and David R. Johnson assert that strong opportunities exist for students with disabilities in this new world of high-stakes testing. If your score counts, *you* will count. Furthermore, schools will care more about curriculum and instruction for students with disabilities. And higher expectations will lead to greater gains. Thurlow and Johnson urge teachers and administrators to be actively involved in constructing and implementing tests that are truly fair to students and to schools.

In the second selection, Pixie J. Holbrook shares the struggles of her students, who are trying hard to jump the hurdles posed by a statewide test that is based on high-level academic skills and that must be passed before a high school diploma is granted. She knows that her students—and her own son—are able to develop skills that will serve them well as adults in the working world, but she agonizes over the possibility that their spirits will be crushed as they pursue a goal that is unattainable—and irrelevant.

As you read these selections, consider these questions: Is it fair to include students with disabilities in high-stakes testing when it is already known that they are doing poorly in school? Can high-stakes testing be designed and implemented to be fairer to all students? Would the "average" score be more reachable if the results of all children were included? Will the confidence of students with disabilities be destroyed by high-stakes tests, or will they—and their schools—rise to the challenge set for their peers? Who is accountable in your state? What happens when standards are not met?

**Martha L. Thurlow and
David R. Johnson**

 **YES**

High-Stakes Testing of Students
With Disabilities

High-stakes testing is becoming a common component of educational re-form. When the stakes are high for students, there is always concern about the potential for unintended consequences, such as increased rates of students dropping out of school. There are increased concerns when students have disabilities. Despite the apparent potential for unintended consequences, there are also intended effects to be considered—benefits to students and others....

Testing students with disabilities is not something new. These students take a series of individualized assessments when their eligibility for special education services is first under consideration. After that, they may be given additional tests to measure their progress toward the goals listed on their Individualized Education Plans (IEPs). Every 3 years, they are again administered a wide range of assessments designed to determine whether they are still eligible for services. These kinds of assessments have been in place for 25 years, since the enactment of Public Law 94-142, the Education of All Handicapped Children Act.

What is new is the requirement that students with disabilities participate in assessments that in many places were developed for students not receiving special education services. These tests include the state and district tests used to document how students are performing. Sometimes these tests are norm referenced, providing comparisons of children across the nation, and some-times they are standards based or criterion referenced, providing comparisons with specific standards.... [S]tates must document the number of students participating in the tests, report on their performance, and develop alternate assessments for students unable to participate in existing state or district tests. Guidelines must be developed to assist in deciding which students take state and district assessments and which take an alternate assessment. Performance reports are to be made available to the public with the same frequency and in the same detail as reports that are provided to the public for students without disabilities.

IDEA 97 [Individuals with Disabilities Education Act Amendment of 1997] added these new requirements for several reasons. Researchers had documented

From Martha L. Thurlow and David R. Johnson, "High-Stakes Testing of Students With Disabilities," *Journal of Teacher Education*, vol. 51, no. 4 (September/October 2000). Copyright © 2000 by The American Association of Colleges for Teacher Education. Reprinted by permission of Corwin Press, Inc. References omitted.

that when students are excluded from state or district assessments, several un-intended consequences occur. In addition to concerns about inappropriate re-ferrals to special education and increased rates of retention in grades prior to those tested, there are concerns about the focus of instruction for students not included in assessments. Teachers had reported how their students with disabil-ities were sent on field trips on the day of districtwide testing; parents told of receiving phone calls from the school principal suggesting that their son or daughter stay home on the day of testing to avoid a testing process that would be much too stressful for their child. These students, however, missed impor-tant experiences and instruction that other students received, simply because they were not taking the test. Eventually, excluded students suffered in many ways because expectations for them were lowered, and their access to the gen-eral education curriculum and to the benefits of standards-based reform was limited. Requirements to include students with disabilities in state and district assessments and to report on their performance recognize that students with disabilities benefit from being held to high standards, from having access to the general education curriculum, and from being part of the student body for which educators are held accountable for teaching.

Including students with disabilities in state and district assessments has always been done to some extent. Typically, however, only those students who could take the test in the same way that everyone else took the test (i.e., under standard administration conditions) were included in the assessments....

What It Takes for Students With Disabilities to Participate in Assessment Systems

Beginning from the assumption that it is beneficial for students with disabili-ties to participate in state and district assessments, and also beginning from the need to comply with federal law, it is important to ask what is required for these students to take state and district assessments in a way that best reflects what they have learned—what they know and can do. These are three basic consid-erations: (a) purpose of the assessment, (b) accommodations, and (c) alternate assessments.

Purpose.   Most of the initial discussion about the need for students with dis-abilities to participate in assessments occurred without considering the differ-ent purposes of state or district assessments. Initial concern was that schools were not being held accountable for teaching these students. Little thought was given to the assessments that were used for student accountability—to deter-mine whether students were promoted from one grade to the next or whether they received a diploma. High-stakes testing that has consequences for students with disabilities, however, becomes a tricky issue because of the students' dis-abilities, which may interfere with learning and with the student being able to actually demonstrate what she or he knows and can do.

Accommodations.   It is generally recognized that providing accommodations increases the participation of students with disabilities in assessments. Yet, controversy surrounds for use of accommodation, especially certain accommodations. This is evident in court cases about the use of scribes and word processors as well as new cases involving the use of spell checkers and readers. States and districts often have complex policies about the use of accommodations, and these policies often differ from one place to the next.

Despite the controversy, it is generally recognized that accommodations are an important aspect of the assessment of students with disabilities, just as they are for instruction. Examples of accommodations used during assessments are extended testing time, marking answers in the test booklet rather than on a separate sheet, being tested individually, and having directions repeated. There is much variability in the nature of accommodations, from setting and timing changes to changes in how the test is presented or how the student responds. There is also variability in how easy it is to provide accommodations to students. The logistics of providing accommodations is a concern with which schools are now dealing, sometimes with more resistance than necessary.

Alternate assessments. Alternate assessments are new in most states and districts. They are measures for students unable to take state or district assessments, usually less than 2% of the total student population (about 20% of students with disabilities). Most states are in the process of developing these assessments. Surveys indicate that states are taking a variety of approaches to alternate assessment procedures, from versions of paper-and-pencil tests to checklists to portfolios. In some places, alternate assessments are a way for some students to show that they have met the graduation requirement.

Including Students With Disabilities in Assessments With High Stakes for Students

The consequences of educational accountability systems for schools and educators are much better understood than are those for students. The consequences of high-stakes systems for students with disabilities are much less understood. Tests should be considered as high stakes for students with disabilities when the results are used to make critical decisions about the individual's access to education opportunity, grade-level retention or promotion, graduation from high school, or receipt of a standard diploma versus an alternative diploma (e.g., special education diploma, certificate of completion). The decisions all have immediate and long-range implications for the student. The use of exit exams to determine whether a student earns a high school diploma, for example, has lifelong consequences and directly affects an individual's economic self-sufficiency and well-being as an adult.

Access to Educational Opportunity

For students with disabilities and for others who experience difficulties on these tests, there is a variety of possible system responses. Test results, either favorable or unfavorable, are designed to have an effect on the content in focus as a curriculum, instructional strategies, intervention strategies to improve the learning of all students, professional development support for teachers and administrators, the use of assessment results, and the use and nature of test preparation materials. These and other examples are the intended consequences of using student test scores as an index of system performance. Information on student test scores can be used to revisit and modify the curriculum, instructional approaches, and strategies and to identify the skills teachers and administrators may need to address critical areas where students' scores are found to be poor.

There are, however, several unintended consequences for students, including students with disabilities who perform poorly on state and local tests. Observable consequences may include (a) increased referrals to special education for services, (b) lowered expectations of students as learners, (c) narrowing of the curriculum and instruction to focus on the specific learning outcomes assessed in state tests, (d) teaching to tests, (e) using test preparation materials that are closely linked to the assessment without making changes to the curriculum, (f) limiting the range of program options students can participate in because of intensified efforts to concentrate on areas of weakness identified by testing, and (g) the overall impact test scores have on judging whether a student will graduate from school with a standard education diploma. Although these consequences certainly affect all students, students with disabilities in particular are significantly affected by high-stakes testing programs.

These and other consequences potentially limit access to educational opportunities. A primary concern is that scores on high-stakes tests will be used to place students with disabilities in low-track classes, where they learn less than they are capable of learning. Research shows that when students with disabilities are placed in low-track classes, they do not catch up with their peers in other tracks. For students with disabilities, the IEP team, with general education involvement, should strive to maintain high standards and expectations for students, to provide meaningful access to the general education curriculum through appropriate accommodations and support systems, and to actively engage general education and special education teachers in collaborative instructional arrangements to support students in meeting state standards.

Retention and Social Promotion

State tests also become high stakes when they are used for grade-level retention and promotion decisions. Increasingly, states are requiring that schools and school districts use state test scores to determine whether students should be promoted to the next grade level.... Retention has been referred to as a kind of academic *redshirting,* that is, the act of keeping students back a grade to improve test scores. Retaining students could be viewed as an appropriate intervention; however, there is little research evidence to suggest that this is the case. Persuasive evidence indicates that repeating a grade does not improve the achievement of students with disabilities overall.

A second concern is based on documented increases in the dropout rate for students who have been retained. Dropping out of school is one of the most serious and pervasive problems facing special education programs nationally, yet very limited data are presently available on dropout rates among youth with disabilities. The last congressionally mandated study of the secondary school experiences of students with disabilities found that nearly 40% had left school by dropping out.

Graduation Requirements and Diploma Options

Some states have attached high-stakes exit exams to graduation since the late 1960s and early 1970s. Requirements that states set for graduation can range from Carnegie unit requirements (a certain number of class credits earned in specific areas) to the successful passing of minimum competency tests, high school exit exams, and/or a series of benchmark exams. States may also require almost any combination of these. Diversity in graduation requirements is complicated further by an increasingly diverse set of possible graduation diploma options. The standard high school diploma is not the only exit document available to students, including students with disabilities, at high school completion. Among the array of diploma options are special education diplomas, certificates of completion, occupational diplomas, and others. There is a critical need to better understand the implications of state graduation requirements because of findings that students with disabilities experience significant negative outcomes when they fail to earn a high school or equivalent diploma. There are also data to suggest that more stringent graduation requirements may be related to higher rates of dropping out of school among students with disabilities compared with the dropout rates of their counterparts without disabilities.

Currently, 16 states have had their exams in place long enough to affect the graduating class of 2000. Approximately 9 other states have developed graduation exams that students in future graduating classes will have to pass to receive a standard diploma. Additional states have legislated exams that are now being developed; add to these numerous local exams to determine whether students will receive diplomas. The states with active graduation exams have diploma options that reflect the array of diplomas and certificates and the criteria for earning them. . . .

As with other students, those with disabilities are allowed multiple opportunities to take exit exams. States with graduation exams generally have more diploma options available to students overall. Many states also offer students with disabilities additional flexibility in meeting standard diploma requirements. For example, most states with only course credit requirements for graduation allow their students with disabilities to meet requirements by taking modified coursework or completing IEPs or by having IEP teams or districts decide the requirements. More than half the states that require both credits and exams to earn a standard diploma allow changes in requirements for students with disabilities.

Implications for Teachers and Teacher Educators

As more and more states and school districts implement performance standards and tests in an effort to improve educational accountability, they are faced with several critical questions. Many of these questions apply to all students, yet there are several that specifically address the experiences of students with disabilities.... For example, how do we ensure that results on state tests do not unnecessarily limit educational experiences and opportunities? What steps must be taken to ensure that states carefully align current grade-level retention and promotion policies with newly emerging state tests and related performance standards? What do schools need to consider about using state test scores to retain or promote students with disabilities? What is the role and importance of accommodations in supporting student participation in these and other exams? Is the standard diploma the only option that should be available to students, or should there be some type of diploma for students who do not pass the test but who meet other criteria? If more than one type of diploma is available, what specific requirements should be aligned with each diploma option? These are difficult and complex questions. Exploring the answers to them produces several suggestions for including students with disabilities in high-stakes assessments.

Maintain high expectations for students with disabilities. For students with disabilities, the IEP team should serve as the focal point for discussions about student participation in state testing and standards-based accountability systems. The IEP must indicate whether the student is to participate in the assessment and the nature and scope of accommodations that might be required by the student.... The IEP team must work to ensure that high expectations for learning and achievement are maintained for students with disabilities. If students experience difficulties in passing state tests, efforts must be undertaken to ensure that they remain on a full curriculum track, with learning expectations that guide the instruction of general education students.... General education teachers, in collaboration with special education personnel, must determine the strategies, accommodations, and overall supports needed to ensure that students meet high standards and have access to the full range of curricular options available to other students. Difficulties in test performance should not result in lower expectations, narrowing of curricular options, or displacement of the student from the general education curriculum....

Accommodating the test situation. IEP team members need to think about the link between assessment accommodations and instructional accommodations. It is important that assessment accommodations are familiar to students and that they be used prior to test administration....

Nonapproved accommodations. There are several accommodations that are considered to change the construct tested, such as reading a reading test to a student, and therefore are not approved for use. Nonapproved accommodations are needed for some students to be able to take the test. For example, students who are blind and have not learned Braille are essentially denied access to the test if it is not read to them regardless of whether the test's content is mathematics, reading, or some other content area. This same situation occurs for students with significant reading disabilities and other conditions as well. Denying access to the assessment because of the effects of a disability, especially when the assessment provides access to a benefit (such as a diploma), raises many concerns. Simply denying diplomas or providing certificates of attendance for these students does not seem to be reasonable because it can be argued that they have met standards and simply are not being allowed to appropriately show their mastery of them. One approach is to have a special request process, through which students needing nonapproved accommodations could request permission to use them, with the reason for needing each accommodation documented. For these students, test performance might be just one part of a larger body of evidence required for meeting graduation requirements.

A phase-in approach to testing.   Historically, students with disabilities either have been excluded from the general education curriculum or have received a watered-down version of it, although there are examples in which students have indeed had the same exposure and opportunities that other students have had to master the general education curriculum.... As a result, questions can be raised about whether it is appropriate to expect that today's ninth-grade students have had equal access to the general education curriculum and standards. Because of questions about opportunity to learn, educators might want to ask for an extended phase-in of the requirements for students with disabilities. For example, those students now in elementary school would be the first required to meet state graduation requirements.

Providing retesting opportunities.   How retesting interacts with disability issues should be considered. Retesting must be available to students with disabilities just as often as it is to other students. This means that special editions of the test are needed and that accommodations need to be provided during retesting. IEP teams need to determine whether to request additional accommodations with each retake, thereby recognizing the possibility that the accommodations are needed even though the student may have hoped not to use them. Changing rules about test format, administration procedures, or accommodations for retesting must be addressed.

Available appeals and waiver processes.   It is important that teachers and those who train them know whether any procedures are available for students to appeal a poor test score or to obtain a waiver from taking a test. An appeals process that ensures consideration of individual student needs or a process for requesting a waiver from testing may reduce the number of problems students encounter. However, it is important for these students to still be held to high standards. Alternative ways for them to show that they have met high standards should be pursued.

Teacher Educators Influencing Policies on Inclusive Diploma Options and Graduation Policies

It is critical for teacher educators to know about the existing policies that affect students, which in turn affect teachers. Beyond that, it is important for teacher educators to speak up about policies that are implemented or that are being considered. More than half the states do not yet have graduation exams, but most are thinking seriously about adding them. It is a good time to get involved in discussions about these exams. Many states that have graduation exams are rethinking some of their policies. Knowing what is being thought about and adding input to the discussion are equally important. There are several points that might be considered in relation to graduation requirements and graduation exams for students with disabilities.

Recognize that not all students demonstrate high knowledge and skills in the same way. Just as this calls for alternative testing practices, it also can mean that there should be other avenues to diplomas, such as an appeals process. Only 1% to 2% of the total student enrollment (i.e., students with severe disabilities) should require alternate tests or special accommodations to participate in testing programs at any level.

Clarify the implications of different diploma options for continued special education services. It is important for parents and educators to know that if a child graduates from high school with a standard high school diploma, the student is no longer entitled to special education services. Special and general education teachers should carefully work with students and families to consider what it actually means to receive a standard high school diploma. In some cases, it may be advisable to delay formal receipt of a standard high school diploma until the conditions (goals and objectives) of the student's IEP have been fully met, including all transition service requirements outlined in IDEA 97. A pressing concern is to ensure that the agreed-on goals and objectives in the student's IEP have been fulfilled by the educational agency and that students have been connected with the adult services needed to support postschool education, employment, and independent living needs.

Consider the views of others about diploma options and policies. Postsecondary education representatives need to determine whether they will accept an alternative diploma as part of their admission requirements. The question is whether graduating from high school with a special education diploma or other certificate of completion grants students who earn them access to postsecondary education programs. High schools and postsecondary programs should thoroughly discuss the meaning and rigor of these alternative diplomas and agree on their use for postsecondary education admissions. This issue is not the same as concerns about the meaning of grade point averages or class ranks earned by students (regardless of disability) who have taken easier classes or programs of study.

Employers need to be consulted and informed about the types of diplomas students receive on graduation. Although it is unfair to generalize on the motivations of employers, it is fair to say that employers are interested in hiring the most qualified individuals they can. If members of the business community are not engaged in discussions about plans to use an array of alternative diplomas, employers may view these alternative diplomas as a convenient screening mechanism for new employees. Students who hold a standard high school diploma might thereby be viewed as more desirable candidates for employment than those with an alternative, or "lesser," diploma. . . .

Conclusions

The consequences of high-stakes testing for students with disabilities, particularly of tests used to determine graduation status or type of diploma, last well beyond the time a student is in school. Participation in postsecondary education programs, employment and future earnings, civic participation, and the individual's overall social and emotional well-being are affected by the credential they receive in high school and carry forward into adulthood. A substantial body of research has documented the negative consequences of dropping out of school, yet limited research has been conducted on the consequences of receiving less than a standard high school diploma.

There may indeed be high-stakes consequences related to granting students an alternative diploma rather than the standard high school diploma. Some educators and policy makers have expressed concern that the current diploma and graduation requirements may give students with disabilities an unfair advantage over students without disabilities who may be held to higher standards. Alternatively, receiving less than a standard high school diploma may limit an individual's future opportunities to access postsecondary education and employment.

These issues, coupled with the possibility of lower expectations, off-target teaching, and denial of responsibility for students with disabilities, form an unfortunate set of unintended consequences that surface when addressing the participation of students with disabilities in educational accountability systems. Balancing these against a desire to be fair to students and not to harm them creates significant challenges for states and districts today. Teachers must take a major role in raising and addressing the tough questions as high stakes affect students' educational opportunities, retention or promotion, and graduation from high school.

Pixie J. Holbrook

When Bad Things Happen
to Good Children

Sarah is in fourth grade. She's the daughter of two professional parents and has an older brother, whom she lovingly describes as a "pain in the neck." Every time she writes an entry in her journal, she's eager to include one of her brother's adventures. Her teacher has taught her to start each entry with a line that grabs the reader's attention. "My, what a week this has been!" or "You're not going to believe what my brother did this time!" Sarah loves to write, always filling a page or two with ease. She's bright and clever, eager and creative. Her words are engaging and her stories pull you in.

But Sarah can't read her own writing, and I can't either. She brings her weekly journal to my special education resource room each Thursday, and together we labor over the confusion of half words and reversed letters. The sentences are literally endless, with that one capital and maybe that final period. In the middle are wonderful ideas, but we can't figure out where they start and end. Little by little, word by word, Sarah and I piece together the writing. She says, "Oh yes, I remember, that's the word *uncle*. My uncle had a flat tire." And I ask, "Sarah, could that be the word *shaking?* Was your dog shaking?"

The story takes form, but Sarah's luster is fading. She knows her failings. She knows that, as hard as she tries, she can't spell or read like other students. She knows that, as fast as these stories emerge, she can't reread them. Ideas start and stop in her mind, but she can't find them on her paper. Sarah has a learning disability that affects all that she does during the school day. Social studies, science, and math all require reading and writing, which Sarah labors over daily. School is a struggle from beginning to end, but Sarah perseveres with the support of her family and teachers.

Sarah has been tested, and her intellectual potential is above average. Through a series of subtests that involve verbal and nonverbal tasks, it's discovered that Sarah has the learning potential of students her age and older. However, on certain tasks that involve the perception of visual information, her brain confuses the images. It's particularly evident when she encounters symbols. When asked to reproduce those skewed images in writing, her brain once again confuses the message. Her coordination is weak, and the letters are

From Pixie J. Holbrook, "When Bad Things Happen to Good Children: A Special Educator's Views of MCAS," *Phi Delta Kappan* (June 2001). Copyright © 2001 by Phi Delta Kappa International. Reprinted by permission of *Phi Delta Kappan* and the author.

labored and poorly formed. Her writing is a series of words with omitted, misordered, or illegible letters. In terms that we can relate to, Sarah reads, spells, and writes like a student at the end of first grade. She has the interests, experiences, and enthusiasm of a 10-year-old, but her work in school is that of a 7-year-old.

When Sarah was in kindergarten, her ability to master readiness skills was strong. She was well socialized and had good background information from an enriched home life and some preschool experience. Her parents and teachers were prepared for her to experience school success in all ways. However, by the middle of first grade, Sarah's progress was slowing. As the demands of decoding the symbols for letters and numbers increased, Sarah was not moving forward. Her peers were already building an automatic sight vocabulary and were playing with the phonic units of reading and spelling. All this eluded Sarah. She was struggling with the basic deciphering of the very *direction* of the symbol or with associating a cluster of visual information (letters) with its meaning as a word.

By the end of first grade, it was recommended that Sarah get the help of a remedial reading teacher. Thanks to the enthusiasm of this teacher, Sarah was able to maintain her love of stories and writing. Second grade brought little change, and Sarah's official referral for a complete evaluation came at the end of that year. By third grade Sarah was placed in special education, and in fourth grade, with daily services by a trained professional, she made a substantial leap in reading, going from preprimer (early first grade) to the mid-second-grade level.

Days in school can be very long for Sarah, but weekends bring relief. She is a fine athlete and excels at soccer. Her weekends are filled with cheering crowds and team hugs. There are sleepovers and dinners with grandparents. She has pets, a new clarinet, and a Diskman. She's a friend to many and is well liked by her peers and teachers. Back at school, her classmates chose her to be a peer mediator, an esteemed role that many students aspire to. Sarah will certainly succeed in that role, too. She's an average, healthy, middle-class, suburban girl. The only thing that separates her from thousands of other 10-year-old girls is a learning disability.

Our board of education says that we have to assess all students. We need to track their progress and be certain that we have set our expectations high. We need to help all students access the curriculum, and we need to support them and recognize their achievement. I want nothing less for Sarah. I test her individually at the beginning and end of every year. I want to see how I have helped her, and I share the results with her so that she too can mark her progress. We enjoy seeing how she has changed, comparing her two spelling tests and giggling over how she read that same word back in September. These tools help me create an individual program for Sarah. Her needs are unique, but this kind of assessment, coupled with my training and experience, allows me to select the appropriate techniques and materials that will ensure her progress.

Sarah took the MCAS (Massachusetts Comprehensive Assessment System) test this spring. It was her first time taking it and my second time giving it. I have opposed this one-dimensional, trivia-laden test since its inception. But I have an obligation as a professional to administer this test to my special-needs students. I had already separated out the two children who qualified for the "alternate" assessment. The state allows me to choose between 1% and 3% of my students for this option. It is like being in a Biblical story. Whom shall I sacrifice? I sent those two bewildered but grateful students to the library for 15 hours over two weeks to work with learning packets and play educational games under the supervision of our paraprofessionals. The other two special education teachers in my building had done the same.

My two students joined several others, who grew increasingly irritated by the change in their schedule and unfamiliar activity. "Why can't we come back to your class?" they asked me each day. "Because the governor wants to know how all the children in Massachusetts are doing," I replied, offering my best explanation. One was grateful; the other, insulted. "Thanks for getting me out of that one," exclaimed one. "Sure. I'm not smart enough!" said the other. It hurt no matter what I did.

As a special-needs student who did not qualify for the alternative assessment, Sarah is entitled to certain "allowable accommodations" for the MCAS that were determined at her team meeting. I can help Sarah in several ways. I can administer the test in a small-group setting in my resource room. I can read all directions until I'm certain she understands. I can read all parts of the test to her, "except for the English Language Arts test," I kept repeating to myself. This makes absolutely no sense. None at all.

Now they are really losing me. How is this "accommodation" fair to a disabled reader? She must pass the reading section of the MCAS for graduation; yet by 10th grade, Sarah will still be a highly disabled reader. Does anyone imagine that she will be *un*disabled by 10th grade and so able to read 10th-grade material? Do blind people suddenly see in 10th grade in order to take the MCAS without using Braille? Sarah has a reading disability, but I can make no adjustments to the reading section of the MCAS. I can read all the other sections, but not that one. Yet, ultimately, all the Sarahs in Massachusetts must pass that one in particular for graduation.

❧

I came to the testing session with a positive attitude. I can do this, I told myself. I'll make this as productive a day as I can for my students. Correction. I mean as productive a two weeks as I can. I'm upbeat, and this will spread to my students, I reassure myself.

With the help of the other two special education teachers and our paraprofessionals, we have arranged a complicated schedule in order to administer the test with the proper accommodations for individual test-takers. Some will have the allowable sections read to them, some we will scribe for, and several just need the directions clarified. But because of the special reading and scribing arrangements, we have to do this one-on-one. How can we write for more than one student at a time? For our students who are not in grade 4, substitutes have been hired, and we have provided materials and activities so that their programs will be as little disrupted as possible. Perhaps I am making this sound easy, but any teacher would shudder at what this entails. It is instructional time used unwisely, it's an additional expense for substitutes, and it's a great deal of extra work for us. We resent this, but we are trying to be professional, and, above all, we are trying to ensure that all our students are comfortable and using their time productively.

Sarah is my student, and we will spend about two hours a day together for the next several days, working through the test. The subtests are untimed, which is both a blessing and a curse. There will be no pressure to rush for Sarah, who processes everything slowly. But by the same token, she is a perfectionist and is likely to need a great deal of time to select her answers or develop her ideas for the open- response questions. There are three sessions for English/ language arts, two for math, two each for science and history. The "long essay" had been done the week before.

Sarah is smiling, cautious but ready to work. Her parents and regular class-room teacher have prepped her well. She is a shy girl who is wary of making mistakes. It's a condition she is used to, and she compensates for it with a fixed smile and a feigned positive attitude. Her face is quite flushed as we begin.

The first reading selection is manageable, and she chooses to read silently. She can independently answer the comprehension questions, though I can see that there are many errors. The second exercise takes 45 minutes, the equivalent of a daily reading lesson together. Sarah's face reddens when she sees the next page, and deep sighs are audible. The next selection is a poem, and I estimate that she can read perhaps one out of four words. She reads silently and answers all the questions wrong. We can't fool Sarah anymore. She knows she doesn't know. And she knows that I know she doesn't know. This is so very humiliating.

Her eyes are wet now, but she's silent and stoic. I check in, and she reassures me she's fine. She appears to be on the verge of weeping, but she will not be deterred. I cannot help her in any way; I can only sit nearby and return a false smile. I can offer a break, nothing more. Later, I calculated the reading level of this selection. Sarah reads like a second-grader, and the poem is at the high end of the fifth- grade scale. Her eyes are now just scanning the paragraphs. I know she has stopped reading and is just glancing and gazing. It's meaningless, and it hurts. Yet she attempts to answer every question.

It is now 2½ hours, and my anger is growing. This is immoral and has become intolerable. This is professionally irresponsible. And it's only the first day.

That night my desire for dinner is gone, and I unload my frustrations on my understanding husband, long into the evening and night. How can I meet my professional obligations to my administrators and to the intent of the assessment, while meeting my obligations to nurture and support the development of these special young people? My priority is always the children. Maybe I should tell Sarah, "Just skip them. You tried, and this test is just too hard. Forget it. You tried." But this is not the way I teach. I would never approach a lesson with my students in this way. I always want them to give it their all. To compromise my values as a teacher hurts deeply.

Finally, I resolve to try a new plan, after discussing it with Sarah the next day. Having seen the next session of reading and noting that the reading levels are even higher, I commit to not having her experience a higher level of defeat and frustration. Sarah is paler today, and there are dark circles under her eyes for the first time. I know she will work another long day without complaint. We decide to skip all the sections except one. Together we select the easiest one, and she agrees to read it aloud to me. In this way she and I can be certain that she has really read the passage, rather than breezed over the text, pretending to read. Sarah is a conscientious student and tells me that she's worried what "they" will say if she doesn't read everything. I reassure her that "they" will like it if she does well on just this one.

Her reading is halting and labored. She struggles with words like *medium*, *altogether*, and *participate*. I can't help her, though her eyes seem to plead for my help. She pushes on, and her comprehension of the passage slips away. She is just going through a meaningless exercise. Sarah cannot read critical words, and she has no understanding of what she has just read. The multiple-choice questions follow. She reads them aloud and takes cautious guesses. The selections are random, and she gets only one out of eight correct.

Sarah has an organic, physiological disability, and the blind are being asked to see. Learning disabilities are invisible, and the board of education is requiring this reading-disabled young lady to read at grade level—in fact, above grade level. Does this make any sense to anyone?

I value this child, I support her struggle, and I am dedicated to her special form of education. But I participated in hurting Sarah. I took away a piece of her pride, her joys, and her dreams. I forced her to face the fact that she is less than normal and that she will be judged as such. She'll receive a letter in the early fall, just before the excitement of a new school year, that will state definitively that she is a "failure." It will arrive in her home mailbox, and like other children her age, she'll enjoy the anticipation of the daily mail and will open the letter that is addressed "To the Parents of Sarah B." She can't read the long sustained text, but she can read a graph. And the graph will show that small black bar at the bottom that designates "failing." Members of the board of education, how dare you do this to all these fine children? Or to 10? Or to one? How dare you!

⌁◉⌁

I am sorry to say that I know this firsthand. Our disabled and complex son took the MCAS three years ago as an eighth-grader and boycotted it in his 10th-grade year. He was not about to be subjected to that experience ever again. It was not for a political statement as much as for the necessity of acting as responsible parents that we told the school to make other provisions for our son. He was *not* to take that test. However, three years ago, we knew less than we do now, and we allowed him to take the MCAS with our daily support and encouragement. His teacher fed him donuts and soft drinks to help secure his and his friends' compliance. Seven learning-disabled boys, reading at the third-grade level, took the eighth-grade MCAS and played along. Each day, our son would arrive home telling us he couldn't answer any of the questions. "I can't do any of it, Mom," I can still hear him say.

My son loves to walk our long rural driveway and deliver our mail to us each day. He can read "To the Parents of...", and the day the letter arrived, he knew it was the MCAS results. It was too late for me to stop him. He scanned the text and read the graph. He threw an angry glare at me and tossed the wadded letter across the room. "I told you I was stupid!" he yelled. My heart broke, broke in pieces. How dare they do that to our son! After his years of holding his fragile self-esteem intact, of walking through that school door one more time and facing yet another day of being less able than everyone, the state board of education informs him that he's a failure.

Sarah is only one of my 24 students. That's a reasonable amount of students to attend to, but what the state board is asking of them is not reasonable. Sarah is privileged with intelligence and a healthy home. Not so for Mandy, who has cerebral palsy and mild retardation and who would not qualify for the alternative assessment. Not so for Cynthia, who isn't sure whether her mom will be home each night and who chews the skin off the tips of her fingers and has to have every direction repeated. She, too, won't qualify for the alternative assessment. How about D.C., whose dad is in prison and whose mom is a heroin addict? He lives with his mom in the local shelter, and as a third-grader he enjoyed shocking us by imitating a needle plunging into his arm. He reads three grade levels lower than his agemates, but still he has to take the MCAS. Paul is autistic and spins in his chair repeating TV commercials when he's stressed. He's very bright and reads years above his age level—but with no comprehension of what he just encountered. Sorry, he doesn't qualify for the alternative either.

And there are many more. They live in condos, raised ranches, tenements, and converted chicken coops. They play in city parks, cornfields, groomed soccer fields, and back alleys. They are your neighbors and your nieces—perhaps your own child. They are developmentally delayed, have attention deficits, are autistic, abused, and neglected. They have compulsive disorders, expressive language delays, and are scared about their fragile lives. Do I need to go on? Please make me stop because this is just the beginning, and their faces parade before me. And none of this makes any sense.

My disabled fourth-graders cannot take the MCAS in its present form. They still cannot read. There is a critical point in students' education when they go from learning to read to reading to learn. This typically takes place in the third or fourth grades. My students have not yet made that transition. For my fourth-graders, the present MCAS is a ridiculous waste of time, emotion, and self-esteem. By eighth grade, these same students may have made the basic reading transition, but their understandings will still be far behind those of their peers, and their progress will be at a decidedly slower pace. By eighth grade, the average disabled reader is probably reading at the third-grade level. By 10th grade, if their motivation can be sustained, they might achieve seventh- or eighth-grade levels in reading. These children have a disability. Their brains don't work in the same way as yours and mine. More services will help, and we should always expect a little more for each of them. But let us be realistic: the disability won't go away, just as blindness, deafness, or cerebral palsy won't vanish.

However, with seventh- or eighth-grade reading skills, they can function in the world of work in many capacities. Remember, they are disabled *readers*— not disabled *people*. A specific learning disability is often accompanied by average or above-average intelligence and a host of strengths in such areas as spatial relationships, social perception, problem solving, fine motor coordination and dexterity, mechanical ability, aesthetic senses, and empathy and compassion. (The MCAS does not assess these skills for any student.) Reading is only one aspect of their abilities, only one tool for learning, only one portion of a developed human being. Young people with disabilities can graduate with the motivation to continue to learn on the job and from travel, television, discussions, cinema, and their family members and friends. They will be providing services in the fields of day care and hospitality and in medical reception and computer repair. They can be our police force, design our gardens, process our banking, and make the music we listen to. The possibilities are vast. But without a diploma and without self-esteem, none of these things will happen.

Are there any solutions? Yes, many. I would *not* recommend exemptions from such accountability measures as MCAS for disabled children. I am committed to equal access to public education. All students must be assessed, disabled and nondisabled. But changes in the current MCAS must be made.

Many teachers, parents, and advocates for disabled students have the answers. Just ask us. For starters, we could stop using the word "failure." Such language is powerful, but it is not productive. For standardized testing, let's use the Iowa Tests of Basic Skills, a shorter and easier test that is nationally normed. Revise the present MCAS, making it easier, and lower those inflated readability levels. Base this new MCAS on agreed-upon frameworks, and eliminate social studies and science. End the use of the single paper-and-pencil task as a determinant for graduation. Use broader, more diverse, and more authentic assessment techniques such as portfolios and videotaping. Assess students' multiple intelligences by means of projects, public speaking, or science fairs. Expand the criteria for the alternative assessment to include 80% of the disabled students, not just 1% to 3%. Maybe we should even try this broader view of assessment for *all students*. Now there's an idea!

On several occasions, I have been asked to ponder this question: Does the disabled student deserve the same diploma that the valedictorian receives? My response is, yes! The world of work will determine what the value of the diploma is. And the disabled student doesn't necessarily want the job that the valedictorian wants, and the valedictorian doesn't necessarily want the job that my disabled son seeks. However, without a diploma our son will not be able to be a landscaper—grooming people's lawns, paving their walkways, and advising them on proper fertilizer or drainage stone. The valedictorian has options for higher education in a four-year college and even for graduate-level work. The disabled student can enter the work force with basic knowledge and perhaps additional vocational skills from one of our state's fine technical high schools. That disabled student can continue his or her education at work or in a two- or four-year college, with the support and understanding of peers, educational institutions, and employers.

If children are marked as "failures" at age 10, again at 14, and again at 16, their motivation will die, and they will spiral downward. They will be robbed of an education and marked forever as failures who have no worth. Surely, this is not what our state board of education intended. We must stop MCAS in its present form, before more harm is done.

Postcript. In early September 2000, I sent this article to the then lieutenant governor of Massachusetts, Jane Swift. She immediately contacted me and came to my school to meet with me and my students. We had a lengthy discussion about what it is to be learning disabled and about the effects of the MCAS on these young learners. In addition to this meeting, hundreds of parents and educators across Massachusetts have voiced their opposition to the current MCAS.

As of spring [2001], the state allows a new set of "nonstandard accommodations." A teacher can now read the reading sections of the test to the student, and the student can dictate the "long essay" to the teacher to write down. The state tells us that if a student passes the 10th-grade MCAS with these "nonstandard accommodations," he or she will receive a diploma. I recognize this as an important step for disabled students but look forward to other critical revisions of the test.

POSTSCRIPT

Do Students With Disabilities Benefit From Participating in High-Stakes Testing?

The furor over high-stakes testing is voiced on many fronts. Writer-lecturer Alfie Kohn regularly decries the unfairness of standardized testing, which he feels forces students into molds and plays a cruel game of rewards and punishments. Senator Paul Wellstone sees high-stakes tests as harsh punishment for all children, especially those who live in poverty or have disabilities. He has proposed an amendment to the Elementary and Secondary Education Act Reauthorization that would prohibit using the results of one single standardized test for high-stakes decisions.

Local legislators feel that high-stakes testing is essential to validate the impact of the billions of dollars spent on education reform and to guarantee that high school diplomas are meaningful. Federal legislators believe that participation of all students is essential to ensure that students with disabilities are not shunted aside and relegated to substandard educational programs.

A small number of legal suits have shed interesting light. In *Brookhart v. Illinois State Board of Education* (1983), the court ruled that students with disabilities could be held to the state standard of needing to pass a minimum competency test for graduation. However, the 18-month notice provided by Illinois was deemed to be too short to make up for the length of time that the students had not had access to the general curriculum.

The state of Oregon settled a class action suit brought by parents whose children with learning disabilities were not permitted to utilize accommodations that were a regular part of their educational programs to take the test. The parents argued that without the accommodations, their children were unable to show what they know and can do. The state maintained that the accommodations compromised the test. However, the settlement agreement permitted the use of many of the accommodations that were used daily as part of the students' educational programs.

Most students with disabilities do require some accommodations. Many teachers believe that these are fair ways for a student to participate. Others think that accommodations make tasks too easy, providing unfair advantages rather than leveling the playing field. Current research on accommodations investigates the line that separates using an accommodation to level the playing field (by removing the effect of the disability) and using an accommodation to change the playing field (making tasks easier or changing their nature substantially). Especially in this time of high-stakes testing, the first is much more desirable than the second.

Contributors to This Volume

EDITOR

MARYANN BYRNES is a practitioner and an academic in the field of special education. She is a member of the faculty of the Graduate School of Education at the University of Massachusetts–Boston, serving jointly in the teacher education and special education programs. Dr. Byrnes consults with schools and districts on issues of assessment, focusing on the effective participation of all students. Her other school-based activities include long-term consultation for system change, curriculum alignment, and staff development, as well as program and budget evaluation. She has taught at elementary, middle, high school, and graduate school levels, served as a special education administrator for 18 years, and is a former president of the Massachusetts Association of Administrators of Special Education (ASE). Dr. Byrnes earned her B.A. at the University of Chicago, her M.Ed. in learning disabilities at Northwestern University, and her Ed.D. in learning theory at Rutgers University. She has written numerous articles on inclusion, the appropriate use of accommodations, and special education finance.

STAFF

Theodore Knight   List Manager
David Brackley   Senior Developmental Editor
Juliana Gribbins   Developmental Editor
Rose Gleich   Administrative Assistant
Brenda S. Filley   Director of Production/Design
Juliana Arbo   Typesetting Supervisor
Diane Barker   Proofreader
Richard Tietjen   Publishing Systems Manager
Larry Killian   Copier Coordinator

AUTHORS

THOMAS ARMSTRONG is an award-winning author and speaker with 28 years of teaching experience, from the primary through the doctoral level, and over 1 million copies of his books in print on issues related to learning and human development. His articles have appeared in hundreds of newspapers and journals, including *Parenting* and *Mothering,* and he has given over 400 keynotes, workshops, and lectures in 40 states and 12 countries in the past 16 years. His books include *Awakening Your Child's Natural Genius* (Association for Supervision and Curriculum Development, 1998) and *ADD/ADHD Alternatives in the Classroom* (Association for Supervision and Curriculum Development, 1999).

BEN BAHAN is a professor in and chair of the Department of Deaf Studies, with a joint appointment in the Department of ASL, Linguistics, and Interpretation, at Gallaudet University in Washington, D.C. The recipient of the President's Distinguished Faculty Award for 2001, he is also vice president of DawnSignPress in San Diego, California, and co-investigator for the American Sign Language Linguistic Research Project. He earned his Ph.D. in applied linguistics from Boston University in 1996, and he is coauthor of *The Syntax of American Sign Language: Functional Categories and Hierarchical Structure* (MIT Press, 2000).

THOMAS BALKANY is the Hotchkiss Professor in and vice chairman of the Department of Otolaryngology in the University of Miami School of Medicine. Board certified by the American Board of Otolaryngology, he earned his M.D. from the University of Miami in 1972. His interests include otology, neurotology, and cochlear implants, and he is coeditor, with Nigel R. T. Pashley, of *Clinical Pediatric Otolaryngology* (Mosby, 1986).

SHELDON BERMAN is superintendent of the Hudson Public Schools in Massachusetts. He is on the board of directors of the Compact for Learning and Citizenship, and he is a founder and former president of Educators for Social Responsibility. He is the author of numerous articles and the book *Children's Social Consciousness and the Development of Social Responsibility* (New York Press, 1997).

TOM BERTLING is an author who has been hearing-impaired since age five. Among his books are *No Dignity for Joshua: More Vital Insight Into Deaf Children, Deaf Education, and Deaf Culture* (Kodiak Media Group, 1997) and *An Intellectual Look at American Sign Language: Clear Thinking on American Sign Language, English and Deaf Education* (Kodiak Media Group, 2001), which he edited.

FREDERICK J. BRIGHAM is an assistant professor of special education in the Department of Curriculum, Instruction, and Special Education at the Curry School of Education of the University of Virginia. He has also taught at Dickinson State College and served as director of special education for the West River Special Education Unit in Dickinson, North Dakota. He earned his M.Ed. from Bowling Green State University in 1983 and his Ph.D. from Purdue University in 1992.

PAUL D. CALALUCE, JR., is the principal of Humiston School and director of Pupil Personnel Services for the Cheshire Public Schools in Cheshire, Connecticut.

GARY M. CHESLEY is the superintendent of the Bethel Public Schools in Bethel, Connecticut.

SCOT DANFORTH is an assistant professor in the Department of Behavioral Studies at the University of Missouri–St. Louis. He has also taught at the University of South Florida, and he is cofounder of the Disability Studies in Education Special Interest Group of the American Educational Research Association. He earned his M.Ed. from the University of North Carolina, Chapel Hill, in 1987 and his Ph.D. from the University of South Florida in 1994. He is coauthor, with Joseph R. Boyle, of *Cases in Special Education,* 2d ed. (McGraw-Hill, 2001) and *Cases in Behavior Management* (Merrill, 2000).

LAWRENCE H. DILLER practices behavioral pediatrics in Walnut Creek, California. He is an assistant clinical professor at the University of California and the author of *Running on Ritalin: A Physician Reflects on Children, Society, and Performance in a Pill* (Bantam, 1998).

CHESTER E. FINN, JR., a scholar, educator, and public servant, has devoted most of his career to improving education in the United States. He has been a professor of education and public policy at Vanderbilt University since 1981 (currently on leave), and he is the John M. Olin Fellow at the Manhattan Institute and president of the Thomas B. Fordham Foundation. He is also a distinguished visiting fellow at Stanford University's Hoover Institution and an adjunct fellow at the Hudson Institute, where he worked from 1995 through 1998. Among his many publications is *Charter Schools in Action: Renewing Public Education,* coauthored with Bruno V. Manno and Gregg Vanourek (Princeton University Press, 2000).

ALAN GARTNER is a professor of educational psychology and dean of research in the Graduate School and University Center at the City University of New York. He has published a number of books, including *Inclusion and School Reform: Transforming America's Classrooms,* coauthored with Dorothy Kerzner Lipsky (P. H. Brookes, 1997).

MICHAEL M. GERBER is a professor in the educational leadership and organizations emphasis in the Graduate School of Education and director of the Center for Advanced Studies of Individual Differences at the University of California, Santa Barbara. He is the principal investigator for Case-Link, an interactive, multimedia Web development project in special education, and he was coprincipal investigator on Project TEECh, one of the first large-scale research projects focusing on microcomputer access and use by students with mild to moderate disabilities.

MICHAEL F. GIANGRECO is a research associate professor in the Center of Disability and Community Inclusion at the University of Vermont. His professional interests focus on how to plan, adapt, coordinate, implement, and evaluate educational programs and services for students with disabilities who are included in general education classrooms. He is the author of *Ants* *in His Pants: Absurdities and Realities of Special Education* (Peytral, 1998) and *Vermont Interdependent Services Team Approach: A Guide to Coordinating Educational Support Services* (P. H. Brookes, 1996).

LARRY S. GOLDMAN is an associate professor of clinical psychiatry at the University of Chicago in Chicago, Illinois. He is also a member of the Council on Scientific Affairs of the American Medical Association.

KENNETH W. GOODMAN is founder of the Forum for Bioethics and Philosophy at the University of Miami, where he is currently director of the Bioethics Program. He also holds appointments in the university's Department of Medicine, Department of Philosophy, School of Nursing, and Department of Epidemiology and Public Health. He has written extensively about science, medicine, and science policy, and he is coauthor, with James G. Anderson, of *Ethics and Information Technology: A Case-Based Approach to a Health Care System in Transition* (Springer, 2002).

DANIEL P. HALLAHAN is a professor of education in and chair of the Department of Curriculum, Instruction, and Special Education at the University of Virginia in Charlottesville, Virginia. He earned his Ph.D. in a combined program in education and psychology from the University of Michigan in 1971, and he received the Council for Exceptional Children Research Award in 2000. Among his many publications is *Exceptional Learners: Introduction to Special Education,* 8th ed., coauthored with J. M. Kauffman (Allyn & Bacon, 2000).

EDWARD M. HALLOWELL is a child and adult psychiatrist and founder of the Hallowell Center for Cognitive and Emotional Health in Sudbury and Andover, Massachusetts. He is also on the faculty of the Harvard Medical School. He is the author of seven books on various psychological topics, including *Worry: Hope and Help for a Common Problem* (Pantheon, 1997) and *Connect: Twelve Vital Ties That Open Your Heart, Lengthen Your Life, and Deepen Your Soul* (Pantheon, 1999).

FREDERICK M. HESS is an assistant professor of education and government at the University of Virginia in Charlottesville, Virginia. He is the author of *Spinning Wheels: The Politics of Urban School Reform* (Brookings Institution Press, 1999) and *Bringing the Social Sciences Alive* (Allyn & Bacon, 1999).

ANNELLE V. HODGES is an associate professor and chief of audiology in the Department of Otolaryngology at the University of Miami School of Medicine. Her clinical interests include cochlear implants, deaf education, and audiology, and her current research focuses on objective methods of setting cochlear implants in infants and small children. She earned her Ph.D. from the University of Virginia.

ROBERT HOFFMEISTER is an associate professor of education and director of the Center for the Study of Communication and Deafness at the Boston University School of Education. His research has focused on the acquisition of American Sign Language (ASL) by Deaf children, Deaf people as a bilingual/bicultural minority group, and other areas related to the Deaf culture. He holds an M.Ed. from the University of Arizona and a Ph.D. from the University of Minnesota.

PIXIE J. HOLBROOK is a special education teacher for the Northampton Public Schools in Massachusetts and a private consultant. She has worked in public and private education in Connecticut and Massachusetts for 30 years, teaching and advocating for children with special needs in urban, suburban, and rural settings.

JERRY JESNESS is a special education teacher at Las Yescas Elementary School in Los Fresnos, Texas. His extensive writings on many aspects of education have appeared in such publications as *Principal, Reason,* and *Teacher.*

DAVID R. JOHNSON is an associate professor in the Department of Educational Policy and Administration at the University of Minnesota, where he is also director of the Institute on Community Integration. A member of the National School Boards Association and the American Association on Mental Retardation, his articles have appeared in such publications as *Career Development for Exceptional Individuals* and *Journal of Disability Policy Studies.* He earned his M.S. in rehabilitation counseling from Mankato State University in 1977 and his Ph.D. in educational policy and administration from the University of Minnesota in 1987.

K. FORBIS JORDAN is a professor emeritus in the Department of Educational Leadership and Policy Studies at Arizona State University. He is coauthor, with L. Dean Webb and Arlene Metha, of *Foundation of American Education,* 3rd ed. (Prentice Hall PTR, 1999).

TERESA S. JORDAN is an associate professor in and chair of the Department of Educational Leadership at the University of Las Vegas, where she has been teaching since 1990. She has also served as director of research and evaluation in a large Arizona school district and as head of a private consulting firm that provided staff development and special education support services to public school systems, private school administrators, speech-language pathologists, and special education early childhood teachers. Her policy and research expertise is in public school finance, particularly funding for special-needs youth, state-level educational accountability systems, and school improvement programs. She holds an M.S. in communication disorders and a Ph.D. in educational leadership and policy studies from Arizona State University.

JAMES M. KAUFFMAN is the Charles S. Robb Professor of Education at the University of Virginia in Charlottesville, Virginia, where he also serves as director of the doctoral program in special education. His primary areas of interest in special education are emotional and behavioral disorders and learning disabilities. He is coeditor of *Behavioral Disorders,* the journal of the Council for Children with Behavioral Disorders, and he is coprincipal investigator of the Center of Minority Research in Special Education (COMRISE). Among his many publications are *Characteristics of Emotional and Behavioral Disorders of Children and Youth,* 7th ed. (Prentice Hall PTR, 2000) and *The Least Restrictive Environment: Its Origins and Interpretations* *in Special Education,* coauthored with Jean B. Crockett (Lawrence Erlbaum, 1999). He received his M.Ed. in teaching in the elementary school from Washburn University in 1966 and his Ed.D. in special education from the University of Kansas in 1969.

ASHLEY THOMAS KING is a bilingual coordinator at Kwethluk Community School in Kwethluk, Alaska. He has also taught special education in California and English as a second language/English as a foreign language in Canada and the Czech Republic.

REX KNOWLES is a retired college professor living in Claremont, California.

TRUDY KNOWLES is an associate professor of education at Westfield State College in Westfield, Massachusetts, where she helps coordinate the middle-level education program. She is actively involved in the education of young adolescents through her work in local schools, the Commonwealth of Massachusetts Middle-Level Educators, the New England League of Middle Schools, and the National Middle School Association. She is coauthor, with David F. Brown, of *What Every Middle School Teacher Should Know* (Heinemann, 2000).

HARLAN LANE is the University Distinguished Professor in the Department of Psychology at Northeastern University in Boston, Massachusetts, where he specializes in speech, language, deafness, and Deaf culture, and a research affiliate in the Research Laboratory of Electronics at the Massachusetts Institute of Technology. He has also taught at Université de Paris VII, Harvard Medical School, and the University of California, San Diego. He earned his M.A. from Columbia University in 1958 and his Ph.D. from Harvard University in 1960. His publications include *The Mask of Benevolence: Disabling the Deaf Community,* exp. ed. (DawnSignPress, 1999) and *When the Mind Hears: A History of the Deaf* (DIANE, 1998).

MARK LEVINE works in the Behavioral Counseling and Research Center of the California Department of Education and is on the board roster of the California Association for Behavior Analysis, a statewide organization that represents and promotes the interests of the behavior analysis profession.

DOROTHY KERZNER LIPSKY is director of the National Center on Educational Restructuring and Inclusion at the City University of New York. She is the author of *Inclusion and School Reform: Transforming America's Classrooms* (Paul H. Brookes, 1997).

DONALD L. MACMILLAN is the Distinguished Professor of Education at the University of California, Riverside. His major research interests include classification of mild disabilities, risk factors related to school disabilities, social and affective characteristics, and conduct problems of children. He has served as vice president of the American Association on Mental Retardation's Education Division and of the Council for Exceptional Children's Division on Research, and he has won several awards, including the Outstanding Research Award, Special Education Special Interest Group, from the American Educational Research Association in 1998. He earned his M.A. and Ed.D. from the University of California, Los Angeles.

SUSAN UNOK MARKS, a project staff member of SRI International, is currently on the advisory panel for the Special Education Elementary Longitudinal Study (SEELS), a project funded by the Office of Special Education Programs. She is coauthor, with Russell M. Gersten and Scott K. Baker, of *Teaching English-Language Learners With Learning Difficulties: Guiding Principles and Examples for Research-Based Practice* (Council for Exceptional Children, 1999).

NATIONAL ASSOCIATION OF THE DEAF (NAD) is a private, nonprofit organization that works to safeguard the accessibility and civil rights of 28 million deaf and hard of hearing Americans in education, employment, health care, and telecommunications. Headquartered in Silver Spring, Maryland, the NAD's programs and activities include grassroots advocacy and empowerment, captioned media, the certification of American Sign Language professionals, legal assistance, policy development and research, and youth leadership development.

NATIONAL COUNCIL ON DISABILITY (NCD) is an independent federal agency that makes recommendations to the president and Congress on issues affecting 54 million Americans with disabilities. The NCD is composed of 15 members appointed by the president and confirmed by the Senate. The NCD's overall purpose is to promote policies, programs, practices, and procedures that guarantee equal opportunity for all individuals with disabilities, regardless of the nature or severity of the disability, and to empower individuals with disabilities to achieve economic self-sufficiency, independent living, and inclusion and integration into all aspects of society.

JAMES M. PATTON is a professor of special education and associate dean of admissions and student services at the College of William and Mary of Virginia. He directed professional development and teacher education and evaluation programs for the Commonwealth of Virginia for three years, and he has also taught special education in the public schools of Louisville, Kentucky. His major research interests include the educational and psychosocial development of African Americans, particularly those with gifts and talents; the social, political, and economic correlates of mild disabilities; and the analysis of policies that affect people of color and those from low socioeconomic circumstances. He is coauthor, with Bridgie A. Ford and Festus E. Obiakor, of *Effective Education of African American Exceptional Learners: New Perspectives* (PRO-ED, 1995).

ARUN K. RAMANATHAN is a student in the Lynch Graduate School of Education at Boston College.

DANIEL J. RESCHLY is a professor of education and psychology as well as chair of the Department of Special Education at Vanderbilt University in Nashville, Tennessee. He is an authority on special education and school psychology professional practices, the assessment of students with disabilities, and minority representation issues in educational programs. He chairs the National Research Council (NRC) Committee on Disability Determination for Mental Retardation, and he is a member of the NRC's Committee on Disproportionate Representation in Educational Programs. He earned his M.A. from the University of Iowa in 1968 and his Ph.D. from the University of Oregon in 1971.

CARL SCHRADER works in the Behavioral Counseling and Research Center of the California Department of Education.

SUSAN SHAPIRO-BARNARD is a lecturer in education at the University of New Hampshire in Durham, New Hampshire. She is also affiliated with the university's Institute on Disability, for which she has coauthored a number of booklets and manuals.

RUSSELL J. SKIBA is an associate professor in counseling and educational psychology and director of the Institute for Child Study at Indiana University. A member of the School of Psychology faculty, he teaches and publishes in the area of school discipline and cultural diversity. He was a member of the expert panel for the President's Early Warning, Timely Response Guide for school safety and the upcoming Early Warning Toolkit. His areas of research include school violence and school discipline, behavior management, minority disproportionality, and school reform.

JEFFREY R. SPRAGUE is codirector of the Institute on Violence and Destructive Behavior at the University of Oregon. He is a nationally recognized researcher on school-based violence prevention, severe behavior disorders, functional behavioral assessment, positive behavioral support, and school safety.

JOHN PAUL STEVENS is an associate justice of the U.S. Supreme Court. He worked in law firms in Chicago, Illinois, for 20 years before being nominated by President Richard Nixon to the U.S. Court of Appeals in 1970. He served in that capacity until he was nominated to the Supreme Court by President Gerald Ford in 1975.

CLARENCE THOMAS is an associate justice of the U.S. Supreme Court. A former judge on the U.S. Court of Appeals for the District of Columbia, he was nominated by President George Bush to the Supreme Court in 1991. He received his J.D. from the Yale University School of Law in 1974.

MARTHA L. THURLOW is director of the National Center on Educational Outcomes, where she addresses the implications of contemporary U.S. policy and practice for students with disabilities. She has conducted research involving special education for the past 25 years in a variety of areas, including assessment and decision making, learning disabilities, early childhood education, and integration of students with disabilities in general education settings. She has authored or coauthored numerous books, including *Improving Test Performance of Students With Disabilities: On District and State Assessments,* coauthored with Judy L. Elliott (Corwin Press, 2000), and she has published more than 200 articles and reports. In 1995 she assumed the position of coeditor of *Exceptional Children,* the research journal of the Council for Exceptional Children.

HILL M. WALKER is a professor in and codirector of the Institute on Violence and Destructive Behavior at the University of Oregon and director of the

Center on Human Development. He is an international leader in the assessment and treatment of antisocial behavior. Among his publications is *Making Schools Safer and Violence Free: Critical Issues, Solutions and Recommended Practices,* coauthored with Michael H. Epstein (PRO-ED, 2001).

CAROLYN A. WEINER is president of Syndactics, Inc., in Phoenix, Arizona. She is coauthor, with Judith M. Creighton and Teresa S. Lyons, of *K-TALK: Kindergarten Teacher-Administered Language Kit* (Communication Skill Builders, 1989).

NANCY J. ZOLLERS is an assistant professor of teacher education in the Department of Counseling, Developmental, and Educational Psychology at Boston College in Chestnut Hill, Massachusetts. Her research interests include school culture, inclusion, urban schools, severe disabilities, qualitative research, and charter schools. She holds a Ph.D. from Syracuse University, and she is coauthor of *Conversations in Excellence: Integrating Mission* (National Catholic Educational Association, 1997).

G. E. ZURIFF is a professor of psychology at Wheaton College in Norton, Massachusetts, and a clinical psychologist at the Massachusetts Institute of Technology. His research interests include the philosophy of psychology, especially behaviorism and psychoanalysis, and public policy on mental disorders, and his teaching interests include learning and perception. He holds a Ph.D. from Harvard University.

Index